To Ca Then
Have you Enjoy The book !

Ce

The Media and Entertainment Industries

Readings in Mass Communications

Albert N. Greco, Editor
Fordham University

Allyn and Bacon
Boston • London • Toronto • Sydney • Tokyo • Singapore

Vice President, Editor in Chief: Paul A. Smith
Series Editor: Karon Bowers
Editorial Assistant: Scout Reilly
Marketing Manager: Jackie Aaron
Editorial Production Service: Chestnut Hill Enterprises, Inc.
Manufacturing Buyer: Megan Cochran
Cover Administrator: Jennifer Hart

Copyright © 2000 by Allyn & Bacon
A Pearson Education Company
160 Gould Street
Needham Heights, MA 02494

Internet: www.abacon.com

Between the time web site information is gathered and published, some sites may have closed. Also, the transcription of URLs can result in typographical errors. The publisher would appreciate notification where these occur so that they may be corrected in subsequent editions.

Library of Congress Cataloging-in-Publication Data

Greco, Albert N.
  The media and entertainment industries : introduction / Albert N.
Greco.
    p.   cm. -- (Media economics series)
  Includes bibliographical references and index.
  ISBN 0-205-30010-3
  1. Mass media--United States.   I. Title.   II. Series.
P92.U5G74   2000
302.23'0973--dc21   99-22845
                                                         CIP

Printed in the United States of Amerca

10   9   8   7   6   5   4   3   2   1   04   03   02   01   00   99

Contents

Preface

It is hard to imagine what life was like before the introduction and wide acceptance of the media and entertainment industries. These formats, from books to the Internet, have had a dramatic, revolutionary impact on the political, social, economic, intellectual, educational, and religious life in this nation and in the world. As we enter the next millennium, it appears that media and entertainment products and services will continue to exert a wide-reaching, profound influence on all aspects of our existence.

MEDIA AND ENTERTAINMENT USAGE AND EXPENDITURES

According to statistical data released by the United States Department of Commerce, Bureau of the Census, U.S. consumers have embraced media and entertainment products wholeheartedly. In 1999, the average American above the age of eighteen spent 3,405 hours utilizing this media; and the prognosis through the year 2001 is upbeat, with total media usage expected to increase to 3,440 hours (+1.12 percent).

However, a review of this data revealed an intriguing conundrum: (1) all media and entertainment products and services are purchased (or rented) with discretionary dollars. After all, the average consumer does not have to see a film, purchase a paperback romance novel, or subscribe to an Internet service; and (2) America's media and entertainment industries are in the midst of a "zero sum game." In order for one media format to grow substantially, beyond the Commerce Department's projections of gradual incremental increases hovering near the 1 percent mark, it must take time (and consumer spending) away from another format. This business problem centers on what is, in reality, an "entertainment glut" in this nation. There is far too much "product" available to the average American. Consumers have literally thousands of entertainment options before them on a daily basis, from a numbing number of cable channels, feature films on videocassettes and in theaters, music CDs, over 1.5 million book titles in print, print and online versions of newspapers and magazines, local radio stations (and hundreds available through the Internet), and so on. How and why consumers decide to allocate their funds and time is the pivotal question facing everyone working in or studying the media and entertainment industries today.

Formats

Television provides a glaring example of what can happen to a dominant medium when it is confronted by intriguing, seductive substitutes. Starting in the early 1950s, television dominated media usage in this nation. However, network television viewing has been declining steadily since the early 1990s. Clearly, cable television made substantial inroads into television viewing patterns, and the projected growth of cable through 2001 is expected to continue to cut deeply into network viewing statistics, raising the specter of a possible advertiser backlash against network advertising rates.

Radio has long been viewed as the "forgotten" medium. But radio is local, personal, niche driven, and portable—assets of great significance to advertisers. Although total usage will decline somewhat by 2001, it will remain an influential force in this nation as it seeks to take consumer and advertising dollars from daily newspapers.

The print formats face similar problems. Newspapers continue to experience declines in usage because of television and, to a lesser degree, the Internet, as do magazines. Books, on the other hand, have demonstrated the importance of this format in U.S. life (while holding its own against incursions of other formats), and the prognosis through 2001 is quite positive.

Home video continues to play a substantial role in film viewership in this nation; film attendance in theaters has plateaued, revealing the fact that more and more consumers prefer to watch films at home in the comfort of their living rooms (while saving money because of low rental fees). The highly touted Internet will continue to grow through 2001, but it lags significantly behind almost all the mass media in terms of total usage and media expenditures.

Table 1 outlines these trends between 1996 and 2001. The term *pay cable* refers to pay-per-view cable television; *home video* refers to rented or purchased prerecorded videocassettes.

Expenditures

A review of media-expenditure statistical data revealed a picture of important consumer preferences. In 1999, Americans spent $616.66 per capita on all media and

TABLE 1   Media and Entertainment Usage Hours per Person per Year: 1996–2000

Format	1996	1997	1998	1999	2000	2001
Total Media Usage	3,395	3,402	3,402	3,405	3,429	3,440
Television	1,567	1,564	1,552	1,548	1,555	1,551
Networks	803	759	730	690	666	642
Independents	177	183	177	183	188	188
Basic Cable	498	528	547	571	592	612
Pay Cable	89	94	98	104	109	109
Radio	1,091	1,089	1,085	1,076	1,074	1,072
Recorded Music	289	296	303	313	325	336
Daily Newspapers	161	158	157	155	154	153
Consumer Magazines	83	81	80	80	79	79
Consumer Books	99	97	96	97	98	99
Home Video	49	52	54	56	58	60
Movies in Theaters	12	12	12	12	12	12
Home Video Games	26	29	31	33	35	37
Consumer Internet Access	16	22	30	33	37	39
Educational Software	2	2	2	2	2	2

Source: U.S. Department of Commerce, Bureau of the Census, *The Statistical Abstract of the U.S. 1998* (Washington, DC: GPO, 1998, p. 565).

entertainment products and services. Of that total, cable (including pay-per-view) accounted for $178.23 (28.90 percent of these expenditures). In second place for most of the 1990s were consumer books, at $92.38, representing 14.98 percent.

Filling out the top spots in 1999 were home video's $96.33 (15.62 percent), recorded music's $64.40 (10.44 percent), and Internet access provider's $40.88 (6.68 percent). Table 2 outlines these patterns. Cable and pay-per-view tallies were added together by the Commerce Department. Obviously, after a television or radio set is purchased, there is no additional expenditure except for electricity or batteries to run the unit, assuming no cable connection is utilized.

THE SCOPE OF THIS BOOK

A review of the mass-media-published literature revealed the need for a concise book that addresses the divergent media and entertainment industries. Although these formats are covered in all the basic mass-media studies, detailed material on specific business issues, from the structure of the media and entertainment industries to basic media economic issues, is often covered in a brief manner.

This book contains detailed chapters written by experienced academics, many of whom have extensive background working or consulting in these businesses. The goal of each author was to present extensive analyses, supported by numerous statis-

TABLE 2   Media and Entertainment Expenditures per Person per Year: 1996–2001

Format	1996	1997	1998	1999	2000	2001
Total	$512.05	$545.63	$582.63	$616.66	$651.37	$685.18
Television						
Basic Cable	140.37	155.70	168.75	178.23	187.60	196.62
Recorded Music	57.33	59.21	61.54	64.40	67.99	71.56
Daily Newspapers	50.99	51.59	52.62	54.05	55.27	58.31
Consumer Magazines	36.63	37.22	37.92	38.91	39.96	40.92
Consumer Books	82.96	84.67	88.09	92.38	97.68	102.86
Home Video	77.43	82.51	88.79	96.33	104.76	113.72
Movies in Theaters	27.04	26.39	26.62	27.13	27.35	27.56
Home Video Games	14.92	16.86	18.59	19.88	20.84	21.65
Consumer Internet Access	20.01	27.23	35.30	40.88	45.35	49.32
Educational Software	4.38	4.26	4.43	4.46	4.53	4.66

Source: U.S. Department of Commerce, Bureau of the Census, *The Statistical Abstract of the U.S. 1998* (Washington, DC: GPO, 1998, p. 565).

tical data, to engage readers eager to understand more completely the burgeoning, influential, and exciting media and entertainment industries.

I must thank all the authors for their cooperation and numerous suggestions. This book would not have become a reality without the splendid editorial and marketing staffs at Allyn and Bacon, especially the efforts of Paul Smith and Karon Bowers. I must also thank the following reviewers whose suggestions were most helpful: Marshell Rossow, Mankato State University; Roger Soenksen, James Madison University; and Sandra Wertz, University of South Carolina.

I must also thank a small group of people keenly interested in the workings of the media: Elaine, Albert, Timothy, John, Robert, Teresa, and Gabrielle Greco; John Sterling and Michael Kay, two individuals who always exhibit grace under pressure; Ernest J. Scalberg, Ev Dennis, and Bill Small, colleagues at Fordham who allowed me to work on this project; and of course Don, Paul, Constantino, Bernie, Joe, and Derek from 161st Street and River Avenue in the Bronx!

Albert N. Greco
Fordham University
Graduate School of Business Administration

1

The Structure of the
Book Publishing Industry

Albert N. Greco
Fordham University
Graduate School of Business Administration

How many books are published in this country? How many book categories are there? How many titles are returned by booksellers and distributors? Why are there book returns? What are the major channels of book distribution in the United States?

TITLE OUTPUT: 1880–1996

Jean Peters explored United States frontlist (i.e., a new title) output in "Book Industry Statistics from the R.R. Bowker Company"; backlist titles were excluded.[1] A backlist book is an old title that remains in print and continues to sell months and possibly years (and sometimes decades) after its original publication. There are more than +1.5 million distinct titles in print according to Bowker's definitive *Books In Print.*

Peters revealed that more than 1.8 million new titles were issued between 1880 and 1989. Of that total nearly half (49.56 percent; 913,197 books) were issued by U.S. book publishers between 1970 and 1989.

Table 1-1, which is based on a statistical analysis of the data in Peters' article, reveals the surge in title output.

TABLE 1-1   Total U.S. Book Output by Decades: 1880–1989

Decade	Total Title Output	Percent Change from Previous Decade
1880–1889	37,896	—
1890–1899	50,011	+31.97
1900–1909	83,512	+66.99
1910–1919	107,906	+29.21
1920–1929	79,006	−26.78
1930–1939	98,480	+24.65
1940–1949	91,514	−7.07
1950–1959	124,675	+36.24
1960–1969	256,584	+105.80
1970–1979	402,911	+57.03
1980–1989	510,286	+26.65
Total: 1880–1989	1,842,781	—

Source: Jean Peters, "Book Industry Statistics from the R.R. Bowker Company," *Publishing Research Quarterly 8* (Fall 1992): p. 18.

In 1990 it reached 46,738, off from 53,446 in 1989. Tallies for the rest of the decade indicated publishers were curbing the avalanche of titles evident in the 1980s: 1991, 48,148; 1992, 44,276; 1993, 49,756; 1994, 51,563. By 1996 title output surged to 62,039. More than 200,000 new titles reached the U.S. market between 1990 and 1994.

Book Industry Trends 1998 (published by the Book Industry Study Group; BISG) revealed that $156.5 billion worth of books, representing 20.15 billion copies, were sold by U.S. publishers between 1989 and 1997. BISG's projections for 1998–2002 were upbeat.[2]

Table 1-2 outlines these trends covering the years 1989–2002.

BOOK CATEGORIES

Book Industry Trends 1998 utilized nine distinct book categories (1) trade (adult and juvenile, fiction and nonfiction; both issued in hardcover and paperback versions); (2) mass market paperback (fiction and nonfiction); (3) book clubs (fiction and nonfiction; hardcover and paperback); (4) mail order books (fiction and nonfiction; hardcover and paperback); (5) religious (mainly nonfiction; hardcover and paperback); (6) professional (business, law, scientific, technical, and medical; all nonfiction; hardcover and paperback); (7) university press (almost entirely nonfiction; hardcover and paperback); (8) ELHI (elementary and high school textbooks, related readers, etc.; fiction and nonfiction; hardcover and paperback); and (9) college (textbooks, related readers, etc.; fiction and nonfiction; hardcover and paperback).

TABLE 1-2   Total Book Sales: 1989–2002 (Millions of Dollars; Millions of Units)

Year	Net Dollar Sales	Percent Change from Previous Year	Net Unit Sales	Percent Change from Previous Year
1989	14,110.8	+11.18	2,142.0	+6.92
1990	14,855.2	+5.28	2,144.3	+0.11
1991	15,568.7	+4.80	2,181.0	+1.71
1992	16,329.1	+4.48	2,192.3	+0.52
1993	17,394.4	+6.52	2,221.9	+1.35
1994	18,249.3	+4.91	2,280.0	+2.61
1995	19,303.7	+5.78	2,335.5	+2.43
1996*	20,108.1	+4.17	2,369.0	+1.43
1997*	20,576.0	+2.33	2,287.7	−3.43
1998*	21,476.6	+4.38	2,305.8	+0.79
1999*	22,513.4	+4.83	2,332.0	+1.14
2000*	23,562.1	+4.66	2,361.9	+1.28
2001*	24,611.2	+4.45	2,392.3	+1.29
2002*	25,671.5	+4.31	2,423.2	+1.29

Source: Book Industry Study Group, *Book Industry Trends 1998* (New York: Book Industry Study Group, 1998), pp. 2–4 through 2–9.

*Indicates a BISG estimate or projection.

Trade Books

Most Americans read trade books and bestsellers. In 1998 trade books held the largest market share in both dollar ($6.15 billion, representing 27.32 percent of all book sales in this country) and unit sales ($860.3 million units; 35.84 percent of all units sold). Adult trade book sales exceeded the $4.7 billion mark, with hardcovers capturing more than $2.75 billion and paperbacks in the $1.91 billion range. This is also the most visible book niche since fiction and nonfiction bestsellers traditionally come from this group.

The *New York Times Book Review* is the preeminent list of best-selling titles in this nation. On September 20, 1998, the fiction hard-cover list included works by some of the country's most successful authors, who tend to dominate the best-seller list year after year.

Tom Clancy held the number one slot with *Rainbow Six,* his latest thriller. Other well-established authors on the fiction list included Sidney Sheldon (*Tell Me Your Dreams*), Richard North Patterson (*No Safe Place*), Judy Blume (*Summer Sisters*), Patricia Cornwell (*Point of Origin*), John Irving (*A Widow for One Year*), and John Grisham (*The Street Lawyer,* still on the list more than seven months after its initial release date in February 1998).

The nonfiction winners represented a more eclectic mix of authors and genres. While Christopher Anderson's *The Day Diana Died* (first place) capitalized on the one-year anniversary of the tragic demise of Diana, Mitch Albom's second place title *Tuesday with Morrie* (on the list for forty-eight weeks) described this sportswriter's weekly visits with his old college mentor, then near death. Other successful titles included entertainer Jimmy Buffet's *A Pirate Looks at Fifty,* Frank McCourt's *Angela's Ashes* (his difficult childhood in Limerick), Bill Bryson's *A Walk in the Woods* (humor and hiking on the Appalachian Trail), and Thomas Cahill's *The Gifts of the Jews.*

For the most part, the paperback lists replicate in essence the hard cover lists. This was noticeable among the fiction results, which contained its usual smattering of popular authors, including Danielle Steele's *Special Delivery,* Sidney Sheldon's *The Best Laid Plans,* Nora Roberts' *Rising Tides,* and Charles Frazier's *Cold Mountain.* The nonfiction list encompassed its usual mix of "star" books (television personality Drew Carey's *Dirty Jokes and Beer* and comedian George Carlin's *Brain Droppings*) along with serious works by Stephen E. Ambrose (*Citizen Soldiers,* the U.S. Army in Europe during World War II), Jonathan Harr (*A Civil Action;* industrial polluters), and Katherine Graham's autobiography (*Personal History*).

The ever-popular "Advice, How-to, and Miscellaneous" lists demonstrated the intense popularity of titles in this genre. Among the hard-cover titles John Gray's *Men Are From Mars, Women Are From Venus* was on the *Times* list for 235 weeks, sharing the spotlight with H. Leigh Steward, et al. (*Sugar Busters,* a diet book), Suze Orman's *The 9 Steps to Financial Freedom,* and Peter J. D'Amamo's *Eat Right 4 Your Type.*

The paperback collection also listed diet books (Robert C. Atkin's *Dr. Atkin's New Diet Revolution* and Michael R. Eades' *Protein Power*) along with self-help (Richard Carlson's *Don't Sweat the Small Stuff . . . And It's All Small Stuff*) and the trendy *The Beanie Baby Handbook 1998* (Les Fox and Sue Fox).

Juvenile titles comprise the second part of the trade list. BISG reported that 335 million units were sold in 1991, 327.9 million in 1992; tallies for 1996 (379.9 million) and 1997 (343.8 million) were unimpressive.[3]

October 16, 1995 bestseller data from *Publishers Weekly* revealed that Jon Scieska's *Math Curse* and Sam McBratney's *Guess How Much I Love You* held down the top two positions on the juvenile picture bestseller list. On the fiction list, (1) Lois Lowry's *The Giver* and (2) Dick Kink–Smith's *Babe: The Gallant Pig* were top ranked, as were (1) R. L. Stine's *Goosebumps* and (2) Ann M. Martin's *Babysitters Club* on the paperback juvenile series list. Top sellers on the nonfiction list included two titles by Joanna Cole: (1) *The Magic School Bus in the Time of the Dinosaurs* and (2) *The Magic School Bus Inside a Hurricane.*

Mass Market Paperbacks

Mass market paperbacks are popular and ubiquitous. In 1998 they accounted for $1.5 billion in sales (a 6.73 percent market share) but 483.7 million units (a hefty

20.15 percent of all U.S. unit sales). The basic mass market paperback marketing strategy has not changed since the days of Ian Ballantine: low prices; high volume; and a "no guts, no glory" selling concept.

The top names on the October 16, 1995 mass market bestseller list are familiar ones: (1) Tom Clancy and Steve Pieczenik's Tom Clancy's *Op-Center 11: Mirror Image;* (2) Sidney Sheldon's *Nothing Lasts Forever;* (3) Dick Francis' *Wild Horses;* (4) Robert Jordan's *Lord of Chaos;* and (5) Nelson DeMille's *Spencerville.* Other "brand name" authors included Danielle Steel, John Irving, and Mary Higgins Clark. Only John Grisham and Crichton were missing.

Book Clubs

Growing from a solid sales revenues base in 1989 of $704 million (and 111.7 million units), tallies by the late 1990s were strong. Dollar sales were steady in 1996 ($1.09 billion) and 1998 ($1.21 billion), but unit sales in both 1996 (135.5 million) and 1998 (141.6 million) indicated a sharp increase, up 32.71 percent between 1992–1998.

Mail Order Books

The mail order book market was in a state of "free fall" by the late 1990s, a clear indication its traditional market was being challenged seriously by superstores, Internet sales, and price clubs. Annual dollar sales declined steadily between 1989 ($796.8 million) to 1998 ($470.5 million); unit sales figures closely followed (1989, 157.2 million units; 1998, 76.1 million).

Projections through 2002 were bleak. Dollar sales were pegged to decline 4.18 percent between 1997–2002. Unit sales will decline to 58.4 million units in 2002, down 31.86 percent between 1997–2002.

Religious Publishing

While some politicians might express dismay at what they perceive to be a moral decline in this nation, religious publishing was in the midst of a veritable renaissance by the late 1990s. Dollar sales increased sharply between 1989 ($737.1 million) and 1998 ($1.18 billion), as did unit sales (1989: 131.7 million; 1998: 170.5 million, +29.5 percent).

This niche has two distinct categories: (1) bibles, testaments, and so on; and (2) other religious publications. In the bible/testament group, dollar sales were strong although unit sales seemed lackluster between 1989 ($201 million; 21.3 million units) and 1998 ($296 million; 26.2 million). Dollar sales through 2002 should top the $325.7 million mark; unit sales will inch up to 28.1 million.

The "other religious" category (inspirational works, biographies, autobiographies, histories, etc.), dollar sales grew from $536.1 million in 1989 to $882 million in 1998; by 2002 revenues should be in the billion dollar range. Unit sales were also impressive between 1989 (110.4 million) and 1998 (144.8 million); 159.6 million units are anticipated to be sold in 2002.

Professional Publishing

Professional titles are grouped by BISG into four categories: business, law, medical, and technical, scientific, and other; however, many industry analysts combine scientific, medical, and technical into one pool (called STM). One might assume that most professional titles are issued in hardbound format; the opposite is the case. Of the 170.3 million professional books sold in the U.S. in 1998, 64.1 million were hardbound and 101.1 million were paperback. Yet dollar revenues came predominantly from hardback sales ($3.02 billion); paperbacks totaled $1.13 billion. Professional titles have been issued in both print and electronic formats since the 1970s, and additional electronic inroads will occur by 2003.

Interest in business titles has grown steadily since 1989 due to a combination of factors: uncertainty about the economy after the stock market crash of 1987 and the recession of the early 1990s; concerns about the impact of mergers and acquisitions on American business life; and a surge in the total number of students registered in business degree programs and courses (including continuing education programs).

Dollar revenues jumped from $481.7 million in 1989 to $852 million in 1998, representing 18.48 percent of the professional market. By 2002 this market should reach $1.16 billion. Unit sale increases were modest (1989: 36.8 million; 1998: 53.7 million) with 72.9 million expected to be sold in 2002.

While many editorial writers quibbled over the state of the legal profession in this nation in the 1990s, sales of law books exploded, jumping from $883.3 million in 1989 to $1.5 billion in 1998. Unit tallies were not as dramatic, reaching the 25.5 million unit plateau in 1998. By 2002 dollar revenues should grow ($1.98 billion) although unit sales will be more modest (27.9 million).

Medical publishing also grew because of the information explosion in the STM field. Revenues increased from a healthy $490.5 million in 1989 to $919 million in 1998. The prognosis for 2002 is an impressive $1.1 billion. However, the medical publishing field will also undergo a metamorphosis as more products are released electronically, cutting into print unit sales, which slid upward from 15 million units in 1989 to 19.2 in 1995 (the 2003 outlook is for 19.0 million).

The last component is the eclectic technical, scientific, and other areas. As long as English remains the primary international language in this field, the sale of American printed products (and eventually electronic formats) should continue unimpeded throughout the remainder of this decade. Results for 1989 ($737.6 million) through 1998 ($1.06 billion) augur well for the future (2003: projected sales of $1.17 billion).

University Presses

University presses publish serious nonfiction titles in a wide array of disciplines from economics (*Poverty and Inequality in Latin America: The Impact of Adjustment and Recovery*) to film studies (*Alfred Hitchcock: The Legacy of Victorianism*) to literature (*Internal Difference and Meanings in the "Roman de la Rose"*). Twenty-five presses issue titles in original fiction (e.g., Southern Methodist and Arkansas) and twenty-eight publish poetry (e.g., Illinois and Nevada). The goal of a university press is to transmit knowledge and extend the classroom into the community. While small in number (approximately 114 presses belong to the Association of American University Presses and output, their reach is felt in the publishing community because of cutting edge STM research and critical studies of America's political and cultural institutions.

BISG calculated total sales to be $391.8 million in 1998 (up from $227 million in 1989). Unit data was 18.5 million in 1998 (versus 14.4 million in 1989). The 2002 estimate was 20.0 million units. Paperbacks (10.9 million units) sold more briskly than hardcovers (6.9 million).

Peter C. Grenquist, Executive Director of the Association of American University Presses insisted, in an interview with this author on July 14, 1995, that BISG's sales revenue calculations were too high. He based his conclusions on research studies conducted by his office among AAUP members. In 1989 Grenquist's predecessor took the same position in another interview with this author, casting doubts on BISG's data collection procedures for university press dollar and unit sales.

ELHI

The elementary and high school (ELHI) textbook, reference book, and related materials market is a big business, accounting for 14.3 percent of the nation dollar sales ($3.3 billion, up from $1.986 billion in 1989) and 12.5 percent of all units (302.2 million) in 1998 (up from 222.9 million in 1989). The preponderance of ELHI titles are paperback (177.1 million in 1998).

Some media critics insist that electronic publishing products will make substantial inroads into the printed ELHI market. In light of the precarious state of education in this nation, tight budgets, a changing student population in many urban centers, and a national average of fifteen students per classroom computer, it seems difficult to believe that a radical transformation will occur in this decade (or even by 2005).

Another mitigating factor relates to the need of ELHI students to use printed workbooks and textbooks in order to perform homework assignments. There are a variety of different home computer machines (MACs; IBMs), operating systems, and programs (WordPerfect, MS Word); and most computers are in the homes of families with +$35,000 in annual income. Educators who seek to rely on adopting electronic publications in a nation that is not 100 percent computerized will create electronic "haves and have-nots," hardly an acceptable formula from an ethical or legal point of view.

In all likelihood, BISG's estimates for 2002 sales figures ($3.67 billion) and unit sales (271.5 million) should be realized since this niche is not ready to go electronic from a technology, economic, or public policy point of view.

College

How can a market survive when the price of textbooks has become astronomical? For example, one of the best accounting textbooks on the market in the mid-1990s is Horngren and Harrison's *Accounting,* retailing at $85.00 (hardcover) in 1999. Is the price of a textbook so high that publishers will price themselves out of the market?

College professors select texts and other assigned readings, not the consumers who must purchase the item. As long as instructors are not sensitive enough to price issues, the marketplace will determine the retail cost of new (and used) textbooks. Yet the used textbook market, along with other practices (students sharing or copying textbooks), have made serious inroads into what is a lucrative publishing niche.

BISG's unit figures covering 1989 (148.4 million) to 1998 (175.9 million) illustrate the plight of college textbook publishing: the student market is growing faster than the textbook market.

Electronic published works will penetrate the college textbooks market. A sizable number of colleges have invested substantial amounts in fiber optic lines and computer centers. A small number of schools insist that every entering student purchase a computer. Textbook publishers wait for the day when they can sell a textbook on-line rather than printing copies on speculation; while that day will come, the outlook (and into the 2005–2015 decade) is certainly "optimistic" for the defenders of print.

The BISG outlook for 2002 is 207.2 million units. Dollar figures are healthier, reaching the $3.9 billion level in 2002. The publishers' strategy is crystal clear: charge more on fewer units.

U.S. BOOK RETURNS

Can the domestic U.S. book market absorb this outpouring of titles? Even with the emergence of superstores, price clubs, and viable global markets, one must wonder about the elasticity of the marketplace to consume this plethora of new books.

Between 1984 and 1989, the U.S. book industry drowned in a recorded $7.88 billion of returns. This meant that 23.87 percent of all books published during those years were returned to America's publishers for full credit, a sad waste of financial and natural resources.

This massive return of books undermined seriously the stability of the book industry, causing many publishers to question the efficacy of a system that failed to operate successfully during a period of exceptionally stable business conditions. This was a period, after all, free from high rates of interest or inflation, recession, or a war.

The *Publishers' Monthly Domestic Sales* reports, issued by the Association of American Publishers (AAP), provided detailed information on gross sales, total returns, and net sales in twelve key market segments. These reports are based on the voluntary submission of confidential information by (approximately) 110 AAP members each month. These firms, overall, represent a cross section of the entire publishing community, but they account for upwards of 80 percent of all books sold in this nation.

AAP revealed that U.S. book sales grew at an 85.82 percent pace during the years 1984 through 1989, easily exceeding the 15.24 percent rate of inflation (as measured by the Consumer Price Index). Both juvenile niches emerged as market segment leaders; paperbound titles reported an enviable +229.06 percent increase; and hardbound juvenile books grew at a solid +189.19 percent rate. Adult trade hardbound titles posted a +111.14 percent pace, with the always important technical–science–business–medical (STM) category reporting in at +103.48 percent. However, the largest growth rate was recorded by the bible–testament–hymnal–prayerbook niche, which exceeded +2,005.00 percent.

Between 1984 and 1989, the U.S. book industry posted $7.88 billion in domestic book returns. The mass market paperback segment withstood the greatest onslaught of returns, topping the $2.9 billion mark and generating 36.83 percent of all returns.

The college market was second with $1.36 billion, surpassing the adult hardbound niche's $1.25 billion tally. This volatile pattern caused deep concern among textbook publishers, especially because part of the problem centered on the intractable used textbook market. Eventually textbook houses would adopt shorter revision cycles (e.g., issuing a textbook every two or three years), a strategy that proved to be ineffective. "Print on demand" textbooks (a process whereby an instructor selects chapters from various books in an order he or she deems to be appropriate) held out some hope in a bleak marketplace. "Electronic" formats (CD-ROM, computer disks, on-line) might address effectively what has emerged as a nightmare to publishers and authors (but a boon to college bookstores and consumers).

This data also revealed wildly uneven sales patterns in most of the market segments, especially in the adult trade paperback, book club, and mail order categories. It appears that book sales personnel failed to grasp what the market could absorb (and overordered print runs) or responded to unrealistic sales quotas by convincing bookstore managers that "this title cannot miss." The bottom line was a disaster.

What patterns emerged in the net sales of books? The AAP data revealed a lack of "stable" business cycles. Overall, two of the largest niches (specifically the adult trade and book clubs) posted acceptable numbers in 1985, slipped in 1986, rebounded in 1987, and declined again in 1988. Mass market reported lamentable results in 1985 and 1986, jumped upward in 1987, and regressed in 1988 and 1989. Overall, the university press categories were cheerless, with the paperback niche generating a –5.91 percent decline in 1986.

However, when these niches were analyzed using annual percentage changes, an alarming phenomenon was evident. All twelve segments recorded erratic patterns and steep negative declines, a sign the industry was skating on thin ice.

How severe was the glut of book returns? Only one niche (bibles–testaments–hymnals–prayerbooks) was in single digits (at 5.31 percent); the next smallest tally was 12.02 percent, posted by juvenile paperbacks.

Which categories sustained the deepest returns? Mass market paperbacks posted returns in excess of forty percent. Adult trade hardcover was second, and book clubs were third, an unsettling event since the clubs claim to have a firm grasp of both the market and their members' preferences.

The Book Industry Study Group conducted some additional research on book returns addressing the years 1992–1997. They discovered that, in almost every book category, publishers withstood sharp increases in return rates. The adult trade hardbound niche sustained increases in returns between 1992 (27.8 percent) and 1997 (36.3 percent), a fate that also befell adult trade paperbacks (1992: 21.5 percent; 1997: 23.6 percent).

Juvenile hardbound books posted a slight decline (1992: 17.6 percent; 1997: 17.3 percent); juvenile paperbacks, on the other hand, jumped upward from a 22.5 percent return rate in 1992 to a 26.4 percent level in 1997.

Mass market paperbacks continued to exhibit volatile trends with returns in a staggering percent range (1992: 43.8 percent; 1997: 46.4 percent), topping all categories during these six years. Mail order books was the only other niche posting high rates (1992: 18.0 percent; 1997: 25.2 percent).

More moderate upswings were recorded for book clubs (1992: 21.0 percent; 1997: 20.0 percent), technical, scientific, business, law, and medicine (1992: 15.0 percent; 1997: 15.5 percent), both university press categories (hardbound 1992: 18.7 percent, 1997: 17.6 percent; and paperback 1992: 19.7 percent, 1997: 20.3 percent), and college (1992: 21.6 percent; 1997: 23.2 percent).

The Causes of Book Returns

Book printers, binders, and freight companies make a good living because of the overprinting of titles and their returns; publishers and bookstores do not profit since it costs them a significant amount of time and money to pay for books that fail. Authors also abhor the return system because every return represents a lost opportunity to reach a reader.

If returns are a drag on the economic stability of retailers and publishers and the livelihoods of authors, why do they exist? The bookselling market demands a return policy since bookstore owners are reluctant to buy books by unknown authors, works of serious fiction, and poetry. After all, they posit, why tie up capital, scarce shelf space, and other resources on books that probably will not sell? If you stick to known commodities (the "Tom Clancys" of the world) and steady selling backlist titles, you can make a living. Book publishers are compelled to discount titles and offer a full refund to the bookseller if the book does not "turn" (i.e., inventory "turn-over").

The paperback revolution, which began after World War II, was dependent on the mass distribution of hundreds of new and reprinted titles every month. Some of the early leaders in the "paperbacking of America" were originally in the periodical industry, so they drew upon their own extensive business experiences to fashion an effective distribution system.[4] Magazine distributors were asked to stock book racks in drugstores, bus and train terminals, and five-and-ten-cent stores, the precursors of the K-Marts, the Wal-Marts, 7-11's, airline terminals, and supermarkets of today. Because newspapers and magazines could be returned for full credit, mass market paperback publishers had to adopt this policy. Do other industries utilize this type of system? In reality very few do, and they are mainly in the perishable food industry.

Solutions to Book Returns?

Over the years many "solutions" have been offered to curb massive returns. Some of them include: (1) increase the discount rate and refuse to accept any returns; (2) keep the current discount structure and refuse to accept any returns; (3) develop incentive policies that penalize wholesalers with high return rates; (4) reduce the number of copies printed; (5) control the number of new titles (especially in the literary fiction category) issued each year; (6) stop or curtail the publication of mid-list books; (7) increase the development of "attractive, innovative" titles (e.g., cookbooks, cat books, etc.); (8) convince book retailers to adopt rational ordering procedures; and (9) curb the puffy rhetoric and aggressive tactics of sales personnel.

Perhaps all of these scenarios have merit and will end the return nightmare; perhaps none of them will work; perhaps it is time to think about adopting and modifying those marketing ideas and practices that do seem to work rather effectively for other industries in this nation.

BOOK SALES BY CHANNELS OF DISTRIBUTION

Book publishers rely on a variety of channels to distribute books in this nation. Many industry analysts have been critical about the entire distribution system, which often adversely affected sales and the ability of consumers to find titles in stock at local bookstores. Overall the system seems to work because of the proliferation of superstores and price clubs, the development of regional and national book distribution firms, and the advent of innovative marketing opportunities (including "800" numbers, the Internet, and web sites). Supplementing this network is a vast library system able to supply titles to local patrons. Nevertheless, the distribution of books could stand some creative procedures to maximize the availability of more titles to more people.

General Retailers

If England was a nation of shopkeepers in the nineteenth century, in this century America is the land of retailing, ranging from small "mom and pop" establishments to national giants (Wal-Mart, K-Mart, etc.). This vast network of establishments forms the firm bedrock of one of the world's most sophisticated merchandising systems, an infrastructure book publishers cultivated in the last three decades.

Traditionally the retail channel is the largest, most important channel of book distribution in this nation. In 1997 it accounted for $6.65 billion in total sales (representing 32.04 percent of all revenues) and 1.078 billion units (47.14 percent). Barring unforeseen economic downturns, BISG anticipates America to witness a veritable explosion of retail activity in the years through 2002, resulting in these firms accounting for $8.059 billion in sales (+31.08 percent); unit sales will keep pace, reaching 1.159 billion in 2002.

There has been a dramatic shift in book retailing in this nation; independents have sustained an erosion in sales; and non-bookstore retail establishments captured more than half of all book sales in 1997.

The College Market

Starting in the 1960s college bookstores became general trade bookstores (as well as "general stores" selling computers, music CDs and cassettes, and clothing). So it is not surprising that book sales to college stores in 1997 topped the $3.279 billion level. The outlook for 2002 is certainly upbeat, with projected sales of $4.33 billion and 297.4 million units.

Libraries and Institutions

In spite of steep declines in book purchases, libraries and institutions remain an important component of the book distribution system. In 1997 they purchased 4.26 percent of all books sold in this nation, representing 95.5 million units and $1.829 billion in sales dollars (8.81 percent of sales revenues).

Respectable growth patterns were projected by BISG for 2002, growing 27.26 percent in dollar sales ($2.3 billion) and units (+9.11 percent; 104.2 million).

Schools

The school book market is gigantic in this nation; and it will retain this position of importance for the next ten to fifteen years in spite of the development of electronic products. In 1989 schools bought 245.9 million books (for $2.28 billion); by 1997 these tallies jumped to 308.6 million books and $3.3 billion.

By 2002 BISG anticipates schools to consume 301.3 million units and $3.848 billion.

Direct to Consumers

The "direct to consumers" is the second largest dollar channel of distribution in this nation.

Growing from annual sales of $2.856 billion in 1989, 1997's totals exceeded $3.82 billion. A solid $4.7 billion is possible for 2002.

Unit sales declined from 315.7 million in 1989 to 290.9 million in 1997. Sales in 2002 will hit 300.1 million.

Sales to Wholesalers and Jobbers

One of the most important channels is the invisible but highly significant wholesalers and jobbers niche (supplying titles to general retailers, colleges, libraries and institutions, schools). Gross sales reached $2 billion in 1989 and $3.03 billion in 1997. It is likely that this market will post strong gains, reaching the $3.77 billion mark in 2002.

Unit sales were also impressive, growing from 474.1 million units in 1989 to 509.2 million in 1997, and 2002 tallies should reach 534.1 million.

CASE STUDY

The Changing Library Market for Books

Libraries comprise a significant but declining niche for book sales. A review of the six sales categories tracked by BISG indicated that libraries and institutions generate consistently the highest average dollars-per-book unit. While the national mean for all books sold in the United States stood at $5.49 per unit in 1986, libraries paid $11.89 per book (a differential of $6.40); this trend continued into 1993 when libraries topped the $17.18 mark while the national median was $8.04 (for a sizable difference of $9.14 per title).

Table 1-3 outlines these trends covering the years 1986–1994.

While consumers were able to take advantage of heavily discounted books at superstores, price clubs, supermarkets, and other retail outlets, libraries appeared to be captives of a relatively rigid two-tier channel of distribution. Table 1-4 addresses the years 1995–2002.

While library material expenditures increased 104.56 percent between 1987–1999, book purchases grew 78.07 percent. The end result was that books as a

TABLE 1-3   Publishers' Average Dollars-Per-Unit Sales by U.S. Sales Categories: 1986–1994

Categories	1986	1987	1988	1989	1990	1991	1992	1993	1994
General Retailers	$ 3.56	3.97	4.18	4.43	4.66	4.86	5.16	5.51	5.70
College	7.56	8.02	8.37	8.73	9.33	9.59	9.89	10.25	10.44
Libraries & Institutions	11.89	12.83	13.73	14.29	14.89	15.41	16.13	16.69	17.20
School	6.97	8.04	8.62	9.06	9.41	9.71	9.80	10.13	10.09
Direct to Consumer	7.72	8.29	8.74	9.05	9.54	9.95	10.65	11.20	11.70
Other	1.30	1.41	1.50	1.56	1.66	1.75	1.82	1.92	1.96
Average Total for All Books	5.49	6.04	6.34	6.64	6.99	7.20	7.45	7.83	8.00

Source: Book Industry Study Group, *Book Industry Trends 1993* (New York: Book Industry Study Group, 1993), p. 2–186; Book Industry Study Group, *Book Industry Trends 1994* (New York: Book Industry Study Group, 1994), p. 2–186; and Book Industry Study Group, *Book Industry Trends 1998* (New York: Book Industry Study Group, 1998), p. 2–184.

percentage of total library expenditures have been shrinking steadily since 1987, when books represented 54.1 percent of all library expenditures. By 1993 their share barely topped the 50 percent mark; and it dipped to 49.68 percent in 1994. The prognosis for 1998 is a 47.35 percent mark.

TABLE 1-4   Publishers' Average Dollars-Per-Unit Sales by U.S. Sales Categories: 1995–2002

Categories	1995	1996	1997	1998	1999	2000	2001	2002
General Retailers	$ 5.77	5.88	6.17	6.31	6.48	6.64	6.80	6.95
College	10.87	11.31	11.95	12.40	12.93	13.37	13.84	14.29
Libraries & Institutions	17.96	18.53	19.16	19.76	20.34	21.16	21.80	22.35
School	10.31	10.53	10.71	11.33	11.99	12.60	13.21	13.81
Direct to Consumer	12.25	12.50	13.13	13.63	14.09	14.56	14.97	15.37
Other	2.05	2.02	2.17	2.22	2.29	2.35	2.41	2.47
Average Total for All Books	8.27	8.49	8.99	9.31	9.65	9.98	10.29	10.59

Source: Book Industry Study Group, *Book Industry Trends 1993* (New York: Book Industry Study Group, 1993), p. 2–186; Book Industry Study Group, *Book Industry Trends 1994* (New York: Book Industry Study Group, 1994), p. 2–186; and Book Industry Study Group, *Book Industry Trends 1998* (New York: Book Industry Study Group, 1998), p. 2–184.

These BISG calculations may have factored in the real and potential impact of electronic publishing and the communications highway. Even if these issues were part of the calculus, the rapid rise in importance of these two areas (and the plethora of multimedia computers with built-in CD-ROM equipment) indicates that a steeper decline in book purchases may become a reality.[5]

Table 1-5 reports on this library phenomenon.

Why did this occur? By the early 1980s, America was deeply immersed in the "information age," and libraries were compelled to change the way they serviced their patrons' diverse information needs.[6] Most people need detailed and timely data on a variety of personal or business matters, and serials (magazines and journals) played a significant role in the efficient transmission of information. Traditionally, the U.S. library has been one of the primary consumers of serials, especially in the high visibility scientific, technical, and medical (STM) niche.[7]

Since 1980 total page output and library subscription rates for these items have increased dramatically, exceeding significantly the cost of any other published product. Librarians have been hard pressed to keep up with these surging levels.[8]

When the cost of a book exceeds $100.00, it is cause for alarm, and many STM serials have library subscription prices far in excess of that amount. For example, the average annual subscription to the most prominent medical journal published in Holland topped $900.00 in 1993, and one chemistry journal reached the $13,000.00

TABLE 1-5   U.S. Library Purchases: 1987–1999 (Millions of Dollars)

Year	Total Library Material Purchases	Percent Change from Previous Year	Book Purchases	Percent Change from Previous Year	Books as a Percentage of Total Library Budget
1987	1,987.5	—	1,075.3	—	54.10
1988	2,124.6	+6.90	1,125.9	+4.71	52.99
1989	2,358.4	+11.00	1,260.4	+11.95	53.44
1990	2,507.8	+6.33	1,321.8	+4.87	52.71
1991	2,565.7	+2.31	1,322.9	+0.08	51.56
1992	2,655.6	+3.50	1,354.1	+2.36	50.99
1993	2,808.9	+5.77	1,413.7	+4.40	50.33
1994	3,014.0	+7.30	1,497.5	+5.93	49.68
1995	3,244.7	+7.65	1,586.3	+5.93	48.89
1996	3,452.7	+6.41	1,672.2	+5.42	48.43
1997	3,669.9	+6.19	1,751.5	+4.74	47.73
1998	3,857.9	+5.12	1,828.9	+4.42	47.41
1999	4,065.7	+5.39	1,914.8	+4.70	47.10
Totals	34,533.40	+91.60	17,496.10	—	—

Source: Book Industry Study Group, *Book Industry Trends 1993* (New York: Book Industry Study Group, 1993), pp. 3–28 through 3–30; and Book Industry Study Group, *Book Industry Trends 1995* (New York: Book Industry Study Group, 1995), p. 3–28.

annual subscription rate, steep prices for any library regardless of endowment! While university and research libraries are the primary customers for these specialized and critically important periodicals, many public library systems maintain subscriptions.[9]

When queried, journal publishers respond, quite accurately, that information is expensive to collect and costly to disseminate; these economic facts dictate the high library subscription rates for journals, along with a needed and predetermined profit margin. Association based serials (e.g., *The New England Journal of Medicine*) tend to have lower subscription prices in this nation (because of association subsidies and a tax-exempt status) than periodicals released by profit-making companies unable to obtain subventions and compelled to pay taxes on their revenues.

Unfortunately, the staggering growth in journal price increases materialized at a time when the vast majority of American libraries faced forbidding budgetary obstacles. Connecticut, for example, requested that all of the state's public libraries reduce their 1992 budgets by 10 percent, a trend that continued into the middle of the 1990s. Some industry observers reported that 45 percent of American libraries expected to undergo reductions in 1992.

What compounded this conundrum was the fact that American libraries reported a sharp 4.3 percent increase in circulation demand between 1988–1989, and additional circulation increases are anticipated throughout the 1990s. How do librarians trim budgets, keep pace with the plethora of new book releases, augment budgetary allocations for needed periodicals, and keep their patrons happy when they request more services?[10]

John Berry, editor-in-chief of *Library Journal,* believes that electronic versions of serials could provide librarians with the "ultimate answer" to their fiscal problems. While Berry conceded that print journals will not disappear in either the short or long run, it is obvious that on-line and CD-ROM versions of serials could be the intermediate answer to the "serials crisis." Berry cautioned, however, that readable, user-friendly, and cost-efficient computer technologies, and the concomitant purchase of electronic publications, just might provide libraries with the "magic bullet" to elude the debilitating serials price spiral that has aggravated all librarians since 1980.[11] However, this scenario is costly. Hardware and software would have to be purchased, and some library patrons might resist the introduction of electronic periodicals.

Document Delivery Systems

There is another option available to librarians: "document delivery systems."[12] This approach provides a librarian with a plethora of intriguing options. A survey could be undertaken to ascertain the most frequently used serials and those that merely attract dust. The library can then cancel costly subscriptions to journals that are not used or are marginally of interest to patrons. If an individual wants to read a particular article in a canceled journal, the library can contact one of the document delivery systems and order on demand a copy of the specific article. This allows a library to cancel little used journals while providing needed budgetary relief, and, ironically, obtaining a copy of an article for a patron, thereby keeping "peace in the family." This "pay for only what you use" concept has captured the attention of many librarians.[13]

One of the most interesting national document delivery services is offered by the Colorado Alliance of Research Libraries (known simply as CARL to librarians). CARL provides access via a computer to over 12,000 journals and periodicals. Using a consumer or corporate credit or debit charge card, an individual can access CARL's extensive "UnCover" service and acquire a complete fax copy of any article in their collection. The cost for this service, which is paid by the patron and collected by the librarian, is a reasonable $6.50 per article plus a mandatory copyright fee. As for delivery time, CARL has a twenty-four hour turnaround time. Anyone familiar with the publishing industry realizes that this service's potential impact on librarians, users, and the publishing industry is unlimited. Obviously, there are "problems" or "challenges" associated with marketing and pricing these services.

This procedure shifts costs from the library to the consumer willing and eager to obtain a needed article. This first became popular at research libraries; however, by 1995 many libraries offered this service. For example, every public library in New Jersey can obtain articles through a state library association managed consortium.

Regional Library Consortiums

Another option available to librarians is the creation of regional consortiums.[14] One of the most interesting ones is the Bergen County (New Jersey) Cooperative Library System (BCCLS; known as "buckles"), servicing a large suburban region of +825,380 individuals. Bergen County, the thirteenth largest populated area in the United States, is nestled next to New York City, Rockland and Orange Counties in New York State, and Hudson County in New Jersey.

BCCLS, a federation of seventy public libraries with sizable holdings of almost 4.5 million books, 7,374 serials, 1,121 musical scores, 8,907 "talking books," 40,000 audio cassettes, 30,000 music CDs, and 50,000 videos. It was ranked eleventh in the United States in 1992 for total library expenditures ($29.1 million), ahead of Boston (twelfth; $27.9 million) and Baltimore (seventeenth; $23.6). Chicago was ranked first ($67.6 million), followed by Los Angeles (second; $64.3 million), New York (third; $62.2 million), and Philadelphia (fourth; $44.2 million). BCCLS also placed thirteenth in both population and materials expenditures ($4.2 million; Los Angeles was first at $8.3 million). Yet it placed fifth in the nation on library per capita expenditures of $36.10 (among all U.S. regions with at least a 500,000 population base). Regions surpassing BCCLS included Cleveland (first; $62.29), Boston (second; $48.55), Cuyahoga County (Cleveland; third; $43.16), and Seattle (fourth; $42.39). In addition BCCLS's circulation figures placed it eighteenth in the United States while its total number of volumes was ranked eighth.

BCCLS serves a total population of over 825,380; in 1993 the system had 535,534 registered borrowers (with 64,755 newly registered). Over 6.06 million books were checked out by patrons, and BCCLS employed a DEC VAX 6610 computer with 380 MB memory (augmented by a DEC 7410 Alpha processor and other equipment) to handle its automated circulation system, a LePAC CD-ROM electronic union catalog of holdings (185 CD-ROM units were in place), OPAC (Online Public Access Catalog listing author, title, or subject), and an online magazine index.

Robert White, the Executive Director of BCCLS, reported that "it was started in 1979 to improve access to library materials, expand automated bibliographic access to information, enhance the quality of reference services, and strengthen the facilities management of libraries."[15]

White indicated that BCCLS's libraries pay an annual membership fee (ranging from $6,000 to $25,000) to cover costs associated with the computerized circulation system and other related services. Individuals who live or work in any of the communities serviced by BCCLS can use any of the libraries free of charge (there are no transaction fees), and over 1.04 million titles were taken out utilizing their reciprocal BCCLS borrowing service in 1993; 127,613 of these books were through electronic loans. The libraries enjoy access to 4.449 million titles (532,017 individual titles are on the system), and 617,398 new books were added that year. White stated that "this represents 35,731 unique titles. BCCLS libraries enjoy the luxury of a reduced rate structure when purchasing titles (without the hassle of a joint purchasing system) and a county-wide inner-loan system paid for by Bergen County's Board of Chosen Freeholders (i.e., County Executives).

Patrons include, according to White, "new immigrants from developing countries, well-known authors who reside in our communities, prominent athletes [from the New York Yankees and the New York Giants football team], television and Broadway personalities, and Ph.D. candidates. These people have an insatiable appetite for books." This type of regional association works because books, literally millions of them, are made available to individuals who do not want to purchase them. BCCLS participates in a document delivery system.

A review of the demographic profile of BCCLS's patrons was quite revealing. Over 16.91 percent of these individuals were juveniles (under the age of fourteen). More than 21.07 percent were more than sixty years of age, while the vast majority of patrons (62.21 percent) were between fifteen and sixty, facts that have a direct impact on the types of titles ordered.

However, "macro" circulation data reveals conclusively that BCCLS patrons are interested in other types of books. In 1993 6,061,093 items were checked out by BCCLS patrons; 21.45 percent of the total (1,300,146) were nonfiction while 25.02 percent (1,516,621) were fiction titles. The remaining tallies included juvenile (2,229,420; 36.78 percent), multimedia (767,063; 12.14 percent), and periodicals (187,563; only 3.09 percent). The strong showing of multimedia illustrates the importance and popularity of this growing format, another significant fact publishers should ponder.

Circulation figures for the top libraries in the BCCLS system (ranked according to total circulation) are also revealing because they demonstrate that active reading patterns are found in all types of communities, from "blue collar" towns (Garfield) to middle-class communities (Teaneck, Paramus, and Bergenfield) to affluent ones (Ridgewood and Wyckoff).

The specific holdings of the BCCLS libraries reveal a strong commitment to all six principal formats; however, holdings do not always mirror circulation patterns. Of the 4.5 million items in the BCCLS collection, 36.26 percent are nonfiction. Fiction (20.07 percent) was underrepresented, as was juvenile (27.54 percent), in terms of consumer demand. Periodicals (8.46 percent) do not circulate with the same frequency as fiction and nonfiction titles, but they are a mainstay in libraries, which explains this high percentage figure. The tally for reference seems low at 3.87 percent.

When do Bergen County residents use their public library? Are there circulation "peaks" and "valleys"? Again, the BCCLS data is quite revealing because it seems to contradict prevalent bookselling patterns.

The busiest month is July, with December recording the smallest circulation figures. Overall, circulation seems to pick up momentum after Christmas in the cold January–March period. February's tallies are light because it is a short month. Warmer spring weather appears to depress reading activity until the summer vacation period. There is a steep decline in September with only modest increases before Christmas, patterns that defy normal bookselling trends.

Daily circulation numbers varied dramatically, however, ranging from a high of 40,437 on July 6th (a Wednesday and the first business day after the Fourth of July holiday) to a low of 21,021 on May 18th (a Tuesday).

In 1995 BCCLS added two new options. The first allowed patrons to access the BCCLS's computer databank (including the electronic card catalog system) via a home computer with a modem. This innovative service, which generated over 2,800 inquiries in the first three weeks of operation, allowed patrons to search through the computerized card catalog and reserve a title. Other features included a list of the *New York Times Book Review* and general information about all of the BCCLS libraries. Information about magazine and newspaper articles was added to the system in October 1995.

The second feature was NJPIX (the North Jersey Public Information Exchange), which offered patrons the opportunity to search for local, state, and national information and databases and library catalog listings. In essence NJPIX brought Internet resources directly to consumers without utilizing one of the commercial services (Prodigy or America On-Line). Each dial-up session was limited to sixty minutes.

A review of the dial-in access system revealed that BCCLS libraries were purchasing fiction bestsellers in sizable amounts, but nonfiction acquisitions were lagging. For example, on July 14, 1995, the BCCLS libraries had on hand 353 copies of John Grisham's *The Rainmaker* (then the nation's number one bestseller) but only eighty-seven copies of *The Hot Zone* (the number one nonfiction title). Copies of the top ten fiction bestsellers tallied 1,566, whereas nonfiction copies trailed at 535.

While BCCLS may or may not be representative of the typical regional library system, it is clear that community libraries participating in this organization provide an invaluable service to their patrons: free and timely access to a bountiful supply of books (including the Internet). The role of public libraries in the transmission of knowledge and information is of paramount importance to readers and the entire publishing industry.

A Small Town Library Confronts Electronic Issues

Bergenfield is a "typical" small town library serving the reading needs of over 25,000 residents. Ms. Mary Joyce Doyle, the town's librarian, decided it was prudent to join forces with her colleagues because the Bergen County consortium provided her patrons with the best possible access to books, periodicals, and other audio and video products at a realistic cost. Book circulation figures in her library are healthy, and demand for periodicals has also increased dramatically in recent years.[16]

This coordinated system enabled Bergenfield's librarians to manage their time and resources more effectively. They were free from a myriad of numbing, time consuming chores. Now a computer monitored many of these functions. This allowed Doyle's librarians to develop supplemental programs for children (notably an innovative summer reading program) along with a special "home-bound" library service to individuals unable to visit the library.

In spite of this efficient system, Doyle's library still subscribes to 477 periodicals (302 in print and 175 on microfiche). Why? "People want immediate access to a wide variety of major periodicals, so we must keep them on the shelves." Ms. Doyle revealed, however, that Bergenfield is considering purchasing CD-ROM versions of various publications because of the stiff costs of printed versions of these products.

Are there encumbrances associated with electronic publications? Doyle conceded that "if we purchased a twenty-four volume encyclopedia on CD-ROM, we would have to buy a CD-ROM reader, and only one person could have access to that encyclopedia at a time. A paper version could accommodate theoretically twenty-four people at the same time. I am very concerned about meeting the needs of our readers. At the current time, price and usability are a concern." Of course a related issue centered on the need to collect and remit user fees for document delivery services.

Publishers and Serials

Most publishers remain sanguine about electronic publishing's future. Martin Brooks, a Vice President of Electronic Publishing at R.R. Bowker, insisted that "electronic publishing services are invaluable. They provide the user with quick and accurate searching capabilities and immediate access to large databases."[17]

Brooks stated candidly that information collection and processing is expensive. *Ulrich's International Periodicals Directory,* issued by Bowker, catalogs in excess of 175,000 different serials, and this three-volume title is updated constantly. Brooks insisted that "Bowker has been able to establish prices for our CD-ROM products [including *Ulrich's*] that are competitive with print versions."

However, even defenders of electronic publications realize that printed serials are portable, easy to use, and an accepted part of our print-oriented culture. This is a major problem for the academic community, the bastion of the "publish or perish" philosophy. Is an electronic book or journal the same as a printed book or journal? Should the same standards be observed, for example, for printed peer review journals and electronic publications? Deans and department chairs at the major research universities have, obviously, discussed these matters, but little agreement has been reached on the print versus electronic format quandary.

Yet it is likely that economic considerations will compel many, if not a clear majority of, librarians to face the harsh reality of fiscal constraints and begin to purchase more serials in electronic formats in the coming years.[18] It is possible that university deans will adopt a similar stance for tenure reviews, although it is unlikely that this will occur quickly.

The Serials Crisis Affected Book Purchases

Many librarians have been compelled to confront a difficult decision. Should they increase or decrease the percent of expenditures for books or other materials?

It appears that the majority of libraries have been unable to keep pace with inflation along with surges in costs for books and periodicals and materials; in some instances, budgets were slashed by hard pressed municipalities. The need to upgrade existing holdings became a severe problem; audio and video products became immensely popular among library users, and the emergence of electronic hardware and software systems changed forever the way large and small libraries conduct their business.

To accommodate the increased demand for serials, in essence to confront the real challenges associated with the "information age," many librarians were compelled to allocate a larger share of their budgets for non-book items.

Total expenditures for all U.S. libraries (public, school, college and university, and specialized) is expected to grow 108.39 percent between 1986–1997; books will probably increase 90.03 percent during those same years; and serials are anticipated to be up a staggering 192.12 percent between 1986–1997.

The actual budgetary ratio between books and periodicals is changing at an abrupt rate. Books are expected to drop from a 54.42 percent market share in 1986 to only 47.10 percent in 1999. The projected growth rate of serials will erode seriously the position held by books. Table 1-6 highlights this trend.

Libraries serve many different constituencies, so their specific needs for serials are rather diverse. Table 1-7 outlines the four key library segments and their purchase of periodicals between 1986–1997. All U.S. libraries have been forced to allocate larger percentages of their hard pressed budgets for periodicals.

TABLE 1-6 Percentage of Book and Periodical Expenditures by U.S. Libraries: 1986–1999

Year	Library Expenditures for All Materials	Percentage of Books among All Library Expenditures	Percentage of Periodicals among All Library Expenditures
1986	1,827.4	54.42	33.35
1987	1,987.5	54.10	34.39
1988	2,124.6	52.99	35.95
1989	2,358.4	53.44	36.33
1990	2,507.8	52.71	37.41
1991	2,565.7	51.56	38.80
1992	2,655.6	50.99	39.79
1993	2,808.9	50.33	40.83
1994	3,014.0	49.68	41.85
1995	3,244.7	48.89	46.30
1996	3,552.7	48.43	43.73
1997	3,669.9	47.73	44.70
1998	3,857.9	47.71	45.22
1999	4,065.7	47.10	45.75
Totals	$32,692.4	—	—

Source: Book Industry Study Group, *Book Industry Trends 1994* (New York: Book Industry Study Group, 1994), pp. 3–3 through 3–30; Book Industry Study Group, *Book Industry Trends 1995* (New York: Book Industry Study Group, 1995), 3–28.

The picture on America's college campuses is unsettling. In 1986 serials captured 54.63 percent of all library purchases. Because of the information explosion and the splitting of academic disciplines (called "twigging" in the academy), and the inordinate needs of scientists to obtain data quickly, serials have become the print category for many academic instructors and researchers; books are now a secondary format. The outlook for the rest of the 1990s confirms this fact.

Library Book Purchases

What categories of books are purchased by America's libraries? The BISG data revealed some interesting trends. Public libraries in 1986 allocated 43.82 percent of all book purchases for hardback trade; the next leading categories included 22.53 percent for juvenile hard and soft titles, and 14.22 percent for professional works. By 1992 this pattern changed. Trade hardbacks slipped to 40.14 percent, juvenile surged to 26.47 percent, and professional books essentially held steady (14.25 percent).

School library book acquisition patterns are very specialized, with the preponderance of funds allocated for juvenile titles. In 1986 almost 28 percent of school library budgets went for juvenile works versus 16.82 percent for adult trade and

TABLE 1-7   Percentage of Budget Spent for Serials Purchased by Specific U.S. Libraries: 1986–1997

Year	Public Libraries	School Libraries	College and University Libraries	Specialized Libraries
1986	13.36	12.55	54.63	42.03
1987	13.29	12.50	56.36	43.58
1988	13.73	12.67	58.50	43.76
1989	13.11	12.55	58.99	44.76
1990	13.36	13.03	59.80	45.59
1991	13.71	13.24	61.50	46.51
1992	13.70	13.96	62.39	47.20
1993	14.21	13.87	63.55	48.48
1994	13.57	13.64	64.71	49.26
1995	13.33	13.21	66.00	50.17
1996	12.93	12.92	66.99	50.05
1997	12.47	12.89	68.06	49.57

Source: Book Industry Study Group, *Book Industry Trends 1993* (New York: Book Industry Study Group, 1993), pp. 3–28 through 3–30; Book Industry Study Group, *Book Industry Trends 1994* (New York: Book Industry Study Group, 1994), pp. 3–28 through 3–30.

16.21 percent for professional. Allocations for mass market paperbacks were quite strong (12.76 percent), a trend that continues into the 1990s. Professional titles were sizable, topping $55.2 million in 1994.

College and university libraries sustained the most pressure because of the serials crisis.[19] Ever vigilant to maintain viable collections to meet the pressing demands of faculty and students, as well as satisfying standards established by accreditation boards, these institutions have been whipsawed by the staggering increases in serial prices. This compelled university librarians to evaluate their holdings and purchasing patterns. The end result was, in some instances, debilitating.

Total library expenditures for books and all materials grew 92.03 percent between 1986–1994. Allocations for books increased 50.3 percent during those same years. Yet the share held by books versus all materials dropped precipitously. In 1986 colleges allocated $265.4 million for book acquisitions, representing 35.13 percent of total outlays. Each year this share of the pie declined: 1987, 34.0 percent; 1988, 32.31 percent; 1989, 31.51 percent; 1990, 32.02 percent; 1991, 30.34 percent; 1992, 29.39 percent; 1993, 28.37 percent; 1994, 27.5 percent.

These colleges allocated 2.13 percent of their acquisition budget for university press titles in 1986; this slipped to 1.70 percent in 1994, a sign that the traditional market for university press monographs was changing dramatically.

A detailed review of college library purchasing patterns revealed the fact that professional books remained the second largest book category between 1986 and

1994; however, its share of the total budget dropped from 7.12 percent in 1986 to 6.13 percent in 1994. This pattern was repeated with trade books (1986: 9.61 percent; 1994: 7.46 percent) and subscription reference (0.6 percent to 0.41 percent).

Traditionally, special libraries' (i.e., libraries maintained by bar associations, medical and dental societies, etc.) book purchases are heavily weighted in the professional category. This trend remained constant between 1986 and 1994.

NOTES

[1]Jean Peters, "Book Industry Statistics from the R.R. Bowker Company," *Publishing Research Quarterly* 8(Fall 1992): p. 18. For a response to this research study, see John P. Dessauer, "The Growing Gap in Book Industry Statistics," *Publishing Research Quarterly* 9(Summer 1993): pp. 68–71.

[2]Book Industry Study Group, *Book Industry Trends 1998* (New York: Book Industry Study Group, 1998), pp. 2-4–2-6.

[3]Jim Milliot, "Book Purchases Increased 1.6% in 1994," *Publishers Weekly,* 16 October 1995, p. 10.

[4]John Tebbel, *Between Covers: The Rise and Transformation of American Book Publishing* (New York: Oxford University Press, 1987), pp. 421–438. Also see Leonard Shatzkin, *In Cold Type: Overcoming the Book Crisis* (Boston: Houghton Mifflin, 1982), pp. 97–122; and Ronald J. Zboray, "Book Distribution and American Culture: A 150-Year Perspective," *Book Research Quarterly* 3(Fall 1987): pp. 37–59.

[5]Jim Milliot, "Veronis, Suhler See Solid Growth in Book Spending," *Publishers Weekly,* 25 July 1994, p. 8.

[6]Jerry L. Salvaggio, ed. *The Information Society: Economic, Social, and Structural Issues* (Hillsdale, NJ: Lawrence Erlbaum Associates, 1989), pp. 6–34.

[7]Dennis P. Carrigan, "Publish or Perish: The Troubled State of Scholarly Communication," *Scholarly Publishing* 22(April 1991): pp. 131–142.

[8]Dennis P. Carrigan, "Research Libraries' Evolving Response to the 'Serials Crisis,'" *Scholarly Publishing* 23(April 1992): pp. 138–151.

[9]Lawrence J. White, *The Public Library in the 1980s: The Problems of Choice* (Lexington, MA: Lexington Books, 1983), pp. 1–78.

[10]E. J. Josey and Kenneth D. Shearer, *Politics and the Support of Libraries* (New York: Neal–Schuman Publishers, 1990), pp. 23–51. Also see Richard N. Katz, "Academic Information Management at the Crossroads: Time Again to Review the Economics," *Serials Review* 18, 1–2 (1992): pp. 41–44.

[11]Interview with John Berry, November 10, 1992.

[12]Malcolm Getz, "Electronic Publishing: An Economic View," *Serials Review* 18 1–2 (1992): pp. 25–31. Also see Getz's *Public Libraries: An Economic View.* Baltimore, MD: Johns Hopkins University Press, 1980.

[13]Fay M. Blake, "What's A Nice Librarian Like You Doing Behind a Cash Register?" In *User Fees: A Practical Perspective,* ed. Miriam A. Drake. Littleton, CO: Libraries Unlimited, 1981.

[14]John Bendel, "'Looming Colossus' of the Library World," *New York Times,* 11 July 1993, sec. 13 [New Jersey], pp. 1, 13.

[15]Interview with Robert White, July 1, 1994.

[16]Interview with Mary Joyce Doyle, November 8, 1992.

[17]Interview with Martin Brooks, November 12, 1992.

[18]Czeslaw, Jan Grycz, "Economic Models for Networked Information," *Serials Review* 18, 1–2 (1992): pp. 11–18. Also see Steven Harnad, "Interactive Publication: Extending the American Physical Society's Discipline-Specific Model for Electronic Publishing," *Serials Review* 18 1–2 (1992): pp. 58–61, and Karen Hunter, "The National Site License Model," *Serials Review* 18 1–2 (1992): pp. 71–72.

[19]Scott Bennett, "The Boat That Must Stay Afloat: Academic Libraries in Hard Times," *Scholarly Publishing* 23 (April 1992): pp. 131–137. Also see Paul Evan Peters, "Making the Market for Networked Information: An Introduction to a Proposed Program for Licensing Electronic Uses," *Serials Review* 18, 1–2 (1992): pp. 19–24; Jerry L. Salvaggio and Jennings Bryant, eds., *Media Use in the Information Age: Emerging Patterns of Adoption and Consumer Use* (Hillsdale, NJ: Lawrence Erlbaum Associates, 1989).

2

The Structure of the Magazine Industry

Charles Daly
Formerly CEO, Thomson Business Information

Patrick Henry
Editorial Director, Printing News

Ellen Ryder
President, Ellen Ryder Communications

A FINE ROMANCE

It's not unusual on a weekday lunch hour to witness a whole range of human emotion at Eastern Lobby Shop, the biggest and perhaps busiest of the newsstands in the Metropolitan Life Building over Grand Central Station in midtown Manhattan. More than 3,800 magazines are on sale in less than 900 square feet. Customers squeeze by each other, stand on tiptoe, raise chins, and angle for a good view of the new titles, displayed on racks reaching from floor to ceiling and in stacks in front of the cashiers. Impatient businesspeople looking for an edge on the competition elbow each other to scan the headlines in *Variety, Advertising Age, Economist, Publishers Weekly*. Oblivious to clerks unpacking and stocking the new issues, an engaged couple stops gazing into each other's eyes for a moment and gathers up bridal magazines for ideas and advice. Deskbound travelers stoke their dreams by checking out destinations in *Islands, Condé Nast Traveler, Travel & Leisure,* and any of the dozens of city and regional magazines on display. One customer is brought up short by the cover photograph on the new issue of *Newsweek,* strategically positioned by the cash register. Another picks up five computer magazines for help with a purchasing decision. Frantic for reading material on the train ride home, a commuter grabs one of the few remaining copies of *People.* A student enlists a clerk in a search for the new issue of a respected foreign policy magazine, which her professor mentioned in class the other night. A few customers furtively leaf through magazines with photographs of nude women.

This single urban spot attracts scores of browsers, researchers, news gatherers, romantics, business executives, travelers, cooks, gardeners, teachers, students, parents, and teenagers, and every magazine on display caters to a special interest they might have. Because of its size, this isn't a typical newsstand—just as midtown Manhattan isn't a typical American community. But the Eastern Lobby Shop scene—repeated hour after hour as an estimated 125,000 purchases are made each day—is indicative of American magazine publishing today. The activity at Eastern Lobby Shop represents the vitality, diversity, intense competition, and concerns inherent in this industry. The frenetic pace here is clear evidence of why publishers and editors *must* have a passion for the magazines they produce. In a marketplace crowded with choices and competition, it is creative and energetic work that gets noticed and attracts new readers.

As exemplified by a busy Manhattan retail outlet, magazine publishing in America is a thriving business and a snapshot of our culture. That means there's a big story waiting to be told. How then can we even begin to describe our relationship with the beautiful, dazzling array of words and images in print that we call magazines?

We might start by considering this: As a nation of magazine consumers, we're engaged in a serious and complicated romance. For generations, Americans as diverse as Frank Munsey, Fletcher Harper, Malcolm Forbes, Eric Utne, Grace Mirabella, and Martha Stewart have all experienced the thrill of seeing their name in a magazine title. As readers, we're variously challenged, informed, outraged, and transported to new places by magazines. Advertisers understand and depend on the appeal of magazines to sell their products and services; yet they also often struggle to justify the money spent to appear in their pages, requiring publishers to produce extensive research and employ sophisticated marketing techniques. Marketers and promoters of magazines—including editors and advertising and circulation executives—are preoccupied with mushrooming production and manufacturing costs as well as with aggressive competition everywhere from the corner newsstand all the way to cyberspace.

Nearly everyone reads magazines. Some magazines are pure entertainment, others are required on-the-job reading, still others are used to fill time—waiting in doctors' offices and in grocery store lines. Some people treat magazines like part of the family, loyally subscribing year after year. The tactile pleasure of turning pages, the portability, photography, design, and authority of the published word all contribute to the distinctive appeal of magazines.

Magazines have been described as a reflection of a nation's political, social, and cultural life. Our magazines tell us about ourselves. The articles and artwork published in the pages of a magazine, the launch of a new magazine, the demise of an established title are all windows on the lives of a reading public—and a buying public. In the 1860s, a bicycle craze swept America. The novelty and new availability of bicycles sparked a spate of new magazines into existence.[1] Bicycle owners and would-be bicycle owners were eager to learn everything about the new contraption, and magazines filled a need. More than a century later, in the mid-1990s, several large publishing companies began testing and launching magazines devoted to home renovation and remodeling—based on industry projections that in the coming decade families would spend billions of dollars on renovating their homes, rather than building new ones.[2] With magazines as a record of our special interests, it's understandable why historians find the study of them a rich resource.

A magazine is also a powerful vehicle for extending discussion and debate on a topic among interested, motivated readers. Without the constraints of regular news reporting of newspapers, magazines have been freer to publish analysis and opinion. Magazines have given voice to new views on current issues on a local, regional, and national level. The abolitionist movement and women's suffrage movement provided the editorial direction for scores of magazines. From 1858 to 1863, Frederick Douglass published *Douglass' Monthly,* containing his own work and argument, as well as reports on legislation, speeches, and the activities of abolitionist societies and individuals. It became the most influential African-American magazine of the period.[3] Before she edited her own magazine, *Revolution,* reformer and feminist Elizabeth Cady Stanton's first writing on women's rights appeared in the popular periodical *Lily, A Ladies Journal Devoted to Temperance and Literature,* which was published from 1849 to 1856.[4] In 1972, the great-great-great granddaughters of *Lily*'s readers were introduced to new perspectives on feminism when Gloria Steinem founded *Ms.*

While magazines help promulgate common interests, they are also commercial ventures and quickly respond to changes in the economy. Editors and publishers must constantly evaluate their magazines' position in the marketplace. In the early 1990s, Time Inc. Magazines, publisher of *Life*—the magazine that gave prestige and glamour to photojournalism—was considering closing the historic, now money-losing title. The magazine, which had become a monthly in 1972, was suffering from the defection of both subscribers and advertisers, not in small part because it was competing for readers and advertisers with dozens of new entertainment and general interest magazines. But instead of closing the magazine, the company decided to make its business operations leaner by cutting staff and the magazine's page size, and by refocusing the magazine's editorial offerings on "softer" features and photography. In 1994, commenting on the redesign of *Life,* managing editor Daniel

Okrent told a *New York Times* reporter: "*Life* is a window, not a mirror. We use pictures to create a sense of community. We do essays on people and we do much less celebrity coverage than we used to."[5] These editorial changes at *Life* were seen as one reason the magazine's issues in 1994 had advertising page increases of up to 78 percent over the same issues published in the previous year.[6]

Discovering the right combination for editorial and commercial success in a competitive, quickly changing marketplace is not the exclusive domain of big, mass market consumer magazines like *Life*. In a study of music magazines launched in the 1980s, researchers found that in addition to serving a community of readers dispersed throughout the country, these primarily small-circulation magazines were "the most economical means for advertisers to reach a market for their products."[7] Advertisers of guitars, sound systems, and other music services found these magazines the best way to reach a buyer in their small, highly specialized and widely dispersed market.

No good romance endures without clear-eyed understanding of the other forces at work. Through the years, the advent of automobiles, motion pictures, radio, and television all affected—or threatened to affect—American magazine publishing. Today, magazines are being profoundly shaped by developments in communications technology as well as the explosive growth in computer usage at home and work. In addition, developments in interactive media will continue to affect how we conduct business and obtain information, entertainment, and news—requiring magazines to adapt to new competition.

Change is inevitable in the magazine publishing industry. What won't change is the industry's continuing need for informed analysis, evaluation, and new ideas.

TOWARD A DEFINITION

What is a magazine anyway? Easy, you might say. Simply go to any newsstand or coffee table—and point. A magazine is 8 1/2 inches by 11 inches with articles and colorful pages. It has photographs. Ads. Subscribers. Letters to the editor. But *must* it have subscribers to be called a magazine? Must it be printed on glossy paper? Must it even have pages? Must it be published more than once a year? Must it have advertising? What if it only has one or two readers? Where do magazines on CD-ROM fit? Magazines that look like newspapers? The magazine in your Sunday newspaper? 'Zines? Comic books?

Just what makes a magazine a magazine? The word itself comes from the Arabic word *makhazhin,* meaning a place where goods or supplies (especially ammunitions) were stored. In 1731, the British publishers of the *London Gentleman's Magazine* were most likely the first to use the word in a publication title, deriving it from the French *magasin*.[8] So, with such linguistic roots, today's magazines hold and dispense information.

Here's a most basic definition, adapted from dictionaries. A magazine is published periodically on paper with a collection of any or all of the following: articles, reportage, essays, fiction, artwork, photography, other editorial features. But that definition doesn't help much when so many other words to describe magazines are used, seemingly interchangeably. *Journal, review, periodical, house organ* can all refer to what we commonly know as magazines. Further compounding the confusion, in industry jargon magazines are called *books. Vogue* is a fashion book, *House Beautiful,* a shelter book. Even the U.S. Postal Service, which has never been accused of being stingy with *its* definitions, doesn't include a definition of *magazine.* A second-class mailing permit (which most magazines have) can be given to a publication that is bound or unbound. (The Pulitzer Prize–winning magazine historian Frank Luther Mott contended in 1943 that a magazine must be bound to be a true magazine.[9]) Neither is the post office picky about the type of stock a magazine is printed on. The Postal Service manual says that an approved publication can be printed on sheets that "may be die cut or deckle-edged and may be made of paper, cellophane, foil. . . ."[10]

Magazines are usually referred to as *periodicals,* especially in official definitions. In its Census of Manufacturers, the U.S. Department of Commerce says "publications are classified as periodicals rather than newspapers if their news and editorial presentations do not appear to be directed to the public at large."[11] This government definition hits on an important distinction: a magazine is a regularly published periodical that targets a select audience, a group of readers defined by their demographics or interests. And, because most magazines need advertising dollars to support the costs of publishing, a publisher will also identify categories of businesses that want to sell products and services to those same readers. Newsletters and some newspapers could conceivably elbow their way into this definition, and many even have all the above-mentioned characteristics of a typical magazine. Many have color photography, a regular publication schedule, contributing writers, and a targeted audience. Most newsletters, though, contain *highly* specialized information and reporting and are geared to an audience even more select than that of magazines. For instance, a single newsletter could be successfully marketed to music festival organizers, attorneys who represent adoptive parents, or food service managers at colleges. Newsletter subscription costs can be in the hundreds of dollars—out of reach for the average magazine reader. There's also a difference in *style*—which is difficult to describe in a tidy way. Magazines as a group have more sophisticated art direction, more personality, more flair, and more entertainment value than their newsletter cousins. Magazines also have unique requirements in the areas of circulation marketing, advertising, staffing, and production that set them apart from newsletters, newspapers, and, of course, the cyberspace versions of magazines appearing on computer screens. While their production and distribution are unique, magazine supplements in newspapers are usually considered magazines because their editorial and advertising standards are similar.[12]

Comic books and 'Zines (the independently produced, small circulation, mostly literary magazines that burst onto the publishing scene in the 1990s with the advances in desktop publishing) are considered to be in separate publishing categories. As single titles, comics, puzzle books, and other theme publications are not large enough to generate significant revenue. But as a group, they contribute significantly to revenues for their parent companies. Dell Puzzle Magazine Group's 30 puzzle magazines generated about $40 million in revenue in 1995, and the *Ellery Queen's Mystery Magazine* and *Alfred Hitchcock Mystery Magazine* generated about $12 million.[13] Comic books have a long, colorful publishing history, and many do have sophisticated circulation and advertising goals. But neither comic books nor 'Zines—which typically have print runs of 200 copies and production costs of only about $500[14]—account for significant revenues or impact in the periodical publishing world.

Here are the basic points to remember about magazines:

- A magazine has a defined audience.
- A magazine need not have subscribers. It can be sold exclusively on newsstands or given away.
- A magazine can be printed on paper of any quality, but it must have pages.
- A magazine can be published in any frequency—from a one-time test issue to once a week.
- A magazine needn't publish the advertising of other companies. In 1994 the 10-year-old *Garbage Magazine* joined a list of consumer magazines—including *Consumer Reports* and *Ms.*—when its publishers decided to discontinue advertising and rely solely on circulation revenue.

A magazine can be classified as either a *consumer* or a *specialized business* (or *trade*) title. Within the consumer classification, literally hundreds of publishing categories and niches exist. Name a hobby, sport, major city, cultural activity, computer system, and chances are very good there's a magazine (or two or three) devoted to the subject. Consumer magazines appeal directly to an audience of readers who are targeted as potential readers by virtue of where they live, their interest in a specific topic, or their demographics—age, sex, profession, income level, race, religion, or nationality. *Esquire, Redbook, Atlantic Monthly, Field & Stream, Texas Monthly, Premiere, Seventeen,* and *Modern Maturity* are all examples of national consumer magazines and all have markedly different core audiences. *Esquire's* editor and publisher have designed their magazine for men aged 18–49 with an interest in fashion, sports, and politics. *Redbook* seeks out women readers who are most likely married with children. *Atlantic Monthly* readers are mostly professional, well-educated men and women with an interest in politics, business, and the arts. *Field & Stream* appeals to outdoor enthusiasts, *Texas Monthly* to residents of that state, *Premiere* to movie buffs, *Seventeen* to teenage girls, and *Modern Maturity* to men and women over 55. When the potential number of readers and advertisers can support publication of a magazine, the categories within the major niches can become even narrower. There are magazines for residents of particular neighborhoods of a city, for women who play volleyball, for people who like to smoke cigars, for expectant parents, for teenagers who skateboard.

Consumer magazines have two other things in common besides targeting a specific group of readers: advertising and availability. Most consumer magazines sell pages of advertising, and the income from advertising is essential to their survival. Some consumer magazines *can* be viable without advertising income, but it is the exception in today's marketplace. For many readers, too, the advertising in consumer magazines is part of their enjoyment of the magazine. Readers of *Vogue* pore over fashion advertising. *Philadelphia* magazine's restaurant and entertainment advertising is a resource for city residents and visitors. Readers of *Crafts Magazine* turn to its advertising pages to find new techniques, tools, and materials. Consumer magazines are easy for readers to find. In most cases, the publisher works hard to identify potential readers through direct mail marketing techniques. Consumer magazines are readily available and accessible to readers by subscription or on the newsstand, at a friend's house or in doctors' waiting rooms.

The other major classification of magazines is specialized business magazines. We'll refer to these throughout this text with the commonly used term *trade publications*. Contrary to what some people think, trade magazines are not limited to those about construction, plumbing, refrigeration, or other jobs where hands-on work is involved. Trade magazines are written and edited for readers who have a need for more information about their particular job, industry, or profession. They can be devoted to technical, scientific, professional, or marketing subjects. The editorial contained in trade magazines may include information on products, applications, technological changes, industry news and statistics, government regulations and political news, personnel changes, and new techniques in marketing and production.

Trade magazines usually do not directly compete (for either readers or advertisers) with consumer magazines. In comparison to a typical consumer magazine, the circulation of the typical trade magazine is smaller and much more specialized. A trade magazine may or may not publish advertising, but most do. In comparison to the consumer field, the total revenue generated by trade magazines is limited. Each year, *Folio:* compiles its *Folio:* 500 list, ranking magazines in terms of revenue. In 1997, the magazines on this list had $24.9 billion in cumulative revenues, with trade publications accounting for only about one-sixth of that total.[15] Not readily available on newsstands, trade magazines may have a comparatively high subscription price. For example, in 1998 *Publishers Weekly,* directed to people working in the book publishing industry, had an annual subscription rate of $169, compared to *Newsweek's* basic annual subscription rate of $41.08. A trade magazine is often office or "homework" reading for many professionals. Other trade magazines are sent free to eligible readers. In order to get the magazine delivered to them, readers must hold specific job titles or responsibilities. Such a defined audience of readers makes the magazine very attractive to advertisers. This kind of distribution is known as *controlled circulation.*

There is yet another category of magazines known collectively as *public relations magazines.* Clubs, corporations, colleges, manufacturers, institutions, and other entities can all publish bound, glossy, high-quality magazines that are designed to appeal to a group of readers with very specific interests and information needs. Magazine expert James Click outlined six different categories of public relations magazines: those for employees, customers, stockholders (or corporation members), salespeople, dealers, and technical service providers.[16] While numerous, public relations magazines are in a separate category from the two broad classifications—trade and consumer—because their marketing and circulation objectives are extremely narrow. They exist to communicate to small, self-defined audiences: graduates of a college, salespeople at an international company, employees at a health management organization. These publications may, of course, have high editorial standards, but as a group they stand apart from those based on many of the principles we'll be exploring in this chapter.

MAJOR NICHES

The variety of experiences and subject matter addressed by magazines—as well as developments in how we sell and market goods and services—has created identifiable categories of magazines or *niches. Bacon's* publishes an annual directory of magazines, organized into 225 "market classifications"—from advertising to woodworking.

Here are the major niches—but remember, it's only a partial list. These are collected here because of their high proportion of readers and advertisers.

Automotive. Magazines such as *Car & Driver* and *Motor Trend* are often referred to as "buff books" because they're read—with a special voraciousness—by car enthusiasts.

Boating. Examples include *Sail, Boating, Yachting,* and *WoodenBoat.*

Associations, clubs, and institutions. Organizations big and small publish magazines: *Harvard Alumni Magazine, Audubon, Smithsonian, Modern Maturity* are all examples. Civic and fraternal magazines—published by groups such as Elks, Kiwanis, VFW—are also included in this category.

Epicurean. Magazines about food, restaurants, cooking, and wine. In the 1980s, new titles featuring lean cuisine and quick recipes were launched by publishers to capitalize on Americans' new interest in healthy eating.

General interest. If magazines had college diplomas, the publications in this niche would hold liberal arts degrees. These contain a little bit of everything for readers who are curious about ideas, people, news, and trends (both serious and not-so-serious). Examples are: *Harper's Magazine,* the *New Yorker, Reader's Digest, Utne Reader, Vanity Fair.*

Home. This category includes magazines focusing on decorating, renovation, and gardening, such as *House Beautiful, Martha Stewart Living, Condé Nast House and Garden.* In publishing industry jargon, these magazines are sometimes referred to as "shelter books."

Inflight, in-hotel, and other passenger magazines. Distributed free to hotel guests or passengers on airlines or trains, containing subject matter on the transportation company, its services, and articles of interest to the traveler or visitor.

Men's. For example: *GQ, Esquire, Playboy, Details, Men's Journal.*

Women's. A category with a long history and many titles, ranging from how-to service magazines to the more fashion-oriented *Vogue, Harper's Bazaar,* and *Elle,* to magazines with various levels of emphasis on women's health, fitness, relationships, family, and work. The largest-circulation women's titles are known as the "Seven Sisters" (*Better Homes and Gardens, Family Circle, Good Housekeeping, Ladies' Home Journal, McCall's, Redbook,* and *Woman's Day*).

Music/entertainment. Magazines in this category range from magazines for rock musicians, opera fans, moviegoers, and people-watchers.

Outdoor/sport. Name the sport and there's most likely a magazine (or two): From the generalist's *Outside* and *Sports Illustrated* to the particular enthusiast's *Triathlete, Volleyball Monthly, Windsurfing.*

Parenting and family. Magazines for every stage of a family: *American Baby, Child, Family Fun, Parenting.*

Photography. Ranging from magazines for the specialist (*News Photographer* and *Industrial Photography*) to the consumer enthusiast, professional, and aspiring amateur (*American Photo* and *Popular Photography*).

Science/technology. Magazines focusing on the natural and technological sciences, including computer magazines, and the more generalist publications such as *Scientific American, Sciences, Discover.*

Ethnic. Magazines that are directed to readers sharing a racial, ethnic, or ancestral characteristic. Examples range from *Essence* and *Ebony* (which have been publishing since 1970 and 1945, respectively) to relative newcomers such as *A.* (for Asian Americans) launched in 1990.

Youth. For young men and women there is a teen category (*Seventeen, American Girl, YM, Boy's Life*) and for even younger readers: *Sports Illustrated for*

Kids and *Highlights for Children.* The Cricket Magazine Group in Peru, Illinois, publishes four titles targeting children from toddlers (*Babybug*) to early teens.

Regional. A category that has its own association, the City and Regional Magazine Association, and includes magazines that target readers and advertising in a city, region, state, or section of the country. Editorial focus may be either on personalities, news, and lifestyle or on business in that region. *South Florida, Utah Business, Oregon Business, New Orleans, Arizona Highways,* and *Midwest Life* are all examples.

Political. Those magazines with a stated political point of view and usually a devoted, loyal readership. Examples are *American Spectator* (monthly, 300,000 circulation); *Commentary* (monthly, 30,000), *The Nation* (weekly, 86,000), *National Review* (bi-weekly, 262,000).

Farm. *Farm Journal* (circulation 815,000), *Successful Farming* (500,000), and *Progressive Farmer* (450,000) are distributed nationally throughout the U.S. farm belt. Smaller-circulation farm magazines focus on regions of the country and on varieties of growing, chemicals, and fertilizers. Standard Rate and Data Service lists 256 farm titles in 12 categories.

Medical. As with the agricultural magazines, the significance of this category of publishing is often underestimated. For instance, *JAMA: Journal of the American Medical Association* is ranked number 91 in the *Folio: 500,* with revenues of $64 million. Consider the range of disciplines (nursing, radiology, pediatrics, psychology, cardiology, surgery) and you'll understand why *Bacon's* lists more than 757 magazines in the medical category. It's been estimated that there is a total of more than 3,500 medical periodicals.[17]

COUNTING MAGAZINES

How many magazines are there? The short answer: No one really knows. But we can make an educated guess.

Magazine historian John Tebbel estimates that 22,000 magazines are published in the United States. He includes in his figure all manner of magazines—from the 2,000 magazines that have the most visibility and significance in the marketplace (*TV Guide, Farm Journal, Modern Bride, Business Week,* etc.) to the numerous public relations magazines published by colleges, hospitals, corporations, and other entities exclusively for constituents.[18] In 1995 Gale Directory of Publications reported the number of U.S. periodicals at 10,387[19]—but that figure includes scholarly journals, comics, yearbooks, and other periodicals. The Standard Rate and Data Service listed 2,276 consumer and farm magazines that sold advertising, about 750 more than a decade earlier.[20] Each year Samir A. Husni of the University of Mississippi counts up the number of new consumer magazines (whether they sell advertising or not), and in 1994 he found that 832 new magazines were launched. (The number that fold is too difficult to monitor.) His estimate: 4,000 consumer magazines.[21] Estimates of the number of trade magazines published today vary widely. One observer estimates 12,000[22] but most listings range from 2,400 to 3,200. The Association of Business Publishers listed 689 active member magazines in 1995,[23] but acknowledges there are many more individual titles, many published by multi-title publishers. There's simply no accurate way to count public relations magazines, especially because very few sell advertising space and are not eligible for second-class mailing privileges. There may be as many as 10,000. Tebbel's estimate of 22,000 magazines seems right if we project that there are 4,000 consumer, 8,000 trade, and 10,000 public relations magazines.

An international code is used to help count the number of magazines in the world. Most publications with a regular publication schedule—which, in addition to magazines, includes journals, yearbooks, and comics—have an assigned International Standard Serials Number. This is the internationally accepted, concise, unique, unambiguous code of identification of serial publications, consisting of seven numbers with an eighth "check" digit used to verify the number in computer processing. A hyphen is printed after the fourth digit, as a visual aid. The acronym ISSN precedes the number. The number is assigned by one of the more than 50 national centers worldwide. The centers form a network coordinated by the ISSN International Centre in Paris. The ISSN aids in ordering, billing, inventory control, abstracting, and indexes. There's no charge to get an ISSN, but a publisher must supply bibliographic evidence of the serial, including a copy of the title page and cover.

Where are magazines published? For the past decade, four states—New York, Illinois, California, and Pennsylvania—have been home to more than half the publishing companies in the U.S.[24] New York City is the headquarters of most multi-title magazine publishers, but isn't—and wasn't always—the only address for a successful magazine business. In 1885, William Dean Howells (who, four years earlier, had left his editor's desk at the *Atlantic Monthly* to devote more time to his own writing[25]) moved from Boston to take an editorial post at *Harper's,* and a great uproar ensued about how the center of publishing was moving from "literary" Boston to "commercial" New York.

Time and *Newsweek* have headquarters in New York; their primary competitor, *U.S. News and World Report* is based in Washington, D.C. All three news weeklies also have editorial branch offices all over the world. Meredith Corporation—which publishes about 60 titles, including *Better Homes and Gardens*—has its corporate headquarters in Des Moines. *Outside* magazine moved from Chicago to Santa Fe in 1994. Northampton, Massachusetts (population 30,000), is the home of two national magazines, *FamilyFun* and *Family PC.* The National Magazine Award–winner *Wired* magazine set up shop in San Francisco in 1994. Public relations magazines are published everywhere—from major metropolitan areas to rural communities.

A BASIC TENET: THE THREE-LEGGED STOOL

American publishing is big business. Multi-title companies dominate the consumer market. The "top tier" of the nation's big circulation magazines are published by large media companies—Condé Nast, Hearst, Meredith, Hachette Fillipachi, and Time Warner among them. Only about 160 magazines are responsible for 85 percent of the industry's total revenues. With an estimated 22,000 magazines, that means magazine publishing is a *small* business, too. Magazine publishing has always been an appealing venture for entrepreneurs, for men and women with a cause, for editors with ideas.

What the giants of the industry today share with titles having a fraction of their circulation, revenue, and resources is a basic tenet of magazine publishing: Success rests on the three-legged stool of editorial, advertising, and circulation. The three-legged stool is a commonly used metaphor for magazine publishing because weakness or shortcoming in any "leg" affects the others—as well as the stability of the entire venture. What happens with editorial decisions affects how many copies are sold on the newsstand—which in turn affects how many new subscribers a magazine can expect. Advertisers make their decisions based on how many people buy the magazine. The three functions are intimately entwined.

Here's an example. Most magazines sell advertising pages to outside companies. For a magazine to sell the pages, the title's advertising director must be able to tell advertisers exactly who's buying and reading the title. Without that information, few companies will hand over the money it costs to advertise. Advertisers must be assured that a certain number of readers buy the magazine, either through subscription or on the newsstand; and that this number won't fluctuate wildly from month to month. The magazine's circulation department, for its part, must have both faith and knowledge that the editor and the editorial department will maintain their implicit promise to readers (and advertisers) to deliver a consistent editorial message. Imagine, for instance, a gardening magazine treasured by readers for its beautiful photography of flowers and practical information on how to create the best garden. Imagine this magazine's suddenly arriving one month in homes and on newsstands featuring a cover story on a world-famous supermodel giving a behind-the-scenes guided tour of her fabulous backyard garden in the Hollywood Hills. You'd expect longtime readers to object by canceling subscriptions. "This isn't the magazine I decided to buy!" they'd complain. Of course, some readers—new to gardening or fans of supermodels—might be thrilled at the celebrity turn the magazine had taken. Most of the established, core audience, however, would probably find reason to stop subscribing. Advertisers who had signed on to reach readers interested in buying tools for the garden wouldn't find any value in trying to reach movie star watchers. Who can prove celebrity watchers are also spending time in their gardens? This editorial decision would affect circulation and advertising. Celebrity gardening is not what readers or advertisers were promised. An editorial move would result in a loss of core customers and income— a detrimental effect on both the advertising and circulation effort.

Three functions—advertising, circulation, and editorial—must work in concert. Along with principles of production and finance, they are the keys to publishing a successful magazine. To have a fuller understanding of contemporary trends in magazine publishing and in these three critical functions, let's look at how we got where we are today.

AMERICA'S MAGAZINE HISTORY: WHERE TODAY'S TRENDS TOOK ROOT

The story of America's first magazine is more important for the trends it established than for a particular literary or journalistic milestone. In a foreshadowing of decades of competition, rival Philadelphia printers Andrew Bradford and Benjamin Franklin engaged in a race to be the first magazine publishers in the colonies. Bradford won, publishing *American Magazine, or A Monthly View of the Political State of the British Colonies* on February 13, 1741, beating Franklin's *General Magazine, and Historical Chronicle, for All the British Plantations in America* by three days. Six months later, both magazines were out of business—due, some historians say, to lack of reader interest.[26]

In addition to the elements of competition and business risk, the early attempts at magazine publishing in America also tell the story of how distinctly American magazines began to evolve. In the emerging democracy, a cacophony of voices and opinions found a home in periodicals. Many of these early magazines were conceived and published by an individual with strong political views, eager to let the world know of his philosophies and beliefs.

But not all the early titles were publishing brash, revolutionary reading. Up until the early 1800s, many of America's early magazines were indistinguishable from their British counterparts. Lax copyright practices and a lack of access to original writing meant that entire pages of British magazines could be reproduced—without compensation to either the author or original publisher—in American magazines. Some magazines were launched not because of a publisher's burning need to get his ideas to a wide audience, but because he (and the publisher then was most likely a *he*) saw a way to make money. *Harper's Magazine* started life in New York City because the industrious Harper brothers—whose successful book business was thriving—realized that idle presses could be put to use during downtime. They began publishing a "new monthly magazine" in 1850 and soon thereafter a weekly magazine. Fletcher Harper himself referred to the beginnings of the magazine that would make news and influence national opinion for well over a century as "a tender to our business,"[27] serving to extend the already purchased work of their book authors to an even wider audience. *Collier's,* the *Atlantic Monthly,* and *Putnam's New Monthly Magazine* (the magazine historian Frank Luther Mott called "the first genuinely civilized magazine in America"[28]) were also spun off successful book businesses. In 1888, Peter Collier founded a periodical called *Once a Week* (later renamed *Collier's Weekly*), which was sold in conjunction with his low-priced library sets. These popular "instant libraries" were sold on the installment plan by book agents. *McCall's* started life in 1873 because the tailor and pattern maker James McCall saw a way to promote his dress-making designs.[29]

As the population in American cities grew and businesses began thriving, literacy increased. With the reading public and buying public growing, new magazines were born. Americans were interested in reading magazines, talking about them, and having them in their home libraries. Soon it became acceptable to be a professional writer or editor. Bylined articles appeared. The *North American Review* and *Saturday Evening Post* led the way with hiring regular staff writers and paying livable salaries. Editors' personalities and points of view became known.

Author and feminist Sarah Josepha Hale was at the forefront of shaping women's magazines in the nineteenth century. Widowed in 1822 with five children, she began publishing her writing to support her family. Publisher Louis Godey hired her in 1837, by buying the magazine she was editing, *Ladies' Magazine,* and made her editor of his *Godey's Ladies Book*—a post she held for more than 40 years. Her great cause was women's education, and she pushed Godey into publishing articles on history, travel, music, art, famous women, healthy care of children, cooking— along with the popular color illustrations of fashion. Under her leadership, the magazine's circulation grew to a stunning 150,000.[30]

A most important milestone for American magazine publishing occurred in 1879 when Congress passed the first of two acts that lowered postal rates for magazines. The second decrease occurred in 1885, followed by the creation of a rural free-delivery system in the 1890s. It became less expensive to mail and distribute magazines to a mass audience. That led to stunning growth. In 1885, there were 3,300 periodicals in the United States. Less than 20 years later, the list had doubled. More than 7,000 magazines were founded in a 20-year period. While half that number eventually folded or merged, this is considered the Golden Age of Magazines, with magazines attaining an important place in shaping public opinion and providing a forum for new ideas. The importance of the magazine's cover image was realized during this period. It was a trade magazine—*Inland Printer*—that became the first to change the cover illustration from issue to issue. Soon after, magazines began changing the cover images, enlisting the newly popular illustrators of the day to help create the magazine's particular personality."

But not everyone was thrilled with this unleashing of reading material on the public. Francis Browne, editor of *Dial,* believed that mass readership of the early 1890s "great circulation" magazines (the ones that boasted circulations of up to 200,000) led to mediocrity, saying that such magazines were "bound to be conservative because they cannot afford to offend."[31]

A distinct difference began to emerge between the journalism in magazines and the reporting in newspapers. Newspapers recounted stories and events. Magazines assimilated information and brought the perspective and opinion of the author to the forefront. *Harper's, Nation, Scribner's, Atlantic Monthly,* and other journals established a new level of sophistication in magazines. Emphasis was placed on public affairs and what editors believed the public needed to know. In the pages of these "thought leader" magazines, some of the most memorable opinion and essays of the age were published. Commentary and reports on labor problems, income tax, direct election of senators, child labor laws, and women's suffrage all appeared in magazines. *McClure's* became known for publishing reports chronicling abuses in employment, food packaging, and false advertising claims. *Leslie's* from its beginning published crusading articles; especially noteworthy was its series on the unsanitary conditions of dairies supplying New York and corruption among milk producers and distributors. *McClure's* and its crusade against the patent medicine business helped push Congress to establish the Food and Drug Administration. *Collier's* lobbied for the repeal of prohibition.

Magazines also began marking newsworthy, world-shaking events with commemorative issues—another trend that continues today. *Collier's* might have been the first with its "special number" dated May 5, 1906, published two weeks after the San Francisco earthquake, complete with Jack London's article and 16 pages of pictures.[32] Today, big sports and entertainment news, the end of a year, beginning of a decade, or death of a celebrity prompt a magazine publisher to bring out a special issue. Even war can get the presses rolling. When the United States entered the Gulf War in 1991, *Life* for several months produced an unusual weekly devoted to patriotic news and feature stories about America's role in the conflict.

Illustration and photography became increasingly important to magazines. The invention of halftones and advances in printing technology in the 1880s enabled printers to make even more attractive, readable magazines. By the 1890s, high-speed rotary presses were perfected. The low-priced, illustrated magazines especially benefited from this development. Instead of expensive fine line engravings in wood, photographs and illustrations could be printed for a fraction of the cost. *Century* magazine, for instance, paid $300 for a page-size woodcut—but less than $20 for a halftone.[33] Color reproduction was rare before 1900. After 1910, photography played an important role in magazine publishing. Jimmy Hare's photographs in *Collier's* were popular, leading *Life* to offer him a lucrative, exclusive contract to lure him to its pages.[34] Illustrators such as Charles Dana Gibson (the "darling of the 1890s"), Maxfield Parrish, Edward Penfield, Frederic Remington, and Jessie Wilcox Smith were also sought-after contributors to magazines.

Premiums (the gifts given by magazine publishers to encourage subscriptions and renewals) were instituted during this period. *McCall's* used patterns for premiums in the 1900s. Color photographs, calendars, bookmarks, and other items also made appearances. In one extravagant plan, a magazine publisher offered new subscribers free life insurance.

It would be a long time before mass mail solicitations by a publisher to new and renewing subscribers became widespread. Sophisticated direct mail techniques were still a hundred years away; yet magazine publishers early on realized the importance of trying to bring lapsed subscribers back into the fold and often encouraged them to renew with a personal letter.

From just before the Civil War up to the early 1900s, the nation experienced explosive political, social, and economic changes. New manufacturing technologies along with changes in how goods were marketed and advertised helped magazines prosper. Advertising in magazines grew in importance. What first seemed tawdry and demeaning to some publishers (Fletcher Harper turned down Singer's $18,000 bid to advertise sewing machines in *Harper's Magazine* because he believed it would lower the quality of the publication[35]), quickly became an essential part of the business of publishing. Families were buying goods such as cameras, typewriters, and sewing machines directly from manufacturers who recognized magazines as a way to get their messages to this purchasing public. By the 1890s, a national railroad system was operating, to bring these goods directly to retail establishments and families across the country. Automobile manufacturers started advertising in magazines other than trade publications in the early 1900s. Advertising agencies were established to handle manufacturers' needs to create and place ads. Magazines began seeing their editorial distinctiveness as attractive to advertisers—as salable. The *Ladies' Home Journal* was probably the first magazine to offer an advertiser an "adjacency"—the opportunity to place an advertisement at the end of a piece of fiction—at an added cost. Publishers became sophisticated about soliciting advertising, engaging their own salespeople to work with agencies and manufacturers.

Publishers made no effort to account for their magazines' circulation until advertising became important. Before advertisers demanded proof of the number of readers that publishers were claiming, creative guesswork and outright lying were the rules in magazine circulation. In 1914, to bring order to this state of affairs, a group of advertisers and publishers established the Audit Bureau of Circulations to monitor publishers' circulation. The ABC and its counterpart for trade magazines— Business Publications Audit, Inc. (BPA)—are still the two auditing bodies for magazine publishing today.

After World War I, the news and picture magazines—*Life, Time, Newsweek,* and others—made their mark on the culture. By the 1930s and 1940s, a handful of magazines were reaching record-breaking circulation numbers. George Horace Lorimer is considered by some to be the first great contemporary magazine editor. He held the top job at the *Saturday Evening Post* for 38 years and made that magazine an intrinsic part of the American cultural landscape. Lorimer's *Post* and the popular *Ladies' Home Journal* were the first magazines to reach a circulation of one million.

With television on the horizon, such stunning readership numbers wouldn't last, however. By the 1960s, advertisers of cars, soap, cereal, tobacco, and other products could easily reach 100 million American households with a commercial on *The Ed Sullivan Show. Life,* even with its record-breaking 8.5 million readers, couldn't compete with the audience numbers television offered. General interest magazines such as *Life, Look,* and the *Saturday Evening Post* suffered the most from the sea change in marketing goods and the defection of advertisers. But while television had captured audience and advertiser attention with huge numbers, hundreds of new magazines and new magazine companies were able to define a slice of the mass market and serve up a magazine to appeal to a specific group of readers. Magazines did what television couldn't do: reach targeted audiences with special interests.

THE PEOPLE BEHIND THE IDEAS

Successful magazines today are not merely the result of a marketing formula concocted to reach a specific group of readers. America's recent magazine history is rich with the stories of men and women who helped shape the publishing industry and our culture with their editorial vision and inventions. Helen Gurley Brown's eternal "Cosmo Girl," Harold Hayes's shepherding of the spirited "New Journalism" into the pages of *Esquire,* young Jann Wenner's idea for *Rolling Stone,* Lewis Lapham's often-imitated "Harper's Index"—to name just a few. Ideas still drive magazines. Many contemporary magazines owe their success to editors whose editorial inventions as well as entrepreneurial spirit not only have been inspirations for scores of magazine editors and publishers, but also have sparked some of today's biggest magazine publishing businesses into existence. Here's a look at three such stories.

Twenty-eight-year-old DeWitt Wallace refined his magazine idea while recuperating in a French army hospital from wounds he received during the Meuse-Argonne offensive in 1918. Impatient with what he considered the needless length of articles in copies of the *Saturday Evening Post, Vanity Fair,* and *Scribner's* sent to soldiers, he practiced a technique he had already formulated: condensing articles so that the "practical articles" of "lasting interest" could be cut to a quarter of their original size and still retain "their essence."[36] Returning to the United States, Wallace, in partnership with his wife, Lila Acheson, borrowed $5,000 and began publishing the *Reader's Digest* in 1922 in a Greenwich Village apartment. He selected the articles for his conveniently sized, inexpensive magazine on the basis of three criteria: applicability, lasting interest, and constructiveness.[37] The combination struck a chord with the postwar middle class interested in self-improvement, information, and good reading when time was at a premium. Circulation grew to record-breaking levels. Originally, the Wallaces wanted their magazine to be free of advertising, but in 1955 they decided not only to accept advertising but also to sell advertising at higher rates than any other magazine. The magazine grew richer and diversified into other areas, including book publishing and record distribution. In the late 1990s the international publishing company based in Pleasantville, New York, had revenues of more than $500 million and the flagship magazine is second only to the Bible in worldwide readership.[38]

For Condé Nast, the way to publishing success was through "quality circulation," not amassing high numbers of subscribers. The St. Louis–born Nast was a lawyer by training but found the work uninspiring. When his college friend Robert

Collier asked him to work for his family's weekly, he discovered advertising as a second career. As advertising director of *Collier's* he quickly revitalized the circulation of the magazine and engaged in strategic marketing by showing individual advertisers how they could benefit from advertising in *Collier's*. He spent ten years at *Collier's* and during that time became exposed to the opportunities offered by *Collier's* fashion and home pattern market divisions. Under his direction, advertising revenue at the *Quarterly Style Book* grew from $1,500 in 1907 to $180,000 in 1908.[39] With this background, he decided he wanted a magazine of his own and purchased a small, highly regarded but struggling society and fashion magazine called *Vogue* in 1909. He worked feverishly and successfully with editor Edna Woolman Chase to bring the magazine to the attention of the elite, rich, and stylish. Chase and Nast pioneered charity fashion shows of exclusively American designers, and gained the respect and admiration of the social leaders of the day.[40] Nast subsequently purchased *Vanity Fair* and *House & Garden* and incorporated his holdings as Condé Nast Publications in 1922. He saw his task thusly: "To bait the editorial pages in such a way as to lift out of all the millions of Americans just the 100,000 cultivated people who can buy these quality goods."[41] Today, the Condé Nast Publications is part of Advance Publications, the Newhouse family-owned company, which includes the *New Yorker,* newspaper and cable operations, and book publishing houses. *Vogue* has a circulation of 1.2 million and nine international editions.

It has been said that modern magazine publishing began with Henry Luce and Briton Hadden.[42] In their early 20s, the Yale graduates decided that Americans were woefully uninformed about the world and needed a publication that gave them facts, in an easy-to-read, summarized format. An initial 7,000-piece mail solicitation sent in 1922 describing the magazine they wanted to publish got an extraordinary response. Well over 6 percent of the households receiving their letter responded positively.[43] Buoyed by the popular interest in a magazine focusing on news, not comment, the partners launched *Time* in 1923 by raising money from family and friends. They were both listed as editors on the masthead, and devoted themselves to developing an identifiable style and creating a news magazine that could be read in less than an hour. Circulation rose quickly (more than doubling to 70,000 within only two years) and advertisers followed. The publishers quickly began exploring other magazine opportunities. They recognized the early potential of *Saturday Review of Literature* and started a monthly digest of advertising news. In addition to their entrepreneurial skills, Luce and Hadden excelled at identifying *audiences* for their magazines. Hadden died unexpectedly in 1929 at the age of 31. Luce went on to start *Fortune*—a revolutionary business magazine—just before the Depression hit. When he launched *Life* in 1936, it was "the most remarkable instant success in the history of magazine publishing."[44] After merging with Warner Communications in 1989, Time Inc. Magazines became part of a mammoth communications and entertainment conglomerate. Because he also had direct editorial involvement in the startup of *Sports Illustrated,* a total of four of the company's core magazines owe their existence to Henry Luce.

NOTES

[1]John Tebbel and Mary Ellen Zuckerman, *The Magazine in America, 1741–1990* (New York: Oxford University Press, 1991), 64.

[2]Deirdre Carmody, "Sensing Trend Toward Renovation and Remodeling, Home Magazines Are Adding Up," *The New York Times,* June 8, 1995.

[3]Tebbel and Zuckerman, *The Magazine in America, 1741–1990,* 44.

[4]Frank Luther Mott, *A History of American Magazines,* vol. 2, 1850–1865 (Cambridge: Harvard University Press, 1938), 50–51.

[5]Deirdre Carmody, "A Rejuvenated Life Magazine Bounces Back," *The New York Times,* September 26, 1994.

[6]Carmody, "A Rejuvenated Life Magazine Bounces Back."

[7]P. Theberge, "Musician Magazines in the 1980s, the Creation of a Community and Consumer Market," in *Cultural Studies,* October 1991, 5(3): 270–293.

[8]William H. Taft, *American Magazines for the 1980s.* (New York: Hastings House, 1982), 19.

[9]Mott, *A History of American Magazines,* vol. 2, 69.

[10]U.S. Postal Service, Domestic Mail Manual, 44 9-1-95, 3.0, E211.2.7.

[11]Census of Manufacturers, 1992.

[12]The Commerce Department includes magazines distributed as newspaper supplements in their statistics on U.S. periodical publishing.

[13]"The Ad Age 300," *Advertising Age,* June 19, 1995, 5–17. In March 1996, Penny Press, Inc., a privately owned business, acquired all of the approximately three dozen Dell Magazines.

[14]David M. Gross, "Zine Dreams," *The New York Times Sunday Magazine,* December 17, 1995, 72–74.

[15]"Folio: 500," *Folio:* July 1998, 61.

[16]J. William Click and Russell N. Baird, *Magazine Editing and Production.* (Dubuque, Iowa: William C. Brown, 1990), 23–24.

[17]Click, *Magazine Editing and Production,* 25.

[18]Tebbel and Zuckerman, *The Magazine in America,* 44.

[19]Gale Directory of Publications.

[20]SRDS, February 1995.

[21]Deirdre Carmody, "On the Annual Scoreboard of Magazines, It's Sports 67, Sex 44," *The New York Times,* June 12, 1995.

[22]Carmody, "On the Annual Scoreboard of Magazines."

[23]Telephone interview with Nancy Schlick, Director of Communications, ABP, June 7, 1995.

[24]Census of Manufacturers, 1992.

[25]Mott, *A History of American Magazines,* 510.

[26]Tebbel and Zuckerman, *The Magazine in America,* 4.

[27]Tebbel and Zuckerman, *The Magazine in America,* 21.

[28]Mott, *A History of American Magazines,* 320.

[29]Tebbel and Zuckerman, *The Magazine in America,* 99.

[30]Tebbel and Zuckerman, *The Magazine in America,* 33.

[31]Mott, *A History of American Magazines,* 632.

[32]Mott, *A History of American Magazines,* 458.

[33]Mott, *A History of American Magazines,* 710.

[34]Deirdre Carmody, *The New York Times,* September 26, 1994.

[35]Tebbel and Zuckerman, *The Magazine in America,* 143.

[36]John Heidenry, *Theirs Was the Kingdom, Lila and DeWitt Wallace and the Story of the Reader's Digest,* (New York: W. W. Norton, 1993), 40.

[37]Tebbel and Zuckerman, *The Magazine in America,* 185.

[38]Heidenry, *Theirs Was the Kingdom,* 224.

[39]Tebbel and Zuckerman, *The Magazine in America,* 105.

[40]Tebbel and Zuckerman, *The Magazine in America,* 106.

[41]Amy Janello and Brennon Jones for Magazine Publishers of America and American Society of Magazine Editors, *The American Magazine* (New York: Harry N. Abrams, Inc., 1991), 72.

[42]Tebbel and Zuckerman, *The Magazine in America,* 158.

[43]Tebbel and Zuckerman, *The Magazine in America,* 161.

[44]Tebbel and Zuckerman, *The Magazine in America,* 169.

3

The Structure of the Newspaper Industry

ROBERT PICARD
Turku School of Economics and Business Administration

JEFFREY H. BRODY
California State University, Fullerton

The growth of broadcast and other electronic media and the increasing linkage of computers and telecommunications has for several decades led futurists to make prognostications about the imminent demise of the newspaper industry. Those technological changes, along with changes in the circulation and advertising markets, have led newspaper industry personalities, associations, and publications to emphasize the idea that the industry is in serious difficulty by accepting and using the language of crisis. Michael Crichton, a futurist and author of *Jurassic Park,* has fueled the fears of the future by calling newspapers "mediasaurs,"[1] and *Washington Post* media critic Howard Kurtz says the industry is now permeated with "the smell of death."[2]

Speeches made before industry conferences have emphasized the need "to alter our image problem," "to defend our turf," and "to fight back" with marketing strategies for advertising and circulation sales. Industry publications have been filled with news about newspapers suffering "sales slides" and "economic stress," of the industry "reeling," and of publishers "fearful of the future." Task forces, committees, and conferences have sought and promoted strategies to overcome and respond to "obstacles" and "challenges" in the industry. And numerous publications have offered advice to newspaper owners and managers on how to "survive" the current environment.[3]

Publishers and editors have used existing organizations and founded dozens more to serve as industry support groups to address the crises and needs of the modern newspaper industry. Newspaper managers could easily spend a week each month attending conferences aimed at improving circulation and advertising practices, marketing, and editorial content and newspaper design to make papers more desirable in the face of the perceived threats to their existence.

Newspaper industry associations and specialty reporting organizations have responded with programs and seminars aimed at saving the newspaper and making it more desirable to advertisers and audiences. Industry associations and organizations—whose purposes are to educate members, help members respond to contemporary problems, and represent member interests—have wrestled with perceived threats to their continued existence in national, state, and regional meetings.

Newspapers themselves have banded together to meet the challenges of the Information Age, with publishers establishing cooperative ventures to share technology and create networks of newspapers for the electronic era.

Despite the nearly overwhelming impression that it is a declining industry whose future is in great doubt, the newspaper industry is today vibrant, lively, and fundamentally sound. Although the environment in which the industry operates is being altered, thus inducing change in newspaper operations and management, newspapers are still one of the most stable of all business enterprises. The newspaper remains the primary medium used by audiences and advertisers for in-depth news, features, and commercial information. Newspapers are well distributed throughout the nation to serve every economically viable town and city.

Although some newspaper managers and casual media observers project rapid decline for the industry, investors and serious researchers of the industry recognize the fundamental strengths and condition of the industry and do not accept or convey the same sense of fear. "Newspapers remain the cheapest way to get mass amounts of any kind of information," says John Morton, newspaper analyst for the Wall Street firm Lynch, Jones & Ryan. "And this will probably remain true well into the time when the so-called electronic information superhighway into the home becomes widely available." Papers should survive even if the traditional print form becomes no longer desirable or possible at a point in the distant future, he says, because "newspapers are already producing through digital electronic systems right up to the printing press. This makes newspaper information already compatible with whatever kind of electronic transmission system is developed to reach most consumers."[4]

Morton's views are echoed by others. Standard & Poors' investment report on the newspaper industry, for example, indicates that the high level of concern about the impact of on-line services is premature. "The threat from on-line services, as well as future services from cable television, which is expected to add digital interactive capabilities that will result in the availability of hundreds of channels, has had in our opinion a minimal impact on newspapers thus far," it said in its 1995 report.[5]

Part of the reason that investors and newspaper industry researchers exhibit less anxiety about the industry is that they place it in a broader context. By comparison to other manufacturing industries, the newspaper industry is about the same size as the textile products, lumber and wood products, and petroleum and coal products industries in the U.S. It is larger than the tobacco, furniture and fixtures, and petroleum refining industries. Newspapers account for more than $45 billion in activity each year. More than 60 million newspaper copies are purchased every day, and 55 million copies of paid and free circulation weekly newspapers circulate each week.

Most people conceive of the newspaper industry as being comprised of relatively large-circulation daily newspapers that are experiencing declines in circulation, household penetration, and advertising. They describe an industry in which most owners are large public newspaper companies. They envision a product that consists of dozens of pages each day, a product that increasingly uses large photographs and color printing, and a product that is being overwhelmed by and finding it increasingly difficult to compete with television and new information delivery systems.

Such conceptions of the industry are erroneous, however, because they ignore the scope and breadth of the industry, fail to distinguish the great differences in purposes, size, frequency, and scope among newspapers, and accept trends affecting some highly visible papers and industry segments as exemplary of the industry as a whole. This book will explore the broader context and operations of the industry to show the far greater scope and health of the industry and why such general conceptions of the industry are in error.

NEWSPAPERS AS MANUFACTURING AND SERVICE COMPANIES

In simple manufacturing terms, newspaper firms create an editorial and advertising product, manufacture copies of that product, and then sell and distribute those copies to customers. The process involves the acquisition and creation of content (both advertising and editorial), selection and editing of content, design and layout of the newspaper, production preparation and printing, collation of various sections and inserts and bundling of groups of papers, and distribution of the papers. Circulation marketing and sales operate concurrently (Figure 3-1). The life cycle of that product is short—only twenty-four hours for a daily and seven days for a weekly—so com-

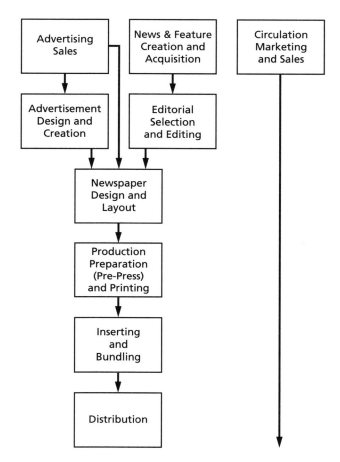

FIGURE 3-1   Stages in the Creation and Production of a Newspaper

panies are constantly engaged in the creation, manufacture, sales, and distribution processes.

That brief description belies the complexity of the operation, however, because the economics and operations of the newspaper industry differ significantly from other types of manufacturing due to the unique nature of the creation and production of newspapers, their marketing, their distribution, and their social functions. A major difference arises from the fact that newspaper firms are not merely manufacturers of a single product, but simultaneously produce a manufactured product and provide a service.

Newspapers operate in two markets at the same time. They create, manufacture, and sell the physical product—a newspaper copy—to readers while simultaneously selling a service—access to those readers—to advertisers. The two separate markets are interdependent and the performance in each affects the performance of the other. The success of a newspaper in attracting readers with news and information makes it more attractive to advertisers, and its success in attracting advertisers provides financial resources and advertising information that help attract readers.[6]

In the creation of the content for each issue, newspaper firms acquire a wide variety of information and features from scores of news and feature services and syndicates, as well as produce information and features on their own. These activities create a large pool of information and features from which newspapers select, edit, and rewrite editorial materials. Although some of the material from news and feature services is increasingly available to readers through other means, it is the reading and selection of materials from scores of sources, the creation of original materials, and the packaging of materials that is the value added by newspapers for which readers are willing to pay and can be used to provide competitive advantages over other information providers. Although there are some general similarities, each newspaper's emphasis and packaging of materials is somewhat different, giving it an institutional personality through the types of materials, tone, general appearance, and perspectives it conveys. Editors and publishers who pay close attention to the interests and values of readers in their local markets can emphasize those elements in their news and information choices to help create the newspaper's personality and develop strong bonds between the reader and the paper.

Concurrent with the development of these editorial materials is the sale of advertising access to companies, organizations, and individuals. When sales are made, advertising materials are provided by the advertisers or its advertising agency, or newspaper personnel are used to design and create the material. This advertising material is critical because it provides the primary source of revenue for newspapers. U.S. daily newspapers are among the most dependent upon advertising for revenue among newspapers throughout the world (Figure 3-2). Advertising is also crucial because it provides the majority of the content for the newspapers (Figure 3-3).

After the editorial and advertising material is complete for an issue, the reproduction of that material takes place through preparation and printing. After printing, the copies are then distributed to subscribers and made available for single-copy purchase. Issues relating to methods of distribution and access to distribution systems are increasing as technology provides new opportunities for conveying information and advertising to readers.

There are great differences in the types, functions, and operations of newspapers within the industry. Understanding these differences and the nature and scope of the industry are crucial for understanding the variety of operational issues and

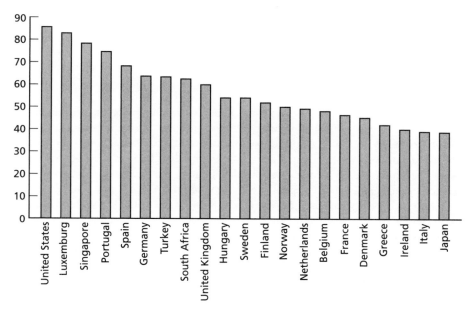

FIGURE 3-2   Advertising Income as a Percentage of Newspaper Revenue in Selected Nations

Source: International Federation of Newspaper Publishers, 1995.

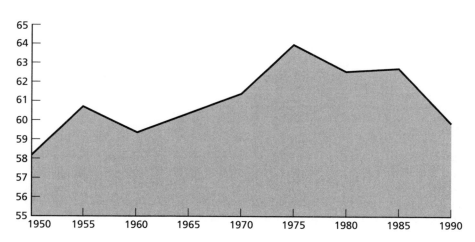

FIGURE 3-3   Advertising as a Percentage of Content of Daily Newspapers, 1950–1990

problems facing different branches of the industry as well as individual newspaper companies.

DEFINITION OF A NEWSPAPER

The definition of a newspaper has always been and will undoubtedly remain nebulous because there is no single industry-wide agreement on elements such as publication frequency, size dimensions of pages, the average number of pages and stories produced, and the format that makes a publication fall within the scope of the term. As a result, in the United States and in other nations, there are wide differences in frequency, size, and format of publications that call themselves newspapers.

Although the newspaper industry itself has never established a single agreed-on definition, a variety of government bodies and agencies, including the postal service, legislatures, courts, and city councils, have established criteria defining newspapers for a variety of purposes. A generally agreed-on definition for legal purposes describes a newspaper as "a publication, usually in sheet form, intended for general circulation, and published regularly at short intervals, containing intelligence of current events and news of general interest."[7]

The postal service definition must be met in order to receive the fiscal advantages of reduced postal rates offered under a second-class mail permit. The United States Postal Service defines a newspaper as a publication that is published at regularly stated intervals, in which editorial content averages at least 25 percent of the total content, and that more than 50 percent of the publication's circulation is paid.[8]

Legislatures have established definitions for regulation and tax purposes. And many government bodies and agencies have established definitions of "official" newspapers for the purpose of establishing the locations in which public acts, resolutions, and other legal and official notices should be published. The U.S. Congress, in writing the Newspaper Preservation Act in 1970, defined the newspaper as "a publication produced on newsprint which is published in one or more issues weekly . . . and in which a substantial portion of the content is devoted to the dissemination of news and editorial opinion."[9]

Numerous private efforts have been made to forge a clear definition of a newspaper, but all have failed to gain universal acceptance. Some definitions have included the ideas that a newspaper is linked to a specific geographic location (such as a city, county, or state) or that it is printed on newsprint, but these elements have tended to disappear from definitions in recent years as regional, national, and international newspapers have strongly developed and as many firms have begun using types of paper other than newsprint for some or all of their newspapers. Although newspapers have traditionally focused on a wide range of news and information intended for a general audience, the definition has been expanded in the past century to include some publications emphasizing special topics, especially publications that focus on business and finance.

If one reviews the various definitions, however, several elements are universal: the publication should contain news, it should be produced using a printing press, the publication should appear regularly, and it should be available to the general public. The newspapers under discussion in this book are based on those universal elements and encompass a wide variety of the newspapers available.

TYPES OF NEWSPAPERS

When considering the many differences in newspapers, nine general categories of papers are clear: (1) international and national daily papers; (2) metropolitan and/or regional daily papers; (3) local daily papers; (4) non-daily general audience papers; (5) minority papers; (6) papers published in secondary languages; (7) religious papers; (8) military papers; and (9) other specialty newspapers.

International and national papers are the types of papers that most often generate intense public discussion. These are papers intended for broad distribution and are not as clearly linked to a single location in terms of the news and advertising that they carry. Such newspapers maintain bureaus in many cities in the nation and throughout the world and usually publish several editions of the newspaper designed for distribution in different parts of the nation or the world. This category includes publications such as *USA Today, Wall Street Journal, New York Times,* and *Washington Post.* These papers emphasize reporting on national and international topics and are written in a way that accounts for the fact that readers may be unfamiliar with local personalities, locations, and issues when they cover events involving specific states or cities. Only about a half dozen such papers are found in the United States.

Large metropolitan and regional newspapers represent a second tier of daily newspapers that tend to be published in major cities and whose content is highly influenced by events in those cities and their surrounding metropolitan areas. In some cases, these papers serve readers well beyond the boundaries of the metropolitan area. The *Boston Globe,* for example, provides coverage of and is circulated throughout New England and the *Des Moines Register* dominates the entire state of Iowa. In recent years, however, many such metropolitan newspapers have reduced their circulation areas to cut unprofitable circulation and thus reduced the influence they once had over larger areas surrounding their place of publication. Major metropolitan and regional newspapers tend to maintain news bureaus in Washington, DC, and sometimes New York City, Chicago, and other major regional cities in the United States, as well as in the capital and other major cities of the state in which they are located. They often operate their own advertising sales offices in New York City and other major financial and advertising locales. Metropolitan/regional newspapers tend to be published seven days per week, with especially large circulation sales on Sundays. About fifty of the slightly more than 1,500 daily newspapers in the nation fall into this category.

Local daily newspapers are those tied to smaller metropolitan areas, specific cities and towns, whose primary purpose is to provide local news coverage and local advertising service. This group includes papers such as the *News-Journal* in Pensacola, Florida, and the Wichita (Kansas) *Eagle.* Local papers tend to publish only one edition daily and to maintain only a local reporting and sales staff, obtaining statewide, national, and international coverage from news services and using the services of nonstaff sales representatives or advertising networks that represent many papers throughout the nation to achieve some national advertising sales. This type of paper accounts for about 95 percent of the daily newspaper segment of the industry. Such papers normally publish at least five days per week and in larger cities are available six or seven days per week. Readers of newspapers in this group that are not published on Sunday tend to purchase the nearby metropolitan/regional newspaper on that day.

The nondaily general audience newspaper category covers the largest group of newspapers, those published less than five days per week. These traditionally include papers that appear once per week or several times each week. Such papers tend to serve counties, small communities, neighborhoods of a larger city, or as a complementary paper to a daily newspaper by providing coverage and advertising services that are not available from the daily. Nondaily papers include publications such as the *Forsyth County News* in Cumming, Georgia, and alternative newspapers such as the *Bay Guardian* in San Francisco. The circulation sizes of nondailies range from a few hundred copies to hundreds of thousands of copies, but their total circulation is rapidly approaching the same level as total daily newspaper circulation. The number of papers in the nondaily press is more than five times as large as the number in the daily newspaper categories.

Minority newspapers are intended to service the needs of specific English-speaking minority groups in the nation's population. Most minority newspapers are nondailies. The largest and most active minority newspaper category includes papers that identify themselves as serving the black community, such as the Chicago *Daily Defender* and the Birmingham, Alabama, *World.* Few other racial or ethnic minority groups maintain as active an English-language press as blacks, although a few newspapers exist to serve the needs of other minority ethnic groups, such as the national *Indian Country Today,* which serves Native Americans, and the *American-Arab Message,* which serves Americans of Arab descent. Gays and lesbians are served by an active nondaily press including such papers as the New York *Native* and the *Bay Area Reporter.*

An important and often ignored segment of the newspaper industry includes papers published in languages other than English. This segment includes both daily and nondaily newspapers published at the national, metropolitan/regional, and local levels. These secondary language papers provide news and advertising in languages ranging from German to Vietnamese, from Spanish to Korean, from Russian to Chinese. Papers in this group include the local and regionally oriented *El Diario-La Prensa* in New York and the *Chinese Times* in San Francisco. Other papers, such as the German-language *Wochen-Post* and the Norwegian *Nordisk Tidende,* serve readers nationwide. These papers are designed to serve not only the information needs of immigrants but also those of citizens who have been born and live in communities in which English is a minority language. They also serve English speakers who wish to preserve the languages of their ancestors for cultural or other reasons.

Papers intended for minorities are not typically major players on the national scene but are important for the the service they provide to their communities. In metropolitan areas with large minority populations, these papers sometimes wield considerable influence on the political and social life of the community.

Religious organizations and individual members of a number of religions publish newspapers, usually nondailies, intended to provide coverage about activities and issues associated with the religions, as well as general news reported from the perspectives of those religions and their members. Among the largest and best-known segments of this portion of the newspaper industry are Jewish and Catholic newspapers, which are published and widely available throughout the United States. These papers include both national and local publications such as the *National Catholic Register* and the *Jewish Times* in Baltimore. This segment of the newspaper industry also includes papers such as the *Baptist Record* in Jackson, Mississippi, and the *Adventist Review* in Silver Spring, Maryland.

Another major category of newspapers, primarily nondailies, is comprised of papers associated with military bases. These papers are operated either by military personnel or private parties and cover base activities and provide news and advertising for surrounding communities. Such papers include the *Hawaii Navy News,* which serves U.S. Navy personnel from Pearl Harbor, the *Quantico Sentry,* which serves the U.S. Marine Corps base in Quantico, Virginia, and the *Fort Leavenworth Lamp,* which serves the U.S. Army facilities at Fort Leavenworth, Kansas. Although some papers have longer histories, most of these papers developed during and after World War II and were strongest during the Cold War when the number of military personnel was at its highest point.

Other specialty papers focus on topics including law, business, labor, sports, and fashion. This category includes both daily and nondaily publications. Well-known examples of this type of paper include *Investor's Business Daily, Women's Wear Daily, Chicago Daily Law Bulletin, Daily Variety,* and the *Daily Racing Form.*

NUMBER OF PAPERS

No single, accurate figure exists for the number of all types of newspapers in the United States, because federal and state governments do not require official registration of publications and because private organizations tracking newspapers normally include only those that fit into a few of the eight general categories of newspapers discussed above. Between 9,500 and 10,000 newspapers are published in the United States, and fewer than 15 percent are daily papers. Privately compiled, regular counts of daily and weekly newspapers have been maintained only for the past four decades, but they reveal that the segments of the industry that they track have undergone significant changes over time.

Daily Newspapers

Despite the perception that the number of newspapers has dropped dramatically in the past five decades, the total number of daily newspapers published in this country remained relatively stable from 1950 to 1980, declining by less than 2 percent (Figure 3-4). The distorted perception of newspaper mortality was fueled by the deaths of a large number of competing secondary papers in mid- and large-sized cities as populations moved to new suburban communities. But concurrent with the development of those communities came the establishment of new dailies to serve their needs, so the aggregate number of newspapers remained relatively stable. The 1980s, however, brought about a significant and rapid decline in the number of daily newspapers, with the number decreasing from 1,745 in 1980 to 1,611 in 1990, a drop of nearly 8 percent. Although that number is dramatic, the decline did not leave communities without newspapers, nor did it indicate a dramatic decrease in competition nationwide, because the majority of the closures came in second editions or "sister publications" of newspapers that did survive. The primary closures occurred in afternoon editions published by morning newspapers.

There are a variety of explanations for the declining interest in these second newspapers, including the extension of urban areas that began requiring readers to

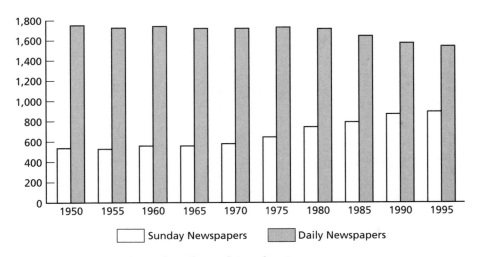

FIGURE 3-4   Number of Daily and Sunday Papers

commute by auto rather than traditional public transportation systems that earlier spurred afternoon readership. In addition, many metropolitan afternoon papers had established a working-class orientation and personality, and did not adjust when the type of workers commuting to metropolitan cities began shifting to the professional and managerial classes.

Because many of the newspapers that died between 1950 and 1980 were afternoon newspapers, many observers of the newspaper industry came to believe that afternoon papers could not survive. This belief was underscored in the title of a popular book about newspaper closures called *Death in the Afternoon*.[10] The belief gained credibility despite the fact that about 80 percent of all newspapers were afternoon newspapers throughout most of the second half of the twentieth century (Figure 3-5). Although a significant number of large metropolitan afternoon newspapers were closed, it was not merely because they were afternoon papers but because they were secondary papers in their markets and unable to withstand the population shift to the suburbs and advertiser preferences for the newspaper with the largest circulation in a metropolitan area. In fact, as suburban papers were established, they were usually afternoon papers. It was not until the 1980s, when publishers of morning newspapers began a wave of closures of their afternoon editions and a significant number of publishers of afternoon papers converted to morning publication, that the number of afternoon papers declined significantly. Even today, however, about two-thirds of all newspapers are published as afternoon papers.

Sunday Newspapers

Only about half of the nation's newspapers publish on Sundays, but that number has increased by about 50 percent since 1960, growing from 563 papers to 863 in 1990

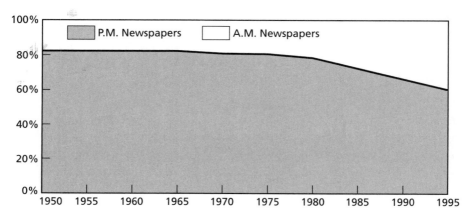

FIGURE 3-5   A.M. and P.M. Papers as Percentage of Dailies

(Figure 3-4). Sunday papers typically have larger circulations than their daily counterparts because they are popular among readers who do not believe they have time to read during the week and because metropolitan Sunday papers are often used by readers of local papers that do not publish a Sunday edition of their own. The larger readership of Sunday papers and the greater amount of time spent with Sunday papers by readers results in greater advertising placement, so Sunday editions typically contain a far greater amount of advertising material than weekday papers.

Other Categories

The number of weekly and non-daily newspapers published has fluctuated greatly in the past three decades with a peak of more than 8,000 in the 1960s. Today the number stands at approximately 7,500 newspapers (Figure 3-6).

The number of papers in other categories is not regularly tracked but various directories list approximately 250 religious newspapers (of which 185 are Catholic), 150 military newspapers, 80 papers serving the black community, 50 foreign language papers, and over 24 gay and lesbian newspapers.

LOCATIONS OF DAILY NEWSPAPERS

The existence of newspapers is influenced by a variety of geographic and demographic factors, including distribution, size, and proximity to other newspapers.

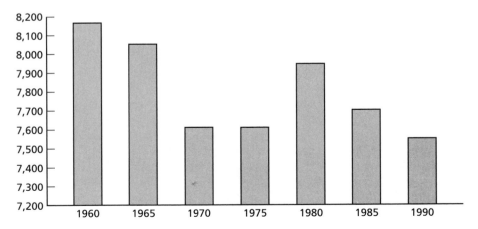

FIGURE 3-6   Number of Weekly Newspapers, 1960–1990

Newspapers are well distributed throughout the nation, ranging from two in Delaware and the District of Columbia to 111 in California, but Delaware and the District of Columbia both have a statistically lower than average number of daily papers per state or district (Table 3-1). California, Illinois, Indiana, New York, Ohio, Pennsylvania, and Texas have statistically larger than average numbers of papers. Together these seven states with a larger than average number of newspapers contain almost 40 percent of all newspapers in the country. California alone accounts for about 7 percent of all daily papers, almost half of all the papers found in the western states. Clearly, the populations of these seven states create the potential for a larger number of readers, as will be discussed below.

The daily newspaper industry is concentrated in the central and eastern U.S. Considering the geographical distribution, one finds that about 40 percent of the papers are located in eastern states, nearly half are located in central states, and about 15 percent in western states.

The number of newspapers in a state is influenced both by its physical size and its population. If the number of papers is considered using a state size measure (total area in square miles), the number of square miles per paper ranges from thirty-five in the District of Columbia and 202 in Rhode Island to 14,150 for Utah and 84,429 for Alaska. Only Alaska falls outside the statistical norm (Table 3-2). Because Alaska is the nation's largest state in terms of square miles and is the third smallest state in terms of population, only ahead of Wyoming and Vermont, its presence highly skews the statistical analysis. If Alaska is removed, seven other states have an unusually large number of square miles served by each newspaper: Idaho, Montana, Nevada, New Mexico, North Dakota, Utah, and Wyoming.

The differences shown here are important because they influence the number of competitors and potential competitors faced by the papers, the sizes of their coverage and circulation areas, and the sizes of the audiences they serve. The figures also quickly reveal some of the major differences faced by urban and rural publishers that significantly affect their operations and costs.

Nationwide, the average daily paper serves about 2,972 square miles, an area slightly larger than the state of Delaware and a little more than twice the size of Rhode Island.

If one considers the distribution of daily newspapers based on state populations, the range is from 1 paper for every 47,000 persons in Wyoming to 1 for every 345,000 persons in Delaware. The nationwide average is 1 paper per 163,000 persons in a state. This means that the average paper serves a population about the size of the cities of Orlando, Florida, Salt Lake City, Utah, or Syracuse, New York. A statistically lower than average population per newspaper is found in Arkansas, Indiana, Iowa, Kansas, Montana, North Dakota, Oklahoma, South Dakota, Vermont, West Virginia, and Wyoming (Table 3-2). A statistically higher than average population per newspaper is found in California, Delaware, District of Columbia, Florida, Maryland, New Jersey, New York, and Utah.

TABLE 3-1 Number of Newspapers by State

	Number of Dailies	Location
Alabama	27.0	E
Alaska	6.0	O
Arizona	19.0	W
Arkansas	31.0	C
California	111.0^{+3}	W
Colorado	23.0	W
Connecticut	19.0	E
Delaware	2.0^{-1}	E
District of Columbia	2.0^{-1}	E
Florida	42.0	E
Georgia	34.0	E
Hawaii	6.0	O
Idaho	11.0	W
Illinois	69.0^{+1}	C
Indiana	72.0^{+1}	C
Iowa	37.0	C
Kansas	46.0	C
Kentucky	23.0	E
Louisiana	26.0	C
Maine	7.0	E
Maryland	15.0	E
Massachusetts	41.0	E
Michigan	52.0	C
Minnesota	25.0	C
Mississippi	22.0	E
Missouri	44.0	C
Montana	11.0	W
Nebraska	20.0	C
Nevada	8.0	W
New Hampshire	9.0	E
New Jersey	20.0	E
New Mexico	18.0	W
New York	68.0^{+1}	E
North Carolina	49.0	E
North Dakota	10.0	C
Ohio	84.0^{+2}	C
Oklahoma	46.0	C
Oregon	18.0	W
Pennsylvania	88.0^{+2}	E
Rhode Island	6.0	E
South Carolina	16.0	E
South Dakota	13.0	C
Tennessee	27.0	E
Texas	95.0^{+2}	C
Utah	6.0	W
Vermont	8.0	E
Virginia	30.0	E
Washington	24.0	W
West Virginia	23.0	E
Wisconsin	36.0	C
Wyoming	10.0	W
Total	1555.0	
Mean	30.5	
Median	23.0	
Mode	6.0	
Standard Deviation	25.6	

Based on 1992 data.
Superscript indicates number of standard deviations above or below average.

Location: E = eastern states, C = central states, W = western states, O = other.

TABLE 3-2   Average Number of Square Miles and Population per Daily Newspaper by State

	Sq. Miles	Adj. Sq. Miles[*]	Population
Alabama	1,915	1,915	153,000
Alaska	84,429[+6]	—	98,000
Arizona	5,700	5,700	202,000
Arkansas	1,662	1,662	77,000[-1]
California	1,368	1,368	278,000[+1]
Colorado	3,589	3,589	151,000
Connecticut	239	239	173,000
Delaware	1,023	1,023	345,000[+2]
District of Columbia	35	35	295,000[+1]
Florida	1,364	1,364	321,000[+1]
Georgia	1,636	1,636	199,000
Hawaii	1,079	1,079	193,000
Idaho	6,964	6,964[+1]	97,000
Illinois	817	817	169,000
Indiana	489	489	79,000[-1]
Iowa	1,521	1,521	76,000[-1]
Kansas	1,788	1,788	55,000[-1]
Kentucky	1,757	1,757	163,000
Louisiana	1,705	1,705	165,000
Maine	4,158	4,158	176,000
Maryland	697	697	327,000[+2]
Massachusetts	207	207	146,000
Michigan	1,126	1,126	181,000
Minnesota	3,376	3,376	179,000
Mississippi	2,168	2,168	119,000
Missouri	1,584	1,584	118,000
Montana	13,368	13,368[+2]	75,000[-1]
Nebraska	3,868	3,868	80,000
Nevada	13,820	13,820[+3]	166,000
New Hampshire	1,031	1,031	123,000
New Jersey	339	339	339,000[+2]
New Mexico	6,755	6,755[+1]	88,000
New York	692	692	266,000[+1]
North Carolina	994	994	140,000
North Dakota	7,070	7,070[+1]	64,000[-1]
Ohio	475	475	131,000
Oklahoma	1,428	1,428	70,000[-1]
Oregon	4,854	4,854	165,000
Pennsylvania	498	498	136,000
Rhode Island	202	202	168,000
South Carolina	1,830	1,830	225,000
South Dakota	6,426	6,426	55,000[-1]
Tennessee	1,505	1,505	186,000
Texas	2,723	2,723	186,000
Utah	14,150	14,150[+3]	302,000[+1]
Vermont	1,068	1,068	71,000[-1]
Virginia	1,199	1,199	213,000
Washington	2,621	2,621	214,000
West Virginia	2,373	2,373	79,000[-1]
Wisconsin	1,560	1,560	139,000
Wyoming	9,781	9,781[+1]	47,000[-1]
Mean	4,569	2,972	163,000
Median	1,636	1,610	163,000
Standard Deviation	11,916	3,482	83,000

Based on 1990 data.
[*]Removing Alaska from statistical calculation.
Superscript indicates number of standard deviations above or below average.

NEWSPAPER CIRCULATION

The circulation of weekday newspapers grew steadily until about 1970 when it reached a plateau. Today the figure is slightly less than 60 million copies sold daily (Figure 3-7). Between 1950 and 1990, daily circulation overall increased 15.8 percent, but during the period from 1970 to 1990 circulation increased by only 216,629, representing only 2.5 percent of the total growth from 1950 to 1990.

Consideration of the average (mean) circulation per newspaper, however, presents a more positive picture of the health of newspaper circulation. It rose 27.4 percent between 1950 and 1990 (Table 3-3), almost at twice the rate of total daily circulation, and it experienced 9 percent growth between 1970 and 1990 (Figure 3-8). Between 1990 and 1995 the figure declined, primarily due to publishers' decisions to reduce unprofitable circulation in outlying areas and to cease publishing afternoon editions of morning papers, as well as closures of secondary papers in a few communities.

The growth in total circulation and average circulation has clearly been affected by the decline in the total number of daily newspapers, but it also indicates that surviving daily papers benefited from the decline in competition and that, despite mistaken beliefs to the contrary, the average newspaper has tended to gain rather than lose circulation.

Although the average circulation per newspaper has risen, its circulation size (38,020 in 1995) indicates that most daily newspapers are relatively small. This is underscored when one categorizes daily newspapers by their circulation size. More than half of daily newspapers have circulations under 25,000, and more than two-thirds have circulations below 50,000. Only about a quarter have circulations be-

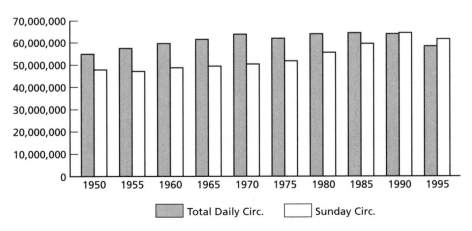

FIGURE 3-7   Daily and Sunday Circulation, 1950–1995

TABLE 3-3   Average (Mean) Circulation of Daily and Sunday Newspapers, 1950–1995

	Daily	Sunday
1950	30,378	84,849
1955	31,902	85,855
1960	33,339	84,722
1965	34,370	84,722
1970	35,531	93,987
1975	34,542	79,963
1980	35,646	74,383
1985	37,450	73,717
1990	38,687	72,578
1995	38,020	69,081

tween 50,000 and 500,000, and fewer than 5 percent of the nation's dailies exceed 500,000.

Population changes need to be taken into account when reviewing the growth of circulation over time. If one adjusts changes in daily newspaper circulation using a circulation per 1,000 population figure, a rapid decline in overall use of newspapers is readily apparent (Table 3-4). The figure dropped 34 percent, from 356 per 1,000 population to 234 per 1,000 population, between 1950 and 1995. This development is significant because it indicates that the penetration of newspapers—the degree to which they are reaching audiences—is declining.

These aggregate trends are not indicative of the situation in all states and the District of Columbia, however. Between 1980 and 1990, for example, twenty-nine states showed increases in daily newspaper circulation within their borders, while

TABLE 3-4   Daily Newspaper Circulation per 1,000 Population, 1950–1995

Year	Circ/Pop
1950	356
1960	328
1970	305
1980	275
1990	251
1995	234

twenty-two states had decreases. Daily circulation changes during the period ranged from a decline of 15.6 percent in Kansas to an increase of 37 percent in Arkansas (Table 3-5).

Important differences are also found in terms of daily circulation per 1,000 population. In 1990, for example, the figure ranged from a high of 333 in the District of Columbia (Connecticut had the state high of 295) to a low of 163 in Utah.

Between 1980 and 1990, a decline in circulation per 1,000 population occurred in thirty-five states, while fifteen experienced increases and one remained the same (Figure 3-8). The change ranged from a 40.5 percent increase in the District of Columbia (Arkansas had the highest percentage increase for any state at 34.6) to a 27.3 percent decrease in Missouri (Table 3-6).

The percentage of households in the states and the District of Columbia covered by daily newspaper circulation declined in forty-six of the fifty-one cases between 1980 and 1990. Like the circulation per 1,000 population figure reported above, household coverage also provides a measure of penetration. The four cases in which increases per household occurred include Arkansas, District of Columbia, South Dakota, and Wyoming (Figure 3-9). By 1990 the percentage of households covered by daily circulation ranged from a low of 46 percent in Mississippi and Missouri to a high of 81 percent in the District of Columbia and Massachusetts (Table 3-7). The average state had a household coverage of 62 percent in 1990 and experienced a decline of 7.8 percent between 1980 and 1990.

The decline in newspaper circulation per 1,000 population and in terms of household penetration needs to be considered in light of lost circulation from competing secondary newspapers and evening editions of morning papers that disappeared in recent decades, as well as the fact that many newspaper readers purchased both papers in such towns. The statistics of circulation per household and household coverage have never accounted for these issues, so these figures can only be expected to decline with the disappearance of those papers.

The circulation of Sunday newspapers has risen steadily, concurrently with the increase in the number of Sunday papers, and it is now at about the same level as weekday papers (Figure 3-7). From 1950 to 1995 Sunday circulation increased 32.6 percent (Table 3-3). Because that circulation was being spread among an increasing number of Sunday papers, however, the average circulation of Sunday papers declined by 18.6 percent in the same period (Figure 3-10). Nevertheless, the circulation of Sunday newspapers increased in forty-seven states and declined only in Delaware, Michigan, Missouri, and West Virginia between 1980 and 1990 (Table 3-5). Changes in that decade ranged from a decline in Sunday circulation of 3.6 percent in Missouri to an increase of 154 percent in Alaska.

The circulation of weekly newspapers has also increased steadily during the past thirty years and there is no indication that the growth in those numbers has begun to diminish (Figure 3-11). Circulation for weekly papers rose from 20.9 million in 1960 to 55.2 million in 1990. The average (mean) circulation of weeklies rose from about 2,500 in 1960 to 7,300 in 1990.

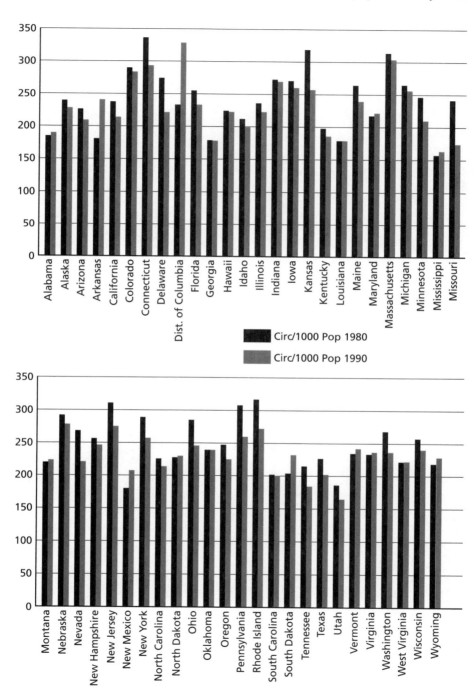

FIGURE 3-8   Daily Circulation Per 1,000 Population

TABLE 3-5   Change in Newspaper Circulation by State, 1980–1990

	Daily Circulation			Sunday Circulation		
	1980	1990	% Change	1980	1990	% Change
Alabama	722,217	772,184	−6.9	675,033	771,140	14.2
Alaska	97,202	126,022	29.6	55,086	140,014	154.2
Arizona	619,894	769,306	24.1	595,048	848,341	42.6
Arkansas	414,642	568,043	37.0	451,060	696,224	54.4
California	5,652,386	6,393,497	13.1	5,338,903	6,638,934	24.4
Colorado	84,7301	943,696	11.4	917,854	1,118,706	21.9
Connecticut	1053,233	973,490	−7.6	877,304	980,737	11.8
Delaware	164,709	147,352	−10.5	178,271	176,086	−1.2
District of Columbia	149,345	201,325	34.8	159,083	168,403	5.9
Florida	2,505,214	3028,873	20.9	2,636,463	3,759,720	42.6
Georgia	982,783	1,159,180	17.9	966,057	1,249,140	29.3
Hawaii	217,399	247,557	13.9	234,514	264,530	12.8
Idaho	201,036	201,642	0.3	191,159	227,311	18.9
Illinois	2,726,647	2,555,705	−6.3	2,811,028	2,849,835	1.4
Indiana	1,514,860	1,511,712	−0.2	1,253,829	1,373,435	9.5
Iowa	802,603	713,280	−11.1	718,245	724,304	0.8
Kansas	752,035	634,482	−15.6	624,098	650,588	4.2
Kentucky	724,427	688,757	−4.9	616,876	663,561	7.6
Louisiana	759,176	761,738	0.3	783,488	834,303	6.5
Maine	301,100	296,366	−1.6	137,035	297,198	116.9
Maryland	919,896	1,063,148	15.6	994,557	1,163,924	17.0
Massachusetts	1,790,394	1,819,587	1.6	1,468,398	1,635,504	11.4
Michigan	2,440,473	2,374,103	−2.7	2,394,885	2,333,785	−2.6
Minnesota	1,011,263	925,016	−8.5	972,837	1,139,924	17.2
Mississippi	39,173	422,480	5.8	357,484	430,349	20.4
Missouri	119,263	903,187	−24.6	1,111,418	1,071,354	−3.6
Montana	17,815	178,268	2.6	174,490	181,904	4.2
Nebraska	460,035	439,000	−4.6	385,883	405,093	5.0
Nevada	216,582	264,901	22.3	214,501	297,104	38.5
New Hampshire	236,119	273,144	15.7	167,315	243,469	45.5
New Jersey	2,262,444	2,140,318	−5.4	2,453,331	2,558,066	4.3
New Mexico	235,122	313,051	33.1	229,723	297,689	29.6
New York	5,087,520	4,642,759	−8.7	4,680,462	4,852,155	3.7
North Carolina	1,320,265	1,413,435	7.1	1,101,748	1,391,657	26.3
North Dakota	148,947	146,648	−1.5	83,713	140,265	67.6
Ohio	3,099,114	2,673,270	−13.7	2,519,888	2,833,608	12.4
Oklahoma	729,266	756,625	3.8	756,184	895,124	18.4
Oregon	654,032	639,559	−2.2	571,545	645,854	13.0
Pennsylvania	3,681,491	3,106,415	−15.6	2,938,749	3,028,980	3.1
Rhode Island	302,836	275,912	−8.9	241,901	286,983	18.6
South Carolina	631,465	69,7941	10.5	541,589	752,895	39.0
South Dakota	140,962	162,194	15.1	128,074	130,372	1.8
Tennessee	979,373	899,877	−8.1	88,4228	984,212	11.3
Texas	3,255,750	3,426,136	5.2	3,578,158	4,333,092	21.1
Utah	273,948	283,936	3.6	272,744	325,718	19.4
Vermont	121,307	137,883	13.7	103,705	115,768	11.6
Virginia	1,273,210	1478,103	16.1	1,145,969	1,389,655	21.3
Washington	1,118,778	1155,879	3.3	107,3625	1,179,415	9.9
West Virginia	434,140	400,144	−7.8	367,471	36,2144	−1.4
Wisconsin	1,227,000	1,186,659	−3.3	1,054,287	1,185,478	12.4
Wyoming	103,427	104,591	1.1	85,469	91,469	7.0

TABLE 3-6   Daily Newspaper Circulation Per 1,000 Population by State

	1980	1990	% Change
Alabama	184	190	3.3
Alaska	236	227	−3.8
Arizona	221	206	−6.8
Arkansas	179	241	34.6
California	236	211	−10.6
Colorado	288	284	−1.4
Connecticut	272	295	8.5
Delaware	275	219	−20.4
District of Columbia	237	333	40.5
Florida	250	229	−8.4
Georgia	177	176	−0.6
Hawaii	222	221	−0.5
Idaho	209	200	−4.3
Illinois	238	223	−6.3
Indiana	274	272	−0.7
Iowa	274	258	−5.8
Kansas	316	255	−19.3
Kentucky	196	187	−4.6
Louisiana	179	181	1.1
Maine	266	239	−10.2
Maryland	217	220	1.4
Massachusetts	312	301	−3.5
Michigan	263	255	−3.0
Minnesota	246	210	−14.6
Mississippi	157	164	4.5
Missouri	242	176	−27.3
Montana	218	224	2.8
Nebraska	291	278	−4.5
Nevada	263	213	−19.0
New Hampshire	252	242	−4.0
New Jersey	307	276	−10.1
New Mexico	177	204	15.3
New York	290	257	−11.4
North Carolina	223	211	−5.4
North Dakota	227	231	1.8
Ohio	287	246	−14.3
Oklahoma	238	241	1.3
Oregon	244	223	−8.6
Pennsylvania	310	261	−15.8
Rhode Island	318	274	−13.8
South Carolina	200	198	−1.0
South Dakota	203	233	14.8
Tennessee	211	183	−13.3
Texas	225	200	−11.1
Utah	183	163	−10.9
Vermont	234	243	3.8
Virginia	236	236	0.0
Washington	267	234	−12.4
West Virginia	221	225	1.8
Wisconsin	259	242	−6.6
Wyoming	213	233	9.4

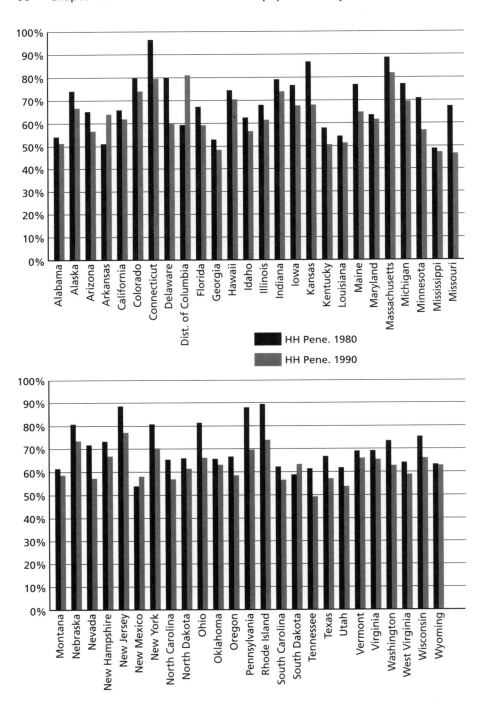

FIGURE 3-9 **Household Penetration of Daily Circulation, 1980 and 1990 (Percentages)**

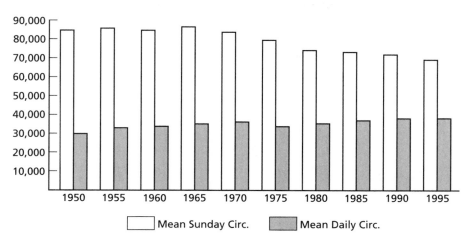

FIGURE 3-10   Change in Average Newspaper Circulation, 1950–1995

NEWSPAPER REVENUE

Newspapers can obtain revenue from the sales of both advertising and circulation (subscriptions and single-copy sales). Some nondaily general circulation newspapers, minority papers, and military papers are distributed at no charge to readers and are fully dependent on advertising sales for revenue, but the greatest bulk of papers charge for circulation and receive revenue from both sources.

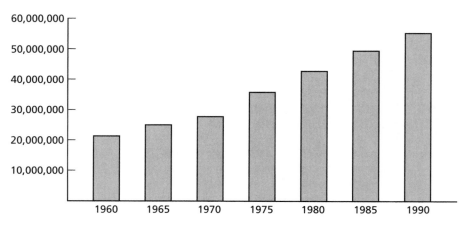

FIGURE 3-11   Total Circulation of Weekly Newspapers, 1960–1990

TABLE 3-7   Household Coverage of Daily Newspaper Circulation by State

	1980	1990	% Change
Alabama	53	51	−3.8
Alaska	71	66	−7.0
Arizona	62	55	−11.3
Arkansas	50	64	28.0
California	64	60	−6.3
Colorado	78	73	−6.4
Connecticut	95	79	−16.8
Delaware	78	59	−24.4
Dist. of Columbia	59	81	37.3
Florida	65	58	−10.8
Georgia	51	48	−5.9
Hawaii	72	69	−4.2
Idaho	60	56	−6.7
Illinois	67	61	−9.0
Indiana	78	73	−6.4
Iowa	75	67	−10.7
Kansas	85	67	−21.2
Kentucky	56	50	−10.7
Louisiana	53	51	−3.8
Maine	75	63	−16.0
Maryland	62	60	−3.2
Massachusetts	87	81	−6.9
Michigan	75	69	−8.0
Minnesota	69	56	−18.8
Mississippi	47	46	−2.1
Missouri	66	46	−30.3
Montana	60	58	−3.3
Nebraska	79	73	−7.6
Nevada	68	55	−19.1
New Hampshire	71	65	−8.5
New Jersey	88	76	−13.6
New Mexico	52	57	9.6
New York	80	70	−12.5
North Carolina	63	56	−11.1
North Dakota	64	61	−4.7
Ohio	80	65	−18.8
Oklahoma	64	63	−1.6
Oregon	64	58	−9.4
Pennsylvania	86	69	−19.8
Rhode Island	88	73	−17.0
South Carolina	60	55	−8.3
South Dakota	57	63	10.5
Tennessee	59	48	−18.6
Texas	64	56	−12.5
Utah	59	52	−11.9
Vermont	67	65	−3.0
Virginia	67	64	−4.5
Washington	71	61	−14.1
West Virginia	62	59	−4.8
Wisconsin	73	65	−11.0
Wyoming	60	62	3.3

Data on advertising and circulation revenue is incomplete for most segments of the newspaper industry because government statistics, industry associations, and advertising researchers typically do not report more than aggregate data or data mixed with nonnewspaper publications. Available data often exclude large segments of the newspaper industry. The most reliable and available statistics cover only daily newspapers and primarily involve advertising. These data reveal, however, that industry advertising revenues have risen strongly over time and that daily newspaper advertising continues to account for the bulk of total advertising expenditures.

Advertising sales by dailies rose from $2 billion in 1950 to more than $36 billion by 1995 (Figure 3-12). By 1994, daily newspapers had $34.2 billion in advertising sales. The dollar value of sales grew 78 percent during the 1950s, 55 percent during the 1960s, 159 percent in the 1970s, and 188 percent in the 1980s. The percentage of total sales resulting from advertising sales is 85 percent, well above that of other industrialized countries with well-developed newspaper industries. In Japan, for example, the figure is 40 percent; in the United Kingdom, 63 percent; and in Germany, 65 percent.[11]

If one considers newspaper advertising expenditures in relation to population, one sees that per capita spending increased from $13.68 in 1950 to $136.63 in 1995

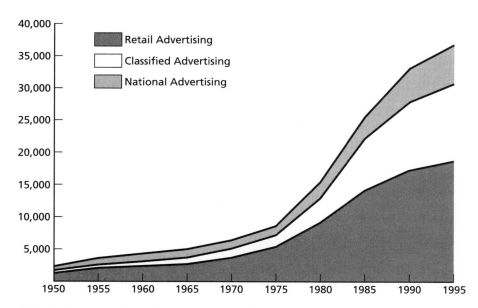

FIGURE 3-12   Advertising Revenues for Daily Papers, 1950–1995 (Millions of Dollars)

TABLE 3-8 Per Capita Spending for Daily Newspaper Advertising

Year	Amount
1950	$ 13.68
1960	20.53
1970	28.07
1980	65.30
1990	129.79
1995	136.63

(Table 3-8). Accounting for inflation, newspapers today receive almost three times the amount of advertising per capita that they received in 1950.

Newspapers continue to gain the largest share of advertising expenditures of any medium, currently about 23 percent of total advertising expenditures. The share of advertising dollars used to purchase newspaper advertising declined from 29 percent to 22.4 percent between 1970 and 1995, a trend evident throughout most of the last half of the twentieth century as more choices became available to advertisers. Although some wish to blame the maturation of television and cable television advertising for the decline in advertising share, changes in the shares over time indicate that the shift to the electronic media was greatest in the 1970s and that much of the gain for television was at the expense of magazine advertising shares. In the 1980s the advertising share for television clearly stabilized at about 20 percent, but the newspaper advertising share continued to drop because advertisers shifted shares to direct mail (Figure 3-13), which has become the primary print competitor for traditional newspaper advertisers.

Despite shifts in advertising shares among media, newspaper advertising revenue has increased in the three different advertising submarkets in which it operates: classified, national, and retail. During the past four decades classified advertising

TABLE 3-9 Rate of Increase in Revenue by Advertisement Category

Source	1950–1970	1970–1990	1950–1990
National	.72	3.63	6.96
Retail	1.80	4.06	13.17
Classified	3.04	6.57	29.52
Total Ad Revenue	1.76	4.66	14.59

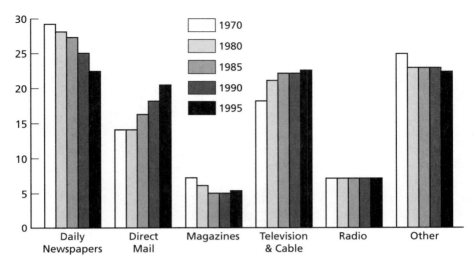

FIGURE 3-13   Shares of Advertising Expenditures by Medium (Percentages)

revenue grew at an explosive rate, increasing nearly 3,000 percent, more than twice the growth rate of retail ad revenue and four times the rate of national advertising revenue (Table 3-9). Classified advertising was the third source of revenue in 1950 and had become second by 1960. It has provided an increasingly larger share of revenue. Classified advertising provided less than one-fifth of total revenue in 1950 but by 1995 it provided more than 36 percent of all income (Table 3-10). This increase was due, in large part, to the growing use of classifieds by automobile dealers and real estate agents. The increasing importance of classified advertising as a revenue source can also be seen in the fact that the percentage of advertising revenue contributed by national advertising was cut in half during that same period.

Statistics on circulation revenue are not as readily available in government and industry reports as are statistics on advertising, but in 1994 circulation sales pro-

TABLE 3-10   Percentage of Daily Newspaper Advertising Revenue by Category

Category	1950	1960	1970	1980	1990
National	25.0	21.1	15.6	13.3	12.8
Retail	56.8	57.1	57.7	58.2	51.6
Classified	18.2	21.8	26.7	28.5	35.6

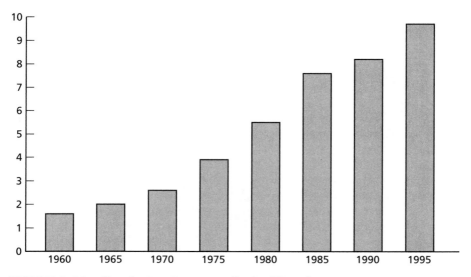

FIGURE 3-14   Circulation Revenue (in $ Billions)

vided approximately $9.5 billion in revenue, about 15 percent of the total revenue of daily newspapers in the U.S. Available data indicate that circulation revenue rose from $1.6 billion in 1960 to approximately $19.7 billion in 1995 (Figure 3-14). Circulation revenue per capita rose from $8.95 in 1960 to $24.14 in 1980, and to an estimated $37 in 1995 (Table 3-11).

Taken as a whole, these revenue figures indicate that the average newspaper in 1994 had a mean annual turnover (income from advertising and circulation sales) of $28.4 million. The total annual turnover value of each copy of paid circulation was thus approximately $740.[12]

TABLE 3-11 Per Capita Spending for Daily Newspaper Circulation

Year	Amount
1960	8.95
1970	13.96
1980	24.14
1990	35.00
1995	37.43

SUMMARY

Despite concerns among some observers that the newspaper industry is troubled, this overview has shown that the industry is much broader and much healthier than is generally believed. It has also shown that the average daily newspaper is small, serving a market of about 163,000 persons within 2,972 square miles, and that the overwhelming majority of newspapers are nondaily papers, many designed to serve the needs of subgroups in the population.

The data show that the general perception of daily newspapers as being large and suffering from economic ills is highly distorted. The average daily newspaper has a daily circulation of only about 40,000, and its circulation has been growing slowly and steadily at about .50 percent per year. The average daily has no other local newspaper competition and has been experiencing growth in both advertising and circulation revenues.

NOTES

[1]"Silicon Valley Nerds Herald Newspapers of Tomorrow," *South China Morning Post,* 2 March 1994, Media Supplement.

[2]Michael Moran, "Downcast News," *Evening Standard,* 23 November 1994, 62.

[3]Two well-known book titles that have helped fuel the impression of a struggle to keep papers alive are Philip Meyer's *The Newspaper Survival Book: An Editor's Guide to Marketing* (Bloomington: Indiana University Press, 1985) and Jim Willis's *Surviving in the Newspaper Business: Newspaper Management in Turbulent Times* (New York: Praeger, 1988).

[4]John Morton, "Worried Publishers Enter the Information Age," *San Francisco Examiner,* 24 April 1994, A15.

[5]"Newspaper Industry Making Headlines with Comeback in 1994 and 1995," *Standard and Poor's Emerging & Special Situation,* No. 4, 17 April 1995, 3.

[6]For economic discussions of these phenomena see Robert G. Picard, *Media Economics: Concepts and Issues* (Newbury Park, CA: Sage Publications, 1989).

[7]4 Op. Attys. Gen. 10; *Black's Law Dictionary* (St. Paul, MN: West Publishing, 1968).

[8]Public Law 233, 65 Stat. 672.

[9]Public Law 91-353, 84 Stat. 466, 15 U.S.C. sections 1801–1804 (1970).

[10]Peter Benjaminson, *Death in the Afternoon: America's Newspaper Giants Struggle for Survival* (Kansas City, MO: Andrews, McNeel and Parker, 1984).

[11]International Federation of Newspaper Publishers, *World Press Trends* (Paris: International Federation of Newspaper Publishers, 1995).

[12]Average (mean) annual turnover per newspaper is calculated by dividing total turnover (i.e., revenue) by the number of newspapers. Annual turnover value of each copy of paid circulation is calculated by dividing total turnover by total circulation.

4

The Structure of the Recorded Music Industry

GEOFFREY P. HULL
Middle Tennessee State University

BASIC FUNCTIONS

In order to produce income, a record company, usually referred to as a "label," gains control over a master recording of a performance by an artist and then sells copies to consumers. Usually this takes the form of getting the artist to sign an exclusive recording agreement with the label, producing a recording, then manufacturing and marketing copies of that recording for purchase by consumers. The label therefore has two basic functions that it must perform: acquire masters and market those masters. The acquisition of masters is usually referred to as the A & R (artist and repertoire) function. This chapter examines the overall market structure of the recording industry, the structure of its component firms, the economics of pricing and profitability, and the importance of independent labels in a market dominated by five major firms.

OLIGOPOLY

From almost every perspective the recording industry is either already in an oligopolistic state or heading towards oligopoly. *Oligopoly* is usually defined as a "few" sellers occupying the market, with "few" being everything between one firm (monopoly) to many firms (pure competition). A more useful definition, which takes into account the concentration of the market in the number of sellers, defines three levels of oligopoly. In a *dominant firm* oligopoly, one firm holds 50 to 90 percent of the market. In a *tight oligopoly,* a concentration of four firms holds more than 60 percent of the market. If it takes more than four firms to reach 60 percent of the market, but less than "many," that is still an oligopoly but would be deemed *"effective competition."*[1]

It should be noted that oligopoly is not a "four-letter word," either literally or figuratively. There is nothing inherently bad about an oligopoly existing in any given market. Oligopoly is simply a word that describes a market in which there are certain kinds of conditions. Generally, markets are described by four significant factors: the number of firms, the seller concentration, the product differentiation, and the barriers to entry.[2] The number of firms involved in the distribution of recordings is relatively small, as discussed below, but the number of individual labels is large. Looking at market share of the leading individual labels (Table 4-1), one can see a market that is fairly well spread. If one considers label ownership, on the theory that the individual labels do not operate autonomously within their corporate organizations, then there is a much higher concentration of sellers. Although all labels sell the same basic products, recordings, there is usually very high differentiation among those recordings. That is why some recordings find favor with consumers and are "hits" and others are not. That is why some recordings are the toast of the critics and others are panned. That is why consumers have favorite artists and favorite recordings. On the label side, the barriers to entry are not as great as they once used to be. There are many acts wanting to record, costs of recording are lower than they used to be, and the label does not have to manufacture its own recordings. From the perspective of the distribution of recordings, there are high barriers to entry. Setting up a nationwide distribution system for recordings entails warehouses, inventory, and personnel, all creating high barriers to entry. On the other hand, if recordings are distributed through cyberspace on the Internet, then barriers to entry are very low.

Oligopoly from Birth to the Fifties

For most of its existence the recording industry has been in a state of "tight oligopoly." Thomas Edison's monopoly lasted only nine years from the invention of the "talking machine" in 1877. The founding of his Edison Speaking Phonograph Company in 1878 led Alexander Graham Bell to create a better cylinder and player and form the American Graphophone Company in 1887. Edison first started offering cylinders for sale to the public in 1889. Shortly thereafter Columbia was formed and started offering cylinders for sale for coin-operated players. By 1901 the Victor Talking Machine Company was formed and began offering Emile Berliner's (the German who invented disk recording) disk players and recordings. Columbia began to market both cylinders and disks under patent licenses. By 1909 the three companies with patent monopolies (or licenses) controlled the market: Edison, Columbia, and Victor. A three-firm tight oligopoly continued until the 1950s, although the firms comprising the top three changed over time. Edison folded in the market crash of 1929, but Decca emerged in the 1930s.[3] By 1950 RCA Victor and Decca claimed 67 percent of *Billboard*'s Top Pop Records chart. Mercury and Capitol were emerging as significant labels with a 10 percent share each and Columbia had dropped to a less than 4 percent share.[4] The popularity charts of *Billboard* magazine are a convenient and reasonably accurate way to measure a record's or label's success. Although the methodologies used in compiling the charts have changed somewhat over time, they have always included a significant sales component.

During the early 1950s, more labels and artists began to emerge but the tight oligopoly remained. Phonograph players became more plentiful in the home market. Jukeboxes became more plentiful. As late as 1953 the top four firms, Columbia (reenergized by Broadway cast albums, MOR hits, and Mitch Miller recordings), Capitol, Mercury, and RCA Victor, controlled 78 percent of the charted records.[5] Only seven labels had any chart action at all. As R&B, country, and folk became more popular more labels appeared in the year-end chart summary. In 1954 fourteen labels reported Top 30 chart activity but there was still a tight oligopoly with RCA Victor, Capitol, Mercury, and Columbia controlling 62 percent of chart activity.[6]

Mom and Pop and Rock 'n' Roll

The birth of rock 'n' roll in 1955 ended the tight oligopoly and brought effective competition with the emergence of many independent labels, especially R&B, into the top charts. In 1955 it took the top six labels to garner a 60 percent share. In 1956 the top six labels controlled only 53 percent of the top chart share. *Billboard* reported twenty-five R&B hits on the charts and twenty rock hits (many of them cover versions of R&B songs by pop artists such as Perry Como).[7] The public's demand for the new music drove sales of recordings up with a 44 percent increase in sales volume from 1955 to 1956. The new artists came from everywhere, on dozens of new labels, and the chart share of the independents skyrocketed to 76 percent in 1958.[8] Even as albums began to replace singles as the dominant selling product in the early 1960s, it was clear that the oligopoly was broken. The 1962 *Billboard* album chart summary showed forty-two labels with at least one charted album and the top six firms controlled less than 50 percent of those records.[9]

Back to Oligopoly

Over the next twenty years the major corporations began to assert more control through branch distribution (in which a major corporation would set up regional branch warehouses) and mergers. By 1972 the top five labels only controlled 31.4 percent of the album charts, but the top five *corporations* controlled 58.2 percent of those charts. The industry was returning to a tight oligopoly (four firms controlling more than 60 percent) with the top four corporations controlling 52.6 percent of the album chart (WEA 26.2 percent, CBS 13.1 percent, A&M 7.7 percent, Capitol and RCA tied at 5.6 percent).[10] As the 1970s wore on into the 1980s the oligopoly became more pronounced. The most significant independent labels joined the branch distribution system. In 1979 A&M joined RCA distribution followed by Arista and Ariola in 1983. United Artists merged with Capitol in 1979. In 1983 Chrysalis went to CBS distribution and Motown went to MCA. In the flurry of consolidation and merger of the late 1980s and early 1990s, *ownership* became the key factor. Large labels bought out smaller labels. The identity of the smaller label may have been retained but ownership was usually in the hands of a large entertainment conglomerate.

The 1990s and Beyond

By the 1990s the structure of the industry had returned to a tight oligopoly. The top four distributing firms controlled about 62 percent of the market in the United States for the first half of the 1990s. WEA averaged about 21.5 percent, Sony about 15.5 percent, and PolyGram (PGD) and BMG about 12.8 percent each. Independent labels had been increasing their share of the market, from 14.6 percent in 1993 to 21.2 percent in 1996.[11] (Figure 4-1 shows details.) The likelihood is that the tight oligopoly will continue. Even if the share of independent labels continues at 20 percent, the remaining 80 percent would still be divided among five companies. If the big five divided up their 80 percent evenly (one-fifth of 80 is 16), and there is no indication that would happen, four of them would control 64 percent of the market. As indicated above, once an independent label begins to show significant market share and profitability, it is subject to being purchased by one of the big five. Unlike the situation in the late 1950s, the large companies do not ignore new musical genres or trends.

In 1998 two of the major record companies, Universal Music Group and PolyGram, merged. Universal's purchase of the PolyGram Music Group from its corporate owner, Royal Philips Electronics of Netherlands, was valued at $10.6 billion. The resulting record company, Universal Music Group, became the largest record company in the world. The worldwide market share of the combined company was estimated at 23 percent.[12] The market share in the U.S.A., as indicated by Figure 4-1, was about 25 percent. Although there was some hint of resistance in the European Community[13] due to anti-trust considerations, the deal is treated for the rest of this chapter as "done."

THE BIG FIVE[14]

Five large international conglomerates own and control the bulk of the recording industry in the world, not just the United States. In case there is any doubt that the recording industry operates on an international level, one only has to look at the

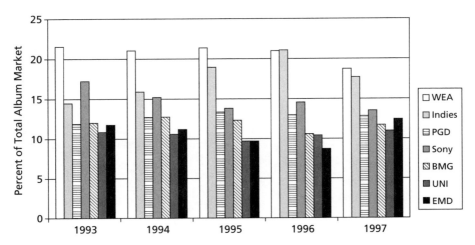

FIGURE 4-1   Market Share of Total Album Sales by Distributor

Source: SoundScan data reported in *Billboard*, 24 January 1998: 76; 20 January 1996: 55; 21 January 1995: 54.

ownership of the five largest record companies: Warner Music Group is owned by a U.S. company, Time Warner; Sony Music is owned by the Japanese Sony Corporation; BMG is owned by Bertlesman A.G. in Germany; EMI, Ltd. is a U.K. firm; Universal is owned by the Canadian Seagram's Ltd. Not every one of the large entertainment conglomerates breaks out the earnings or sales of their music divisions. Where that information is available it is given in the discussion of the "big five" that follows.

Warner Music Group

Time Warner Entertainment Company is the world's largest entertainment company. It got even larger in 1996 with the merger of Turner Broadcasting System. Warner Brothers records began as the music division of Warner Brothers film company to control music interests for its film productions in the 1920s. In the depression of the 1930s, Warner sold off its music publishing interests. In 1958 it reformed its music publishing and record labels, primarily to promote and sell its film and television related music. Warner Brothers had early 1960s success with the Everly Brothers and Bill Cosby comedy recordings and bought Frank Sinatra's MOR label, Reprise, in 1963–1965 (they purchased the label in halves). In 1967 Warner Brothers purchased Atlantic Records and was in turn purchased by 7 Arts. In 1969 the Kinney Corporation (not the shoe company, but a building services, construction, and parking company) purchased 7 Arts and changed its name to Warner Communications, Inc. With the addition of the Elektra Records label purchased in 1970,

Warner/Elektra/Atlantic Distribution (later just WEA Distribution) was formed. Time Warner was formed by the merger of print publishing giant Time, Inc., and "electronic" publishing giant Warner Communications, Inc. The music division of this giant is Warner Music Group, which consists of the labels and Warner/Chappel Music Publishing. In addition, it owns WEA Inc., which consists of WEA Corporation, the branch distribution system, WEA Manufacturing, which owns CD, CD–ROM, and videocassette manufacturing facilities, and Ivy Hill, a printing and packaging arm.[15] The Time Warner parent corporation also owns twenty-four magazines, book publishing, film and television production and distribution, a TV network, cable systems and cable programming, and theme parks. Time Warner reported 1996 operating revenues as $10 billion, with total assets of $35 billion. Warner Music Group labels are: Warner Brothers, Atlantic, Atco, Elektra/Asylum, Reprise.

Sony Music

Sony Corporation, the Japanese electronics manufacturing company, saw the importance of developing software industries to complement its hardware manufacturing when it entered into an agreement with CBS Records to create the Digital Audio Disc Corporation, the first manufacturer of compact discs in the United States. The cornerstones of Sony Music are Sony Music Publishing and the venerable label Columbia Records. Columbia, originally the Columbia Graphophone Company of pre-1900, existed as a separate entity until the depression saw the merger of Columbia Graphophone, Gramophone Company, and Parlophone to create Electric and Musical Industries, Ltd. (EMI) in England. EMI sold its American stock to the American Record Corporation (ARC). Columbia Broadcasting System (CBS) purchased ARC in 1938 and revitalized the Columbia label. Columbia seceded from EMI in England in 1952. Sony built its music interests primarily through the acquisition of CBS Records group for $2 billion in 1988 from CBS, Inc. Sony's music group revenues amounted to about $4.6 billion in 1997, that is about 56 percent of Sony's entertainment business revenues of $8.2 billion, and about 10 percent of Sony's total revenues for that year. Sony also owns film production and distribution interests in Columbia Pictures and Tri-Star Pictures, as well as home video production and distribution, television production companies, and a large consumer electronics division. Sony Music labels are: Columbia, Epic, and Epic Associated Labels. Sony Music also owns half of the Columbia House record club; Warner owns the other half. Sony also owns a branch distribution system (Sony Distribution) and CD and tape manufacturing facilities in the United States.

BMG

BMG is part of the German corporation, Bertlesman, A.G. BMG used to stand for "Bertlesman Music Group" but that was shortened to BMG. BMG's record business took off in the United States when it acquired Arista Records from its founder Clive Davis in 1979. In 1986 BMG purchased all the RCA Victor interests from General Electric (which had earlier that year acquired RCA Corporation's recording interests for $6.4 billion). BMG labels include: Ariola, RCA, LaFace/Arista, Zoo Entertainment, Private, Windham Hill, Disques Vogue, Jive/Silvertone, Wired, Mushroom, Deconstruction, American Recordings, Absorbing, Gun, Red Rooster, Goldrush, K&P, Chodwig, MSM, Expressive, Coconut, Nahsa, MCI, Sing Sing, Jupiter, and Lawine. BMG's labels operate under BMG Entertainment. Under that same group are BMG Music Publishing and BMG Music, the distribution and manufacturing operations, and the record club, BMG Music Service. The parent company also owns television and radio stations (outside of the United States), film production and distribution, magazine publishing, book publishing, and newspapers. Bertlesman owns in whole or part over two hundred entertainment and publishing entities throughout the world and continued to expand in the mid-1990s, acquiring 73 percent of Ricordi (the largest Italian independent record company) and 50 percent of the New Age label Private Music in 1994.[16] Net revenues in 1996 were DM 21.5 billion (about $15.6 billion) with total assets of DM 12.3 billion (about $8.9 billion).

EMI

EMI began with the merger of three labels in the United Kingdom in 1930. Columbia Graphophone, Gramophone Company (the "His Masters Voice" folks), and Parlophone joined to create Electric and Musical Industries, Ltd. (later just EMI, Ltd.). EMI remained a primarily European operation until 1956 when it acquired Capitol Records in the United States. Capitol had been formed in the United States in 1942 by Johnny Mercer, Buddy DeSylva, and Glenn Wallichs. In the United States, Capitol–EMI Industries grew into a major label with a branch distribution system. In 1974 EMI acquired the rights to the substantial Decca U.K. catalog. (There were two Decca record companies until 1974. Decca U.K. was formed in 1929 and U.S. Decca in 1934.) Thorn EMI, PLC was formed in 1979 when electrical/electronics company Thorn merged with EMI. The new company began expansion with the acquisition of Chrysalis Records in 1989, SBK Entertainment World in 1990, Filmtrax and Thames Television in 1990, the Virgin Music Group in 1992, Sparrow Corporation (a gospel label) in 1992, Toshiba–EMI Music Publishing and Star Song publishing in 1994, and Priority Records in 1996. In 1996 Thorn and EMI demerged. The resulting EMI Group contained two divisions: EMI Music Group operated the sixty-five labels and twenty-three music publishing companies, including Capitol, EMI Records, EMI Music Publishing, Virgin Records Ltd., and Capitol–EMI Music. The Music Group also includes EMD (EMI Music Distribution, formerly Cema Distribution) distribution, and manufacturing facilities. The HMV group operated a retail division consisting of 240 record stores, 144 of which were outside of the United Kingdom. Profits of the EMI music division were estimated at

$547.8 million the year of the demerger with profits of the HMV Group estimated at $29.9 million.[17] The demerger fueled speculation that EMI would be purchased by some other conglomerate, at a speculated price of $9+ billion.[18] Total revenues in 1997 were $6.4 billion, with total assets of $3.5 billion.

Universal Music Group

The early history of Universal is particularly interesting. It began in New York 1924 as a talent agency (MCA) and moved to California in 1937 to add film talent to its operations. Television talent booking was added in 1949. The company moved into the production business in 1959 with the purchase of Universal Studios film facilities. MCA added recordings in 1962 when it purchased U.S. Decca and shortly thereafter the Coral and Kapp labels. The ABC–Dunhill labels were added in 1979. MCA purchased about 20 percent ownership of Motown Records in 1988 but later sold that interest for $60 million in 1993 when Motown was purchased entirely by PolyGram. Ownership of MCA moved to Japan in 1990 when the electronics giant, Matsushita Electric Industrial Company, purchased it for $6.13 billion. MCA added Geffen Records to the label roster in 1991 and the company changed the name of its branch distribution system to Uni Distribution. A recent acquisition of note is 50 percent of the rock and rap label Interscope for a reported $200 million in 1996.[19] The Seagram Company, Ltd. of Canada (the beverage company) purchased 80 percent of Matsushita's ownership of MCA in 1995 for $5.7 billion. The new parent, Seagram, earned about 63 percent of its revenues from the sales of beverages, spirits and wines, and 37 percent from its holdings in MCA. After renaming the music division Universal Music Group and prior to the merger with PolyGram, Seagram reported revenues of $8.9 billion in 1996 and total assets of nearly $21.4 billion. Universal labels include MCA, Geffen, DGC, and GRP. Universal continues to own film and television production and distribution as well as the record labels, the record and video distribution system, and music publishing interests. PolyGram N.V. was a Dutch (Netherlands) entertainment holding company that in turn was 75 percent owned by Philips Electronics N.V. PolyGram built its recording interests piecemeal. Philips originally purchased Polydor (a German label) in the early 1950s, and then Mercury Records in 1961. MGM Records was acquired in 1972. PolyGram was formed in 1972 when parent company Philips merged Polydor with Phonogram International. In 1989 PolyGram acquired the Island Records Group, in 1990 A&M Records, and then R&B powerhouse Motown in 1993 for $300 million. In 1994 PolyGram acquired a 50 percent interest in Def Jam Records. PolyGram labels include: Mercury, Polydor, London, Vertigo, Verve, Wing, A&M, Island, Motown, Decca, Deutche Grammophon, and Philips Classics. 1996 total assets were about $5.4 billion, with revenues of $5.5 billion. The parent also owned television and film production and distribution, music publishing, manufacturing, and the PGD (PolyGram Distribution) branch distribution system.

TABLE 4-1 Top Album Labels of the Mid-1990s (1993–1997) (by Number of Albums and Position in *Billboard*'s Top 200 Albums Chart)

Label*	Years in Top	Average Rank	Average No. of Albums
Columbia	5	1.6	40.0
Arista	5	2.8	21.4
Atlantic	5	3	34.4
Epic	5	6.2	30.4
Warner Bros.	5	7.8	27.8
MCA	4	5	31.5
A & M	4	8	18
Reprise	4	8.5	24.3
Elektra	4	10.8	22
Capitol	4	17.5	11.5
Virgin	3	6.7	16
Geffen	3	10.3	14.3
Interscope	3	12	12
Mercury	2	10.5	22.5

Source: Billboard, Year End Supplements, 25 Dec. 1993: YE-18; 24 Dec. 1994: YE-24; 23 Dec. 1995: YE-26; 28 Dec. 1996: YE-30; 27 Dec. 1997: YE-30.

*Labels appearing one year were Liberty, East West, Jive, DGC, Island, and Motown.

Hit Makers

The success of the big five at producing the hits is illustrated in Tables 4-1 and 4-2. The success of the various individual labels tends to vary from year to year as shown in Table 4-1. The only independent labels appearing in that table are East West, Jive, and Disney. All others are owned by the big five. The relative success of the major labels is illustrated in Table 4-2. For each of the years 1993–1997 there was a Sony label (Columbia or Epic), a WEA label (Warner Bros. or Atlantic), and a BMG label (Arista). For four of those years, a Universal label (MCA), an EMI label (Capitol), two more WEA labels (Elektra and Reprise), and a PolyGram—now Universal—label (A&M) were in the mix.

An important point about these two tables is that they show significant diversity and lack of concentration when looking at the individual labels (Table 4-1) and much more concentration when looking at the distributing labels (Table 4-2). The top five distributing labels had 80 to 89 percent of the albums in the top 200 in 1993–1997. That represents significant concentration. However if the individual labels function autonomously in terms of A&R and marketing in finding, developing, and promoting new talent, then there is much less concentration of label power and there should be much more diversity of music to be heard, regardless of who the corporate owner of any individual label might be.

TABLE 4-2   Top 200 Albums by Distributing Labels, Mid-1990s (1993–1997) (by Number of Albums and Position in *Billboard*'s Top 200 Albums Chart)

Label*	Years in Top	Average Rank	Average No. of Albums
Warner Bros.	5	2	79
Arista	5	3.2	34.4
Atlantic	4	2.8	52.3
Epic	4	4.3	54.5
Columbia	3	2.3	55.7
MCA	3	4.3	49.7

Source: Billboard, Year End Supplements, 25 Dec. 1993: YE-18; 24 Dec. 1994: YE-24; 23 Dec. 1995: YE-26; 28 Dec. 1996: YE-30; 27 Dec. 1997: YE-30.

*Interscope appeared in the distributing labels top chart one time.

THE STRUCTURE OF RECORD COMPANIES

Corporate Structure

The upper level structure of the big five recording companies is basically the same. As shown in Figure 4-2, each corporate owner usually holds several different businesses in addition to its recording companies. These other businesses range from other entertainment enterprises such as film, television, and magazine publishing, to consumer electronics, to alcoholic beverages. The music group usually includes at least music publishing and record companies, but may also include record retail operations. The record group then usually includes various labels, which tend to operate as free-standing units for purposes of A&R and marketing, the record distribution system, which distributes all labels owned by the company plus others under a variety of agreements, and a manufacturing division, which makes all of the owned labels' CDs and tapes and usually also special orders from outside labels.

The conglomerates have significant vertical integration. That means they seek to own and control all aspects in the production of their products from the raw ingredients to retail sale to consumers. Most of these corporations own labels that control the creative inputs from recording artists. They own music publishing companies, controlling the creative inputs from songwriters. They own manufacturing facilities to make the tapes and CDs that will be sold to the public. They own distribution companies to get the recordings to the retailers. At least one (EMI) owns retail stores where the final sale is made, and three (BMG, Time Warner, and Sony) have ownership interests in record clubs, another form of retail selling. They also seek horizontal integration when they buy up competing labels in order to insure a larger total share of the recording market.

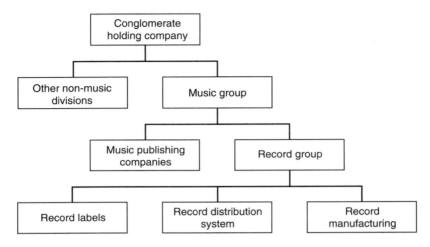

FIGURE 4-2   Typical "Big Five" Conglomerate Structure

Structure at the Label Level

Although the two basic functions of any label are A&R and marketing, any given label may perform those functions in depth, spread across a number of departments and personnel, or simply either not do them or hire an outside organization to provide the service (outsourcing). Figure 4-3 illustrates the divisions likely to be present at a large label. While there is not a great deal of commonality in what a given label may call a particular department, the divisions are typical.

The basic responsibilities of each department are as follows:

Label President

This person is usually someone who has experience in A&R, though not necessarily. Sometimes the presidents come from the business affairs departments and are attorneys, less often they are from the marketing departments. The president oversees all operations, but depending on the depth of his or her personal involvement in A&R, either as a producer or "talent scout," the other divisions may have additional independence. (Note that the business affairs and accounting divisions are "staff" divisions not directly involved in the production and marketing of the recordings.)

Business Affairs

This is usually the legal department of the label. It is in charge of negotiating artist and producer agreements and other licensing arrangements, including sampling and film use. Distribution deals with other labels, soundtrack album deals, and foreign licensing deals are typically finalized by this department. An advantage of

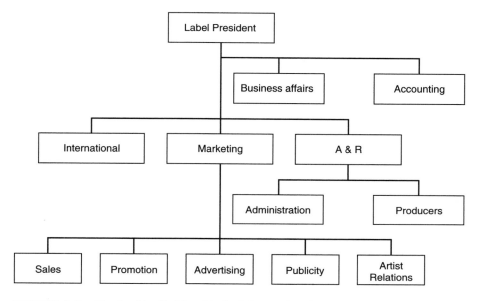

FIGURE 4-3   Typical Individual Label Organization

this split of the negotiating function from the president or A&R people is that it enables the creative people and the marketing people to be at peace with the artist, while any hard-nosed bargaining goes on with individuals who are not as likely to have to deal with the artist in later production or marketing of the recordings.

Accounting

Accounting is critical to the profitability of the company in any business that depends on so many sales of so many different individual units and where there are so many people with an interest in each unit. The counting of sales, returns, free goods, and promotional albums and the payment of royalties to at least three (artist, producer, and music publisher) but as many as a dozen or more interests (multiple artists, multiple producers, a different publisher for each song) per recording is a complex task. The accounting departments can rest assured that artists, producers, publishers, and the Harry Fox Agency (which collects royalties from the labels for music publishers) are all likely to audit the account books for any given album or artist once every year or two.

International Division

This unit works out international distribution deals and coordinates marketing plans around the world. It may be responsible for A&R in foreign territories. Some smaller labels either hire other labels outside of the United States or hire a major U.S. label to take care of international marketing and distribution for them.

Marketing

This is usually the largest division of a label. However, a small independent label may rely on a deal with a major label to supply all of these services while the small label only provides an A&R function. The term "marketing" is significantly more broad than most record companies use the term in their internal structure. Although actual distribution is through a separate distributing company, the responsibility of the marketing department is to get the recordings to the consumer through retail and rack sales, and to promote consumer awareness of the records through radio and TV airplay, print publicity, and advertising in any and all media.

Sales

The sales department is responsible for getting orders for records from rack jobbers, major retail chains, and one-stops. There may be merchandising specialists working in sales whose job it is to visit stores and help set up displays. Sales people may be organized on a national, regional, or local basis, or may be set up by account size or type, then regionalized or localized.

Promotion

The primary job of promotion is to get exposure through radio and video airplay. Some labels separate the radio and video promotion arms. Most large labels have their own promotion staffs and hire independent promotion people as well. Promotion people work with radio and TV broadcast outlets, and work with the artist when the artist is on a tour, whether it be a paying tour with concerts, or a promotional tour with showcases for local media people to hear the act. The promotion staff sees to it that the "right" people from the media and record retail get the opportunity to hear their artists whenever their artist is playing in a given locale. Promotion people may even have to take the artists around to visit local radio and television stations or record stores while the artist is on tour.

Advertising

Advertising personnel create the media plans to go with a given album or single. Because the advertising plan must be careful to promote a unified and consistent image of the artist and album, many labels create the actual advertisements that go to retailers or local radio or television stations. The advertising department will also make national media buys or dispense co-op advertising money to retailers and distributors who come up with advertising plans for label recordings. Co-op advertising money in the recording industry most often means that the label will pay 100 percent of the advertising costs for certain kinds of ads. Sometimes a label will go for a true cooperative advertising plan in which the expense is shared by the label and the retailer.

Publicity

Publicity consists of nonpaid exposure other than radio or music video airplay. This department contains people who write press releases, create press kits including artist bios (biographies) and photos, and try to get the artist appearances as talk show guests or performers on radio or TV. Publicity is probably one of the easiest functions for a label to farm out to independent publicists. In fact, an artist's manager will often have an independent publicity firm working alongside of the label public relations people. The publicity people try to see to it that while an artist is touring there is publicity material flowing to the media in towns where the artist will be performing, but ahead of the artist's actual appearance date. Publicity people will work with promotion people to set up press conferences or "meet and greet" opportunities for local media. The publicity department is also in charge of trying to get album reviews in local and national media.

Artist Relations

This department may go by a number of other names, including product development and career development. Whatever it is called, it has the primary task of coordinating the work of the other departments to be sure that there is a unified marketing plan for every album. People in this department often work with the personal manager of the artist to insure that a uniform image is projected. They may work with the artist or producer during the recording of an album to get a better idea of what the album is about and to develop a marketing plan that the artist will support. They will make sure that copies of the recordings for sales and promotion, as well as advertising and publicity, follow the artist whenever the artist is on tour. Artist relations is a function that labels began to add during the late 1970s as they became aware that marketing plans had to be more sophisticated in order to succeed.

A&R

The A&R (Artist and Repertoire) department is in charge of finding and recording artists. It may also look for songs for artists who do not write their own. Because the A&R department is in charge of delivery of a completed product, ready to be marketed, it also has to perform administrative duties associated with the finished master.

A&R Administration

This is where the coordination takes place for getting mechanical licenses from music publishers and clearances from other labels and music publishers for sampling. The administrative people must make sure that all people who played on an album get proper credits. They may help the producers screen material for an artist if asked. They coordinate delivery of the recording, artwork, and liner notes to make sure that all materials necessary to complete production of the tapes and discs are delivered to the manufacturing plants. They make sure that all musicians, artists, and producers get paid when they are supposed to for the initial production of the album.

TABLE 4-3   Pre- and Post-Recoupment Profitability

	Pre-Recoupment	Post-Recoupment
Wholesale price	$10.50	$10.50
Less: Manufacturing costs	$ 1.00	$ 1.00
Artist and producer royalties	$ 0.00	$ 2.00
Mechanical royalties	$ 0.70	$ 0.70
Distributor charges	$ 1.50	$ 1.50
Gross margin	$ 7.30	$ 5.30

Producers

These people are in charge of the recording process. They may find the talent and record it, record it after others have found it, or screen talent being pitched to the label. They may be "staff" producers who work for a salary and royalty or entirely independent of the label and just work for a royalty and advances.

PROFITABILITY IN THE RECORDING INDUSTRY

In a given year it is likely that less than one percent of records will sell over 250,000 units (see discussion below). The large record labels are fond of saying that less than 20 percent of the recordings they release ever recoup their costs. The high profit margins on compact discs must make one a little suspicious of that calculation. Recording costs and some marketing costs are generally recouped (recovered) out of artist royalties. Table 4-3 illustrates a typical (and somewhat simplified) situation for pre- and post-recoupment profits. Using these figures, the label does not pay the artists their royalties of two dollars per copy until that royalty adds up to the total recoupable amounts. Suppose a major label spends $200,000 in *recoupable* production and marketing costs. Suppose *total* production and marketing costs are $300,000. It will take sales of 100,000 units for artist royalties to equal the "recoupable" amounts. By that time the label's gross profits, after deducting the actual costs of publisher royalties and manufacturing, are $730,000—over $400,000 of actual profits. Even allowing for the label paying for its overhead, that is a substantial figure for a relatively "low selling" album. To reach the *economic* break-even point, where the total fixed costs (production and marketing) are equal to gross profits, only takes sales of 41,096 units (rounded up). That is calculated by dividing the $300,000 production and marketing costs as "fixed" by the $7.30 gross margin per disc sold. Consider the situation of an artist who has a lower royalty rate of only about one dollar per disc. It would take sales of 200,000 units to recoup artist advances. By that time the label would have gross profits of $1,460,000. Even after deducting the $300,000 in fixed costs for production and marketing the label then has a net profit of $1,160,000 on that recording. So, for a lot of artists who never see any royalties on the sale of their albums the record companies *are* making money.[20] Thus, the labels can afford to try to release more albums, even if sales are relatively low. In effect, they are being subsidized by the artists because recoupment of advances at the artist royalty rate is a lot slower than actual recovery of total fixed costs at the label's gross margin per CD rate. This high profitability, particularly on CD sales, also fuels the independent labels.

Price

The price of albums is one thing on which the labels do not compete very much. They behave as oligopolists in a market where there is high product differentiation and tacit coordination of prices but there is no outright cartel or price collusion. Although WEA Distribution had the largest market share, it is not a clear price leader making changes with the other majors following suit. Any of the majors appear to be able to step out as the first to make pricing adjustments. For example, in 1993 WEA lowered wholesale prices across the board on its various CD SRLPs (suggested retail list prices), but moved some individual albums up to a higher price SRLP, and therefore a higher wholesale price. Their $15.98 list and $16.98 list CDs were reduced from $10.30 to $10.18 and $ 10.88 to $10.67, respectively.[21] In late 1995 PolyGram Distribution (PGD) was the first distributor to lower wholesale prices on CDs in response to retailer's demand for more margin in the price wars that had developed between the retail record chains and the mass merchants. PolyGram Distribution's $16.98 list CDs were reduced from $10.65 to $10.50 wholesale and the $17.98 CDs list from $11.39 to $11.00 wholesale.[22] Note the similarity of wholesale prices between WEA and PGD for the $16.98 SRLP albums prior to PGD's adjustment. Wholesale price differentials of a few pennies among the majors has been the norm in the industry for a long time. In 1955, for example, wholesale prices for $3.98 list price vinyl albums varied among the majors by only a few cents from $2.45 to $2.48. Singles prices for $0.89 list singles varied by only $0.03 among the majors from $0.52 to $0.55.[23] In 1979 list prices for the $7.98 vinyl album lines ranged from $4.00 to $4.11.[24]

Price and Demand

While the overall prices of various SRLP lines do not vary much from label to label, there is often movement of albums by particular artists from one category SRLP to another. Moving individual albums up or down to a different SRLP suggests that the labels are very aware that there is high product differentiation in the eyes of the consumer based on the particular artist and particular album. In other words, when a consumer wishes to purchase a particular current recording or a recording by a particular currently popular artist, they will not purchase just *any* recording. Two studies bear this out. A study published in 1978 found that "taste" (as measured by the popularity of singles from the album) was the most important factor in the quantity of an artist's album demanded. The second most important factor was exposure of the artist/recording as measured by a combination of radio airplay and live appearances during the time of release. The artist's status (measured by the success of the previous album) was found to be the third most significant factor. A factor measuring submarket appeal (the ability of the record to cross-over into or out of a sub market such as country or R&B) was found to be more important than price of the album, the last factor of significance. "Price," said the author, "does not seem to be a significant detriment to sales, reinforcing the opinion of some in the industry that 'the public will pay for what it wants, even though it may bitch about the higher cost.'"[25] In another study conducted by a record retail chain in the early 1980s, the price of a popular artist's new record was varied at two outlets of the chain that were in the same city. At one store the album was placed on sale as is common with new releases. At the other store it was carried at the regular "shelf" price of other non-sale albums in the store. After a week, the two stores switched their pricing. At the end of the two weeks the store managers compared sales and found that there was essentially no difference in sales of the "hot" new product at the sale price or at the shelf price.[26]

This is not to say that there is not an overall interest in price by consumers. When vinyl LP list prices were raised across the boards from $5.98 to $6.98 in the mid-1970s, the industry estimated a 14 percent drop in unit sales due to the 16.7 percent increase in price.[27] By the 1990s the industry appeared to have found a more workable mechanism to adjust prices and avoid lost sales. They introduced a new price point (usually higher) by setting it for the new release of a hot artist. If the album proves popular the public is usually willing to pay the higher price. Then other new albums by hot artists can be introduced at the new higher price. Soon, the higher price becomes the norm for new albums by major artists. The older price may be maintained as a catalog price for older albums before moving them back to a mid-line price.

Consumers do appear to be willing to pay a higher price for CDs in general. When CDs were first introduced in the early 1980s, suggested retail list prices ran about $19.00 and wholesale prices about $11.75. As volume of production, sales, and demand increased, the labels began to drop their SRLPs and wholesale prices. By mid-1984 SRLPs had fallen to $15.98 and wholesale prices to around $10.00.[28] As more CD manufacturing capacity came on-line and the volume of sales continued to increase, the cost to manufacture the CDs dropped from nearly four dollars per disc when CDs were first introduced to less than a dollar a disc by 1995.[29] Wholesale prices, however, did not continue to decline. Wholesale prices crept back up to about $10.65 as the typical SRLP rose to $16.98 by 1995. Although there were consumer complaints and a lawsuit by an independent record store alleging price collusion by the major labels, the answer to the question of why CDs cost so much was simply, as *Consumer Reports* put it, "Because people are prepared to pay more for compact discs."[30] In mid-1996 two consumers in Knoxville, Tennessee filed an anti-trust suit alleging that the major labels had "coerced and cajoled" stores into keeping prices high.[31] It should also be noted that the average price paid by consumers for CDs had fallen to a low of about $12.00 in 1990 and remained near $13.00 for the first half of the 1990s. Since Figure 4-4 reflects RIAA figures for all CDs, it is likely that part of the reason for the decline and stabilization is that significant numbers of purchases were of lower-priced catalog product at mid-line and budget price points.

In marketing terms, the perceived value of the CD is significantly higher than that of the cassette. The components of that perceived value are many. CDs do have a significantly higher quality of sound. They do not get hung up in and destroyed by their players nearly as often as tapes. They do not wear out as quickly as tapes. CD players are more flexible than most tape players, allowing the listener to quickly shuttle back and forth between cuts, or even between CDs with the players capable of loading multiple CDs. Most CD players allow the listener to program the order of the cuts they hear or to leave out certain cuts when playing the discs. Most cassette players do not. The technology developed by Phillips and Sony gave consumers a highly desirable product for which they have been willing to pay a higher price.

Price and Profit

As a result of declining manufacturing costs of CDs, increased sales of CDs (from just 22 percent of album sales in 1988 to 81 percent of album sales in 1997), and stabilized wholesale prices, the profit margins of the record labels rose during the late 1980s and 1990s. Certainly there is logic, as far as a label is concerned, to

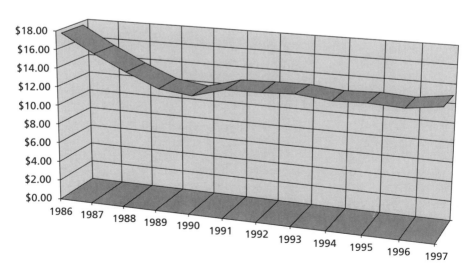

FIGURE 4-4   Average List Price of CDs, 1986–1997

Source: RIAA. Average obtained by dividing dollar value of sales by unit shipments.

raising prices in order to increase profits. The concern must be that they could price themselves out of the market or create an even greater demand for used CDs.

THE "INDIES"

Independent record companies are usually thought of as those not owned by one of the major labels or conglomerates. Such a definition is rather broad, covering every-thing from a small label in a large city with a couple of artists, which just markets recordings on a local or regional level, to Disney, which is part of a major entertain-ment company (just not one of the big five), to a label with a significant artist roster and national distribution through independent distributors, such as Rounder or Alli-gator, or a label that has its recordings distributed by one of the big five but is not owned by them. Some people would argue that the latter is not a true indie because it is not distributed through true independent distributors, but in a time of consolida-tion and vertical integration any label that is not *owned* by a major label is deserving of the title of "indie."

The indies play an important role in the recording industry. They are a develop-ment area for record labels. Several of what might now be called major labels began life as indies, Warner Brothers, Arista, and MCA, for example. The indies provide consumers with diversity and specialty music that the larger labels often ignore be-cause the small volume of sales, in the 3,000 to 30,000 units range, is not enough for a large label to consider. They also provide the larger labels with a source of new talent and new directions in music. The rock and roll explosion began on indepen-dent labels. New Age music began as an independent phenomenon and many of the labels were then bought out by the large corporations as it proved to be commer-cially successful. Rap began on small inner-city independents, then entered the mainstream, then was bought into by the large labels.

Size of the Indie Labels

SoundScan and RIAA data indicate that the independent labels account for about 20 percent of the sales, yet they release about 66 percent of the titles. For example, of over 17,000 titles released in 1995, 11,000 were by independent labels—almost a two-to-one ratio of independent releases to major label releases. The vast majority (90.5 percent) of current releases (not just new, but catalog as well) sell less than 5,000 copies per year. The number of recordings selling over 250,000 per year was just 148 in 1995, but those recordings accounted for over half of the total sales vol-ume. Most of those were released by the major labels.[32]

How do the independent labels survive? The growth of the megastores carrying tens of thousands of titles has provided a place for the independent labels to sell their products to a larger audience. They have also relied on specialty independent stores in larger cities. They keep production and marketing costs low. Coupled with the high profit margins in CDs, low-cost albums can turn a profit with minimal sales. As

Table 4-3 indicates, a typical CD generates a gross margin of over five dollars per copy. If that recording can sell 3,000 units it will earn over $15,000 in profits. If recording and marketing costs are kept low, $10,000 or less, then there is substantial profit. There is even profitability in having more low-budget, low-selling albums than having fewer. Because these recordings are not so costly to make or market, more titles can be released aimed at a very small market. That is the same as it was even back in the 1940s. A *Billboard* article describes indie labels in 1949 as having break-even points on singles of 5,000 units, compared to the majors' break-even points of 15,000 units.[33] The Association for Independent Music (formerly the National Association of Independent Record Distributors [NAIRD]) represents over 1,300 members, mostly small labels, mostly in the specialty music areas of bluegrass, reggae, dance, jazz, classical, and others. That figure does not even count the thousands of custom albums that do not go through independent distribution but are sold by the artists only in their own locales or at their performances.

Indie Labels and Indie Distribution

Although some independent labels are distributed by the majors, most indie records find their way to the marketplace through independent distributors. Most independent distributors operate on a regional basis and some even on a national basis. A trend of the 1990s was the growth in size of independent distributors and the consolidation of independent distribution into fewer firms. For example, in 1995 Passport Music Distribution was formed out of Encore Distribution and Sound Solutions (USA), (an import and budget distributor). Passport, in turn, was part of the largest independent distributor, Alliance Entertainment, which also owns Independent National Distributors and the labels Castle Communications, Concord Jazz, and Red Ant Entertainment.[34]

DIVERSITY IN SPITE OF ITSELF

A particularly popular criticism of the recording industry is that it is run by huge conglomerates that for one reason or another are bent upon shoving much "bad" music down the throats of consumers while "good" music and artists languish without access to the system.[35] To be sure, there is much in popular music at any given time that may not measure up well on some critical scale. The labels are large bureaucratic organizations that tend to be conservative in their releases and follow the patterns of previous successes. At the same time a large label must be aware that, because the majority of releases are not likely to produce much profit, the only way to stabilize revenues is to have a large number of releases so that enough of them will make enough profits to support the superstructure. The big five conglomerates must behave like the investor for a retirement fund. Wall Street analysts know that the best way to minimize risk in the stock market is through a diversity of holdings. That way the main risk is only that inherent in stocks as a kind of investment instead of a particular company. So the large label will release artists that essentially compete with each other as well as those from other labels instead of risking large sums on a single artist who might not catch the public's fancy.[36] Large numbers of releases make it likely that more consumers will find recordings that they like and will buy. The worst problem for the industry would be a market diminished overall because there were fewer releases.[37] The trend, then, should be towards diversity of music being offered rather than towards homogeneity. That trend has been noticed by some observers as not what would have been predicted by the presence of larger and larger conglomerates controlling more and more of the market.[38] In fact one observer predicts that levels of high product diversity are most associated with moderately concentrated markets and that less diversity is associated with low and high levels of concentration.[39] The question is whether the recording industry is at such a high level of concentration (about as high as it could get and still meet the "effective competition" definition earlier) that diversity will begin to suffer.

SUMMARY

In any discussion of the basic structure and economics of the recording industry it is important to remember that there are at least three perspectives from which to discuss the labels. First, one can look at the individual names on individual labels. For some purposes that may be the best way because individual labels, even if owned by the same corporate conglomerate, tend to compete with each other for artists and for the consumers' dollars. Labels can also be viewed based on ownership at the corporate level. From that perspective, the five conglomerates control about 80 percent of the industry. Finally, one could look at labels from the perspective of distribution. The number of distribution firms is smaller than the number of individual labels, or the number of label firms, due to the high costs associated with distribution. The concentration of distribution in the five multinationals is about the same as the concentration of market share by corporate ownership, but there are significantly fewer competing independent distributors and they too appeared to be going through a phase of concentration of ownership in the mid-1990s. The individual label perspective focuses on the A&R function. The distribution perspective focuses on the marketing function. The ownership perspective focuses on the profitability of the "bottom line." All three perspectives can provide valuable insight into the workings of the recording industry.

NOTES

[1]Richard Caves, *American Industry: Structure, Conduct and Performance,* 6th ed. (Englewood Cliffs, NJ: Prentice-Hall, 1987): 10.

[2]See for example, Caves, supra note 1; Paul Keat and Philip K. Y. Young, *Managerial Economics: Economic Tools for Today's Decision Makers* (New York: Macmillan, 1992): 402.

[3]Russell Sanjek and David Sanjek, *American Popular Music Business in the 20th Century* (New York: Oxford University Press, 1991).

[4]"Top Pop Records, 1949," *Billboard,* 12 January 1950: 14.

[5]Nev Gehman, "Poll Clocks 35 Also-Rans for Every Solid-Selling Disk Hit," *Billboard,* 3 January 1953: 1.

[6]Nev Gehman, "The Year's Music Roundup," *Billboard,* 2 January 1954: 11.

[7]Gary Kramer, "Record Firm Rule of Thumb Slips from Fickle Public Pulse," *Billboard,* 22 December 1956: 1.

[8]Bob Rolontz, "72 Labels Landed on Charts in '58—a Feverish Year," *Billboard,* 5 January 1959: 3.

[9]"LP Crown to Columbia, Victor Tops in Singles," *Billboard,* 5 January 1963: 4.

[10]"Columbia and WEA Top Charts for 3rd Straight Year," *Billboard,* 17 February 1993: 1.

[11]Ed Christman, "WEA Remains Top U.S. Music Distributor in '95," *Billboard,* 20 January 1996: 55; Ed Christman, "WEA's '94 Market Share Dips Slightly, But Still Top U.S. Distributor with 21.1%," *Billboard,* 21 January 1995: 54; "SoundScan Releases 1996 Music Industry Figures," Reuters Financial Service, 6 January 1996 (LEXIS).

[12]Don Jeffrey, "P'Gram Accepts Seagram Bid," *Billboard,* 30 May 1998: 1.

[13]Jeff Clark-Meads and Adam White, "Poly/Uni Exec Setup Still Cloudy," *Billboard,* 6 June 1998: 1.

[14]Unless specifically noted, the information for this section comes from several sources, including: Standard and Poor's *Stock Reports* and *Industry Surveys;* Guy A. Marco, *Encyclopedia of Recorded Sound in the United States* (New York: Garland, 1993); Russell Sanjek and David Sanjek, *American Popular Music Business in the 20th Century* (1991).

[15]"Warner Cos. Restructured as WEA Inc.," *Billboard,* 11 November 1995: 60.

[16]Mark Dezzani, "BMG Buys Europe's Last 'Major' Indie," *Billboard,* 20 August 1994: 38; Don Jeffrey, "Acquired by BMG, Private Music Begins a New Age," *Billboard,* 5 February 1994: 6.

[17]Jeff Clark–Meads, et al., "Thorn EMI Demerger Proceeding Smoothly," *Billboard,* 31 August 1996: 1.

[18]Eric Boehm, "For Those with Cash EMI Has the Flash," *Variety,* 12 August 1996: 7.

[19]Chris Morris, "MCA Purchases 50% of Interscope," *Billboard,* 2 March 1996: 13.

[20]See also, Don Cusic, *Music in the Market* (Bowling Green, OH: Popular Press, 1996): 179.

[21]Ed Christman, et al., "WEA Reduces Wholesale Prices on CDs," *Billboard,* 13 March 1993: 9.

[22]Ed Christman, "PGD Reduces Boxlot Prices, Boosting Retail Profit Margins," *Billboard,* 23 December 1995: 5.

[23]"Price List Reflects Firmer Structure in Cost of Disks," *Billboard,* 15 June 1955: 5.

[24]"WEA Raises LP & Single Basic Prices," *Billboard,* 30 June 1979: 3.

[25]Alexander Belinfante and Reuben R. Davis, Jr., "Estimating the Demand for Record Albums," *Review of Business and Economic Research* (Winter 1978–1979): 47, 51.

[26]An unpublished report to the author from a graduate of the Recording Industry program at Middle Tennessee State University who was one of the store managers involved. The name of the manager and chain are withheld by request.

[27]Belinfante and Davis, *supra* note 25.

[28]"CD Prices Start to Tumble," *Billboard,* 7 July 1984, 1.

[29]Susan Nunziata, "CD Plants Expand in Anticipation of Business Boom," *Billboard*, 25 July 1992: 6.

[30]"CD Prices: Why So High?" *Consumer Reports*, February 1996: 17.

[31]David Hinkley, "Suit Calls CD Prices a Steal—for Companies," *New York Daily News*, 11 July 1966, New York Now section: 2 (LEXIS).

[32]Tom Silverman, "Preserving Diversity in the Music Biz," *Billboard*, 18 May 1996: 6.

[33]"Indies' Surprise Survival," *Billboard*, 3 December 1949: 1.

[34]Ed Christman, "Alliance to Acquire Red Ant Entertainment," *Billboard*, 24 August 1996: 3; Jim Bessman, "Indie Distributor Changes More Than Name," *Billboard*, 20 May 1995: 47; Ed Christman, "Alliance Shifts Distrib Gears: Trans World Fills No. 2 Slot," *Billboard*, 5 February 1994: 64.

[35]See, for example, Reebee Garofalo, "How Autonomous Is Relative: Popular Music, the Social Formation and Cultural Struggle," *Popular Music*, January 1987: 77.

[36]A structure observed by Richard A. Peterson and David G. Berger, "Measuring Industry Concentration, Diversity, and Innovation in Popular Music," 61 *American Sociological Review* (1996): 175.

[37]An argument made in Jon Stratton "Capitalism and Romantic Ideology in the Record Business," *Popular Music*, 3 (1993): 183.

[38]Robert Burnett, "The Implications of Ownership Changes on Concentration and Diversity in the Phonogram Industry," *Communication Research*, December 1992: 749.

[39]Peter J. Alexander, "Entropy and Popular Culture: Product Diversity in the Popular Music Recording Industry," *American Sociological Review*, 61 (1996): 171.

5

The Structure of the Film Industry
Windows of Exhibition

Barry R. Litman
Michigan State University

Broadcast television was the first new telecommunication technology and service to appear on the scene and to become a new exhibition window for theatrical films after their domestic and international runs. While the major studios first boycotted this new technology as a threat to their protected position in theatrical exhibition, they soon came to understand that television broadcasting, both network and syndication, provided a fertile ground for subsequent runs after the movie had exhausted its theatrical potential.

They came to establish a special exhibition window for network television, usually two to three years after the theatrical run. Syndication to local television stations would occur after the movies no longer had network earning power. As new succeeding technologies, such as pay cable, VCR, pay-per-view, and now fiber-optic video-on-demand have arrived, the studios welcome them with open arms and adjust their exhibition sequence accordingly to maximize the present value of profits across the many new exhibition windows. While this process of "windowing" has generated much attention, it really is not new in the truest sense since, prior to the advent of television, the second and subsequent theatrical exhibition runs constituted the same type of "windowing" process.

Most important is the underlying economic theory behind "windowing," which is really an application of the second-degree price discrimination model. According to this theory, the firm with substantial market power can maximize profits by segmenting consumers into clearly distinct groupings, with different elasticities of demand, and charging them their "reservation price," that is, the highest price that they would be willing and able to pay for this product rather than just the single equilibrium price that the firm would normally determine under the standard theory of monopoly pricing. In this way, the monopolist/oligopolist would confiscate consumer surplus (the difference between the highest price and actual price) from each segment of demand and turn it into producer's surplus (e.g., excess profits). This process of segmentation of demand would occur so long as price[1] exceeded MC, that is the net addition to revenues exceeded the net addition to cost. While such price discrimination clearly works to the overall benefit of powerful firms by bolstering their excess profits, there is an added benefit to consumers in the sense that output for the industry is greatly increased from what it would be under the single-price monopoly situation. A whole new group of consumers would now be able to purchase product at reasonable prices, whereas they had been excluded before due to a high monopoly type price. In short, price discrimination would clearly improve society's allocation of scarce resources.

For such price discrimination to work effectively, there must be clearly identifiable classes of customers with different elasticities and no arbitrage between the customer classes. In the context of the motion picture industry, the customer classes correspond to the different exhibition windows and the profit maximizing objective of the distributor is to sequence these windows according to whichever customer class is willing to pay the next highest price (or net contribution to revenue). This situation is depicted in Figure 5-1. Each quantity segment corresponds to a different exhibition window. The sequential order is theatrical exhibition (both domestic and international) followed by VCR, pay-per-view, pay cable, network TV, and syndication.[2] When video-on-demand is fully operational in the next millennium, it can be expected to move to the front of the line, perhaps even challenging theatrical exhibition as the primary exhibition window and "launching pad."

One key difference between this application and the price discrimination model in its purest sense is the importance of time as the critical vehicle for separating out the customer classes in product space. The amount of time clearance between windows will be very important (as it was between first and second theatrical runs before the arrival of television) and geographical clearance between countries is also crucial, as well as prevention of piracy/leakage between windows. The price/net revenue factor is also related to time in the sense that the shorter the elapsed time since theatrical release, the greater the value to the household and the higher the price that will be paid.

While some movie patrons must see a new release the first week it debuts, others are willing to wait until it reaches the VCR or PPV markets and pay a lower household price.[3] As one moves sequentially across the different windows, the net contribution to distribution revenue falls and the films are most likely to be sold to

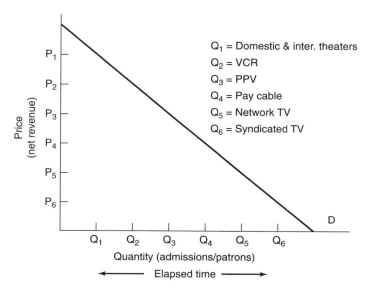

Price (net revenue)

P_1
P_2
P_3
P_4
P_5
P_6

Q_1 = Domestic & inter. theaters
Q_2 = VCR
Q_3 = PPV
Q_4 = Pay cable
Q_5 = Network TV
Q_6 = Syndicated TV

D

Q_1 Q_2 Q_3 Q_4 Q_5 Q_6

Quantity (admissions/patrons)

← Elapsed time →

FIGURE 5-1   "Windowing Model" for Motion Pictures

the different windows as parts of groups. The direct contribution by viewers becomes unclear as advertiser support replaces viewer payment in the broadcast realm.

The goal of the profit maximizing distributor is to determine the optimal sequencing of windows and also the optimal time within a window and clearance between the windows.[4] As long as there is no widespread leakage between windows, the sequencing of windows can be maintained and flourish. It should be noted that a window may move to the front of the sequence either because its net contribution to revenues per household is higher (e.g., PPV) or its total contribution to revenues is higher (e.g., VCRs). It is the balancing act that is maintained between the high profit per household technologies and the high penetration technologies that is the key to maximizing profits for the distributor. Also, the degree of market power and bargaining strength by the distributor in each window will also affect its overall financial contribution and place in line.

The emergence of multiple exhibition windows also complicates other aspects of the production/distribution process. Since each window is populated with consumers of different demographic and psychographic makeup, this means that the average movie will have differential levels of popularity as it moves throughout the windowing process. For example, the moviegoing patron is known to be somewhat younger than the average television viewer while those that frequent video stores tend to be more family oriented, and the international viewer prefers certain genres. What this means is that each and every film must be handled somewhat differently, depending on its genre, age orientation, degree of sex and violence, and other factors.

The time spent within a window may be shortened if a movie is not expected to have a favorable reception. This even applies to shortening the first-run theatrical exhibition if the movie is not expected to be favorably reviewed and moving directly into the VCR market. In fact, some low-budget movies now actually bypass the first-run theatrical market entirely. On the other hand, a very popular theatrical launch may cause the distributors to attempt to tap the VCR "sell-through" market direct to consumers rather than rely on VCR rental driven demand.

Another decision involves the production budget, advertising budget, and even casting. It has always been true that well-known actors and actresses are very popular abroad and concessions have been made to include these people in big-budgeted films to appeal to this foreign constituency. Now, with all the new video windows, TV stars and well-known personalities from other entertainment media will be more highly cultivated for these windows. This is not to diminish the marquee value of true movie stars like Arnold Schwartzenegger, Harrison Ford, Jody Foster, Meg Ryan, or the like but simply to imply that former TV stars like John Travolta, Robin Williams, or Ron Howard can also make it big on the silver screen and in the other subsidiary markets. Finally, according to Owen and Wildman,[5] the prevalence of such an elaborate and dynamic windowing process in the United States means that additional funds can be invested upfront in the production budget that will reap financial returns downstream in the windows. This added budgetary flexibility (plus the added richness of the domestic market) has always been a key factor in enhancing the U.S. film in offshore markets and facilitating the worldwide domination that has always characterized the major studios since the 1920s. We will now examine these subsidiary windows in greater depth.

THE TELEVISION NETWORK MARKET

As has been mentioned above, the motion picture distributors made a truce with the television industry in the mid-1950s and began to supply regularly scheduled series and motion pictures shortly thereafter. In the market for regularly scheduled prime-time programs, the major movie distributors have maintained an extraordinary presence, collectively averaging in excess of 40 percent since the mid-1960s (see Table 5-1), with Universal being the dominant supplier for a long time and Warner and Paramount dominating in recent years. The networks themselves historically produced a small percentage of their prime-time programming needs, concentrating primarily on news, sports, and specials rather than entertainment series. The remainder of prime-time series are produced by independent production houses (also known as "packagers"), many of which have market shares comparable to the major film distributors. As Owen originally noted, the major movie companies have no economic advantage in this programming area since the supply industry is monopo-

TABLE 5-1   Network Supplier Market Shares of Prime Time Hours— 1995 Fall Schedule

Supplier	Network Hours				Netlets Hours		
	ABC	CBS	NBC	Fox	WB	Paramount	Total
Major Networks[a]							
ABC/Disney-Touchstone	8.0				.5	.5	9.0
CBS		7.5	.5				8.0
NBC			6.0				6.0
Fox	3.0	1.5		4.5			9.0
Total	11.0	9.0	6.5	4.5	.5	.5	32.0
Netlets[b]							
Warner Brothers	2.0	1.5	3.0	1.5	3.0		11.0
Paramount	.5	.5	1.0		.5	2.5	5.0
Total	2.5	2.0	4.0	1.5	3.5	2.5	16.0
Major Movie Co.[c]							
Universal	.5	2.0	1.5	1.0		1.0	6.0
Columbia		1.0	1.5				2.5
Tri-Star		.5	.5	1.0	.5		2.5
Total	.5	2.5	3.0	3.5	.5	1.0	11.0
Independents							
Carsey-Weiner	1.5	1.0	1.0				3.5
Brillstein-Grey			1.0		.5		1.5
Witt-Thomas	.5	.5	.5		.5		2.0
Spelling				2.0	2.0		4.0
New World	1.0						1.0
MTM			1.0		.5		1.5
Dreamworks	1.5	.5					2.0
All Others 7.5							7.5
Total	4.5	2.0	3.5	2.0	3.5		23.0
Grand Total 7.5	18.5	15.5	17.0	11.5	8.0	4.0	82.0

Source: Broadcasting and Cable, May 27, 1996, p. 19.

*Fox, Warner Brothers, and Paramount are all major movie company suppliers to other networks.
[a]Excludes movies which have various suppliers each week.
[b]Includes all co-productions with independent suppliers.
[c]Includes all co-productions with non-studio suppliers.

listically competitive due to a well-developed rental market for inputs, minimal economies of scale, and easy entry.[6] Given such competitive conditions, the supply industry has been unable to countervail the coordinated monopsony (buying) power of the historic Big 3 networks. The networks understood that their bargaining advantage was greatest in the initial developmental stages of a television show, when the quality of the scripts and pilot are of unknown value and the future success of the program is uncertain.[7] At this stage, venture capital is scarce because the investment is so risky. Once a show becomes a hit and its true value is known, however, it can command a high price on the open market because its parent network cannot risk its being bid away by another network. The same problem occurred in major league sports and the "reserve rule" and other devices were used to tie the players to their teams.

To prevent such competitive bidding, the networks historically developed a series of parallel steps in the buying process which, if commonly followed, would bind series to long-term "option" contracts prior to knowledge being available regarding their ratings popularity; this would enhance their bargaining power relative to their suppliers. This was known as the "step process" of program acquisition. Thus, the networks became profitable in the programming area because they have been able to control both sources of potential profit—profit from uncertainty of program quality and profit from inter-industry coordination. These two sources of power are intricately intertwined. The tight oligopoly structure of the networks acts as a bottleneck which narrows down the number of potential sources of access for program producers. The profit-maximizing incentive for oligopolists to coordinate their behavior inhibits the emergence of significant inter-network competition for programming. The uncertainty over quality, the large number of competing producers, and the scarcity of venture capital made the producers unable to resist this network power. This was the distressing situation that existed for program packages until the arrival of cable opened up more sources of access and created a more competitive network marketplace.

Historically, theatrical movies represented a different species of network programming because specific knowledge exists concerning their value in the theatrical market. This knowledge includes data on the box office gross and rentals accruing to the distributor, as well as the performance of the movie in the various award categories. This information has been shown in previous studies to be an important determinant in explaining the expected rating of these films on prime-time television. The known "quality" of theatrical movies, in reducing the uncertainty and risk to the networks, also enabled the movie companies to demand prices reflecting the marginal worth of their movies. The networks, in turn, were unable to refrain from intense competitive bidding for exclusive rights to these movies as contrasted with their superior position in acquiring television series.

The major movie companies also have more bargaining power because of a much stronger position in the movie industry as producer–distributors than as television series suppliers. As indicated elsewhere, the major movie distributors clearly dominate the theatrical movie industry. This highly concentrated market structure enabled these distributors to bargain more effectively with the networks over theatrical movie rental terms.

It should also be recalled that the financial success of theatrical movies historically depended on rentals earned in the domestic and foreign theaters. The sale of network television rights was only a secondary consideration. This is in sharp contrast to the financial requirement of TV program producers to obtain network financing, make the network sale, and remain on the network long enough to create value for the series in the syndication market (their real profit center). In short, the movie companies have a greater independence in their financing and more potential profit centers. This flexibility should translate into greater bargaining strength with the networks over theatrical movie rights. Hence, an interesting paradox prevailed in network negotiations with the major distributors. They had the upper hand in the TV series market but were disadvantaged in the submarket for theatrical rights.

Of course, it still would have been possible for the networks to tacitly agree to hold down prices for movies of known quality. For example, the networks could have established a bidding pool that could designate which one of them was to be "highest" bidder for the next hit movie. But the success of such a price-fixing buying cartel would have required open discussions among the networks and a complex allocation scheme. The risk of antitrust detection would have been very high, which probably explains why network competition has been the rule in this sphere of programming.

Movie companies were able to obtain high and increasing prices for their films since the early 1960s. The prices for theatrical movies were always two to three times higher (for the standard two-hour length of time) than the prices of regularly scheduled programs of comparable quality, offering further evidence that movie producers had greater bargaining leverage than series producers. Movie prices started to rise because of increasing network demand, ratings popularity, and internetwork rivalry for theatrical movies. The average price of a theatrical movie rose from $100,000 for two network runs in 1961 to around $800,000 by the end of 1967. During this period the number of hours of prime-time movies increased from two in 1961 to fourteen in 1968 as each network had at least two movie nights each week.[8] By the mid-1970s, the prices once again skyrocketed due to a shortage of acceptable movies for television. This shortage resulted from the fact that the four-year stockpile of network features amassed during the late 1960s ran out around 1972 or 1973, the trend in the 1970s toward R- and X-rated pictures resulted in a smaller percentage of acceptable features for TV, and the major movie studios, addressing a slight recession in their industry, cut back their output significantly, concentrating their efforts on fewer high budget films.

Around 1966 and 1967, the networks attempted to neutralize the power of the movie distributors and stabilize movie prices by producing their own made-for-television movies (a substitute product) and ABC and CBS entered directly into motion picture production. This vertical integration into the production sphere resulted in some eighty theatrical movies during 1967–1971 and 40 to 50 percent of their yearly requirements of made-for-television movies. The effect of such a large foreclosure of product was devastating and sent a clear message to the movie producers that, hereafter, theatrical movie licensing fees would be stabilized.

Private and public antitrust litigation ensued.[9] The motion picture distributors charged that the television networks were in violation of the *Paramount* decrees since they had set up a fully integrated market chain through network distribution, ownership, and affiliation with broadcast exhibition outlets, and now production of theatrical movies. These lawsuits had been filed shortly after the FCC had reduced the ability of the networks to co-venture programming with outside packagers (another form of vertical integration) and had forced the networks to abandon one hour of prime-time programming to open the airwaves to independent sources of supply.

The case ended with a consent decree in 1980 that basically ratified the FCC's "Prime-Time Access Rules" and "Financial Interest and Syndication Rules" and limited the ability of the networks to produce in-house television series. Paradoxically, the decrees did not forbid the networks from producing theatrical movies nor from broadcasting them on their own network after the theatrical run.[10] While ABC and CBS had left the theatrical production industry in 1972 because of the lawsuits as well as an inferior product, all three networks reentered into this arena in the late 1970s and early 1980s. To their dismay, they learned a hard lesson. Success in producing hit TV series did not translate into movie production. None of the networks was even moderately successful.

In the meantime, competition for the limited quantity of available theatrical movies once again caused license prices to increase to roughly $2 million per film. To counteract this problem, the networks increased their requirements for made-for-television movies to all-time record levels. While the increased demand for these tailor-made programs naturally increased their prices, they still cost less than half the rental fee for a theatrical movie.

In 1978, the networks once again tried to stabilize the prices of theatrical films by purchasing television rights before the theatrical movie was released, and often before filming was completed.[11] The rationale behind this change in strategy was to obtain commitments by the movie producers at an early stage in the production process when the quality was uncertain, the risk was high, and the television value was indeterminate. In this way, the networks sought to bind themselves to specific producers and thereby reduce inter-network competition over theatrical movies. It was, of course, a risk for the networks because they would be wedded to the flops along with the hits, but one that had been shown to be acceptable and profitable with regularly scheduled programming. Because of the success of this blind bidding strategy and its growing financial dependence on network advances, the movie distributors eventually demanded "escalator" clauses in their licensing contracts to tie network prices more closely to theatrical rentals, thereby negating the network bargaining advantage. By the mid-----1980s, the entire point became largely moot as the television networks severely reduced their reliance on theatrical movies since they had been pushed further back in line behind other exhibition windows and the plummeting television ratings of these shopworn movies no longer justified such high license prices. The networks continue to reposition their product line to fill a more unique niche in the burgeoning video market; they now prefer program product, such as made-for-TV movies, that has not been shown in other media and is not generally available on videocassette.

THE PAY TELEVISION MARKET

The development of the pay television market and role of motion picture distribution requires an understanding of the basic structure of television broadcasting. The scarcity of space in the electromagnetic spectrum created a natural limitation on the number of available Very High Frequency (VHF) stations in any local market. The necessity of maintaining a buffer zone (a one-channel separation) between adjacent VHF frequencies and the fact that the FCC decentralized the allocation of VHF frequencies, so that smaller cities would have at least one originating broadcast station, further reduced the number of viable broadcast signals in local markets. On average, there were only three VHF commercial frequencies available in the top 100 markets in the country (which account for over 90 percent of all TV households). Given the overwhelming economic incentive to share programming expenses through "networking," and the necessity for networks to have local affiliates to transmit their programs, there was room for only three national TV networks.[12] When the FCC sought to increase the amount of spectrum space for television by adding on a technically inferior Ultra High Frequency (UHF) band to the existing superior VHF band, it created a surplus of unwanted UHF frequencies and the perpetuation of the tight network oligopoly. With only three national network signals and the incentive (imposed by advertising sponsorship) for maximizing ratings by seeking the lowest common denominator of programming, "minority taste" programming went unfulfilled even though public broadcasting sought to fill the void with their own cultural and educational programming.

One new approach toward solving the lack of diversity inherent in broadcasting was that of pay television. Proponents of pay TV argued that direct consumer payment would make programming more sensitive to viewer's preferences than the current advertiser-supported system of "free" television. The zero-priced television system is inconsistent with an efficient allocation of resources among program types since it does not provide information concerning *intensity of consumer demand*. In a pay TV system, this program inefficiency can be cured since viewers can express the strength of program preferences through a pricing system. Although there were experiments with pay TV scrambled over-the-air on under-utilized UHF stations, with the development of cable television during the 1960s a collection mechanism was now in place for excluding "free riders"—the basic market failure problem associated with over-the-air broadcasting and the reason for advertising support in the first instance.

The FCC was lobbied by the broadcast interests in the late 1960s not to permit pay TV to get a foothold since it was anathema to the "free" system of broadcasting that had developed and threatened to fractionalize the audience and "siphon" programming.[13] According to broadcasters, consumers would thereby suffer a loss of welfare since they would now have to pay directly for programs they formerly received free: the World Series, National Football League, and the Miss America Beauty Pageant were some of the examples of prominent programming that were always cited as being in jeopardy if pay TV caught on. Also, such high preference programming would be unavailable to most people due to their inability to receive cable because they resided in a low population density area. The end result of this controversy was a series of FCC rules that permitted pay TV to exist but restricted its programming to those types that were unavailable from commercial broadcasting. There could be no duplication of broadcast programming whatsoever. The most important program area permitted was that of recent theatrical movies for the time interval between their theatrical run and their appearance on network television.

In 1972, Home Box Office initiated a pay-cable program service consisting of recent uncut, uninterrupted movies, Las Vegas night club acts, and special sporting events. This channel (package) of programming was sold on a monthly subscription basis for about $7 to those areas already wired for cable. Yet, the nationwide development of this alternative form of television would not come until the expensive system of microwave transmission was replaced in 1975 by the new cost-effective satellite-to-dish national transmission system. When the FCC failed to liberalize these restrictive programming rules in 1975, HBO decided to appeal their legality through the courts. Finally, in 1977, in the *Home Box Office* case, the U.S. Court of Appeals declared "null and void" all programming limitations imposed by the FCC on pay cable networks.[14] This Declaration of Independence for pay cable networking meant that they could become full-fledged competitors of the three commercial networks and is generally credited with triggering off what has come to be known as the "cable revolution," with penetration in slightly over two-thirds of American households in 1998.

Such movie-driven "premium" networks as The Movie Channel, Showtime, and Cinemax soon joined HBO, the industry leader, to exploit this new pay cable market.[15] In recent years, several specialty networks have entered by differentiating their product in other dimensions (e.g., Disney, Playboy, American Movie Classics, and Bravo [cultural]) rather than offering the full range of motion pictures and entertainment specials as do the leading networks.

In the development years of the late 1970s, the pay cable networks decided on a conscious policy of *nonexclusive* licensing of theatrical movies. The basic strategy was for each network to present a full movie package, including all the box office hits, to overcome viewers' hesitancy in paying for a product that formerly was provided "free" of charge (albeit with commercials). This meant that for the movie component of the pay cable schedule, usually 80 to 85 percent of the total schedule, all the pay networks were virtually identical since the motion picture distributors would license everyone at approximately the same time. At the cable system level, the local cable monopolist would generally license only a single pay network to avoid programming redundancy. Frequently, the local cable system was a part of a nationwide chain (multiple system operators) that, in turn, was a subsidiary of one of the top pay cable networks. As is true for all such vertical arrangements, there was the incentive for self-preference, and the same linkage that had occurred in motion picture distribution/exhibition began to surface in the pay cable industry. Competition for exclusive access to smaller cable systems would necessarily then turn on nonproduct dimensions such as marketing or the percentage split of the consumer's monthly payment between the network and the local system.

Ironically, in these pre-VCR days, in a few markets, consumers expressed a willingness to buy a multiple number of redundant networks in order to gain more viewing flexibility. Soon most cable systems began offering multiple networks, which meant that there would be competition for local patronage even in vertically integrated systems. HBO set up a sister service, Cinemax, to try to capture the extra business, but the genie could not be put back in the bottle and *product competition* became a new reality. Product competition/differentiation meant having exclusive rights for a period of time to certain movies and, of course, not sharing your entertainment or sports specials. While at first the networks continued licensing box office hits on a nonexclusive basis, less successful movies and all-time classics were licensed exclusively. By 1981, exclusive rights were also obtained for many of the former category as well. It should be noted that the license prices for exclusive rights for a single network were significantly higher than when everyone had equal access and could in a sense "split" the total license fee. Throughout this entire period, HBO and companion service Cinemax collectively dominated this market, with a combined market share ranging over 60 percent, twice the size of Showtime. HBO used its monopsony power to reduce the license prices to the motion picture distributors, paying on a "flat" rental basis rather than the customary "per-subscriber" method. HBO followed a "take it or leave it" bargaining strategy, which, given its strategic position, was reluctantly accepted.

In April 1980, a new and potentially explosive element was introduced into the pay cable industry. Getty Oil, a giant multinational oil company and a partner in the ESPN cable network, announced a joint venture with four of the major motion picture distributors (Fox, Universal, Paramount, and Columbia) to establish a new programming network known as Premiere. The Premiere network was scheduled to begin operations on January 1, 1981 and would offer twelve to fifteen films a month, primarily those of the movie distributor partners. The key provisions in this venture were the exclusivity clause that permitted Premiere to withhold the theatrical films of these four companies for a period of nine months from the other pay cable networks and the "formula" for setting the license prices. The Premiere network felt that only through such a product differentiation plan could it possibly compete with HBO and Showtime. This was the first attempt of the major studios to bypass the distribution buying strength of the entrenched giant of HBO. Having control over the key movie product, they felt they no longer needed others for distribution. This should be a natural in-house activity rather than negotiated out with others.

Immediately HBO and Showtime complained to the Justice Department that such a joint venture represented:

> *[a] horizontal agreement among competitors to increase prices, a group boycott, and a concerted refusal to deal. The plan is in violation of both the Sherman and Clayton Antitrust Acts and is an obvious attempt by these film companies, fueled by Getty Oil, to force the public and cable industry to pay higher prices for their films.*[16]

The Justice Department filed a civil antitrust suit against the Premiere principals in August 1980, and an injunction against the network beginning its operations was granted just before the January 1 starting date. Within a month, the Premiere network folded. However, HBO had learned an important lesson; lacking an assured source of films, it was vulnerable to such an "end around" as Premiere. It decided to become vertically integrated through ownership and long-term contracts to avoid future problems. It established a theatrical film subsidiary called Silver Screens, joined CBS and Columbia in launching a new mini-major production–distribution company called TriStar, and signed long-term exclusive contracts for the full line of theatrical films of Columbia, Orion, and CBS.[17]

To counteract this move, in 1983 the owners of Showtime and The Movie Channel, in conjunction with Warner Brothers, Universal, and Paramount, announced a new joint venture under which the #2 and #3 pay cable networks would be merged together.[18] While the principals claimed that these networks would continue to be run separately and that the motion picture distributors would continue to license their theatrical films on a nonexclusive basis, the Justice Department believed that such an amalgamation at the production stage would increase the likelihood of coordinated behavior, with the possibility of price squeezes on nonintegrated downstream competitors.[19] On the withdrawal of the motion picture companies, Showtime and The Movie Channel were permitted to merge, even though neither company was in danger of financial failure and the resulting concentration of market power greatly exceeded the threshold values of the Department of Justice's "Merger Guidelines." Within months, another small player, Spotlight Network, folded and the newly combined Showtime–The Movie Channel signed a five-year exclusive pact with Paramount Pictures.

Since the execution of the merger, many other exclusive arrangements have taken place. For example, Showtime–TMC locked up Atlantic, Cannon, DeLaurentis and Touchstone. As original contracts expired, there were many changes that ensued. Paramount has shifted over to HBO and, of course, Disney Studios were always exclusive with the Disney Channel. The main point is that while some large studios still have *not* signed these agreements and prefer to negotiate picture by picture for either exclusive or nonexclusive rights, a significant share of the movie supply industry became committed to this form of vertical tying arrangement, and this severely restricts a potential new pay cable distributor from gaining access to a sufficient number of box office hits to offer a service competitive with HBO and the other giants. It should be recalled that there are only about twenty or so box office hits any single year (a severe bottleneck), and pay cable distributors like to have a major hit each month to showcase on the cover of their cable guides. Hence, splitting up the top twenty hits, especially if done through exclusive contracts, doesn't go very far and, not surprisingly, hasn't opened this segment of the market to any new entrants. This is a severe deterrent to new full-fledged competition! While HBO–Cinemax and Showtime–The Movie Channel continue to dominate the movie-driven portion of the pay cable market, the market itself has diminished in importance with the arrival and strength of the VCR market whereby consumers can more directly select their own movie lineup.

NEW TECHNOLOGIES

The market for private backyard satellite dishes has developed in recent years as an offshoot and complement to cable technology. While at first cable systems were required to have a ten-foot diameter "dish" (at a cost of nearly $100,000) to receive the satellite transmissions, by 1979 the FCC had totally deregulated dish size requirements, and the cable industry had standardized with the four-and-one-half meter dish (at an initial cost of about $10,000 and later on $5,000). With reception costs significantly reduced, every cable system could now afford to participate in the nationwide satellite delivery system.

As the cable industry continued to develop, more sophisticated television receive-only satellite dishes (TVROs) came on line, and a new unintended use for these TVROs became apparent. In rural areas that were starved for TV signals, individual households could install a slightly cheaper version of the cable dish (for about $2,000 to $3,000) and receive signals from the same satellites as the cable systems. Thus, rural areas that had too low a population density to make cable financially viable could nonetheless participate in the same television phenomenon as their urban counterparts. Hence, the individual household could become a mini-cable system of its own.

While at first advertiser-supported cable services had no objection to the emergence of these backyard satellite dishes, since they increased their nationwide coverage area, the premium channels and especially the industry giant HBO fought bitterly since they represented a "leakage" from the system—nonpaying "customers." HBO became especially enraged when hotels and taverns began installing their own dishes and thereby subverting the system.

The legality of these backyard satellite dishes remained in question. Were these dishes engaged in theft of service (private transmissions) as HBO claimed or rather were these signals of the same class as over-the-air broadcast transmissions and thereby part of the public domain? This issue was finally resolved in the Cable

Policy Act of 1984, which formally legalized the right of consumers to *individually* own a backyard TVRO and *freely* receive satellite transmissions, provided that the satellite network did *not* encrypt (scramble) its signal nor set up a marketing system for collecting payments. During 1985, there was an absolute stampede by consumers to purchase their own dishes and take advantage of receiving so many free signals (especially recent movies) for the one-time installation investment of about $3,000. While there were rumors that scrambling was coming, it was conveniently forgotten or downplayed by satellite dish vendors in the euphoria of such a thriving business. Dishes were even being sold in areas passed by cable, causing cable operators to pressure their network suppliers to speed up their scrambling plans. Some 1.5 million dishes were operational by December of 1985.

Scrambling arrived in January of 1986 when HBO and its sister service Cinemax encrypted their signals and announced a $12.95 per month subscription price for the former and a $19.95 packaged price for the combination. Additionally, consumers would need to affix a descrambler box to their dish at a one-time cost of $395. The scrambling issue created significant confusion in the minds of consumers concerning how many (and which) services would eventually be scrambled, how one actually subscribed to a single service or package of services and became "authorized" to receive them, and whether consumers might have to buy several incompatible descrambler boxes.

During this 1986–1987 period of confusion, consumers significantly curtailed their demand for backyard dishes; sales fell by nearly 65 percent compared to the 1985 benchmark and eventually stabilized at about 20,000 units per month. Nevertheless, by mid-1988, some 2 million households in the U.S. (out of 88.6 million total) had backyard satellite dishes and some 500,000 "addressable" descramblers had been sold.[20] With a dozen major cable networks now scrambled and more on the horizon, with standardization of the descrambler technology and continued declines in basic dish prices, and the emergence of "third party" packagers, consumer confusion ended. The industry continues a steady growth path in those rural or outlying areas where cable cannot efficiently serve (some 10 to 15 million U.S. households). Since 1990, the backyard satellite industry has steadily declined as the cost of running cable became affordable in less dense areas. Furthermore, there were early attempts to replace this technology with a direct broadcast system to the home using a more powerful satellite necessitating a smaller, flat rooftop dish. Since 1995, this DBS system has gradually begun to compete with the other technologies, especially for delivery of pay-per-view networks and now appears on a steadier growth path toward financial stability.

The motion picture distributors should profit from the growth of this home satellite industry since it widens the exhibition market for premium pay TV networks like HBO and should eventually translate into higher license prices for theatrical movies. Furthermore, this industry is currently capable of transmitting movies, boxing and wrestling matches, live concerts, and other special event programming on a pay-per-view basis. This means that the viewer orders (by telephone) a particular performance (play) rather than receiving a bundle of films or the like on a monthly basis. This capability is also available on cable if the home converter has an integrated chip that can receive an authorization signal from the cable system headquarters. Only about 30 million cable households currently have "addressable" converters, but as more cable systems are upgraded over the next decade, this new technology may alter the distribution path for theatrical movies. Instead of a nationwide theatrical release, the movies may be premiered on pay-per-view television, thereby yielding an enormous opening night payoff. This may also cause the movie distributors to directly enter this market rather than rely on intermediaries as is current practice, with Request TV and Viewer's Choice being the dominant pay-per-view distributors.

Yet, an even broader industry can now be envisioned. With the development of the fiber to home information superhighway, there is the potentiality in the near future for true video-on-demand, that is, the consumer can order the movie or video program directly from a computer bank, and then download it for play at the consumer's convenience. Whether this new revolutionary approach to movie distribution will eclipse the theatrical market as the new "launching pad" still remains to be seen and will critically depend on the costs of wiring households and latent consumer demand.

THE VIDEOCASSETTE MARKET

Of even greater importance to the motion picture industry than cable has been the videocassette revolution of the past decade. VCR penetration at nearly 80 percent now exceeds cable penetration by nearly 15 percent and has long surpassed the theatrical box office in revenues generated. Ironically, the motion picture industry stalwartly tried to handicap the development of VCRs just a few short years ago in the *Betamax* case by claiming that their use in taping programs violated the copyright protection afforded motion pictures and TV programs.[21] Having lost that fight, they soon realized the potential for home video as another valuable exhibition window for theatrical films.

The main reason for the popularity of the VCR is its versatility; it permits viewers to "time-shift" programming to escape the temporal tyranny of program times dictated by the networks and local stations; it allows playback of home video photography made by compatible portable video cameras; and finally, and most importantly, it allows consumers to access, through purchase or lease, a wide array of prerecorded videocassettes. In essence, the VCR significantly improves consumer sovereignty and provides the diversity of programming that is absent from commercial television. Within this short thirteen-year period, the VCR industry has reached such an advanced stage of maturity that product differentiation according to content types (genres) already appears to satisfy even the narrowest programming taste. Critically, *this industry is still driven by the theatrical motion picture* (over 70 per-

TABLE 5-2 Domestic Revenues of Home Videocassette Suppliers, 1989–1996 (in $ Million)

Supplier/Year	1989	1990	1992	1993	1994	1995	1996
Disney	439	634	1025	1250	1600	2000	2200
Warner	562	486	602	763	790	1000	1400
Columbia/TriStar	215	416	696	643	620	500	580
MCA/Universal	246	350	492	631	720	670	750
Paramount	310	376	529	315	430	460	450
LIVE Ent.	106	278	167	141	100	100	100
CBS/Fox	272	221	577	519	650	850	1000
Orion/Nelson	191	173	86	51	65	65	65
MGM/UA	223	203	143	200	—	—	—
Goodtimes	67	45	5	—	475	475	450
New Line	—	—	—	150	200	275	250
Polygram	—	—	6	—	120	140	175
Turner	—	—	23	50	65	110	100
Anchor Bay	—	—	—	—	100	100	115
Republic	—	31	29	50	65	80	85
Vidmark	31	34	59	40	65	100	110
Media	123	50	—	—	—	—	—
Video Treasures	—	52	111	—	—	—	—
Academy	—	—	37	—	—	—	—
Prism	—	—	23	—	—	—	—
Starmaker	—	—	17	—	—	—	—
All Others	305	333	350	405	350	475	370
Totals	3,090	3,682	4,977	5,208	6,415	7,400	8,200
CR4	51.2	51.9	58.3	63.1	58.6	61.1	65.2
CR8	79.5	80.5	85.0	85.8	85.5	84.2	86.3
HHI	965.3	961.8	1,151.4	1,271.8	1,223.7	1,287.7	1,380.3

Source: International Television & Video Almanac (annual edition); *S&P Industry Surveys: Leisure Time,* March 14, 1991; *Billboard,* January 25, 1997, pp. 81–83.

cent share of sales),[22] which explains why the motion picture distributors have taken such a keen interest and dominant position.

The key difference between the VCR, television, and cable related markets is that in VCRs, *the majors act as distributors themselves,* while in the latter two markets, they rely on specialized distributors like CBS, HBO, Viewers Choice, and others. In fact, VCR distribution is very similar to that of magazines, paperback books, and records. The market shares for VCR distributors is given in Table 5-2. It is clear that the major theatrical distributors have transplanted their power into this market. Yet, their dominance in VCR software is somewhat smaller than in the traditional theatrical market. This is explained by the persistence of a strong group of independent distributors who specialize in non-movie types of videos such as the "How-To" genre (e.g., "Jane Fonda's Workout Book"), music videos, children's, pornographic, and educational.[23] The independents have also been involved in the distribution of "B" quality movies that purposely have a short theatrical run (sometimes none at all) in order to move more quickly through the VCR and other subsidiary markets. It is the insatiable appetite of these subsidiary markets for product that has caused the growth of the independent production industry and led to a record number of movie releases over the last decade.

It should be noted that these market shares are based on sales of cassettes rather than rentals, even though rentals account for the vast majority of consumer transactions. This is due to the "first sale" copyright provision that permits distributors to only collect copyright payments the first time a cassette is sold, not every time it is rented. Thus retail establishments will pay the wholesale price for theatrical movie cassettes but need not share revenues from renting. To capture some of this producer's surplus, the movie distributors charge very high wholesale prices for their cassettes and the retailers mark them up by their customary margins to yield extremely high retail prices that scare away consumer sales and further encourage the rental market. Occasionally, the wholesale price will be lowered after the first ninety days in order to stimulate the "sell through" consumer market.

One interesting difference between the prerecorded videocassette industry and the other subsidiary markets is the partial integration of the cassette distributors into the manufacturing (duplication) stage but not into the wholesale or retail stages. Because of high capital costs, long-term contracts and vertical integration, the tape duplication stage is very concentrated, with a four-firm concentration index fluctuating between 71 to 94 percent since 1984 and the recent merger between the #1 and #3 firms giving industry leader VCA–Technicolor a market share of 40 to 47 percent.[24] Until CBS–Fox (#3) merged with VCA–Technicolor, it and Bell & Howell–Columbia–Paramount (#2) were the only two vertically integrated firms and accounted for roughly a third to a half of the industry's market. Most of the other distributors have long-term exclusive contracts with duplicators, making new significant entry very difficult. On the other hand, the retail stage is extremely competitive with large discount department chains like K-Mart and Sears in competition with grocery chains and individually owned specialty shops. The availability of videocassette movies is now as plentiful as cigarettes, milk, and bread.

THE INTERNATIONAL MARKET

Historically, the second most important subsidiary market has been the international market which is the aggregation of some 80 or more trading partners of the United States. Going as far back as World War I, the American film distributors have dominated this world market for film, later extended to television and most recently to videocassettes.[25] In fact, U.S. control has been so pervasive that charges of "media imperialism" have been leveled. This refers to the same kind of domination of a country's cultural products that the economic imperialists had over their resources and mercantile goods. Most of all, it is a fear of the loss of cultural identity embedded in a weak indigenous production industry that has led many countries to impose economic and institutional barriers to free trade in cultural products.

The reason why U.S. motion picture distributors have been so powerful rests primarily on the relative size and strength of the U.S. market compared to those of other countries. U.S. motion picture and television producers can largely recoup their production costs from the domestic market alone, and given the public goods nature of the mass media[26] and the fact that the greatest expense is the "first-copy" production cost, distribution prices to foreign lands only need cover the incremental expenses. This pricing practice is often mislabeled as "dumping." Prices are based primarily on the strength of a country's demand (demand driven), providing that they cover the incremental costs of distribution for the particular country. Hence, the richer and more populous countries must pay higher prices for the same video product.

Since foreign countries do not have such a well-developed domestic market as the United States, they must either cut back on production costs (with detrimental effects on production values) or charge higher domestic and/or export prices; either strategy puts them at a disadvantage both within their own country and internationally, because the U.S. market had erected noneconomic barriers to imports through their ethnocentric dislike of foreign films, especially those with subtitles or dubbing.

The leading U.S. film distributors have bolstered their economic advantage by developing the most far-flung distribution networks throughout the world—comparable to their extensive domestic networks. This also includes significant ownership of foreign theaters! Furthermore, with the blessings of the U.S. government (under the Webb–Pomerene Act of 1918), the major movie distributors had a formal export cartel in place for nearly forty years that acted as the sole export sales agent for its members. The Motion Pictures Export Association set general export price levels for each country, terms of trade, and guaranteed the smooth functioning of the distribution process.[27] While the Webb–Pomerene Act was eventually repealed, its effect was long-lasting.

The protectionistic response of foreign countries to U.S. dominance has been the erection of traditional and nontraditional trade barriers. These barriers include import quotas, tariffs, strict licensing procedures, limitations of the percentage of screen time for imported films (and TV programs), and the freezing of local currencies from leaving the country (the most recent occurrence is in the European Common Market). In some instances, the U.S. government has been able to reduce these trade barriers as a quid pro quo for more favorable exchange rates or more open trade in other products. Additionally, foreign governments have provided encouragement to indigenous producers through formal subsidies, production prizes, tax breaks, or loans at favorable (or zero) interest rates.

The U.S. response to such foreign government tactics has been to qualify as indigenous producers within the countries, thereby escaping the penalties associated with being importers while enjoying the benefits afforded local companies.[28] This is one reason why Hollywood has experienced "runaway production" over the last ten to twenty years and so-called foreign coproduction has become more prevalent; the other reasons include the attractiveness and mystique of foreign locales and the cheaper costs in filming abroad.

No matter what barriers have been erected, the major motion picture distributors have successfully hurdled them and prospered. With the proliferation of new TV stations and satellite networks throughout the world, due to deregulation and privatization of formerly state-controlled monopolies, the export market, rather than constricting, appears wide open.

NEW BROADCAST WINDOWS

As has been mentioned, the motion picture studios have tight control over the movie product in the domestic and international theatrical markets but only partial control within the other exhibition windows, the strongest being VCRs. While they have grudgingly been forced to deal with strong network buyers in broadcasting, pay cable, and now in pay-per-view, they have always had the secret desire to form their own distribution networks in these exhibition windows and thereby bypass the powerful bottlenecks they encounter. While attempts have been made at times in the past, such as with the Premiere Cable Network or in conjunction with the Showtime–The Movie Channel merger, these have often been rebuffed by antitrust authorities or unreceptive market conditions.

One transplant that has finally taken hold and that may have started a new trend is the movie distributor's attempt to own and operate their own television networks, thereby bypassing the Big Three networks that have historically disadvantaged the studios in the market for regularly scheduled prime-time series. While conditions were unfavorable for new network entry for over thirty years, by the mid-1980s the economic hurdles in starting a network seemed somewhat less daunting.[29] This stimulated the Fox organization to take a chance in 1986 and then their success was followed in 1995 by Paramount and Warner Brothers on a smaller scale. Of course, the mega-merger between ABC and Disney may have set the course for further significant television involvement by the remaining major studios.

The Fox Network Saga

In the mid-1980s, the television networks were in dire financial straits.[30] Industry critics and financial analysts blamed the networks' problems on excessive costs, poor management techniques, and a failure to be innovative with new programming. Beginning in the mid-1980s, as the networks began to institute various cost controls, such as cutting their news staffs, they simultaneously were put into "play" since it was widely believed that their stock prices were undervalued relative to their earning potential. Shortly thereafter, each of them was acquired or reorganized in highly publicized multibillion dollar deals (NBC by General Electric, ABC by Capital Cities, and CBS by Lawrence Tisch) and new corporate managements installed. Each became a subsidiary of a giant U.S. media conglomerate. This corporate reorganization was also rationalized as a defense against unfriendly takeovers by foreign corporations—a strategy that turned out to be clairvoyant when Sony and Mashushita acquired major motion picture studios at the end of the decade and Rupert Murdoch (News Corporation) first purchased Twentieth-Century Fox and then the Metromedia Broadcast Group to act as a foundation for his proposed fourth television network.

Murdoch believed that a new network that was both innovative in its programming and cost-conscious could selectively compete for viewership against the bigger networks. Even in the face of new competition from cable and other services, Fox believed that the timing was right to establish a fourth network since the technological and regulatory handicaps that made network entry so risky before seemed to be lower due to the entrance of many new independent stations in the top 100 markets as potential affiliates and the newfound possibility of using cable outlets as well. Recognizing the hazards of full scale entry, Fox sought to first establish its presence in the weekend prime-time hours. Furthermore, Fox believed that viewers were ready for a more exciting kind of network programming that contrasted with the staleness and predictability of the traditional broadcast networks and was targeted to youth and young adults. The economics of networking seemed irresistible to both Fox and the independent stations; they could both improve their economic position through forming a network partnership.[31]

During its first several years, the audience for Fox programming continued to grow, and its survival was assured. By 1995, it had developed a consistent lineup of successful programs (*Married with Children, Star Trek, Melrose Place,* etc.) across seven nights of the week and established a very successful children's lineup as well. Even to this day, Fox still has not achieved ratings parity with the Big Three, leaving open the question of why Warner Brothers and Paramount would now enter into this crowded, fiercely competitive marketplace.[32] Industry speculation suggests that Paramount and Warners were positioning themselves for the possibility of a friendly takeover by a giant media conglomerate anxious to have a strong foothold in all kinds of programming.

Understanding the harsh realities of establishing new networks, after six-month planning horizons, both Warner Brothers Television Network and United–Paramount debuted in mid-January 1995. Warner Brothers began with a single night of prime-time programming while Paramount had two nights. As expected, neither network had comparable affiliate clearances to the established networks. By September 1995, UPN had access to 88 percent of the nation's television households while Warner Brothers had only 81 percent. Warner achieved this clearance only after utilizing superstation, WGN, to enter some broadcast markets where no affiliates were available while Paramount was forced to accept secondary affiliation status in many markets, covering some 15 percent of the country, which means that the stations could position the programs in different slots than originally broadcast.[33]

The Paramount network was based around the *Star Trek* franchise program and consisted of hour-long dramatic fare targeted to males, while Warner Brothers utilized half-hour situation comedies to attract a predominantly "yuppie" demographic target. With the exception of *Star Trek,* none of the programs showed acceptable ratings during the abbreviated first season, most earning ratings in the 1 to 3 percent range, which is comparable to that of a basic cable network or an access hour syndicated show. For the next season, Paramount replaced all its shows save *Star Trek,* while Warner Brothers retained its shows, added a second night, and began planning for expansion into the children's market. With widespread losses their first two years of operation, unless their programming achieves acceptable ratings next year, the planned expansion of Paramount may be torpedoed and the fate of these new netlets may be sealed.[34] In fact, during 1996, there were talks about a possible merger between the new networks to provide a stronger, more united, front in affiliates and programs to create a market niche that could be sustainable. While both networks continue to broadcast today, their financial plight is still quite evident and their future quite precarious.

Syndication

The strength of the major studios in supplying prime-time entertainment programming to the networks over the last twenty years or so creates additional benefits in the television syndication industry. After passage of the Financial Interest and Syndication Rules in 1971, the subsidiary syndication rights for network series remained in the hands of the studios, each of which had syndication divisions. In addition to off-network rerun rights, the major studios also had a continuously expanding inventory of old and "classic" films that could be sold in packages to local television stations, cable superstations, and some family oriented "basic" cable networks like USA or The Family Channel.

Beginning in the 1970s, another type of syndicated programs began to catch fire, the first-run talk shows, game shows, and "info-tainment" type fare. These programs were more current than off-network reruns or old movies and they became quite popular during non-network hours of the broadcast day (e.g., mid-morning, late afternoon, and early fringe evening). To keep up with this trend, the movie studios began producing such first-run syndicated programming and, by the 1990s, they were dominating this segment of the syndication industry as well, eclipsed only by King World with its franchise of *Wheel of Fortune, Jeopardy,* and *Oprah Winfrey.*[35]

The prospects for continued studio domination of the syndication exhibition window are somewhat uncertain at the present. While the overall syndication industry continued to grow over the period of the 1980s, the most recent entry of the Warner Brothers and United–Paramount networks has somewhat constricted the open market for all kinds of syndication programming, since each hour of new network programming reduces the demand by these formerly independent stations for syndicated programming. Furthermore, the recent repeal of the Financial Interest and Syndication Rules suggests that the broadcast networks, now including Fox, Paramount, and Warner Brothers, will play a bigger role in off-network syndication in the future as they either produce more prime-time series in-house (the current trend) or they co-venture with independent program packages. Hence, the high and increasing market concentration in the syndication industry, and the market strength of the major movie studios, first noticed in the 1980s, may see some erosion over the next several years.

NOTES

[1]Price and marginal revenue are coextensive in this context.

[2]For more detail on this point, see the pioneering article, David Waterman, "Pre-recorded Home Video and the Distribution of Theatrical Feature Films," in Eli Noam, ed., *Video Media Competition: Regulation, Economics, and Technology,* New York: Columbia University Press, 1985, Chapter 7.

[3]If the movie theaters were to vary their prices according to how long the film had been at a particular location, a certain group of patrons would undoubtedly pay premium prices to see highly publicized movies their premiere night or opening week.

[4]This is equivalent to maximizing a group of simultaneous demand equations for each exhibition window.

[5]Bruce M. Owen and Steven Wildman, *Video Economics,* Cambridge, MA: Harvard University Press, 1992, Chapter 2.

[6]Bruce Owen, Jack H. Beebe, and Willard G. Manning, *Television Economics,* Lexington, MA: Lexington Books, 1974, Chapter 2.

[7]This entire section comes largely from Barry R. Litman, "The Economics of the Television Market for Theatrical Movies," *Journal of Communications,* 29 (Autumn 1979): 20–33.

[8]Owen, Beebe, and Manning, op. cit.

[9]*Columbia Pictures v. ABC and CBS,* U.S. District Court, Southern District of New York, 1972; *U.S. v. CBS, NBC and ABC,* U.S. District Court, Central District of California, 1974.

[10]For more detail on these decrees, see FCC Network Inquiry Special Staff, *An Analysis of Television Program Production, Acquistion and Distribution,* Washington, DC: GPO, 1980, Chapter 8.

[11]Litman, op. cit.

[12]In fact, the DuMont network realized this economic fact in 1955 and exited from the scene, greatly fortifying ABC with whom it had been fighting for the limited number of affiliates. In 1986, with the greater viability of UHF signals transmitted by cable, Fox Broadcasting established itself as the fourth network, although it broadcasts only two nights per week.

[13]This section comes largely from Barry R. Litman and Suzannah Eun, "The Emerging Oligopoly of Pay TV in the USA," *Telecommunications Policy,* 5 (June 1981): 121–35.

[14]*Home Box Office, Inc. v. Federal Communications Commission,* 567 F. 2d 9 (D.C. Cir. 1977).

[15]A corollary market of advertiser-supported cable networks, such as USA, ESPN, CNN, and MTV, and several 'superstations' emerged and was packaged together by local cable systems and sold as "basic" cable service. The premium channels mentioned have always been sold separately (à la carte).

[16]*Variety,* April 30, 1980, p. 158.

[17]It also established a production unit for producing made-for-cable films, ironically called Premiere Films.

[18]*Wall Street Journal,* 10 June, 1983.

[19]Lawrence White, "Antitrust and Video Markets: The Merger of Showtime and The Movie Channel," in Noam, op. cit., Chapter 11. The post merger Hefindahl–Hirschman Index was approximately 4500 and the change in the index was 400 points.

[20]*Satellite Times,* September 7, 1988, p. 1.

[21]They sought to ban the import of VCRs into the U.S., permit only machines that had a playback (as opposed to a record) mode, and levy a copyright surcharge on all blank tapes sold.

[22]For an historical treatment of this issue see Heikki Hellman and Martti Soramaki, "Economic Concentration in Videocassette Industry: A Cultural Comparison," *Journal of Communication,* 35 (Summer 1985) 122–34.

[23]If one narrowly defined the market as theatrical videos, their control would be approximately equal to that of the theatrical movie market. However, just as movies on television must compete with other entertainment and information programming, so must videocassette recordings.

[24]*Videoweek,* January 1988.

[25]This section draws heavily on Thomas Guback, "Hollywood's International Market," in Balio, op. cit. (1985), Chapter 17.

[26]Mass media products possess the "non-rivalry in consumption" attribute of public goods. This means that one person (or one country's consumption of a movie or TV program) does not diminish the utility available for others to consume. On the other hand, with the exception of over-the-air broadcasting, a collection mechanism is available for excluding nonpayers, so the "exclusion" and "free rider" problems of public goods do not apply.

[27]Ibid.

[28]Ibid.

[29]Laurie Thomas and Barry Litman, "Fox Broadcasting Company, Why Now?" *Journal of Broadcasting and Electronic Media,* 35 (Spring 1991): 139–57.

[30]Ibid.

[31]Ibid.

[32]Larry Collette and Barry Litman, "The Strange Economics of New Broadcast Entry: The Case of United Paramount and Warner Brothers Networks," AEJMC Convention paper, Anaheim, CA: August 1996.

[33]Ibid.

[34]Ibid.

[35]Sylvia Chan–Olmstead, "A Structural Analysis of Market Competition in the U.S. Syndication Industry," *Journal of Media Economics,* 4 (Fall 1991): 9–28.

6

The Structure of
the Radio Industry

GEOFFREY P. HULL
Middle Tennessee State University

ALBERT N. GRECO
Fordham University
Graduate School of Business Administration

STAN MARTIN
Formerly Vice President, The New York Times Corporation
Station Manager, WQEW-AM

This chapter explores the economics of the radio broadcasting industry on both a macro and micro scale. Like most mass media, radio broadcasters participate in two markets—a consumer market composed of listeners and potential listeners and a service market of advertisers.[1] To participate in the consumer market, the station offers entertainment, information, and news to potential listeners at no charge. The only cost to the consumer is the purchase price of a receiver. When a station has listeners it can sell access to those listeners to advertisers by selling advertising time during its broadcast day.

Radio is a mature industry. Penetration of radio receivers into the marketplace is over 99 percent, and most people have several receivers in their homes, as well as receivers in their cars and at their offices. Most of the population already listens to radio at some point in their day (83 percent). So the industry is mature in that there are not many new potential listeners who are not already listening to radio at some point in their days. Americans spend more time listening to radio, an average of 1,050 hours per year, than they do consuming any other medium except television.[2] It is mature in another way as well. There is very little spectrum space available to start new radio stations. So the market has about all the "players" it can hold, especially in the larger markets.

A defining macroeconomic characteristic of radio is that it is highly regulated by the federal government. The Federal Communications Commission (FCC) exerts control over which and how many firms can participate in the market through the licensing process. In the interest of preventing monopolies, the FCC kept strict control over the number of broadcast stations that could be owned by any one firm either nationally, or in one market. The FCC also strictly oversees the technical aspects of broadcasting such as antenna height, broadcast frequency, power, and modulation. The FCC is less involved in regulating the content of radio but there are some restrictions there as well. The reasons for the FCC control are primarily due to the nature of the technology of broadcasting and have important historical underpinnings.

A significant microeconomic factor in radio broadcasting is the cost of programming. This was an important reason underlying the creation of radio networks (where a group/chain of stations receives programming from a single source on a regular basis) in the early days of broadcasting, the use of syndication (where a supplier sells programming to stations on an individual basis), and the rise of music as the dominant program content. Single firms that own large numbers of stations can "share" programming, so cost savings is a factor that is part of the drive to create large chains. Restrictions on chain ownership by the FCC and control of programming costs are economic factors rooted in the history of broadcasting.

TECHNOLOGY, THE FCC, AND THE RADIO MARKET

Early History and Creation of the FCC[3]

History records that the first radio, or "wireless" transmission, over a significant distance was that of Marconi, in 1897. Using spark-coil transmitters, he was able to communicate Morse code over a distance of up to eighteen miles from a land station to a ship at sea. By 1901, Marconi had successfully transmitted the letter "S" across the Atlantic Ocean. In 1906, early experimenter Reginald Fessenden successfully transmitted voice and music programs on Christmas Eve and New Year's Eve short distances and from land to sea. The early significant use of radio was in maritime safety. It was for the sake of safety that Congress passed the first regulation of radio in the United States—the Wireless Ship Act of 1910. It required "radio-communication" apparatus on all ships carrying fifty or more persons. That same year, Lee DeForest broadcast a performance of Enrico Caruso from the Metropolitan Opera in New York City to about fifty listeners scattered about the city.

World War I briefly interrupted the development of commercial radio broadcasting but it grew rapidly after the war. Radio was an eight-million dollar manufacturing industry in 1919, about 13 percent of the value of all manufacturing reported by the Department of Commerce. In 1920, there were about 6,000 amateur and 4,600 "commercial" licenses outstanding in the United States. Perhaps the most important of these was that operated by Westinghouse engineer, Dr. Frank Howard, in Pittsburgh, Pennsylvania. As part of his work with Westinghouse in experimenting with radio, Dr. Howard operated a station from his garage licensed as 8XK. He regularly programmed sports and music on Wednesday evenings for two hours. His music programming reportedly gave rise to an early "trade-out" (the exchange of advertising time for barter goods or services) of a new records to play in exchange for a promotional mention of the phonograph dealer who supplied him with the records. The promotional value of the airplay to the phonograph dealer was an increase in the sales of the recordings which Dr. Howard had played.[4] Westinghouse decided to create its own station for the purpose of providing programming to encourage people to buy Westinghouse's manufactured receivers. In October 1920, station KDKA became the first regular broadcast station.[5] It inaugurated service in November that year by broadcasting the results of the Cox–Harding presidential race. The hundred-watt station soon expanded its programming, with the first broadcast church service in January of 1921, boxing in April 1921, band concerts in that spring and summer, and reports of Davis Cup matches in August that same year.

Radio grew rapidly in popularity. In 1926, the RCA Corporation started the first radio network, National Broadcasting Company, with twenty-four stations. That same year there was one radio receiver for every twenty American homes, about an 18 percent saturation. By 1934, the saturation of radios in American homes was over 71 percent. The number of broadcasters burgeoned, adding over 500 to their numbers in 1922 alone. The powers of the Commerce Department in the Radio Act of 1912 were so limited that it could only allocate frequencies for broadcasters in general. The broadcasters competed with each other by adding transmitter power and hours of operation, or by changing frequencies. Interference became so bad that the broadcasters asked Congress for help.

The Radio Act of 1927 created a Federal Radio Commission (FRC) to regulate broadcasting by assigning frequencies, prescribing power and location of transmitters, and minimizing interference primarily through the vehicle of granting a three-year renewable license. Although the number of applicants was greater than the number of stations that could be accommodated without interference, the only criteria which Congress gave the FRC to use in the granting of licenses was whether granting the license would serve the "public interest, convenience, and necessity."

Although the FRC was able to save broadcasting from its own interference, it was not able to regulate the diverse aspects of electronic communication other than radio which had blossomed in the first thirty years of the century. As a result, President Roosevelt asked Congress to replace the Radio Act with a broader Communications Act. The Federal Communications Act of 1934 became the cornerstone of broadcasting for the next sixty years. Station licenses were still to be granted to "serve the public interest, convenience, or necessity" but the new administrative agency created by the 1934 act, the Federal Communications Commission (FCC), was given broad powers to regulate telephone, telegraph, and broadcast communications of all kinds. A seven-member commission (reduced to five in 1983) was to make the regulations. The term of the licenses was eventually extended to seven years for radio, but stations were still subjected to an extensive renewal process. At various times the FCC was more or less involved in the regulation of programming content but became increasingly less involved in the 1980s and 1990s, preferring to let the marketplace regulate content. Though challenged by listeners who did not like having their favorite station change formats, the U.S. Supreme Court upheld the FCC's discretion to let the marketplace rule.[6]

In a sweeping rewrite of the 1934 Act, Congress passed the Telecommunications Act of 1996. The Act was envisioned by some as creating opportunities for competition both within and across media. By 1998, the results were getting mixed reviews. Some complained that by allowing mergers and re-mergers (of the small "baby bells" that were split forcibly from AT&T in 1984) and both horizontal and vertical integration in the electronic media, competition and consumers were not being served.[7] Others argued that the 1996 Act opened up competitive opportunities for new niche companies.[8] Whatever the ultimate outcome may be, the 1996 Act had three significant economic effects on radio; it extended the duration of radio and television licenses to eight years,[9] prompted the FCC's adoption of nearly "automatic" renewal for existing licenses under the new two-step process,[10] and relaxed the guidelines for mergers. All of these enhanced the value of an existing license, made more people want to enter the radio marketplace, while at the same time raising the barriers to entry due to the enhanced value of a license.

Movement toward a Free Market

Throughout the 1980s and 1990s the FCC relaxed its rules regarding the number of broadcast outlets in a single market that could be owned by one entity and regarding the total number of broadcast outlets that could be owned by one entity nationwide. In 1988, the Commission began to allow greater overlap between commonly owned AM and FM stations. In 1992, the Commission changed its rules to allow the same owner to operate up to four stations in markets with more than 15 stations and up to three stations in smaller markets as long as they controlled less than half of the stations in that market. Congress further relaxed the rules with passage of the Communications Act of 1996 (see Table 6-1) with a limit that no single party can own more than half of the stations in a given market. At the same time the national ownership restrictions were being relaxed. In 1953, the FCC rules limited the total number of stations owned by one firm to 7 AM, 7 FM and 7 TV stations (the 7-7-7 rule). Beginning in 1984, the limits were expanded, first to 12-12-12. Then in 1988 radio ownership limits moved to 18-18, then 20-20 in 1990.[11] Finally, the Communications Act of 1996 removed all limits on the total number of stations that could be owned by a single entity.

The relaxation of the ownership limits had the predictable effect. In the early 1990s sales of radio station licenses reached a fever pitch. The reason was the consolidation of ownership into larger and larger chains. Growth-oriented broadcasting owners purchased everything from single stations to entire chains.[12] The removal of all limits by the Communications Act of 1996 led to mega-mergers. Westinghouse Electric purchased CBS, Inc. and Infinity Broadcasting, creating a chain of 83 stations. The Infinity deal cost Westinghouse $3.9 billion but raised its market shares in a number of major markets, including San Francisco (19 percent) and Philadelphia (44 percent).[13] The 1996 mergers totaled more than $25 billion. Although many of those sales were sales of groups involving television and radio stations, the transactions involving only radio stations totaled $2.8 billion.[14]

How much did the merger, acquisition, and consolidation of the 1980s and mid-1990s affect the concentration of radio ownership? *Broadcasting and Cable* ranked the top 25 radio groups based on the average number of listeners in a quarter hour the group "controlled." The top 25 groups controlled 1,372 of the nation's 10,273 commercial radio stations, just 13 percent. When viewed from another perspective, that of listeners reached by the top groups, a different picture emerges. The largest group, Chancellor Media Group/Capstar Broadcasting, controlled nearly 400 stations by the end of 1997, only about 4 percent of the total number of stations. However, that same group had over 8 percent of all the listeners reached by the top 25 firms. Table 6-2 indicates the degree of concentration based on total listeners which was beginning to emerge in the largest firms. Since these firms have consolidated an estimated 80 percent of the top 75 markets,[15] this is significant concentration in a listener sense, if not in a geographic market sense. The consolidation trend was expected to move into smaller markets, the numbers 76 through 200, in the late 1990s.[16]

TABLE 6-1 1996 Communications Act Radio Ownership Limits

Number of Radio Stations in Market	Maximum Total Stations Allowed One Owner	AM/ FM Limits
45 or more	8	5/5
30–44	7	4/4
15–29	6	4/4
14 or less	5	3/3

Source: Section 202(b)(1)(D) of the Communications Act of 1996.

TABLE 6-2   Ownership Concentration in Radio (1997)

	AQH Listeners	Percent of Top 25 Total Listeners	No. of Stations	Percent of Commercial Stations
Top 4 Firms	7,383,900	52	652	6.3
Top 8 Firms	10,462,800	73	907	8.8
Top 12 Firms	11,941,400	84	1070	10.4

Source: "Radio's New Order," *Broadcasting and Cable,* 23 June 1997: 26–37.

Effects of Ownership Concentration

Radio executives predicted that ownership concentration would impact radio formats. "As the market contracts in the number of owners there will be greater program diversity," said Randy Michaels of Jaycor Broadcasting. Another executive predicted that there would be a consolidation down to about fifteen large radio groups over a short period of time.[17] Those predictions are in contradiction to a study, completed before the 1996 Communications Act, which suggested that increasing the total number of stations in a market would have a small effect on the number of available formats for listeners, finding a 10 percent increase in the number of stations would lead to only a less than 2 percent increase in the number of formats. The study concluded, "[R]elaxing ownership rules will generate only small program diversity benefits if only modest increases in either the number of stations or in the incentives to offer different formats or higher quality programming result."[18] The broadcasters' logic which leads to the opposite conclusion is that as more stations per market are owned by the same entity, that entity will choose not to compete with itself, but rather to be able to deliver to advertisers a larger share of the total market. Theoretical models of mass media, and broadcasting in particular, suggest that advertiser-supported media firms cater to delivering as large an audience as possible. That can be done by programming different stations with non-competing formats. The non-competing formats can get a larger total share of the audience by appealing to a larger and more diverse group of listeners. The broadcasting owner can then sell a package deal to advertisers who will buy because they can reach a larger share of the total audience or a niche audience served by a particular station's format. In 1997, both theories remained to be proven.

Listeners are only one of the two markets in which the stations participate. A question for advertisers was whether the increased concentration would mean higher advertising rates. By mid-1997, about a year after the passage of the Telecommunications Act of 1996 that allowed the consolidation, there was no clear evidence that increased concentration in ownership would raise advertising prices.[19] One early 1990s study, as market "duopolies" began to emerge, found that advertising costs in markets with heavily concentrated ownership were actually less than those in more competitive markets.[20] An updated mid-1990s study found the same thing.[21] By early 1998, however, the situation had changed. In some top ten markets, the major group owners increased prices 30 to 50 percent, well ahead of the national averages of radio advertising rate increases during that time period.[22] Complaints such as those prompted the Justice Department to carefully scrutinize proposed mergers and buy-outs. Reports indicated that the Justice Department had allowed some mergers where as much as 53 percent of the advertising revenues in a single market were controlled by one group. By 1998, some merger proposals would have placed as much as 75 percent of the advertising revenues in some markets into the hands of a single group owner.[23]

RECORDINGS IN RADIO

While news is an expensive format to produce, requiring announcers, reporters, editors, and wire service sufficient to fill a day with information, talk and music formats are very inexpensive. For talk, all the station has to provide are hosts, delay line technology, and telephone lines and the callers/listeners provide most of the program content for free, in return for being allowed to speak their minds on some subject. In music formats, most of the music is supplied by record companies and all the station has to provide is an announcer and playback machines and a license fee for the songs (but not the recordings) played. Even if the music is supplied by a syndication service, the service does not have to pay for the recordings and therefore its charge to the station is for its announcers, compiling and recording (if delivered in recorded form) the programs but not for the actual music itself.

The vast majority of broadcasters rely on the popularity of recordings and the popularity of their announcers to attract a listening audience. The presence of that audience in turn helps the broadcaster sell advertising time to clients who want their message to reach those listeners. Record companies rely on radio as the primary means of exposure of their recordings to the public. The labels hope the airplay will interest the public in buying copies of the recordings. In exchange for the airplay, or rather the hope of airplay, the record companies provide the stations and syndicators with copies of the recordings for free. Since the predominant format in radio is the playback of recordings, it is worthwhile to briefly examine the relationship between radio and records.

A Love/Hate Relationship

It is no secret that radio stations and record companies do not sell the same thing. Get any label promotion people and radio programmers in the same room and the programmers will quickly remind the promotion people that radio programming is to sell advertising, not records. None of the top 20 advertisers on radio were record labels, or even their conglomerate owners—they were retail, business, and consumer services, and automobiles and auto accessories. These advertisers accounted for one-third of radio advertising billings.[24] On the other hand, music obtained by playing records is the predominant format content of 70 percent of all radio stations (Table 6-3). Those stations rely mainly on the music they play to attract and hold listeners. From the label perspective, radio airplay still accounts for significant percentage of the exposure of record buyers to new music. Market research done in 1995 revealed that 44 percent of music consumers made their last album purchase because of the influence of radio or television airplay of a record.[25] A 1977 Warner Communications survey noted, "[T]he 43 percent of the total population who listen to music [on the radio] for at least 10 hours per week comprise 54 percent of all buyers and account for 62 percent of the total dollar market."[26] In 1979, CBS records reported to the NARM convention that 80 percent of singles buyers learned about the records they purchased from radio.[27] Researcher Paul Hirsch concluded that radio programmers were gatekeepers who preselected the music that listeners and potential buyers would hear.[28]

The Historical Context: 1920s–1955

From the days of the first commercial radio broadcast in 1922, popular music began to have an impact on radio programming. By playing popular music the stations and networks could attract listeners that the advertisers wanted to reach. Most of the programs were not locally produced but were supplied by the networks with which the local stations were affiliated. The programs were produced largely by the advertising agency, the network (for the sponsor), or by the sponsor itself. Programs with musical content were the most popular. A 1929 survey of the ten most popular programs listed only two non-musical or musical/variety programs, the comedy series "Amos 'n' Andy" and the dramatic series "True Story," at numbers four and five,

TABLE 6-3   Growth of Radio Music Formats*

	1986	1995
Stations with music formats[1]	9,055	11,101
Stations with non-music formats	2,681	4,709
Number of different music formats	12	23
Total stations	11,736	15,810

Source: Broadcasting & Cable Yearbook, 1995, B-653, B-655.

*Only clearly music formats are counted. Thus, foreign language, ethnic, and Indian are not counted as music even though they may contain significant portions of music. The number of formats exceeds the number of stations because a station using a given format for a significant part of the day could report more than one format.

[1]Music formats in 1986 were Adult Contemporary, Beautiful Music, Big Band, Black, Classical, Country, Urban, Progressive, Top 40, Oldies, Jazz and MOR. In 1995 Rock/AOR, Gospel, Classic Rock, Nostalgia, New Age, Blues, Bluegrass, Folk, Reggae, and Disco were added.

respectively.[29] The musical shows usually had live orchestras with guest and regular performers. These programs, together with classical music programs, amateur hours, and a small segment of popular singles programs (with only a 0.7 percent average rating), accounted for just over a 50-percent share of the nighttime radio audience. The dramatic difference between nighttime programming and daytime programming is illustrated by the fact that during the daytime, adult serial drama, talk shows, and juvenile shows accounted for over 82 percent of listenership share.[30] Daytime radio programming in those days was strikingly similar to daytime television programming today.

During the depression it became more of a common practice for local radio stations to fill their non-network time by playing recordings, especially when the quality of the recordings became better with the continued development of electrical recording. While the music publishers did not particularly care in what form a song was played, live or recorded, the record companies and the orchestras who recorded for the record companies at first took a dim view of airplay of records. They attempted to stop radio stations from playing records by marking the labels "Not Licensed for Radio Broadcast" or "Licensed Only For Non-Commercial Use on Phonographs in Homes. Mfr. & Original Purchaser Have Agreed This Record Shall Not be Resold Or Used For Any Other Purpose." Those attempts ended in a 1940 Federal Appeals Court case in New York.[31] Orchestra leader Paul Whiteman had complained of a radio station (W.B.O. Broadcasting) playing records of his musical performances. Whiteman's label, RCA, joined the suit against the radio station and Whiteman, saying that Whiteman had no interest left in the recordings which had not been contracted away to RCA. The court held that having fixed the recording of Whiteman's performance on records and distributed them to the public, neither the label nor Whiteman could complain if radio stations or others then performed the recordings for the public. At that time there were no copyrights protecting sound recordings. Judge Learned Hand commented, "If the talents of conductors of orchestras are denied that compensation which is necessary to evoke their efforts because they get too little for phonographic records, we have no means of knowing it. . . ."[32]

With the legal path cleared to play more recordings, the radio stations of the early 1940s began to do so. The first "disk jockeys" were born. One of them, Martin Block, who aired a program called "Martin Block's Make Believe Ballroom," realized the future importance of radio to the recording industry. Speaking of radio airplay in 1942, Block said, "If the platter is a good one, the most effective type of direct marketing has just taken place. And sales are sure to reflect the airing of the disk."[33] But it was not until the mid-1950s, when television threatened the death of radio, that records became the mainstay of radio programming. The dramatic, comedy, and variety shows that had been the bulwark of radio programming since the early days of the networks could not compete with the visual impact of the same kind of programs aired on television. Radio stations were going off the air, and advertising revenues plunged. In 1955, *Billboard* reported that playing records was the clear trend for radio programming, noting that records were the programming of 53 percent of stations with power of less than 5,000 watts, and 42 percent of the programming of stations with greater than 5,000 watts power.[34] Even so, popular music was not the primary programming of those stations that did play music. Only 12 percent of the stations that did program popular music played it for 75 hours per week (half of the available air time). Twenty-three percent played classical music at least ten hours per week and 16 percent played country music at least twenty hours per week.[35]

Radio Turns to Records

Three other events of the mid-50s combined with the threat of television to transform radio into a predominantly music medium. The introduction of the 45-RPM single in 1949 by RCA Victor brought an easily handled, nearly unbreakable, inexpensive, high-fidelity recording into the marketplace. The 45 took less space than the 78 or the LP (introduced by Columbia the year before). The vinyl material was lightweight, especially in the seven-inch format chosen for the 45, compared to the 10- or 12-inch format for the older 78s. Since the 45 used the same material as the LP but ran at a nearly 50 percent greater speed, it had potentially higher fidelity than the LP. Finally, the 45 was less expensive to purchase than the LP and the players for the 45 were less expensive—factors which would prove attractive to the teen market. Radio initially objected to the 45 single. Many radio stations had built up libraries of 78-RPM ETs (electrical transcriptions). The practice of sending radio stations ETs of programs had developed as a way to distribute high-quality recordings of programs, and music, to stations. Most stations paid for the ETs as part of a subscription service from the labels. Most complaints about the 45s died out when the labels began supplying the new 45s free of charge to all but the smallest stations.

Disk jockey Todd Storz was responsible for the second breakthrough that made radio broadcasters and record companies reluctant partners. In 1955, he introduced the Top 40 format on station WTIX in New Orleans.[36] The concept of Top 40 was more than just playing the forty most popular records. That had been being done for some time. What Storz noticed, allegedly at a bar one night as he observed customers playing a couple of songs over and over, was that listeners wanted to hear certain songs more often than others. He devised a closed play list with a limited number of selections and a rotation that played the most popular songs more often. Now virtually all commercial radio stations with a music format apply this "formula" in one way or another. Many stations have several rotations. How often a record gets played depends upon several factors, including such things as the current strength of the recording, whether it is waxing or waning in popularity, whether it was a recent hit (a "recurrent"), or whether it is a hit from several years past. The result was a sound that attracted listeners, and therefore advertisers. *Billboard* noted, "It was Storz who saved radio from death."[37]

Rock 'n' roll was the other "savior" of radio. From 1951 to 1955 sales of recorded music grew a modest 19 percent to about $230,000,000 as reported by the

RIAA. The 1956 through 1959 sales figures indicated a growth of more than 125 percent to almost $515 million—largely the result of rock. Rock could also deliver a new radio audience that had not been listening to the predominantly middle-of-the-road formats of the early 1950s. It was an audience that had more money to spend and more leisure time than the youth audience had ever had before. Advertisers were attracted to the potential market that could be reached through rock radio and bought air time. Rock radio prospered. By attracting listeners who were not part of the mainstream radio audience the rock stations were able to succeed quickly in markets where it would have taken years to develop a sizable listenership by eating away at the audiences of several other stations. The existence of the rock format stations created a demand for more music to program. As more music was programmed, more was exposed to potential buyers who then made purchases which benefited the labels.

The availability of records made it possible to produce inexpensive programming at the local level and to sell advertising at the local level. Radio advertising revenues increased over 800 percent from 1940 to 1970 from about $157 million to about $1,257 million. During that same time period the share of advertising revenues produced from local billings (as opposed to national or regional networks, or other national) increased from a mere 28 percent in 1940 to 68 percent in 1970. It was no longer necessary to rely on a network that could afford to hire an orchestra and popular entertainers. Those orchestras and entertainers were available on disc to perform at the spin of a platter. As a result, the share of revenues from network billings dropped from 47 percent in 1940 to 4 percent in 1977.[38]

Diversity in Radio Brings Diversity in Music

Table 6-4 illustrates the rapid growth and proliferation of radio stations from a mere thirty in 1922 when the first National Radio Conference began licensing stations[39] to

TABLE 6-4 Growth of Licensed Radio Stations in the United States

Year	AM Stations	FM Stations*	Total Stations
1922	30**	—	30
1935	585	—	585
1955	2,669	552	3,221
1975	4,432	3,353	7,785
1995	4,945	6,613	11,558

Source: Broadcasting & Cable Yearbook, 1995, B-653, B-655.

*The first FM permits were granted in 1940.

**Numbers are of licensed, on-air stations (except 1922 when stations were not licensed), not including those under construction.

over 11,000 stations in 1995. In the forty years between 1955 and 1995, the number of broadcast radio stations increased by 256 percent.

In 1995, radio reached 99 percent of U.S. homes. But not all of the people in the 98 million homes were listening to the same thing. The proliferation of stations brought with it a proliferation of formats. The more stations that existed in a radio market the more they found that they had to have some way to divide the audience pie, and perhaps attract listeners who were not tuned in to the other stations. The stations began to divide the audience pie into smaller shares and look for programming niches. One way to achieve this was by playing different music from the competitors. The demand for different music has led to airplay of a wider variety of music. The radio market has not become homogeneous as some had predicted in the early days of Top 40. In fact, the overall trend for a significant number of years has been to increasing heterogeneity in music available to radio listeners. Even in the decade from 1986 to 1995 the number of radio stations reporting predominantly music formats grew over 2,000 and the number of different music formats reported nearly doubled (see Table 6-3).

The FCC, Technology, and Music

In the early days of radio the Federal Communications Commission adopted the "duopoly rule." The essence of the regulation was that the FCC would not grant a license to an applicant who already owned or controlled another broadcast outlet in the same area so that the two stations would have overlapping service areas. In the early days of FM, the FCC had allowed ownership of AM-FM combinations on the theory that they were not competing services. The rule was changed briefly in 1970 to prohibit AM-FM ownership but that rule was relaxed in 1971 to allow ownership of AM and FM stations in the same market. During the first half of the 1960s many AM-FM combination stations had simply duplicated the AM programming on the FM station. But in 1966 the FCC ruled that jointly owned AM and FM stations had to provide separate programming. FM owners discovered "progressive" rock and music formats that reached audiences beyond the Top 40 and MOR (middle of the road) programming common on the AM dial at that time.[40] By the 1970s FM had become a significant competitor.

The technological reasons leading to the growth of FM were the development of stereo recordings, FM stereo broadcasting, and the widespread use of stereo receivers in homes and automobiles. The FCC first authorized FM *stereo* broadcasts in 1961. At that time, the number of AM stations on the air (3,539) exceeded the number of FM stations on the air (815) by over a four to one margin. By 1971 that margin had shrunk to less than two to one as the number of FM stations increased to over 2,600 in ten years. By 1983, the number of *authorized* FM stations surpassed the number of *authorized* AM stations for the first time and in 1985 the number of *on-the-air* FM stations surpassed the number of *on-the-air* AM stations with 4,888 and 4,754 respectively. By 1995, the number of FM stations on the air exceeded the number of AM stations on the air by over 35 percent (6,788 FM and 4,923 AM).[41] Although the FCC authorized stereo AM in 1982 and adopted a standard broadcasting system in 1993, it never caught on. Music programming in stereo had become the dominant content of FM radio. Although there was still significant music content on AM, by 1995, news, news/talk, talk, religious, and sports accounted for more than 35 percent of AM formats. That same programming accounted for only about 16 percent of FM formats.[42]

RADIO STATION OPERATIONS

Basic Operations

"S." It all started with the letter "S."

In 1896 Marconi received a patent for his innovative "wireless" transmission system, a medium that freed consumers from the constraints of a "wired" communication.[43] Five years later Marconi sent his first trans-Atlantic wireless radio message, the letter "S," triggering a metamorphosis that revolutionized the mass media industry in a way paralleling that of Gutenberg's invention of movable type.

On November 2, 1920, KDKA-AM (http://www.kdkaradio.com) was the first radio station to go on the air, owned then and now by Westinghouse, which later purchased CBS and changed the corporation's name to CBS (http://www.cbsradio.com). Aside from being the nation's oldest station, KDKA-AM was the number-one rated station in the Pittsburgh market, based on Arbitron's Spring 1999 report.

A radio station's call letters identify the station and its country of origin. Call letters were originally issued at the London International Radiotelegraphic Conference in 1912 so that telegraph operators could transmit messages directly to a specific operator in a precise location. Germany was awarded the "A" and "D" letters along with "KAA" to "KCZ." The United States received "KDA" to "KZZ." The Federal Communications Commission awarded all call letters until 1983 using a fairly simple procedure. A U.S. station's call letters began with a "W" if it was located east of the Mississippi River (e.g., WABC-AM) and "K" if west of the Mississippi (KABC-AM). Approximately thirty stations in operation prior to the creation of Federal guidelines continued to use their original call letters regardless of locale, hence KDKA-AM while east of the Mississippi retained its original call letters. A directory of more than 11,000 U. S. radio stations (including mailing address, telephone numbers, station information, format, personnel, target market, etc.) is available through three web sites: (1) http://www.radioinfo.com; (2) http://www.geocities.com/ResearchTriangle/6375/origins.html; and (3) http://www.ipass.net/~whitetho/recap.htm.

KDKA-AM's original format was news, the reporting of the 1920 Presidential election results. On January 2, 1921, KDKA provided the first religious programming. Later that month it hired the first radio personality Harold W. Arlin. On March 4, 1921, it broadcast the Presidential inaugural of Warren G. Harding, the nation's 28th President. Six days later, KDKA created the first musical program, featuring soprano Ruth Roye. Sports would be added, reporting on the exploits of Babe Ruth and the resurgent New York Yankees, changing the way Americans learned about and remained informed about their beloved national pastime.[44]

Slowly, ever so slowly, radio emerged as a commercial format in the 1920s, much to the chagrin of then Secretary of Commerce Herbert Hoover, who wanted advertisements banned from the airwaves.[45] Since the birth of KDKA-AM, radio emerged as a dominant mass media format with certain clearly defined characteristics. It was in 1920, and remains today, local in orientation, intensely personal, portable, and a niche-oriented medium that is second only to television in terms of annual hourly media usage.

To some individuals, radio is the "forgotten" format, easily eclipsed by the innovative, seductive offerings of cable television's hundreds of channels, the Internet, and films (easily available either in theaters or on prerecorded videocassettes).[46] Clearly, radio is not as "big" as it once was, affecting the lives of every American, serving as the platform of choice for politicians, and being able to influence (and possibly mold) the American mind. Yet radio's ability has always been to reinvent itself, developing influential formats of "talk" and sports (including "talk sports") radio, and building on a long tradition of ethnic and college radio formats, along with a stunning coverage of all types of music. The emergence of public radio and the increasing influx of advertising dollars indicates conclusively that radio is alive and well in the United States.

How has radio survived in the face of formidable competition? What is the structure of the radio industry in the United States? What are its strengths and weaknesses? How does it compare, on the pivotal advertising front, with its visual competitors? What are the economic characteristics of radio?

THE DEMOGRAPHIC STRUCTURE OF THE RADIO INDUSTRY IN THE UNITED STATES

In 1999, upwards of 99 percent of America's households had radio sets, averaging 5.6 units per household. This represented a higher market penetration than telephones (93.9 percent), television (98.3 percent), cable television (63.4 percent), or VCRs (81 percent). Radio's place among U.S. mass media formats has remained strong since 1970 in spite of the proliferation of rival mass media formats. Table 6-5 outlines this trend between 1970 and 1998.

This vast listener base supported 9,880 radio stations in 1995, up 36.65 percent since 1970. While AM had been the frequency of choice of Americans for decades (accounting for 61.73 percent of all stations in 1970), the technological advantages offered by FM radio cut deeply into AM's market share. Newer stations tended to go FM in order to create a solid advertising platform. The Commerce Department data revealed that AM radio peaked in 1990 with 4,987 stations (53.17 percent); but it

TABLE 6-5   Radio Use in the United States: 1970–1998

	Percent of Total U.S. Households	Average Number of Sets per Household
1970	98.6	5.6
1980	99.0	5.5
1985	99.0	5.5
1988	99.0	5.6
1989	99.0	5.6
1990	99.0	5.6
1991	99.0	5.6
1992	99.0	5.6
1993	99.0	5.6
1994	99.0	5.6
1995	99.0	5.6
1996	99.0	5.6
1997	99.0	5.6
1998	99.0	5.6

Source: U.S. Department of Commerce, Bureau of the Census. *Statistical Abstract of the United States 1997* (Washington: GPO, 1997), p. 566.

declined steadily to 4,150 in 1995 (holding a 42 percent market share). Table 6-6 outlines the growth of FM stations and the decline of AM between 1970 and 1995.

Radio is a niche market, appealing to individuals who love to listen to Frank Sinatra and Ella Fitzgerald, Motown, social commentators, comics, and sports. Its audience is representative of American society, reaching out to young and old alike, urban youths and rural merchants.[47]

TABLE 6-6   Number of Radio Stations in the U.S.: 1970–1995

	AM	FM	Total	Percent Change from Previous Year
1970	4,463	2,767	7,230	
1980	4,589	3,282	7,871	+8.87
1985	4,718	3,875	8,593	+9.17
1988	4,932	4,155	9,087	+5.75
1989	4,975	4,269	9,244	+1.73
1990	4,987	4,392	9,379	+1.43
1991	4,985	4,570	9,555	+1.88
1992	4,961	4,785	9,746	+2.00
1993	4,994	4,971	9,965	+2.25
1994	4,913	5,109	10,022	+0.57
1995	4,150	5,730	9,880	−1.42

Source: U.S. Department of Commerce, Bureau of the Census. *Statistical Abstract of the United States 1997* (Washington: GPO, 1997), p. 566.

On average approximately 83 percent of the U.S. population listens regularly to radio. Its 1997 listener base was predominantly young, with the highest tallies (91.52 percent) posted by individuals between the ages of 18 and 24. Those in the 25–34 cohort were a close second, with a 90.56 percent rate. "Baby Boomers" (45–54) traditionally have been fairly active listeners (84.50 percent), although older Americans seem less interested in radio (55–64: 77.94 percent; over 65: 58.89 percent). However, as the "Baby Boomers" age, and begin to dominate the 55-plus age group, it is likely they will continue to utilize radio, substantially changing listener statistics and attracting the attention of advertisers and media buyers.[48]

Males (84.66 percent) and females (80.94 percent) tend to listen to radio with the same devotion, with similar response rates among white Americans (82.84 percent), African-Americans (85.30 percent), and Hispanic-Americans (84.06 percent). Table 6-7 provides detailed information about these demographic trends.

Other 1997 demographic data revealed the attractiveness of radio listeners as a market niche: a solid 88.15 percent of college graduates were listeners; 87.96 percent of those who attended college were listeners; and 82.27 percent of those who held only high school diplomas listened in. Of those who had not graduated from high school, 70 percent were radio listeners. Over 90 percent of those who were employed full-time were radio listeners. Over 86 percent of part-time workers listened to radio. Listenership among the unemployed (which includes retirees, students, etc.) hovered near the 70 percent level.

Radio listener rates are high among higher income levels. In the $30,000–34,999 range, 90.50 percent are radio listeners. Of those with annual wages over $50,000, the radio listening rate is 90.10 percent. Similar results were evident in the $35,000–39,999 (85.55 percent) and the $40,000–49,000 (87.97 percent) categories.

TABLE 6-7   The U.S. Radio Audience: 1996–1997

Age/Other	Percent of People Who Use Radio	
	1996	1997
18–24	91.6%	91.52%
25–34	91.0%	90.56%
35–44	89.4%	88.74%
45–54	86.7%	84.50%
55–64	77.8%	77.94%
+65	59.1%	58.89%
Total	83.4%	82.75%
Males	86.0%	84.66%
Females	81.0%	80.94%
White	83.4%	82.84%
Black	84.3%	85.30%
Other	80.1%	72.18%
Spanish Speaking	85.3%	84.06%

Source: U.S. Department of Commerce, Bureau of the Census. *Statistical Abstract of the United States 1997* (Washington: GPO, 1997), p. 566.

The relevant demographic data revealed conclusively that the nation's radio listeners were educated, employed, and earning fairly sizable sums of money—attractive indicators to advertisers and media planners on Madison Avenue.[49] Table 6-8 provides detailed information about these demographic trends.

RADIO FORMATS

In 1997, the Radio Advertising Bureau (RAB) collected data on the radio industry, and their tallies (10,112 radio stations) differed somewhat from those recorded by the Commerce Department. While Commerce's economic data is generally accurate and the most useful barometer of national events, RAB's tallies reflect their ability to monitor closely (on a weekly basis) substantive changes in this industry; so RAB is probably the best source of accurate information on radio formats in this nation.

RAB (http://www.RAB.COM/station/mgfb98/fact36.html) reported there were thirty radio formats utilized in the United States. The most popular format was country, with 2,491 stations (representing 24.63 percent of all stations). A distant second was news/talk, with 1,111 (10.99 percent); adult contemporary (902; 8.92 percent) was in third place, easily beating out the popular oldies (755; 7.4 percent) format.

The vast variety of formats clearly proves several substantive points. First, radio has been able to carve out distinct market niches that satisfies the wants and needs of U.S. consumers.[50] Second, this fragmentation, while somewhat chaotic, provides advertisers with the ability to target carefully intended audiences, some-

TABLE 6-8   Radio Listener Household Educational and Income Levels: 1996–1997

Category	1996	1997
Not H.S. Graduate	72.9%	70.00%
H.S. Graduate	82.5%	82.27%
Attended College	88.4%	87.96%
College Graduate	88.0%	88.15%
Employed Full-time	90.6%	90.27%
Employed Part-time	87.3%	86.33%
Not Employed	71.3%	70.04%
Less Than $10,000	71.8%	70.03%
$10,000–19,999	75.7%	70.96%
$20,000–29,999	79.6%	79.18%
$30,000–34,999	84.8%	90.50%
$35,000–39,999	86.9%	85.55%
$40,000–49,999	85.8%	87.98%
+$50,000	89.7%	90.10%

Source: U.S. Department of Commerce, Bureau of the Census. *Statistical Abstract of the United States 1997* (Washington: GPO, 1997), p. 566.

thing which newspapers (the other local mass media format) also tries to accomplish but far too often lacks the reach of radio.[51] Table 6-9 lists these formats utilized in 1997.

Veronis, Suhler is another major source of data on the radio industry. They rely, however, on information generated by publicly traded corporations with radio holdings, even though many stations are privately owned. Consequently, their results and categories differ from both Commerce and RAB. In spite of their utilization of a "smaller universe," their totals are of great interest to researchers looking for insight into what is, at times, a "semi-chaotic" industry.

They reported that between 1991 and 1996 a sizable number of radio stations changed their formats.[52] The largest change was in the business news niche, with a sharp reduction (–73.7 percent) in the number of stations offering this format, dropping from 57 to 15. The second largest decrease was posted by easy listening

TABLE 6-9   U.S. Radio Formats: 1997

Format	Number of Stations	Percent of All Stations
Country	2,491	24.63
News/Talk	1,111	10.99
Adult Contemporary (AC)	902	8.92
Oldies	755	7.47
Adult Standards	551	5.45
Spanish	474	4.69
Religious	404	4.00
CHR	358	3.54
Soft AC	346	3.42
Rock	262	2.59
Adult Hits, Hot AC	260	2.57
Southern Gospel	255	2.52
Classic Rock	240	2.37
Sports	220	2.18
Black Gospel	208	2.06
Classic Hits	172	1.70
Urban, Rhythm & Blues	169	1.67
Contemporary Christian	159	1.57
New Rock, Modern Rock	137	1.35
Modern AC	134	1.33
Alternative Rock	94	0.93
Jazz	75	0.74
Modern AC	69	0.68
Variety	50	0.49
Easy Listening	49	0.48
Oldies	46	0.45
Classical, Fine Arts	44	0.44
Pre-teen	40	0.40
Gospel	37	0.37

Source: http://www.RAB.COM/station/mgfb98/fact36.html.

stations (–58.2 percent; 268 to 112 stations), barely eclipsing the top 40 format (–56.9 percent; 705–304).

Formats recording increases included alternative/progressive (+345.2 percent; 31 to 138 stations), classic rock (235.4 percent; 127 to 426 stations), and news/talk (+203.2 percent; 404 to 1,225 stations). Table 6-10 outlines these trends.

While the country format is on the largest number of stations, it does not claim the largest share of the listener audience. That distinction belonged in the late 1990s to the news/talk format, as indicated in Tables 6-10 and 6-11. In fact, the share of the top markets belonging to country-formatted stations declined steadily during the late 1990s. Meanwhile, the shares of R & B/Urban and Spanish formats rose steadily during the same time period.

When discussing radio formats, it is important to keep in mind that the categories are, in reality, rather blurred. How much difference is there between, for example, Album-Oriented Rock and Alternative/Progressive? Some industry studies

TABLE 6-10   Changes in Radio Formats: 1991–1996

Format	Number of Stations		Percent Change
	1991	1996	
Country	2,314	2,537	9.6
Adult Contemporary	1,898	1,379	–27.3
News/Talk	404	1,225	203.2
Religious	661	875	32.4
Golden Oldies	729	775	6.3
Classic Rock	127	426	235.4
Standards/Big Bands	457	383	–16.2
Album Oriented Rock	339	366	8.0
Spanish	214	326	52.3
Top 40	705	304	–56.9
Urban Contemporary	191	260	36.1
Soft Contemporary	182	165	–9.3
Alternative/Progressive	31	138	345.2
Easy Listening	268	112	–58.2
All News	40	64	60.0
Jazz	28	60	114.3
Variety	66	59	–10.6
Ethnic	34	58	70.6
Black/Rhythm & Blues	87	51	–41.4
Classical	51	42	–17.6
Full Service	33	15	–54.5
Business News	57	15	–73.7
Total	8,916	9,661	8.4

Source: Veronis, Suhler & Associates. *The Veronis, Suhler & Associates Communications Industry Forecast: Historical and Projected Expenditures for 12 Industry Segments* (New York: Veronis, Suhler & Associates, 1997, p. 140).

combine all news with news/talk; and a Spanish station could be all music or news/talk but is reported by its language rather than its content. Table 6-11 highlights these issues.

RADIO RATINGS

Radio stations are in the business of selling air time to advertisers.[53] So their ratings are pivotal to their economic vitality. The Arbitron Company (http://www.arbitron.com) is the nation's preeminent radio rating service, tracking audiences in 268 local markets and releasing listener and format results quarterly for more than 2,600 stations (who pay a fee to be counted by Arbitron).

Contacting over two million consumers annually, Arbitron collects more than one million diaries in which consumers list the station(s) they listened to on a daily basis. Arbitron also offers station managers its "Maximi$er 98" and the "Media Professional" for advertising agencies. Both offer respondent database data, allowing, for example, a station to customize survey areas, demographics, and time periods. A station manager in Dallas can determine how many people listened to a specific show on all competing stations between 11:00–11:15 a.m. on December 15, 1999.

Since 1995 Arbitron has attempted to increase its diaries in 146 small markets, raise its average response rate to nearly 40 percent, and improve the sample representation for males between the ages of 18 and 34, issues of some concern to station managers and advertisers.

TABLE 6-11   National Percentage Shares of Radio Formats: 1994–1998

Format	Winter 1998	Fall 1997	Winter 1996	Fall 1995	Winter 1994
News/Talk	16.2	16.5	16.5	16.9	16.2
AC	15.1	14.4	15.0	14.1	16.8
R & B/Urban	11.8	11.9	10.7	9.8	8.7
Country	9.8	10.3	11.0	12.1	13.0
Top 40 (CHR)	8.2	8.2	7.2	8.8	9.7
AOR	6.8	6.8	7.7	7.7	8.5
Spanish	6.3	6.2	5.6	5.9	4.8
Oldies	5.7	6.1	6.5	6.6	6.5
Classic Rock	4.7	4.7	3.6	3.4	3.7
Modern Rock	4.0	4.1	4.4	3.9	2.2
Adult Standards	3.5	3.4	3.7	3.2	3.0
Jazz	3.2	3.0	3.2	3.0	—
Religious	2.2	2.0	2.1	2.1	1.9
Classical	1.8	1.7	2.0	1.8	1.9
Easy Listening	—	—	0.4	0.5	1.0
Other	0.5	0.5	0.4	0.3	0.3

Source: Various issues of *Billboard* magazine, based on Arbitron data on top ninety-four markets.

The ten largest markets monitored by Arbitron are: (1) New York; (2) Los Angeles; (3) Chicago; (4) San Francisco; (5) Philadelphia; (6) Dallas–Ft. Worth; (7) Detroit; (8) Washington, D.C.; (9) Houston–Galveston; and (10) Boston.

New York had 43 stations listed in the Spring 1998 Arbitron ratings (out of a total of 87 stations: 33 AM and 54 FM) (http://www.rronline.com/11101001lratingl.htm). The top three were: (1) WLTW-FM (Adult contemporary; 5.9 rating); (2) WSKQ-FM (tropical; also 5.9); and (3) WQHT-FM (rhythm; 5.6). The top AM station was WABC-AM (ninth overall; talk radio, although the station carries all 162 New York Yankee baseball games; 3.2). WQEW-AM (American standards) was 20th overall (1.8) in what is a highly fragmented, harshly competitive market.

Popular formats vary significantly in the top markets. In Los Angeles Spanish Adult Contemporary and Regular Mexican dominate the airwaves, whereas Urban is on top in Chicago. Stations are able to slice the demographic pie in such a way as to satisfy consumers and advertisers alike.

Some Formats

WQEW-AM (1560 AM) is one of only two commercial radio stations owned by The New York Times; the other is WQXR-FM.

Originally the AM arm of WQXR, played only classical music. The management at *The Times* decided in 1993 that New York needed a station playing American standards (the music of Frank Sinatra, Tony Bennett, Count Basie, Nat "King" Cole, Natalie Cole, Ella Fitzgerald, and the gifted Nancy Lamont) after legendary station WNEW-AM (1130 AM), home of William B. Williams, the "Make Believe Ballroom," the "Milkman's Matinee," was converted to an all business news format.

This format was followed for slightly more than five years. On December 27, 1998, *The Times* agreed to lease WQEW-AM to "Radio Disney," and the American standards format was dropped in favor of an "all Disney" children's format.

When WQEW-AM played American standards, it had an exceptionally devoted listener audience covering the entire New York–New Jersey–Connecticut region; individuals in the Middle Atlantic region, the New England corridor, areas east of the Mississippi also picked up the station's signal. While news, the weather, stock reports, and popular medical features were important to these listeners, they tuned in for music. On any given day, listeners heard perceptive comments about songwriters Rogers and Hart, Johnny Mercer, Duke Ellington, Dietz and Schwartz, and the Gershwins; but the sounds of music seduced these listeners; and the music centered on Sinatra. Each weekday between 3:30 and 4:00 p.m., the station played "Sinatra in the Afternoon"; on Saturday between 10:00 a.m. and 2:00 p.m., it was four hours of Sinatra.

On Friday, May 15, 1998, when the world awoke to find out that Sinatra died late on May 14th in California, scores of reporters descended on the station to interview the on-air personalities about the man and his music; and the station went "all Sinatra," playing his recorded 1,307 songs until he was buried on the following Wednesday, duplicating its eighty-one hours of nonstop Sinatra in December 1995 when the singer turned eighty years old. For five glorious years, WQEW-AM was, for hundreds of thousands of listeners, Sinatra's station, where they listened attentively, if not reverently, to "Cheek to Cheek," "My One and Only Love," "The Best Is Yet to Come," "Talk to Me," "Prisoner of Love," or the haunting "In the Wee Small Hours of the Morning."

Yet WQEW was also known as the home of Dinah Washington, Peggy Lee, Nancy Wilson, Matt Munro, and Diana Krall. Every Monday afternoon the "WQEW Cabaret" show featured live entertainers, ranging from Rosemary Clooney to Tony Bennett. Saturday night was "Jazz Straight Ahead"; Sunday evening was the "Broadway" show followed by the "Big Bands." Regardless of the time of the day, or the day itself, this was home to the largest listener audience of American standards in the United States.

Radio stations change formats constantly, a fact of life in a mercurial industry; but the demise of WQEW-AM's American standards format left about 650,000 listeners with a song in their hearts and tears on their eyes.

WBGO-FM (88.3 FM; http://www.wbgo.org) is one of the best known National Public Radio (NPR) stations in the United States.[54] Founded in 1976 in Newark, New Jersey, as the educational radio for the Newark Board of Education, in 1979, it became a not-for-profit, community-based station widely recognized for its jazz programming. Relying on a traditional mix of corporate, business, foundation, listener, and governmental grants, WBGO serves an eclectic community audience (averaging 325,000 individuals each week) that is 14 percent Hispanic-American, 39 percent African-American, and 46 percent Caucasian.

WBGO's programming reflects the NPR spirit with its amalgamation of NPR-produced features and WGBO-generated programs. About 250 NPR stations carry WBGO's "Jazz Set with Branford Marsalis" and Bob Porter's superb "Portraits in Blue." Porter, who has written for *Cashbox, Downbeat,* and *Radio Free Jazz,* was nominated for a Grammy in 1979 and won it in 1980 for his liner notes for the five record box set of "The Complete Charlie Parker on Savoy." A "typical" week at WBGO will highlight the works of Slide Hampton, Harry "Sweets" Edison, Betty Carter, Charles Mingus, Horace Silver, and Carmen McRae. Regrettably, jazz in the United States is an underserved musical format, and WBGO's efforts, and skilled programming, helps keep this all-American format alive and well.

College radio has served as the training ground for generations of future professional radio and television personalities and program directors, along with a sizable contingent of individuals who just loved working at a college station for the fun of it.[55] One of the more interesting college stations is WFUV-FM (90.7 FM; http:/ hvww.wfuv.org), the radio station of Fordham University. Its on-air alumni include Charles Osgood (currently on CBS radio and the host of the critically acclaimed "CBS News Sunday Morning") and Alan Alda.

Relying on a small number of professional on-air personalities (including well-known New York radio personality Meg Griffin) to help train the next generation of radio announcers, disk jockeys, and managers, WFUV's programming is eclectic and reflective of the City's and nation's ethnic mosaic. The station's "City Folk" segments, hosted by Griffin in the 2:00–6:00 p.m. time slot, allows listeners to hear Leon Redbone, the soundtrack from the film "Dead Man Walking," and rare concert performances by Bob Dylan, and Elvis Costello. Ethnic programming includes Irish folk songs and polkas; and Christine Lavin has served as the guest host on the Sunday "breakfast" show. Aside from the traffic reports and NPR features, WFUV also includes some religious programming, coverage of the Fordham Rams' football (once coached by Hall of Famer Vince Lombardi) and basketball games (Denzel Washington played on the JV), lectures by the University's professors, and a weekly interview with Father O'Hare (President of Fordham).

Table 6-12 lists the three most successful formats in the top twenty U.S. markets for the Spring 1998 Arbitron ratings period.

RADIO COMPETITION

Radio competes with every other mass media format for consumer usage.[56] The U.S. Department of Commerce carefully tracks media usage trends in the United States. While the average consumer above the age of 18 (Commerce tracks individuals above the age of 12 for recorded music, films in theaters, and video games) increased his/her annual media usage between 1990 and 1998 (from 3,267 to 3,469 hours—an increase of +6.18 percent), radio usage declined 6.87 percent (from 1,135 to 1,057 hours). Commerce's projections for 1999 and 2000 indicated a modest leveling off to 1,047 hours in each year. Yet radio retained its second place foothold among American consumers (trailing only television's 1,625 hours in 1998); recorded music stood at 315 hours and newspapers at 160 hours.[57]

In essence all of the mass media are in a "zero sum game." With annual increases in total media usage expected to hover somewhere near the 1 percent mark (1997–1998: +0.93 percent; 1998–1999: +0.81 percent; 1999–2000: +1.23 percent), any medium that wants to increase sharply its market share of time must take hours away from competing media. Television's hold over consumers is legendary, and unlikely to shrink dramatically, although cable will continue to cut deeply into the position of the networks. The Internet's surge in annual consumer use will probably plateau in 1999–2000 between 25 and 28 hours, if Commerce's projections hold.[58]

What media are vulnerable to radio's potential inroads? Radio and newspapers are both local in nature, portable, personal, and inexpensive (radio's only costs after the purchase of a unit, which can be obtained for only a few dollars, are electricity or batteries). Newspaper is the one format vulnerable to incursions by both radio and the Internet; and radio marketers and advertising executives have targeted newspapers for confrontations in the traditional marketplace and the Internet's "market space."

TABLE 6-12   Top Radio Formats in the Top Twenty Markets in the United States: Spring 1998

Market	Top Three Stations and Formats		
	No. 1	No. 2	No. 3
New York	WLTW-FM AC	WSKQ-FM Tropical	WQHT-FM CHR/Rhythm
Los Angeles	KLVE-FM Spanish AC	KSCA-FM Regular Mexican	KFI-AM Talk
Chicago	WGCI-AM Urban	WGN-AM News/Talk	WBBM-FM CHR/Rhythm
San Francisco	KGO-AM News/Talk	KOIT-AM AC	KLYD-FM CHR/Rhythm
Philadelphia	KYW-AM News	WBEB-FM AC	WDAS-FM Urban AC
Dallas/Ft. Worth	KHKS-FM Pop	KKDA-FM Urban	KVIL-FM AC
Detroit	WJLB-FM Urban	WNIC-AM AC	WJR-FM Talk
Washington, D.C.	WHUR-FM Urban	WPGC-FM AC Rhythm	WMZQ-FM Country
Houston-Galveston	KODA-FM AC	KBXX-FM Rhythm	KRBE-FM Pop
Boston	WBZ-FM News	WJMN-FM Rhythm	WMJX-FM AC
Miami-Ft. Lauderdale	WEDR-FM Urban	WPOW-FM CHR/Rhythm	WLYF-FM AC
Atlanta	WSB-AM Talk	WVEE-FM Urban	WSTR-FM CHR/Pop
Seattle	KIRO-AM News Talk	KUBE-FM CHR/Rhythm	KBSG-AM Oldies
Minneapolis-St. Paul	WCCO-AM Full Service	KQRS-FM Adult Alt.	KDWB-FM CHR/Pop
San Diego	KYXY-FM AC	KFMB-FM Hot AC	KSON-FM Country
Nassau-Suffolk	WALK-FM AC	WHTZ-FM CHR/Pop	WXRK-FM Alt.
Phoenix	KNIX-FM Country	KZZP-FM Hot AC	KTAR-AM News/Talk
St. Louis	KMOX-AM Talk	WIL-FM Country	KEZK-FM AC
Baltimore	WERQ-FM CHR/Rhythm	KPOC-FM Country	WBAL-AM News/Talk
Pittsburgh	KDKA-AM News/Talk	WDVE-FM Rock	WBZZ-FM CHR/Pop

Source: http://www.rronline.com.

ADVERTISING TRENDS

Commercial radio broadcasters are in business to sell time to advertisers. What is sold are the thoughts and emotions of segmented listeners in a specific market and demographic group—for example, teenagers in Pittsburgh or Reno, African-American women between 18 and 49 in Los Angeles or Atlanta, Hispanic-American senior citizens in Miami or Philadelphia, or Caucasian men over 50 in Iowa City or Cooperstown, New York.

Every advertising platform has certain strengths and weaknesses, and radio is no exception. Its advantages are formidable. It can target audiences with some precision since it reaches individuals in predetermined geographical or demographic cohorts at specific times of the day. Its greatest strength is "drive time," catching consumers going to and from work. Radio also offers advertisers speed and flexibility. Radio's closing period is the shortest of all of the mass media since ad copy can be submitted, or changed, up to air time, allowing advertisers the ability to respond quickly and decisively to changes in the marketplace. Radio traditionally has sold shows, personalities, or segments of a show ("The Chase Cabaret Show"), features that appeal to many advertisers.

In addition, radio's cost to reach every thousand listeners (knows as "CPM") has been among the lowest of all of the mass media, allowing advertisers to repeat their commercials frequently; its use of words and imagery excites the listener's imagination, and it is portable. Lastly, radio has an exceptionally high level of acceptance among consumers because it is personal; radio personalities talk "directly" to the listener, become "part of the family," and address areas of interest and concern to the listener.[59]

Yet there are pronounced disadvantages. People have to listen to the radio, and attentiveness has always plagued it. Listeners might walk out of the room and miss a commercial, batteries in the Walkman unit might die, or the verbal message could be too complicated and soon forgotten. Radio is an audio but not a visual medium; there are no charts, demonstrations, or young actors or actresses to sell a product. Lastly, some advertisers believe there is too much "ad clutter" on the radio, negating its effectiveness, although the most recent study indicated clearly that radio is viewed as one of the least-cluttered mass media formats.[60]

Overall, radio's total advertising revenues increased 226.99 percent between 1980 and 1996, with strong upward ticks in 1993 (+9.28 percent), 1994 (+11.34 percent),1995 (+9.22 percent), and 1996 (+5.76 percent). However, its share of the total U.S. advertising market stood at 6.91 percent in 1980 and 6.99 percent in 1996, barely posting any statistically significant increase.[61]

In essence, radio's advertising revenues plateaued. If it plans to generate meaningful increases between 1999 and 2004, it will have to siphon dollars away from competing media, almost certainly newspapers. Table 6-13 outlines radio's advertising revenue stream between 1980 and 1996.

TABLE 6-13   Radio Advertising Revenues: 1980–1996

	Radio Ad Revenues ($ Million)	Percent of Total U.S. Ad Expenditures
1980	$ 3,702	6.91%
1985	6,490	6.85%
1988	7,798	6.61%
1989	8,323	6.72%
1990	8,726	6.78%
1991	8,476	6.71%
1992	8,654	6.59%
1993	9,457	6.85%
1994	10,529	7.02%
1995	11,500	7.10%
1996	12,105	6.99%

Source: U.S. Department of Commerce, Bureau of the Census. *Statistical Abstract of the United States 1997* (Washington: GPO, 1997), p. 578.

Local radio advertising accounts for the vast majority of dollars extracted from corporate America. In 1980 it accounted for 74.01 percent of all radio ad revenues, jumping to 77.38 percent in 1995 and 78.65 percent in 1996. Network revenues hinged at a paltry 4.94 percent in 1980, decreasing to 4.17 percent in 1995 and 4.21 percent in 1996. Spot revenues also dropped from 21.04 percent in 1980 to 17.03 percent in 1995 and 17.14 percent in 1996. Table 6-14 outlines these trends.

TABLE 6-14   Radio Advertising: Network, Spot, and Local Advertising Revenues: 1980–1996

	U.S. Advertising Expenditures	Network	Spot	Local
1980	$ 53,550	$183	$ 779	$2,740
1985	94,750	365	1,335	4,790
1988	118,050	425	1,418	5,955
1989	123,930	476	1,547	6,300
1990	126,640	482	1,635	6,609
1991	126,400	490	1,575	6,411
1992	131,290	424	1,505	6,725
1993	138,080	458	1,657	7,432
1994	150,030	463	1,902	8,164
1995	161,860	480	1,959	8,869
1996	173,200	510	2,075	9,520

Source: U.S. Department of Commerce, Bureau of the Census. *Statistical Abstract of the United States 1997* (Washington: GPO, 1997), p. 578.

Nationally, the top radio advertising category was retail establishments, spending $394.8 million in 1997 (+17 percent over 1996). Business and consumer services were a close second with $375.3 million (+27.5 percent over 1996); automotive, auto accessories, and equipment rounded out the top three with a +29.8 percent surge in ad allocations, hitting $143.2 million in 1997. These tallies exclude local advertising allocations, which are extremely difficult to track because of radio's market fragmentation. Table 6-15 lists the top twenty national advertising categories in 1996 and 1997.

The top national advertiser in 1997 was the Chrysler Corporation, allocating $58.322 million, split between networks ($43.812 million) and spot national ads ($14.510 million), just eclipsing MCI Communications Corporation's $54.319 million, which spent almost all of its budget on spot rather than national advertisements. The venerable Sears Roebuck & Company stood in third place ($44.034 million), with General Motors Corporation ($39.547 million) and Chattem, Inc. (Gold Bond; Pamprin; $35.165 million; all allocated for network ads) rounding the top five. All of these figures exclude any local advertising expenditures. Table 6-16 lists the top twenty national advertisers in 1997 with total, network, and sport ad sums.

TABLE 6-15   National Radio Advertising Categories: 1996–1997 ($ Million)

1997 Rank	Category	Advertising Expenditures		
		1997	1996	% Change
1.	Retail	$394.8	$337.5	+17.0
2.	Business & Consumer Service	375.3	294.2	+27.5
3.	Automotive Accessories & Equipment	143.2	133.4	+29.8
4.	Entertainment & Amusements	116.4	106.0	+9.8
5.	Publishing & Media	105.6	96.7	+9.2
6.	Food & Food Products	98.3	92.6	+6.2
7.	Travel, Hotels, & Resorts	67.7	75.6	10.4
8.	Insurance & Real Estate	55.8	45.4	+22.0
9.	Computers, Office Equipment, & Stationery	53.6	32.8	+63.4
10.	Confectionery, Snacks, & Soft drinks	38.0	27.2	+39.7
11.	Drugs & Remedies	38.0	35.9	+5.8
12.	Gasoline, Lubricants, & Fuels	31.4	38.2	−17.8
13.	Horticulture & Farming	30.0	25.5	+17.6
14.	Beer & Wine	23.9	29.0	−17.6
15.	Toiletries & Cosmetics	21.1	10.7	+97.2
16.	Electronic Entertainment Equipment	11.3	14.7	−23.1
17.	Direct Response Companies	11.2	15.8	−29.1
18.	Household Equipment & Supplies	8.8	3.7	+137.8
19.	Apparel, Footwear, & Accessories	8.1	7.2	+12.5
20.	Liquor	8.0	2.8	+185.7

Source: http://www.RAB.COM/station/mgPo98/fact27.html.

TABLE 6-16   Radio's Top Twenty National Advertisers: 1997 ($ Million)

Rank	Advertiser	Total	Network	Spot
1.	Chrysler Corp.	$58.322	$43.812	514.510
2.	MCI Communications Corp.	54.319	1.375	52.944
3.	Sears Roebuck & Co.	44.034	37.366	6.667
4.	General Motors Corp.	39.547	18.035	21.512
5.	Chattem, Inc.	35.165	35.165	—
6.	AT&T Corp.	33.634	19.703	13.930
7.	National Amusements Inc. (Comedy Central; Blockbuster, UPN Network)	33.083	3.286	29.797
8.	Warner Lambert Co.	30.270	29.916	0.34
9.	Proctor & Gamble Co.	29.267	22.415	6.852
10.	News Corp. (FOX TV; 20th Cent. Fox)	28.730	4.443	24.287
11.	William Wrigley, Jr. Co.	26.643	23.676	2.966
12.	VISA USA Inc.	25.968	14.367	11.601
13.	Bell Atlantic Corp.	25.904	—	25.904
14.	Pepsico, Inc.	25.731	8.016	17.715
15.	SBC Communications	25.412	—	25.412
16.	Chrysler Corp. Dealer Associations	25.172	—	25.172
17.	USWest, Inc.	24.734	—	24.734
18.	CompUSA Inc.	24.420	—	24.420
19.	Philip Morris Companies, Inc.	22.868	16.420	6.448
20.	U.S. Government	22.022	12.892	9.110

Source: http://www.RAB.COM/station/mgfb98/fact28.html.

FINANCIAL PERFORMANCE CHARACTERISTICS

Statistical data on radio's income and expenditures reveal that historically this mass media format has been a financially profitable endeavor. In 1996, radio generated $8.765 billion in operating revenues and had operating expenses of $7.253 billion.

Veronis, Suhler & Associates projected a 9.3 percent compound annual growth rate between 1996 and 2001 for radio stations, a 4.4 percent increase for radio networks, for an industry total of 9.1 percent. Radio station projected income by 2001 should top the $18.3 billion mark, with the networks accounting for another $650 million. Veronis, Suhler also expects radio operators to "diversify their formats and increase their appeal to underserved states. In the process the overall radio audience will expand."[62] In addition, the emergence of strong, national radio group owners will be able to package group ad buys more successfully, increase the total audience, make radio an even more attractive mass media format, and prod national advertisers to allocate more sums for radio advertisements. The end results will be more ad dollars spent on radio, an increase in efficiency, and a surge in the fiscal strength of radio networks.

Radio revenues and operating incomes increased 26.04 percent between 1993 and 1995, according to U.S. Commerce Department data. In 1993, operating revenues stood at $6.954 billion, increasing to $7.98 billion in 1994 (+14.75 percent) and $8.765 billion in 1995 (+9.84 percent).

Operating expenses also surged ahead, up 14.82 percent between 1993 and 1995. By 1995 expenses stood at $7.253 billion, with payroll accounting for 40.53 percent of that amount. Other major allocations included: benefits, including employer contributions to Social Security (5.68 percent); broadcast rights (4.03 percent); music license fees (2.77 percent); depreciation (6.7 percent); lease and rental (3.3 percent); purchased repairs (1.19 percent); insurance (1.03 percent); telephone and other purchased communication services (1.82 percent); purchased utilities (1.54 percent); purchased advertising (5.64 percent); taxes (1.24 percent); and "other," 24.53 percent.

Entry barriers into radio broadcasting in the forms of obtaining licenses and substantial investments in physical plant and equipment are not as high as for radio's sister communications industry, television. Dun and Bradstreet's *Industry Norms and Key Business Ratios* indicates some key "balance sheet" differences between the two. In 1997, the typical radio station reported fixed assets (plant and equipment) of approximately $480,000, compared to nearly five times that sum ($2.8 million) for the typical television stations. Radio stations tend to be more liquid than television stations, having a higher percentage of their current assets in cash than their video "cousins," 14.8 percent cash for radio compared to 9.3 percent cash for television. Both of these mediums tend to be more profitable than print operations. Except for the lowest quartile of stations, all of them have better profitability ratios than the print media, as indicated in Table 6-17. Radio and television had net profit

TABLE 6-17 Profitability Percentage Ratios of the Mass Media: 1997

	Radio	Television	Newspapers	Periodicals	Books
Upper Quartile					
Return on Sales	15.4	22.8	9.8	11.5	7.9
Return on Assets	15.6	13.0	16.5	23.2	13.8
Return on Net Worth	38.2	28.9	29.0	54.3	28.4
Median					
Return on Sales	6.7	7.9	5.7	5.0	3.2
Return on Assets	5.7	7.8	9.0	8.8	5.5
Return on Net Worth	11.2	12.7	16.3	18.8	12.7
Lower Quartile					
Return on Sales	(.01)	(1.6)	2.6	1.7	.01
Return on Assets	0.4	0.1	4.5	3.1	0.2
Return on Net Worth	0.9	2.1	7.4	5.6	1.7

Source: Dun & Bradstreet. *Industry Norms and Key Financial Ratios* (New York: Dun & Bradstreet Credit Sources, 1998).

after taxes of 7.7 percent and 10.2 percent respectively, compared to newspapers' 6.1 percent, periodicals' 6.3 percent, and book publishing's 4.7 percent.[63]

What is a radio station worth? What, precisely, is purchased? In reality, a station is not just a physical plant with studios, offices, a tower, and a transmitter. Nor is it merely a going concern with accounts receivables, billings, and goodwill. A station is, in reality, an FCC license to do business in a specific geographical area, which is, clearly, a scarce commodity in a highly-regulated mass media industry.

More often than not, the operating license is the station's most valuable asset; it is certainly its most valuable long-term asset since new licenses are simply not available in most major markets. Consequently, the only way to enter such a market is to purchase an existing station and its license at whatever price the market commands.

This is a classic case of supply and demand. While there has been a substantial increase in the total number of AM and FM stations in this nation since the end of World War II, this proliferation did not keep pace with what has been a staggering demand for these licenses. The net result was, overall, a sizable increase in the value of the average station and, in essence, what individuals or corporations were forced to pay in order to go into the radio business.

This pattern has gone on unabated since 1955. That year 242 stations changed hands, and the average selling price was $112,946. By 1965 the average price for a station stood at $143,787 (+27.31 percent). The Consumer Price Index (CPI) grew 30.71 percent between 1995 and 1965, indicating that station prices did not keep pace with inflation.

However, by 1975, the radio industry started to witness the dramatic impact of a strong demand and a limited supply. That year the average station was sold for $361,063 (+151.11 percent over 1965). The growth in the CPI between 1965 and 1975 was only 66.05 percent. This pace picked up momentum by 1985 when 1,558 stations exchanged hands for an average price of $908,098 (+151.51 percent in only ten years while the CPI surged upward 100 percent). By 1995, the average price of the 524 transactions surged well beyond the million-dollar mark when it hit $1,512,290. The next year that sum seemed ridiculously small when 671 stations cost on average $4,233,710.

The average price paid for a station increased more than 3,648 percent between 1955 and 1996. In 1997, individual stations in large markets typically sold for thirteen to eighteen times their cash flows; stations in smaller markets lagged somewhat selling for eight to ten times cash flow. A single station in a major market (e.g., Los Angeles–Glendale, CA) might command as much as $112.5 million. Stations in smaller markets (e.g., Milledgeville, GA or Hampton, NH) were going for about $1 million.

By 1998, merger costs exploded. CBS spent $2.6 billion to acquire the American Radio Systems Corp; and Chancellor Media Corp. purchased the CapStar Broadcasting Corp. for $4.1 billion. Table 6-18 provides information about merger transactions and average prices between 1955 and 1996.

TABLE 6-18 Radio Station Transactions: 1955–1996

	Number of Stations Sold	Total Amount Paid for All Radio Transactions	Average Price Paid per Radio Station
1955	242	$ 27,333,104	$ 112,946
1965	389	55,933,300	143,787
1975	363	131,065,860	361,063
1985	1,558	1,441,886,073	908,098
1995	524	792,440,000	1,512,290
1996	671	2,840,820,000	4,233,710

Source: Broadcasting and Cable Yearbook, 1998, Vol. 2 (New Providence, NJ: R.R. Bowker, 1998, pp. A-104, A-105, A-116); also see Sara Brown, "Living Large in 1997," *Broadcasting and Cable,* 3 February 1993: 32.

CONCLUSION

Radio has changed with the times since the day KDKA-AM went on the air. Radio empires have been created, allowing owners and advertisers to reach a wider audience and to consolidate back-office operations, adding dollars directly to the bottom line. Deregulation offered owners the ability to wage innovative, successful campaigns against newspapers and television in order to increase their share of the total U.S. advertising pool. Radio's niche marketing allowed marketers the ability to reach young, mobile audiences, an exceptionally attractive demographic group. Radio usage stood at approximately 3 1/2 hours per day; and it seemed positioned to keep its audience against the debilitating incursions of the Internet or cable television.

Listeners unable to pick up their favorite station, perhaps former residents of New York or New Jersey living in Orlando, Florida eager to listen to the New York Yankees on WABC-AM could "tune in" via the Internet (http://www. broadcast.com) and catch some baseball heroics described by John Sterling and Michael Kay.

Hundreds of other stations around the country are also available. On any given day, a college student in the Bronx, NY or an individual in Bergenfield, NJ can listen to WDRV-FM (Adult Contemporary) in Pittsburgh, PA, KOGO-AM (Talk Radio) in San Diego, CA, WERO-FM (Adult Contemporary) in Greenville, NC, KSKY-FM (Christian Music and Talk Radio) in Dallas, TX, WQTM-AM (Sports Radio) in Orlando, FL, WARM-FM (Adult Contemporary) in York, PA, or KKZX-FM (Classic Rock) in Spokane, WA.

By the end of the 1990s and the turn of century (the Millennium), radio was no longer the forgotten medium. It was a force in the mass media environment, it made money for owners, and it satisfied the diverse wants and needs of its listeners—business characteristics that would make even Peter Drucker smile.

NOTES

[1]See generally, Robert Picard, *Media Economics* (Newbury Park, CA: Sage, 1989); Alan B. Albarran, *Media Economics* (Ames, Iowa: Iowa State University Press, 1996); Alan B. Albarran and Sylvia M. Chan-Olmstead, *Global Media Economics* (Ames, Iowa: Iowa State University Press, 1998).

[2]U.S. Bureau of the Census, *Statistical Abstract of the United States: 1977 (117th edition),* Washington, D.C., 1997: 565.

[3]General historical references are, Christopher H. Sterling and John M. Kittross, *Stay Tuned: A Concise History of American Broadcasting* (Belmont, CA: Wadsworth Publishing Company, 1978); Gleason L. Archer, *History of Radio to 1926* (New York: Arno Press, 1971, reprint of a 1938 publication by The American Historical Society, Inc., New York); Thomas T. Eoyang, *An Economic Study of the Radio Industry in the United States of America* (New York: Arno Press, 1974, reprint of a 1936 doctoral dissertation, Columbia University, 1936); Hiram L. Jome, *Economics of the Radio Industry* (New York: Arno Press, 1971, reprint of 1925 edition, New York: A. W. Shaw Company); "Brief History of Broadcasting and Cable," *Broadcasting and Cable Yearbook,* 1995: xiii.

[4]Archer, supra note 3, 199.

[5]While WBL (later WWJ) Detroit also has a good claim to being the oldest regular broadcast station, most historians have concluded that KDKA holds the distinction.

[6]*FCC v. WNCN Listeners Guild,* 450 U.S. 582, 101 S.Ct. 1266 (1981).

[7]See, e.g., Alan Sloan, "In the Land of Giants," *Newsweek,* 10 August 1998: 4; Fred Vogelstein, "A Really Big Disconnect: You Call This Reform?" *U.S. News and World Report,* 2 February 1998: 39.

[8]Wendy Beech, "Deregulation: Bonanza or Bust (How to Take Advantage of the 1996 Telecommunications Act)," *Black Enterprise,* May 1998: 93.

[9]47 U.S.C. § 307 (c) 1.

[10]Donald M. Gillmor, Jerome A. Barron, and Todd F. Simon, *Mass Communication Law,* 6th ed. (Belmont, CA: Wadsworth Publishing Co., 1998: 711).

[11]T. Barton Carter, et al., *The First Amendment and The Fourth Estate,* 6th ed. (Westbury, NY: Foundation Press, 1994: pp. 609–619).

[12]See, e.g., "Sage Acquires Stations," *New York Times,* 26 June 1996: C3–national; "Chancellor Agrees to Buy 8 Radio Stations," *New York Times,* 16 May 1996: C4–national; "American Radio Merging with Henry Broadcasting," *Broadcasting and Cable,* 25 March 1996: 14; Cheryl Heuton, "The Large Get Larger: SFX Purchase of Liberty Continues Run on Stations in Big Markets," *Mediaweek,* 4 December 1995.

[13]"The New Empire of the Air," *U.S. News and World Report,* 1 July 1996: 10.

[14]"Radio's New Order," *Broadcasting & Cable,* 23 June 1997: 26.

[15]Sara Brown, "Living Large in 1997," *Broadcasting and Cable,* 3 February 1998: 32.

[16]Ibid.

[17]Donna Petrozzello, "Radio Group Heads Foresee Consolidation, Format Diversity," *Broadcasting & Cable,* 24 October 1944: 3.

[18]Robert P. Rogers and John R. Woodbury, "Market Structure, Program Diversity, and Radio Audience Size," *Contemporary Economic Policy,* January 1996: 81.

[19]Christina Merrill, "Advertising: No Changes in Rates . . . Yet," *Mediaweek,* 15 September 1997: 36.

[20]Gerry Boehme, "The Myth of Duopoly Control," *Radio and Records,* 12 June 1996: 20.

[21]Gerry Boehme, "Duopolies Don't Inflate Market Costs," *Radio and Records,* 10 July 1998: 18.

[22]Michael Freeman, Betsy Sharkey and Rachel Fischer, "The Price is Not Right; Consolidation, LMAs are Raising Broadcast Ad Rates, Buyers Told," *Mediaweek,* 16 February 1998: 8; "Buyers Can See Clearly Now: Prices Are Climbing," *Mediaweek,* 25 May 1998: 14.

[23]Chris McConnell, "Justice Studies More Radio Mergers," *Broadcasting and Cable,* 25 May 1998: 19.

[24]"Study Reveals Top Advertisers," *Billboard,* 13 April 1996: 85.

[25]"Soundata Consumer Panel," *NARM Sounding Board,* March 1996 (Retrieved from NARM's internet site, http://www.narm.com.).

[26]Warner Communications, Inc., "The Prerecorded Music Market: An Industry Survey," reprinted in *NARAS Institute Journal,* Vol. 2, No. 1 (1978): 77.

[27]CBS Records, "Today's Singles Buyer," distributed at the NARM Convention.

[28]Paul Hirsch, "The Structure of the Popular Music Industry," University of Michigan Institute for Social Research monograph (1969).

[29]Edgar A. Grunwald, "Program Production History 1927 and 1937," in *Variety's 1937–1938 Radio Directory* (1937).

[30]*Id.*

[31]*RCA Mfg. Co., Inc. v. Whiteman,* 144 F.2d 86 (2d Cir. 1940).

[32]*Id.,* at 90.

[33]"The Bionic Radio," *Billboard,* 21 May 1977: RS-71 (Century of Recorded Sound Special Issue).

[34]*Id.,* at RS-96.

[35]"Radio Meets the TV Challenge and Re-invents Itself," *Media Week, Radio 75th Anniversary Supplement,* 4 September 1995: Supp. Page 20.

[36]R. Serge Denisoff, *Solid Gold* (New Brunswick, NJ: Transaction Books, 1975), notes the 1955 date at 233. Russell Sanjek and David Sanjek, *American Popular Music Business in the 20th Century* (1991) note it as KOWH, Omaha at 109.

[37]"The Bionic Radio," *Billboard,* 21 May 1977: RS-71 (Century of Recorded Sound Special Issue).

[38]Data from "Radio Billings 1935–1974," *Broadcasting Yearbook* (1976): C-298.

[39]That number represents the number of *authorized* stations at the beginning of 1922. By the end of 1922 there were an estimated 382 broadcast stations in the U.S. Hiram L. Jome, *History of Broadcasting* (New York: Arno Press, 1971: 69, originally published as *Economics of the Radio Industry.* Chicago: A.W. Shaw Company, 1925).

[40]See generally, R. Serge Denisoff, *Tarnished Gold* (New Brunswick, NJ: Transaction Books, 1986); Phillip H. Ennis, *The Seventh Stream: The Emergence of Rocknroll* (Hanover, NH: Wesleyan Univ. Press, 1992); Russell Sanjek and David Sanjek, *American Popular Music Business in the 20th Century* (New York: Oxford Univ. Press, 1991).

[41]"Record of Radio Station Growth Since Television Began," *Broadcasting & Cable Yearbook* (1995): B-655.

[42]"U.S. and Canada Radio Programming Formats," *Broadcasting and Cable Yearbook, 1995*: B-592.

[43]Erik Barnouw, *A Tower in Babel: A History of Broadcasting in the United States, v. I to 1933* (New York: Oxford University Press, 1966, pp. 7–198); and Susan J. Douglas, *Inventing American Broadcasting 1899–1922* (Baltimore: Johns Hopkins University Press, 1987, pp. 17–183).

[44]A highly useful study was written by Joseph E. Baudino and John M. Kittross. "Broadcasting's Oldest Stations: An Examination of Four Claimants." *Journal of Broadcasting* 21 (Winter 1977): 61–83.

[45]Dwight H. Teeter and Don R. Le Duc, *Law of Mass Communications: Freedom and Control of Print and Broadcast Media* (Westbury: The Foundation Press, 1995, pp. 87–89). An exceptionally useful article was written by Louise Benjamin, "Working It Out Together: Radio Policy from Hoover to the Radio Act of 1927," *Journal of Broadcasting & Electronic Media* 42 (Spring 1998): 221–236.

[46]Edward C. Pearce and Everette E. Dennis, eds., *Radio: The Forgotten Medium* (New Brunswick: Transaction Publishers, 1995, pp. xv–xxi).

[47]Geoffrey P. Hull, *The Recording Industry* (Boston: Allyn and Bacon, 1998, pp. 95–105). One of the most useful studies was written by Leo Bogart. *Strategy in Advertising: Matching Media and Messages to Markets and Motivations* (Lincolnwood: NTC Business Books, 1990, pp. 8–115). Also see Albert C. Book, Norman D. Cary, Stanley I. Tannenbaum, and Frank Brady, *The Radio and Television Commercial.* (Lincolnwood: NTC Business Books, 1996, pp. 21–25); and Jodeane Newcomb Brownlee and Michael L. Hilt, "A Comparison of Two Omaha Radio Talk Shows: Local vs. National Issues," *Feedback* 39 (Spring 1998): 8–16.

[48]V. Parker Lessig and C. When Park, "Promotional Perspectives of Reference Group Influence: Advertising Implications," *Journal of Advertising* 7 (1978): 41–47; Michael J. Ryan, "Behavioral Intention Formation: the Interdependency of Attitudinal and Social Influence," *Journal of Consumer Research* 9 (December 1982): 263–278.

[49]Paul Surgi Speck and Michael T. Elliott, "Predictors of Advertising Avoidance in Print and Broadcast Media," *Journal of Advertising* 26 (1997): 61–76; Jonathan David Tankel and Wenmouth Williams, Jr., "The Economics of Contemporary Radio," in *Media Economics: Theory and Practice,* eds., Alison Alexander, James Owers, and Rod Carveth (Hillside: Lawrence Erlbaum Associates, 1998, pp. 185–198).

[50]Richard Vaughn, "How Advertising Works: A Planning Model Revisited." *Journal of Advertising Research* 26 (February/March 1986): 57–66.

[51]Avery M. Abernathy, "Differences Between Advertising and Program Exposure for Car Radio Listening," *Journal of Advertising Research* 31 (April/May 1991): 33–42; Rajeev Batra and Douglas M. Stayman, "The Role of Mood in Advertising Effectiveness," *Journal of Consumer Research* 17 (September 1990): 203–214; and William O. Bearden and Michael J. Etzel, "Reference Group Influence on Product and Brand Purchase Decisions," *Journal of Consumer Research* 9 (September 1982): pp. 183–194; William O. Bearden, Richard G. Netemeyer, and Jesse E. Teel, "Measurement of Consumer Susceptibility to Interpersonal Influence," *Journal of Consumer Research* 15 (March 1989): 473–481.

[52]Veronis, Suhler & Associates, *The Veronis, Suhler & Associates Communications Industry Forecast: Historical and Projected Expenditures for 12 Industry Segments* (New York: Veronis, Suhler & Associates, 1997, p. 140).

[53]Hugh Malcolm Beville, Jr., *Audience Ratings: Radio, Television, Cable* (Hillsdale: Lawrence Erlbaum, 1988, pp. 8–49); see Beville's *Social Stratification of the Radio Audience* (Princeton: Princeton University Press, 1989, pp. 11–21).

[54]Steven Berry and Joel Waldfogel. "Free Entry and Social Inefficiency in Radio Broadcasting," *NBER Working Paper No. 5528*, pp. 1–10; and Steven Berry and Joel Waldfogel, "Public Radio in the United States: Does It Correct for Market Failure or Cannibalize Commercial Stationed, *NBER Working Paper No. 6057*, pp. 1–9.

[55]Peter M. Lewis and Jerry Booth, *The Invisible Medium: Public, Commercial, and Community Radio* (Washington: Howard University Press, 1990, pp. 61–83).

[56]Robert G. Picard, *Media Economics: Concepts and Issues* (Newbury Park: Sage Publications, 1989, pp. 35–51). Also see Albert N. Greco. "Shaping the Future: Mergers, Acquisitions, and the U.S. Publishing, Communications, and Mass Media Industries, 1990–1995," *Publishing Research Quarterly* 12 (Fall 1996): 5–15.

[57]U.S. Department of Commerce, Bureau of the Census, *Statistical Abstract of the United States 1997* (Washington: GPO, 1997, p. 565).

[58]Ibid., p. 565.

[59]This topic has been the subject of a number of major articles, including: C. B. Armstrong, and M. Rubin, "Talk Radio as Interpersonal Communication," *Journal of Communication* 39 (1989): 84–94; and J. Bierig and Joseph Dimmick, Jr., "The Late Night Radio Talk Show as Interpersonal Communication," *Journalism and Mass Communication Quarterly* 56 (1979): 92–96. Also see Joseph N. Cappella, Joseph Turow, and Kathleen Hall Jamieson, "Call-in Political Talk Radio: Background, Content, Audiences, and Portrayal in Mainstream Media," *The Annenberg Public Policy Center of the University of Pennsylvania*, August 7, 1996: 1–3; J. Crittenden, "Democratic Functions of the Open Mike Radio Forum," *Public Opinion Quarterly* 35 (1971): 200–210; Marc Fisher, "Blackout on the Dial," *American Journalism Review* 20 (June 1998): 44–49; S. E. Frost, Jr., *Is American Radio Democratic?* (Chicago: University of Chicago Press, 1937, pp. 32–67); Nathan Godfried, *WCFL: Chicago's Voice of Labor, 1926–1978*. (Urbana: University of Illinois Press, 1997, pp. 1–88); R. C. Hofstetter, M. C. Donovan, M. R. Klauber, A. Cole, C. J. Huie, and T. Yuasa, "Political Talk Radio: A Stereotype Reconsidered." *Political Research Quarterly* 47 (1994): 467–479; and J. Turow, "Talk Show Radio as Interpersonal Communication," *Journal of Broadcasting* 18 (1974): 171–179.

[60]Michael T. Elliott and Paul Surgi Speck, "Consumer Perceptions of Advertising Clutter and Its Impact Across Various Media," *Journal of Advertising Research* 38 (1998): 29–41; and Paul Surgi Speck and Michael T. Elliott, "Antecedents and Consequences of Perceived Advertising Clutter," *Journal of Current Issues and Research in Advertising* 19 (1997): 39–54.

[61]U.S. Department of Commerce, Bureau of the Census, *Statistical Abstract of the United States 1997* (Washington: GPO, 1997, p. 565).

[62]Veronis, Suhler & Associates, *The Veronis, Suhler & Associates Communications Industry Forecast: Historical and Projected Expenditures for 12 Industry Segments* (New York: Veronis, Suhler & Associates, 1997, p. 140).

[63]Dun & Bradstreet, *Industry Norms and Key Financial Ratios* (New York: Dun & Bradstreet Credit Services, 1998). For an analysis of market entry barrier issues, including regulatory matters, see Michael E. Porter, "How Competitive Forces Shape Strategy," *Harvard Business Review* 57 (March/April 1979): 137–145.

7

The Future of the Broadcast Television Industry

JAMES WALKER
Saint Xavier University

DOUGLAS FERGUSON
College of Charleston

PREDICTIONS

The traditional sources of information on industry forecasting continue to release linear-based predictions for broadcast television. Revenues and expenses are expected to grow at a consistent rate, despite inevitable irregularities. For example, local broadcast advertising has been projected to mushroom to $26.7 billion by the year 2001, up from $20.7 billion in 1996, according to investment banking firm Veronis, Suhler, & Associates.[1]

Discontinuities are harder to predict. We focus in this chapter on the various forces that could bring fundamental change to the present system of television broadcasting. Several possible scenarios will be explored.

In order to understand what can change in the future, it is useful to look at what is *not* likely to change. Stability is reasonably certain in three important areas. First, the continuation of free markets and laissez-faire capitalism in the United States is an underlying assumption throughout this chapter. Second, one might expect that leisure time will continue to grow, albeit at a much slower pace. The implication for television broadcasting is that competition among a growing field of video providers will grow more fierce for the attention of audiences. Finally, there is presently no functional equivalent to broadcast television programming: It combines universal and instantaneous delivery of locally-originated sight, sound, and motion at no direct cost, in a way that no other medium can or is likely to do. To the extent that broadcast television can corner the universal delivery market, it can expect to survive forever. To summarize, broadcast television offers:

- Instantaneous delivery
- Universal access by viewers
- Full-motion color video and high-fidelity sound
- No direct cost
- Capacity for local programming

The current status of the broadcast industry relies on present marketing conditions. In the past, it has been costly for the consumer to move from wireless to wired delivery of television programming because a second wire, or ancillary dish antenna, had to be added to each home. But eventually the one-wire world will unfold. Nearly every home already has a twisted-pair phone connection, and that link to the major telephone corporations will eventually evolve into an optical fiber cable with the bandwidth to provide all varieties of video service along with telephone.

Furthermore, universal delivery may not be the virtue that many broadcasters believe it to be. The most important viewers in an advertiser-supported universe are those with money, because many products are targeted to the affluent. This audience is also the one that can afford cable, DBS, and other video services.

The saving grace for broadcasters is that advertisers want universal access to audiences in order to protect brand equity for their clients. Successful brands used by every household (e.g., bathroom tissue) must appeal to all 100 million television households, not just the 66 million with cable. The top advertising rates are earned by the top-ranked programs.

The mass audience may be the goal of the advertiser, but the individual homes that comprise the television universe may have other plans. Portions of the television audience may become demassified, with individuals constructing their own unique video environments from pay-per-view menus of options rather than from predetermined schedules of programs.[2] Although we lack compelling evidence that a significant portion of viewers is interested in interacting with television, new technologies at least give them a chance to try out new vistas. This will become more apparent by 2007, the year that the new all-digital television standard is fully deployed.

Broadcast and multichannel television is a spectator-oriented medium. A key question for the future is how computers will stimulate the desire for participation rather than merely watching. For instance, will viewers be content with channel-surfing as a means of program selection, or will they want menu-driven programming that provides a nonsequential selection process? With newer technologies and eventual diffusion of such innovations, broadcast television could appear anti-quated. Consumers sometimes adopt innovations once a critical mass is reached. For example, reluctant buyers of answering machines and VCRs simply got tired of explaining why they did not own such devices. Clearly, computers will become the next home appliance in the future.

By April 1998, more than 100 million people were hooked to the Internet with predicted electronic commerce to reach $300 billion by 2002.[3] The computer interconnection is so powerful that some predict 10 million users will eventually transmit television signals on the Internet.[4] Such "webcasting" could further dilute the mainstream broadcast programming options. Already "cybernetworks" are showing broadcast-type soap operas on the Internet, each hoping to become a mainstream television network.[5]

Beginning in late 1998, the government stimulated the industry by offering each broadcast television station a new channel to use for delivering high-definition (digital) television.[6] Broadcasters must invest heavily in new transmission equipment to remain competitive with digital wide-screen images promised by cable operators and direct satellite programmers. Although everyone agrees that digital TV is coming and coming fast, it is not clear what that will mean to the average viewer or the industry. Whether the technology will be used to improve the quality of images or to multiply the number of programs offered is far from certain.[7] For example, television stations may decide to divide their single digital channel into multiple channels under the old, low-definition standard rather than one high-definition channel, except in prime time.

Technology is just one force to be considered. This chapter also looks at several other forces shaping the future of the broadcast industry. These include internationalization of media, consolidation of the television industry, convergence of television and computer industries, and expansion of television reality into the larger culture.

INTERNATIONALIZATION

Television networks and the producers who supply them have traditionally been U.S. corporations. The motion picture industry is based in Hollywood and the original three networks sprang from New York City. Foreign-based media evolved at about the same time, but U.S. companies largely dominated world production of filmed entertainment.

Until recently, the most-watched television programs in many countries were dubbed versions of U.S. programs, but the privatization of foreign media has prompted countries to produce their own programs. Still, there is an increasing number of countries to which programming can be sold, and even those countries that have increased domestic production continue to buy U.S. programs. However, new partnerships will be formed to meet the worldwide appetite for sports programming.[8] Already, broadcast networks like NBC, and cable networks like the Discovery Channel, are trying to create global brand names for their programming products.

One likely scenario is that a small handful of global companies will swallow up the dozen or more major players in Europe, Asia, and South America. America has its Ted Turner, Australia spawned Rupert Murdoch, Italy/France/Spain has Silvio Berlusconi, and Germany has Leo Kirch. Together these media titans and their conglomerates strike strategic alliances. For example, Kirch is programming its new digital TV service in Germany with millions of dollars worth of Hollywood material, including a ten-year deal with Disney for exclusive pay-TV rights to existing and future live-action films.[9]

Economics are a key consideration in joint ventures and strategic alliances among global media interests. Although conditions may change in the next century, the 1990s were characterized by improvements in advertising revenues and more money lent from world banks as a result of improvements in the global economy. As other countries privatize their media, there are more opportunities for U.S. companies to defray the costs of mergers with their unmatched capacity to produce high-quality entertainment and information.[10] NBC, on the other hand, withdrew from worldwide markets for its vast news organization because American culture did not translate very well.

CONSOLIDATION OF THE TELEVISION INDUSTRY

We are seeing the convergence of media that were once only competitors, but there are benefits to broadcast television's unique strengths. Before multichannel television was first popularized by cable operators and then by direct satellite providers, the practice of putting programs "on the air" was the dominant method for reaching mass audiences. Broadcast television connected homes to a nearly continuous stream of programming through antennae on set-tops and rooftops.

Cable television originally operated at the fringe of the television industry, in opposition to broadcast television but greatly dependent on it. Television networks lobbied the FCC to impede the growth of cable channels, except in their capacity to extend the reach of over-the-air programs. Over time, however, broadcasters realized the inevitability of a multichannel world and began to diversify into cable. Broadcast networks bought into cable networks when they saw that channels would arise from new arrangements with production studios. NBC begot CNBC and MSNBC, and ABC became a part-owner of ESPN. Fox started its own all-news channel in 1996 to compete with CNN and MSNBC. CBS withdrew from cable after a disastrous attempt to launch a cultural channel in the early 1980s, but ventured back in the late 1990s with its Eye on People channel, which was sold to the Discovery Channel in 1998.

By 1997, the threat of direct broadcast satellites (DBS), also called digital satellite service, sufficiently threatened both broadcasters and cable operators that the two former enemies began to rethink their competition. Some projections forecast 20 million DBS subscribers by the year 2000. Interestingly, some 30 percent of the new DBS subscribers still have cable service, making each a "multiprovider household" (MPH). Such early adopters of DBS are the cream of the cable subscribers, who are far more likely to subscribe to pay-per-month or pay-per-view services. The threat of DBS to conventional broadcast service is particularly sharp when cast against the original projections of 5 million subscribers by the year 2000, yet it is clear that the broadcast networks have less to fear than their local broadcast affiliates. Nothing, beyond affiliation contracts, prevents the major networks from distributing their popular programs and embedded commercials via direct satellite. For them the big question is whether they can compete alongside a cornucopia of choices.

If affiliates become second-class providers of video programming, many broadcasters worry about their futures. Even within the ranks of network broadcasters, some programmers have called for less cutthroat, head-to-head competition among broadcast networks in order to maximize the programming strengths of individual networks. To the extent that networks can optimize their offerings, affiliates and networks alike will continue to prosper, as long as their program suppliers continue to bring the best shows to the networks first, before shopping them to multichannel providers like cable and DBS. This is a real concern for the networks. As newer forms of program distribution evolve, the broadcast television networks may lose their first-refusal status for the best new shows.

The movie studios have branched into broadcast and cable, either by buying networks (as Disney did with Capital Cities/ABC) or founding them (as Fox, Paramount, and Warner Brothers did). The same companies that make the shows also distribute the programs, publish the books and music, and own the cable systems. The three largest conglomerates are Time Warner/Turner, Disney/ABC, and Viacom/Paramount, accounting for 58 percent of the 1994 revenues generated by the top ten media companies.[11]

The largest broadcast merger in 1995 was the Disney/ABC alliance. The new production division combined Walt Disney Pictures, Touchstone Pictures, and ABC Productions. On the distribution side, Disney/ABC boasted eleven owned-and-operated (O & O) television stations and 228 broadcast affiliates. In the multichannel content arena, the merger brought ABC Television into the fold with the Disney Channel and part-ownership of the ESPN, Lifetime, and A&E channels. All told, the deal represented $4.6 billion in cash flow and affected 85,000 employees.

The number of broadcast owners is shrinking as government ownership limits loosen. Westinghouse bought CBS in 1995 and quickly expanded to an array of fifteen owned-and-operated stations, reaching 33 percent of all homes in the United States.

Group owners of television stations are also busy buying up each other. In 1995, three mergers alone accounted for nearly $1.2 billion. More ownership consolidation followed the loosening of restrictions under the 1996 Telecommunications Act. Broadcasters were elated that the new regulations would not charge them for additional digital spectrum, as some in Congress had threatened.[12]

There are three types of mergers: those who want in (e.g., Westinghouse buys CBS), those who want more control (e.g., Disney buys ABC to guarantee distribution for its programs), and those who want to diversify (e.g., newspaper giant Gannett buys television giant Multimedia).[13] Regardless of the reasons for media acquisition, the result is a broader scope for the media giants.

For example, the 1996 merger of Time Warner and Turner Communications resulted in the world's largest media empire, with the possible exception of the AT&T/TCI merger proposed in 1998. The $7.6 billion merger (substantially less than the $19 billion Disney paid to buy ABC, but larger in scope) brought together a staggering array of entities:

Film/TV Programming:	Warner Brothers Television, Warner Brothers Filmed Entertainment, Castle Rock Entertainment, New Line Cinema, Turner Pictures Worldwide, Hanna-Barbera Entertainment, Savoy Pictures (3 percent)
Cable/Satellite TV Channels:	HBO, Cinemax, CNN, Headline News, Cartoon Network, TBS, Turner Classic Movies, TNT, Court TV (55 percent), Comedy Central (50 percent), E! Entertainment (49 percent), Sega Channel (33 percent), Black Entertainment Television (15 percent), SportSouth Network (44 percent)
Broadcast Television Network:	The WB
Cable/Telecommunications:	Time Warner Cable (11.7 million U.S. homes)
Music:	Warner Brothers Records, Atlantic Group, Elektra
Publishing:	Time Inc., Book-of-the-Month Club, Time Life, Warner Books, Sunset Books, Little, Brown & Co., Oxmoor House, and Leisure Arts
Sports:	Atlanta Braves, Atlanta Hawks, World Championship Wrestling
Theme Parks:	Six Flags Theme Parks (49 percent)

In order to understand the future of media mergers, it is useful to consider why they take place in the first place. The media industry has three main characteristics: high fixed costs of production and distribution, high risk of consumer rejection, and static revenues.[14] Only very large companies have the economies of scope and scale to reduce risk and spread costs. Only giant media empires can absorb the high costs of production and can afford to wait for the high returns.[15] Consequently, it is not so much a question of whether broadcasters can afford to merge with new media and others in the vertical chain, but whether they can afford not to. External forces, primarily government restrictions, may limit the number of mergers in the future, but no evidence of a slowdown is apparent today.

THE INFORMATION SUPERHIGHWAY: WILL BROADCAST TELEVISION SURVIVE OR THRIVE?

In the midst of conglomerization of various media, the very stability of television as a medium is under threat from new technologies. The World Wide Web as a means of easy access to the Internet did not exist until 1993. Now, every product and nearly every television program and network is linked to a steady stream of on-line information. Nearly all television stations are putting their call letters between a "www." and a ".com" on the Internet.

In 1996, Philips introduced a product that takes on-line interactivity out of the computer room and into the living room. WebTV combines Internet access with conventional television, using an interface designed by Microsoft. Despite an initial gradual start for WebTV, Microsoft purchased the new venture from Philips in 1997 for $425 million. Microsoft's strategic ventures and alliances with major media corporations (like the MSNBC channel with the NBC television network) point to a future where computers will influence viewing behavior.

For example, one component of viewing behavior is channel flipping. The audience has become sophisticated over time in the use of remote control devices to "channel-surf" during commercial breaks, sometimes creating an unplanned video environment. With the advent of TV-based computer-surfing, viewers are no longer limited to a predetermined number of television channels to view. The audience can surf the networks and surf the web simultaneously. The World Wide Web has already embraced the television networks and syndicated broadcast/cable programming, and vice versa.

The cable television industry seems uniquely poised to take advantage of technological advancements. For example, Cable Television Laboratories established an agreement in 1996 to standardize new digital set-top boxes and digital cable modems. Menu-driven television programming via cable networks or the computer Internet is not that far away.

On the other hand, innovations from the cable industry are often more promise than fruition. In the late 1970s Warner spent millions on an interactive television system known as Qube and learned that the audience was not interested. Maybe the idea was ahead of its time, however, and future viewers, especially those who grew up with home computers and Sega games, will want their television fare served up from menus rather than cafeteria-style.

The Telecommunications Act of 1996 established a context that enabled fundamental changes in the delivery of video programming. For example, the telephone companies and the cable "multiple system operators" (MSO) have begun to offer interactive programming via a "full service network" (FSN). At least in small markets, entrepreneurs can begin providing telephone and video services on one wire.[16] Neither the broadcasters nor the newer forms of distribution have much expertise in offering interactive programming, but both sides have the financial resources to make strategic alliances with companies like Microsoft and other multimedia providers. John Pavlik notes that the new Telecommunications Act exempts DBS from rate and tax regulation. He further speculates that DBS providers will attempt to offer local television stations via satellite.[17]

The key unanswered question surrounding the possible demise of broadcast television is whether viewers are willing to pay for programming that was once free. Even if the viewers are willing, will their finite leisure time justify the incremental expense of pay television?

Baldwin, McVoy, and Steinfield argue that different tiers of nonbroadcast service (*video-on-demand, à la carte* channel packages, broadcast basic) allow consumers to direct their entertainment resources toward the most desirable programs.[18] Just as motion pictures have exhibition "windows" that begin in theaters and end with television syndication, television programs may eventually begin with premium distribution and later appear on "free" broadcast television. To the extent that broadcasters are owned by movie studios, this trend may be controlled, but viewers will nevertheless have more options to see better programs first by paying a fee.

This so-called "consumer underinvestment in television"[19] may mean that there is an untapped demand for television programming that the conventional over-the-air networks will never fulfill. Forecasters have long predicted competition for the broadcast networks,[20] and it eventually materialized.

In the early 1990s, the future looked very dim for the broadcasters. Ken Auletta wrote a scathing indictment of the broadcast industry that led many to predict the networks' demise.[21] By the mid-1990s, as we have seen, the networks were again making record profits and controlling the television industry. The broadcasters themselves wrote books defending the future of their brand of television media.

Gene Jankowski and David Fuchs have argued that the old system is still firmly in place, and is unlikely to change significantly.[22] First, they maintain that the network–affiliate arrangement is presently the sole means of reaching nearly every television home at negligible cost to the viewer. As such, it will have no real competition for some time to come, implying that network hegemony is intact. This "nothing-will-change" assessment is a popular prediction among other media scholars as well. W. Russell Neuman and Clifford Stoll have also predicted a long, happy life for the *status quo* in their books on the future of the media.

Second, Jankowski and Fuchs have convincingly argued against technological determinism by exploring technology issues in the context of three requirements: distribution, programming, and funding. The latter two, the authors contend, are ignored in visions of broadcast television's future. Prognosticators envision new means of distribution without answering the thorny questions of who will pay, given finite consumer resources of money and time, and what mechanism will fill the additional hours of required programming.

Third, Jankowski and Fuchs have characterized the machinations of the cable industry and the telephone companies as protective of their own overpenetrated markets. In their opinion, both industries have run out of ways to make money from their core businesses and are looking to expand into other domains. The largest cable operator, TCI, saw its stock value plummet in the latter half of 1996 because analysts predicted little revenue growth potential in this largely saturated industry. The recent retreat from video services testing by some regional telephone companies may mean that wired competition is not nearly as imminent as once predicted, although Bell Atlantic continues to press forward. As we observe later in this chapter, the transition to a wired nation may take time.

Finally, the new communication technologies appear to be serving small-scale interests, nibbling at the margins of the network audience by presenting old reruns of programs produced by the networks or an ever-dwindling supply of theatrical releases from Hollywood. Jankowski and Fuchs characterized the predicted 500-channel menu as 490 niche services fighting each other over "ever smaller fragments."

It is too simplistic, however, to pit networks against cable at a time when the industries are converging. The future is instead evolving toward more partnerships among the various technologies and the major studios that supply the software. Television icon Ted Turner, for example, looks for partnerships with computer maven Bill Gates.

Those who claim that the future of broadcasting is secure focus too much attention on domestic broadcasting and not enough on the globalization of telecommunication. Broadcasters have begun to look beyond the continental borders for economic opportunities.

Apologists for the broadcast industry still harbor enmity for the cable industry. One oft-repeated argument is that cable has somehow stolen the networks' programs, even though the advertiser-supported system requires that the supplier give away the product to one customer (viewers) in order to maximize the market for the other customer (advertisers).

The most misleading idea espoused by pro-broadcast forces has been that audience circulation somehow connotes quality. When asked how he knew his network had high-quality shows, Bud Grant, former programming chief at CBS, once replied that the high audience ratings proved that the viewers liked what they were seeing.[23] The real truth, of course, is that the viewers, like voters, can only vote for the candidates who make it onto the ballot.

DEMOGRAPHIC TRENDS

A more diverse country will also influence media trends in the twenty-first century. The newer, urban-based television networks (The WB and UPN) have already begun to focus on more diverse programming, sometimes appealing to ethnic viewers in large metropolitan areas. Although situation comedy on the older broadcast television networks has never been particularly adverse to ethnic families, the newer networks have been featuring an even heavier mix of nonwhite casts.

Television has always attempted to reflect the U.S. mainstream, so it is not a surprise that networks are adapting to the more diverse makeup of viewing groups. In the 1950s, shows like *Ozzie and Harriet* and *Leave It to Beaver* showed us an America that was mostly white and middle-class. Until the 1970s, the "typical" viewer was assumed to be Caucasian.

Demographers have noted some trends in population diversity in the latter part of the twentieth century, specifically between 1990 and 1995.[24] For example, white non-Hispanic persons make up nearly 74 percent of all Americans but account for just 38 percent of the population growth. Hispanic persons only make up 10 percent of the total population but account for 30 percent of the five-year growth. The African American population (12 percent) is growing more evenly with a 16 percent increase. At these rates, the ethnic composition of America is destined to change in the next twenty-five to fifty years. As far as television consumption is concerned, one can expect more viewing among nonwhite groups, which traditionally spend more time watching TV.

TELEVISION AS A CULTURAL FORCE

As television evolves into a stronger presence in U.S. homes through the decline of print-based media and the rise of an electronic marriage with the computer, the broadcast (and wired) version of TV in the new millennium is likely to exert an even stronger influence on U.S. culture. To the extent that television replaces other functional alternatives for leisure time, it is conceivable that television will become an integral part of daily life, especially as the telephone and fax machine become linked to computers, as computers are wedded to television sets, as cable television companies compete for local telephone service, and as telephone companies begin to offer video services.

An abundant supply of mediated communication may sound wonderful, but to what extent does the typical person want to be electronically linked to the rest of the world? Baldwin, McVoy, and Steinfield list several drawbacks of increased video services: information overload, irresponsible use of unedited content, increased commercialism to subsidize higher programming costs, social isolationism and alienation, less privacy, and loss of traditional communities.[25] They also discuss the many kinds of technological gaps between the economic haves and have-nots: information gaps, entertainment and sports gaps, social gaps, urban–rural gaps, and freedom of choice gaps.[26]

Some television broadcasters are adamant that academics and social critics have it all wrong about television's potential as a cultural force. According to them, given a choice, "the audience will opt for relaxation."[27] But is it desirable for viewers to become less and less interested in serious information, especially about political campaigns? By giving the viewers what they want, is broadcast television (and its multichannel conspirators) really serving the public interest?

A key question is how much diversity and choice the public can stand. Until now, the "electronic hearth" that broadcast television represents has served to unify the nation under a set of common experiences. For good or bad, network news programs have commanded the audience's attention, providing their interpretations of events and fads. Would that be possible in a world of limitless channel choices?

If culture is based on what is "in" or "out," what mass medium will communicate the "national norm," whatever it should become? If each viewer is watching a different program, what is the incentive for program producers to make a product good enough to appeal to a large audience?

In 1993, Cox Cable executive Ajit Dalvi predicted that the so-called 500-channel universe would become 250 channels for premium movies, 50 channels of pay-per-view events, and a 100-channel "grazing zone" similar to cable television, with another 200-channel "quality zone" providing an additional two channels for each grazing channel.[28] Will there be 100 channels, each with a 1 percent share of the viewing? Beyond the needs of advertisers to efficiently reach the masses, what will address the need for cultural institutions to reach the masses?

POSSIBLE SCENARIOS

Throughout this chapter, we have examined the various influences on the future of the broadcast television industry. Although it is difficult to predict the future, it is still useful to explore the more likely scenarios. Each of the following educated guesses centers on the ultimate victory of either distribution or content forces (or a mixed outcome). We will also discuss the implications for the broadcast television industry.

Distribution Wins

The first and most plausible scenario is that the telephone companies (telecos) will buy their way into every television home. This one-wire solution, as discussed earlier, is the natural outcome of a switchover from coaxial cable to fiber-optic wires. Like universal telephone service, the big telecommunications giants will be common carriers regulated by the government. Content providers will be separate corporations, with the usual program producers (e.g., movie studios, niche channels, full-service networks) at the top level.

Cable operators who had already installed their own fiber wires will be required to lease back their infrastructure to the phone companies, although the telecos will be anxious to purchase the systems outright. The situation is somewhat analogous to pole-attachment fees paid by cable operators to the telecos in earlier times. As it becomes more and more clear that cable will yield to the telecos, the likelihood of massive system buyouts by the phone companies will increase. Cable-multiple system operators will forge strategic alliances with the remaining broadcast companies who provide ancillary wireless communication to unwired homes (e.g., rural homes, houseboats, mobile vehicles, etc.).

In this scenario, broadcasters will still operate as network affiliates carrying local programs, but distribution will be primarily wired instead of exclusively over-the-air. Because legislators could require the phone company to provide free entertainment and information shows to those who cannot afford value-added premium programming as part of the expansion of universal service, an advertiser-supported system of mass appeal network programming probably will survive. The main difference will be that fewer one-time-only events will be provided by the broadcast networks. But because the new-style networks will still have universal access to nearly all viewers, the most popular and successful shows will remain on ABC, CBS, NBC, Fox, UPN, The WB, and any other networks that survive the transition to wired communication. Even before its merger with ABC, Disney had made joint ventures with BellSouth, Ameritech, and SBC Communication to provide content to wired teleco ventures.

How long would it take for this change to occur? By conservative estimates, fiber-to-the-curb (FTTC) and fiber-to-the-home (FTTH) is many billions of dollars and several years away (circa 2030). By that time, direct satellite broadcasting could largely supplant over-the-air broadcasting with "through-the-air" broadcasting. The telephone companies will upgrade all homes except those in the most remote areas, which will have satellite receivers.

Wireless cable, using high-frequency direct-line frequencies originally reserved for educational purposes, could serve as a stopgap for multichannel distribution until all twisted-pair copper wiring is replaced. Moreover, existing coaxial cable systems will be purchased by telephone companies in many locales to aid in the transition to fiber. The merger of phone giant AT&T with cable colossus TCI will pave the way.

Although distribution is the focus, content will remain crucial nevertheless. Less reliance on schedule-based programming will not mean the total adoption of menu-based selection. Most viewers will still opt for relaxation and will continue to seek novelty. The important difference is that, with the advent of Internet-based programming, it is entirely possible to install a "something else" button on every remote control that would promise limitless random choices. Such a device could first run through dozens of mainstream channels, then hundreds of niche channels, and finally thousands of random web channels and pages. The something-else button could easily remember where it had been in the past twenty-four hours to avoid cycling through old options, offering endless choices of thousands and thousands of channels. Instead of singer Bruce Springsteen's refrain of "fifty-seven channels and nothing on," 57,000 channels and nothing on may be the cry in the twenty-first century.

Content Wins

Another possible scenario is that the many entertainment program producers will consolidate into a vertically-integrated distribution system, offering a choice of distribution systems to viewers at different windows of opportunity. In this case, the actual delivery of programs will remain a hodgepodge of terrestrial broadcasting, *digital satellite systems,* conventional cable, *fiber optics,* and *wireless cable.* Content, however, would be controlled by a very small handful of suppliers operating at a global level.

Big-budget productions would be delivered over high-definition digital transmission systems to pay-per-view audiences. Subsequent distribution would cycle through various à la carte windows and pay-per-month schedules. Instead of HBO producing programs for exclusive exhibition on pay channels, for example, premium channels would offer up television shows in the same way that theatrical movies are distributed in today's entertainment world, with all programs eventually available on "free" television channels.

Governments probably would likely regulate these producers' control of distribution channels, but content providers undoubtedly would be allowed ready access to, and part ownership of, the delivery systems. Home video and premium television would continue to offer independent producers reasonable access to audiences, but viewers would primarily watch programs made by the major conglomerates. As discussed earlier, no one but the giants can afford the high costs of production and withstand the momentous risk of predicting changing tastes in programming.

In this scenario, broadcasters would probably fare less well than in the previous distribution-wins model. For many years, television networks have used the unique advantage of their distribution system to maintain high advertising rates. With a system based on programs, the broadcast networks would have little advantage as mere packagers of shows. The motion picture studios would retain a great deal of influence over public tastes, especially when coupled with a news-gathering force (e.g., Disney/ABC). Broadcast networks without strong links to the production of entertainment probably would be forced to sell off their information-gathering expertise to the select number of entertainment program providers.

Nobody Wins

This scenario projects "more of the same," with the attendant ebb and flow of distribution technologies and program formats. Such a future seems unlikely, even though many people expect it to happen. They argue that the evolution of other media formats has not triggered discontinuous change. When film and radio evolved, the newspapers adapted and survived. When television appeared, film and radio adapted and survived. If past is prologue, then broadcast television will adapt and survive, too.

However, this scenario does not imply that there will be no change at all. We can reasonably expect that computers will get faster, moving images will get better, and virtual reality will be perfected. But, cataclysmic reordering is not on the horizon, or even just beyond the horizon. The nobody-wins scenario acknowledges that institutions, governments, and societies exert a powerful inertia.

We believe that this third scenario is the least likely one. Our crystal ball is no better than the readers', but we hope that this chapter has illuminated the issues. We do not believe that the future belongs principally to the television broadcasters, as others have argued.[29] If we had a million dollars to invest, it would likely be with a visionary telephone company. If "let-the-marketplace-decide" forces continue to hold sway, the future may belong to the one-wire world, not the over-the-air broadcaster.

NOTES

[1]Marilyn Rauch, "Veronis Predicts Swell in Communications Biz," *Advertising Age,* July 28, 1997, pp. 4, 33.

[2]William Bradley, "Behind the Megamedia Mergers," *San Francisco Chronicle,* August 6, 1996, Sec. A, p. 19.

[3]Elizabeth Weise, "Net Use Doubling Every 100 Days," *USA Today,* April 16, 1998, p. A1.

[4]Ken C. Pohlmann, "Channel Envy," *Video,* September, 1996, pp. 23–25.

[5]Bruce Haring, "PCs as TVs : Dramas Kick Off Cyberspace Networks," *USA Today,* April 16, 1996, Sec D, p. 3.

[6]Chris McConnell, "FCC Enumerates TV's Future," *Broadcasting & Cable,* August 19, 1996, pp. 17–22.

[7]Joel Brinkley, *Defining Vision: The Battle for the Future of Television* (New York: Harcourt Brace, 1997).

[8]Jim McConville, "Everybody Wants to Get into the Game," *Broadcasting & Cable,* April 8, 1996, pp. 50–51.

[9]Lisa Bannon, "Kirch of Germany Gets Pay-TV Rights to Disney Movies," *Wall Street Journal,* August 30, 1996, Sec A, p. 5–D.

[10]Joe Mandese, "Media World on Brink of M & A Frenzy," *Advertising Age,* July 25, 1994, pp. 1–2.

[11]Douglas A. Ferguson, "A Framework for Programming Strategies," in *Broadcast/Cable Programming,* Susan T. Eastman and Douglas A. Ferguson, eds. (Belmont, CA: Wadsworth, 1997).

[12]Bill Carter, "The Networks See Potential for Growth," *New York Times,* February 2, 1996, Sec D, p. 6.

[13]Douglas Gomery, "Mass Media Merger Mania," *American Journalism Review,* December, 1995, p. 46.

[14]"Meet the New Media Monsters," *The Economist,* March 11, 1989, pp. 65–66.

[15]Mandese, op. cit.

[16]Thomas F. Baldwin, D. Stephens McVoy, and Charles Steinfield, *Convergence: Integrating Media, Information & Communication* (Thousand Oaks, CA: Sage, 1996).

[17]John V. Pavlik, "Competition: Key to the Communications Future?" *Television Quarterly,* 1996, 28:2, pp. 35–43.

[18]Baldwin et al., op. cit., pp. 137–143.

[19]Ibid., p. 8.

[20]Cited in Baldwin et al., op. cit., p. 9.

[21]Ken Auletta, *Three Blind Mice: How the Networks Lost Their Way* (New York: Random House, 1991).

[22]Gene F. Jankowski and David C. Fuchs, *Television Today and Tomorrow* (New York: Oxford, 1995).

[23]From a television program, "CBS Reports: Don't Touch That Dial" (New York: CBS News, 1982).

[24]Peter Francese, "America at Mid-Decade," *American Demographics,* February, 1995, pp. 23–31.

[25]Baldwin et al., op. cit., pp. 384–391.

[26]Ibid., pp. 392–395.

[27]Jankowski and Fuchs, op. cit., p. 163.

[28]Kate Maddox, "The Big Picture: Visions of a New TV Begin to Merge," *Electronic Media,* November 8, 1993, p. 23.

[29]Jankowski and Fuchs, op. cit.

8

The Structure of the Cable and Satellite Television Industries

Patrick R. Parsons
Pennsylvania State University

Robert M. Frieden
Pennsylvania State University

> *Companies of size will be the ones that survive.*
> *It's going to be the waltz of the elephants, and*
> *you want to be sure you don't get stepped on.*
> *—AMOS HOSTETTER[1]*

Amos Hostetter was chairman and CEO of Continental Cablevision, the country's third largest cable television operator. In late February, 1996, he stood at a podium during a news conference to proclaim that his company was not going to get stepped on in the coming information age. He took his place before the reporters with Chuck Lillis, President of US West Media Group, to announce the acquisition of Continental by the parent company of US West Media Group, US West, Inc., the Regional Bell Operating Company serving much of the Western United States. The combination of the cable and telephone giants was worth more than $11 billion. US West Media group already had a 25 percent equity stake in Time Warner Entertainment, the second largest cable operator in the country. With the addition of Continental (later renamed Media One), US West now had ready access to more than 14 million subscribers. US West provides telephone service for customers in fourteen states; now it would also be the cable company for cities from New England to California.[2]

Hostetter's allusion to dancing elephants was apt. The arena for the delivery of video programming and broadband services was expanding rapidly, thanks both to the leaps in the power of the delivery technology and to the relaxation of regulatory constraints on potential players. But that arena was very large and the price of entry was steep. It was widely observed that only the biggest and most heavily financed companies could compete in the emerging telecommunications environment. For example, in the summer of 1998, AT&T, the nation's largest long-distance telephone company, announced its acquisition of the country's largest cable television company, Tele-Communications, Inc. (TCI). The AT&T–TCI and US West–Continental mergers were the most significant combinations but by no means the only ones.

Through the 1990s, small cable companies sought buyers while large companies sought partnerships and alliances. Mergers, acquisitions, and joint ventures proliferated among cable companies, between cable companies and programmers, and between cable companies, programmers, and a host of interested parties from allied fields such as telephone, computer, film, and even the electric utility industry. The elephants were dancing; sometimes it was a waltz, sometimes a jitterbug, but everyone, it seemed, was looking for a partner.

Competition and Convergence

Convergence became the watchword of the telecommunications industry in the 1980s. Initially it described the convergence of communications technologies, the melding of the computer, the television, the telephone, and satellites into a unified system of information acquisition, delivery, and control. Held together by the global network of satellite dishes, copper, coaxial, and fiber wires and the accelerating flow of digital bits and bytes, convergence was a foundation concept for the National Information Infrastructure and the Information Superhighway. It was, and is, an engaging and accurate metaphor for the changes taking place in the technology of personal and mass media in the remaining years of the twentieth century. It soon became apparent, however, that the term had an additional meaning. Convergence described not just the technological changes taking place, but changes in business and ownership structure of the media as well. Convergence characterized the evolving consolidation of heretofore disparate industries and firms.

Critics such as Ben Bagdikian have argued that the media—print, broadcast, and film—have for decades been in the process of accelerating consolidation, the ownership of more and more outlets by fewer and fewer companies.[3] The notion of convergence, in this economic sense, rephrases Bagdikian's argument and draws attention to the cable television industry in its internal structure and to the relationship of the cable industry to all other communications sectors, including broadcast, telephone, and data processing. It envisions not just a technologically unified (or at least correlated) information–entertainment utility, but an economically integrated megaindustry, as well. To achieve favorable economies of scale, companies have vertically integrated into all market segments up and down the food chain, from production to exhibition. To achieve economies of scope, these ventures have diversified into adjacent markets, with broadcasters like NBC exploiting existing personnel and resources to create their own cable networks, such as CNBC and MSNBC.

Given these observations about economic convergence, therefore, it is in some ways counterintuitive that there is also great fanfare about the competitive open market that technology and deregulation have reportedly forged. How is it, one can fairly ask, that intense competition and convergence can be taking place simultaneously?

Two points must be kept in mind. First, we are in some ways in the very early stages of convergence, at the beginning of a process. The technology of the distribution systems, as well as their industrial organization, retain significant distinctions despite their trajectory toward convergence. The structure and operation of the local telephone company is not identical to that of the local cable company or DBS service. Their technology, ownership structures, and business histories, while related, are not the same. One day the industries that had been known as cable and telephone may, in fact, merge and synthesize into a new system. That day may be decades away, however. For the near term, the cable, broadcast, telco, and other distribution providers will approach various markets with differing levels of interest and energy.

This then raises the second important point—that is, distribution platforms are not the same as programming and services. Satellites, cable companies, and telephone companies, technically, can all provide you with your telephone and your video service. This is the sea change that deregulation and technical innovation have brought about; similar but distinct distribution systems, and the industries they have spawned, are now capable of providing customers with a similar set of products and services. In other words, technology and deregulation have *redefined the relevant markets* for this host of industries by collapsing consumer markets that had earlier constituted separate businesses.

Prior to these changes, the telephone companies' switched, narrowband system delivered local and long-distance voice communications and data, and legal barriers in place since the early 1980s kept the local Bell Operating Companies separate from long-distance companies. Broadcasters and cable companies provided television entertainment. Satellite services were primarily middlemen in the communications transport business, invisible to all but those consumers with ten-foot wide dishes in their backyards.

Fiber-optics, digital technology, and deregulation pulled down the walls between these industries, some of them very large, that had not heretofore faced each other in the competitive arena. AT&T's system has faced off against Time Warner's, while General Motors, through its DirecTV DBS business, has taken on the cable industry. The question, in short, is quickly becoming, do you want to buy your Internet and television service—a package deal—from BellSouth or from TCI? This idea is also at the heart of Hostetter's elephants' waltz: companies that were giants in their own, previously separate, industries clashing in a newly created, combined market for content and services. The early results have been predictable. Some firms, as we will see, have gone head-to-head in the new multiservice market, competing vigorously in television, data, and voice telephony. Some people have chosen, like Hostetter, to sell out rather than attempt a competitive struggle that would cost millions if not billions of dollars and the outcome of which was very uncertain. The extent to which this new and contested market will remain competitive and afford consumers lower prices and better services or, alternatively, lead over time to yet another cabal of regional communications monopolists, is yet to be seen. In his news conference, Hostetter prophesied the consolidation of the nation's cable companies into six or eight regional monopolies, following the pattern of the local telephone companies.[4] Others see a more competitive and open market.

Distribution and Programming

This chapter will look at the general structure of the multichannel television and telecommunications industries. It will describe the major players in Hostetter's dance, both the traditional competitors and the new entrants, as well as the programming and services they provide. The arena is populated by several different categories of players. As suggested above, the broadest distinction one can make is between companies that: (1) serve as the transport structure, those that distribute content to the home, and (2) those that create or provide the content and services. The first category includes, for example, your local cable system, while the second category includes programming networks such as Cable News Network and Home Box Office. It is not a perfect dichotomy. Distributors, in fact, provide many services and often fashion their own programming content, and there are deeply intertwined ownership ties connecting the two. In practice, the lines between them are increasingly blurred. Nonetheless, as a beginning point, it is a useful way to think about industry structure. The first category provides the hardware or distribution technology, the wire-based or broadcast infrastructure; the second category provides what some have described as the software of the industry, the programming and the services carried by the distribution network (see Table 8-1).

This chapter considers the structure of and recent developments in the distribution networks of multichannel telecommunications and the nature and control of the competitive delivery systems that bring the services to market.

The Distribution Landscape

By distribution, we mean the manner in which technologies have been organized into coherent systems. The emerging distribution infrastructure can, at least for

TABLE 8-1

Distribution	Programs and Services
Wireline	*Video*
Cable Television	*Programming Networks and Services*
Telephone	Basic Networks
Utilities	Premium or Pay Networks
	Pay-Per-View
Broadcast	Near Video-on-Demand and Video-on-
Terrestrial	Demand
Traditional VHF & UHF Broadcast	*Broadcast Retransmission*
Television	Local Stations
Emerging Multichannel VHF & UHF	Regional, Imported Stations
Television	Superstations
Multipoint, Multichannel Distribution	*Local Cable*
Systems (MMDS)	Local Cable Origination
Local Multipoint Distribution Systems	Cable Access Channels: Leased, Public,
(LMDS)	Educational and Government (PEG)
Satellite	
Satellite Carriers	
Fixed Service Satellites (FSS)	*Telephone*
Direct to Home satellites (DTH)	POTS, Plain Old Telephone Service
Direct Broadcast satellites (DBS)	CAPS, Competitive Access Providers
Television Receive Only (TRVO)	PCS, Personal Communications Services
Satellite Master Antenna TV (SMATV)	*Data*
	Internet and WWW Access
	(E-mail, information, entertainment,
	games, shopping, banking, and so on)
	Telemetry: Fire and burglar alarms
	Distance Education
	Telecommuting
	Paging and Positioning

purposes of exposition, be divided initially between wireline and broadcast platforms. The former includes the cable television and telephone industries along with a smaller player, the utilities industry. Broadcasting includes terrestrial broadcast systems such as the traditional local television broadcaster and wireless cable systems, among others. Satellite broadcasting platforms include DBS and TVRO.

In practice, the nationally and internationally integrated system that brings you television, telephone, and data service uses a combination of wire and broadcasting paths. A given television signal, for example, might travel the airwaves via satellite and terrestrial microwave before reaching the cable company for final wired delivery. Computer data may run through narrowband and broadband conduits, wired and broadcast. The organization of distribution systems presented here speaks more to the nature of the platform in its final stage or stages, the local system that distributes signals in a given community (although in the case of DBS it is clearly a national "neighborhood"). This organizational scheme reflects not just the technical reality of the difference between distribution systems but also the structure of ownership and control. Distribution systems have related but differing histories and organizations. The discussion below is about how distribution technologies have been ordered into rational systems, and also about how and by whom these systems are controlled.

WIRELINE INDUSTRIES

Cable Television

The traditional cable industry is composed primarily of thousands of local cable systems and scores of national Multiple System Operators (MSOs). Local systems are the individual cable systems that serve a particular town or community. Classic cable systems have a tree-and-branch architecture, with a main office, or headend, fiber or coaxial trunk lines, feeder lines, and drops. There are about 11,660 systems in the United States. The number of systems grew slowly but steadily through the 1960s and 1970s then, as Figure 8-1 illustrates, exploded in the early 1980s following deregulation and the rise of satellite-delivered cable networks.

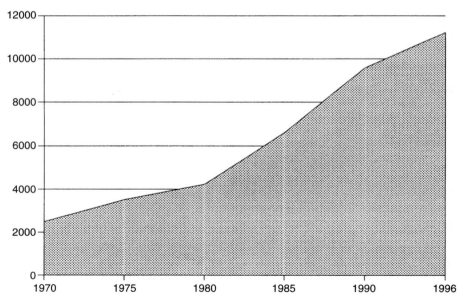

FIGURE 8-1   Cable System Growth, 1970–1996

Source: © 1997 Warren Publishing, Inc., from *Television and Cable Factbook* (2115 Ward Ct. N.W.,Washington, D.C., 20037), F-2.

TABLE 8-2   Systems and Subscribers by Channel Capacity

Channels	Systems	% Systems	Basic Subs	% Subs
54+	1,558	14	27.7 m	46.71
30–53	6,376	57.31	28.5 m	48.16
20–29	1,104	9.92	1.19 m	02.01
13–19	353	3.17	.125 m	0.21
6–12	588	5.28	.219 m	0.37
5	10	0.09	2,732	0.005
<5	4	0.04	517	0.001
NA	1,133	10.18	1.49 m	2.518

Source: © 1997 Warren Publishing, Inc., from *Television and Cable Factbook* (2115 Ward Ct. N.W.,Washington, D.C., 20037), F-3.

The typical system has between thirty and fifty-three channels, with capacity growing steadily as systems rebuild and increase their bandwidth. The introduction of digital delivery technologies in the late 1990s has dramatically expanded capacity as compression multiplies the number of available channels. Systems with fewer than thirty channels tend to be older and located in smaller communities. Cable operations with more than thirty channels account for about 70 percent of all systems and serve more than 95 percent of all cable subscribers (see Table 8-2).

While two-way capacity for cable is critical to its success in competing with the telephone companies and multichannel broadcast services, nationwide the industry is at best only partway through the installation of the equipment necessary for true interactive services. As Table 8-3 shows, the top five MSOs, which lead the industry in modernization of their architecture, have on average less than 50 percent of their total plant at two-way capacity.

Nationwide, cable system wires pass about 97 percent of all television households, and about 66 percent of all TV households in the country, about 64 million, subscribe (see Table 8-4).

While the total number of cable systems is large, the vast majority of those systems are tiny operations serving only a few hundred customers. Most of the

TABLE 8-3   MSO Two-Way Capability

	1996	1997	1998
TCI	20%	35.0%	60.0%
Time Warner	24%	65.0%	90.0%
US West	22%	33.0%	67.0%
Comcast	20%	51.9%	71.2%
Cox	37%	42.0%	64.0%

Sources: CableWorld, 26 February 1996, 1; *Broadcasting & Cable,* 29 April 1996, 12.

TABLE 8-4   Basic Cable Subscription 1975–1996

	Cable Subs (millions)	TV Homes (millions)	Cable Penetration
1996	64.8	97.0	66.8%
1995	63.7	95.4	66.8
1990	55.8	92.1	60.6
1987	44.1	87.5	50.4
1985	41.5	84.9	48.9
1983	34.1	83.3	40.5
1980	17.6	76.3	23.0
1975	9.2	68.5	13.4

Sources: Cable TV Facts (New York: Cable Television Advertising Bureau, 1996), 5; *Cable Television Developments* (Washington, D.C., 1996), 2; *Television and Cable Factbook* (Washington, D.C.: Warren Publishing, 1997); Paul Kagan Associates, Inc., Carmel, Calif.; U.S. Bureau of the Census, *Statistical Abstract of the United States,* vol. 101 (Washington, D.C.: Government Printing Office, 1980), 589; *Broadcasting & Cable,* July 21, 1997, 111.

nation's cable customers are concentrated in a relatively small handful of large systems in major markets. About 42 percent of all subscribers are served by only 2 percent (about 250) of all cable systems; these are systems with more than 50,000 customers each (see Table 8-5). The top 10 percent of all cable systems serve more than 79 percent of the nation's subscribers. About 56 percent, or 8,239 systems, divide up less than 4 percent of the total subscriber base, and some 3,272 systems serve fewer than 250 customers each.

TABLE 8-5   Systems and Subscribers by Number of Subcribers in System

Subs	Systems	% of Systems	Basic Subs	% Total Subs
50,000 +	256	2.3	26.6 M	44.9
20,000–49,999	437	3.93	13.4 M	22.7
10,000–19,999	512	4.6	7.2 M	12.1
5,000–9,999	658	5.9	4.5 M	7.6
3,500–4,999	421	3.7	1.7 M	2.9
1,000–3,499	1,968	17.69	3.7 M	6.3
500–900	1,458	13.1	1 M	1.7
250–499	1,513	13.6	0.5 M	0.9
249 or less	3,272	29.41	0.4 M	0.6
N.A.	631	5.67	—	0
Total	11,126	100.0	59.2 M	100.0

Source: © 1997 Warren Publishing, Inc., from *Television and Cable Factbook* (2115 Ward Ct. N.W.,Washington, D.C., 20037), F-3.

Despite the multitude of small systems, the day of the "mom and pop" cable operation is long over. Most cable systems are owned by large companies that operate groups of systems. These MSOs comprise the dominant ownership structure in the industry. There are more than 600 MSOs in the United States controlling over 90 percent of all cable systems.[5] The bulk of all local subscribers, however, is held by only the top ten or twenty companies. Two MSOs in particular exercise special influence on the business by virtue of their massive size, relative to other MSOs, and through their partnerships with, and equity interests in, other ventures operating in adjacent markets such as programming. They are Tele-Communications, Inc. (TCI), based in Denver, and Time Warner, Inc., out of New York. As Table 8-6 illustrates, they dwarf other MSOs in terms of their overall subscriber base.

Even before its acquisition by AT&T, TCI was the nation's sixth largest media company (not counting the telcos) behind Time Warner, Disney, Viacom, News Corp., and Sony (based on annual revenues). It has assets estimated at more than $20 billion and serves more than 14 million subscribers, 12.5 million through wholly

TABLE 8-6 Top 20 MSOs in the United States

Rank	Company	N of Subs (In Millions)
1.	TCI	13.9
2.	Time Warner	12.1
3.	US West Media Group	5.2
4.	Comcast Corp.	4.2
5.	Cox Communications, Inc.	3.2
6.	Cablevision Systems Corp.	2.8
7.	Adelphia Communications	1.8
8.	Jones Intercable, Inc.	1.4
9.	Marcus Cable	1.3
10.	Falcon Cable TV	1.17*
11.	Century Comms Corp.	1.1*
12.	Charter Comms.	1.07*
13.	Lenfest/Suburban Cable	1.0*
14.	Prime Cable	0.85
15.	InterMedia Partners	0.82
16.	TCA Cable	0.7
17.	Post-Newsweek/Cable One	0.63
18.	Fanch	0.5
19.	Multimedia Cablevision	0.47
20.	Triax	0.45

Sources: Paul Kagan, Associates, Inc. (Carmel, Calif.) in *Cable Television Developments* (Washington, D.C., Spring, 1996); "Databank," *Cable World,* 9 December 1996, 34; "Cable Television's Top 10 MSOs," *Broadcasting & Cable,* 9 December 1996, 79–84; *Broadcasting & Cable,* 16 June 1997, 36–42.

*Subscription figures for Falcon, Century, Charter, and Lenfest are close to one another and vary by source, so rankings may shift.

owned subsidiaries, the rest through equity interests in other cable systems, and through the acquisition of Viacom's cable operations. TCI systems pass about 22.5 million homes. Its revenues, including income from its affiliated programming arm, Liberty Media, grew from $4.9 billion in 1994 to $6.9 billion in 1995.[6] It spent $980 million on system upgrades in 1995 and $260 million on maintenance with a goal of bringing most of its systems up to 550 MHz before 2000. TCI's operating cash flow was $1.8 billion in 1994 and $2.0 billion in 1995, although it posted a loss of $171 million in 1995 and its stock had been stagnant for several years.

Beyond AT&T, TCI has an impressive array of ownership interests, partnerships, and joint ventures. Through Liberty Media, it has full or partial ownership of many leading cable networks, including Encore, the Discovery Channel, BET, QVC and all the Turner channels, including CNN and TNT, and, through Turner, an ownership interest in Time Warner. It owns broadcast properties, clothing stores, and a major interest in McNeil–Lehrer Productions.

Time Warner is similarly situated, although, unlike TCI, cable and telecommunications is not its only nor its primary media business. Time Warner has its roots in publishing, recording, and film, with major subsidiaries in these areas as well as others. Time Warner, following its acquisition of Turner Broadcasting, became the world's largest media conglomerate. A partial list of its holdings includes Time-Life Publishing, the WB Television Network, Warner Bros. films and Warner records, and Turner Broadcasting Systems. More will be said about both corporations throughout the next two chapters. The next tier of MSOs includes prominent and typically long-standing companies such as US West–Media One, Comcast, Cablevision, and Adelphia.

The business philosophies governing the relationships between the MSOs and their individual systems vary, but MSOs typically exercise tight control over the local franchise, managing, often on a regional basis, the hiring and firing of system heads, promotional campaigns, technological innovation, financing and construction, and, most importantly, programming. Large MSOs are in a strong position to negotiate with programmers when they are considering additional channels or services. In the cable television industry, power is concentrated in the corporate headquarters.

Cable Competition

Until the early 1990s the only serious competitor to cable in the area of television programming was the local over-the-air broadcast station, although videotape rental did hinder the development of pay services such as HBO. While deregulation and advances in technology were fundamental in opening the doors to new entrants, these forces were not the only ones at work. Some of the cable industry's own activities nudged the opening for competitors a little wider. The increase in subscriber rates following the 1984 deregulation, the industry's reputation for weak customer service, and the failure to make good on blue sky promises all plowed fertile ground for new entrants. In 1992, for example, TCI President and CEO John Malone announced the dawn of the 500-channel universe. Cable, he declared, would use digital compression to turn on a gusher of new programming, and TCI would deliver the new technology by the end of 1994. Unfortunately, the technology and the programming failed to materialize.

The results were public disillusionment and the failure of cable stocks, including TCI's, to keep pace with a surging market in 1995 and 1996. It made it all the easier for potential competitors to attract consumers. Direct broadcast satellites and wireless cable operators were among the first to begin providing multichannel television to consumers (although C-band satellite services had enjoyed moderate success in some markets previously). While critics claimed DBS would be limited to rural areas where cable was unavailable, the service soon demonstrated it could attract subscribers from urban cable systems. And these services were only the first to demonstrate the competitive reality of the new marketplace. Waiting in the wings were the broadcasters and telephone companies. The task for the traditional cable operators in the latter half of the 1990s seemed to be to successfully roll out digital capacity and begin offering the programming and services long promised. Through recent court decisions and deregulation, cable lost much of its legal market protection; the doors were flung open to new players. The following looks more closely at some of them.

The Telephone Companies

My worst nightmare has to do with Ameritech
saying that they're ready to rock 'n' roll and
that their next concert is in Massillon, Ohio.
—BOB GESSNER, MASSILLON CABLE[7]

Massillon Cable is a family-owned business serving a small town about half an hour south of Akron. Ameritech was one of five multibillion-dollar Regional Bell Operating Companies (RBOC); it provides telephone service to five Midwestern states. Gessner was worried because Ameritech had determined that it was going into the cable television business. By the time Ameritech reached Ohio in early 1996 it already had acquired franchises to build cable systems in a dozen cities. Its first franchise in Ohio was in Hilliard, about one-hundred miles from Massillon and it soon acquired operating rights to Columbus and the suburbs around Cleveland. If Gessner was nervous, he probably had a right to be. The elephants were dancing in his direction.

The entry of the telephone industry into television in the mid-1990s was potentially one of the more important communication business developments of the decade. With the RBOCs and some long-distance carriers entering or considering the video market, cable television faced what some saw as the most serious long-term threat to its historic dominance of the multichannel television business, DBS notwithstanding. Telephone industry competition was not a surprise; in many ways it wasn't even a new event. For example, AT&T was delivering television pictures over coaxial wire before cable television was a gleam in any entrepreneur's eye, and the telephone industry had toyed with various ways of getting into the entertainment business as early as the 1920s. The telephone company had been kept standing enviously on the sidelines of the cable business for decades, prevented from entering the game by the courts and the federal government. As the Berlin Wall of regulatory restraint fell, the two industries prepared for incursions into each other's territory. The telephone industry had to overcome technological challenges in order to deliver broadband services over its narrowband pipe. But innovations such as digital compression, and the simple willingness to spend lavishly to rebuild its infrastructure made real the possibility that the telephone companies would eventually come knocking on consumers' doors with packages full of CNN and HBO.

Of greatest concern to cable operators was the sheer size of the competitive threat. The telephone industry dwarfs the cable industry in almost every measure. It has more wire, more people, and a lot more money, more than $140 billion in annual revenues compared to about $26 billion for cable. The telephone industry has very deep pockets and can afford to use some of that money to explore ways to develop its video enterprises, of which there are many. The telephone companies were engaged, by the mid-1990s, in scores of experiments, test beds, and joint ventures around the country, exploring new technologies, cultivating programming streams, and testing marketing approaches in video and data services. And the trials were not limited to investigating the possibilities of their existing or even expanded fiber and copper network. Telephone companies were looking at alternative delivery systems including DBS, MMDS, and plain old cable systems.

Telco Basics

The major companies in the telephone industry include AT&T, the five RBOCs, the largest independent local operator, GTE, competitive long-distance carriers such as MCI and Sprint, and a host of smaller local and regional companies, including an affiliate of Sprint, Altel, and Continental (not affiliated with the cable company). Basic local telephone service, or POTS (plain old telephone service) is provided by a local exchange carrier (LEC), usually one of the RBOCs or a local independent such as GTE. Long-distance service is provided by AT&T, MCI, Sprint, or one of the smaller long-distance carriers.

It is a world much more complicated and competitive than before the breakup of the Bell system in 1982. Prior to that there was really only one major telephone company, AT&T, the Bell System. A host of medium and small independent companies swarmed around this communications behemoth like flies at a picnic, annoying it, but little more. The forced divestiture broke up the Bell picnic; AT&T was spun off along with seven RBOCs. These "Baby Bells" would continue, as separate companies, to serve as local exchange carriers, while the AT&T long-lines division stayed in long-distance and opened other ventures.

Even before the breakup, MCI took advantage of regulatory opportunities created by the FCC, and frequent and successful litigation, to challenge the almost mythic dominance of AT&T. MCI had been one of many smaller microwave common carriers, which, headed by Bill McGowan, led the way in developing a high-capacity fiber-based national infrastructure and then sank millions of dollars into marketing and promotion. Sprint Telecommunications later followed and by the mid-1980s no family could sit down to a quiet dinner without a telemarketing phone call interrupting the meal while a salesman tried to convince them that they ought to switch their long-distance service. It may be some testimony to the strength of AT&T's name recognition and its advertising that, despite the monumental change that the 1982 divestiture brought to the industry and despite the millions of dollars local companies have poured into television advertising, direct-mail marketing, and annoying sales calls at home, polls have shown that anywhere from 30 to 60 percent of the population still thinks that AT&T is their local phone company.[8]

In fact, for some people, reality may catch up to their mistaken perception. As tangled as the competitive universe of common carriage is, the 1996 Telecommunications Act will increase the number of knots and intersections by deregulating the business even further. Under the Act, long-distance carriers such as AT&T will be allowed to offer local service and the RBOCs can try their hand at the long distance business,[9] all of this in addition to and concurrent with telco efforts to penetrate the video services sector.

AT&T's purchase of TCI was motivated in part by the possibility that the telephone company could use TCI's coaxial plant to provide local telephone service to TCI subscribers. A host of very large telecommunications companies that once fed only on carefully limited common carrier services have been freed to dine from an expansive menu of à la carte items, including home television. The timetable for execution of these market plays is uncertain. A host of legal, technical, and business issues will need to be resolved, but the phone companies are working on several fronts to expand their traditional offerings.

The original seven Baby Bells were reduced to five in early 1996 when Texas-based SBC Communications (formerly Southwestern Bell) acquired Pacific Telesis, and two weeks later Bell Atlantic announced its intention to merge with Nynex. The newly formed SBC serves the Central Southern states, PacTel serves California and Nevada. The new Bell Atlantic (Nynex intended to give up its name while corporate headquarters moved to New York) covers the northeastern seaboard. Those five companies were, as of this writing, poised to consolidate to four with SBC's additional acquisition of Ameritech, the RBOC serving several Midwestern states. The other RBOCs include BellSouth in the Southeast and US West, serving the western and northwestern states.[10] GTE is the largest of the non-Bell LECs. As Table 8-7 shows, each company is a multibillion-dollar enterprise and controls millions of telephone lines. The long-distance carrier AT&T is the largest of the phone companies, and one of the largest companies in the world, with annual revenues of nearly $80 billion.

TABLE 8-7   U.S. Telephone Companies

Company	Revenues	Customer Lines
AT&T	$79.6 bill	
MCI	$15.2 bill	
Sprint	$13.6 bill	
SBC/PacTel	$21.0 bill	30.1 mill
Bell South	$17.8 bill	20.9 mill
Nynex	$13.3 bill	17.0 mill
Bell Atlantic	$13.4 bill	19.7 mill
Ameritech	$ 9.6 bill	18.8 mill
US West	$ 8.2 bill	14.7 mill
GTE	$20.2 bill	18.0 mill

Sources: Financial World, 22 April 1996, 44; *New York Times,* 2 April 1996, D-9; *Cable World,* 7 September 1992, 1; *Cable World,* 8 April 1996.

POTS to PANS.   While much of the telephone industry's history and profitability is grounded in plain old telephone service, the simple call you place to your neighbor is not where the future of the business lies. The POTS segment of the business has been relatively flat for some time and is not expected to grow more than 4 or 5 percent annually. In contrast to POTS, the telcos have been seeking to deliver enhanced services, or what some called PANS, "pretty amazing new stuff." Simple augmented customer services like call-waiting and call-forwarding are seen as helping lift the bottom line, but the serious growth markets are linked to business service and wireless and data communications. The explosion of cellular telephones, fax machines, and computer modems has been so pronounced that the decreasing supply of available telephone numbers has become a serious problem for the industry, and an expanded, more complex dialing regime has evolved, including a proliferation of area codes and a new toll-free dialing prefix (888).

The multichannel video business, therefore, is only one part of the larger picture that the telephone companies are trying to assemble. The ultimate goal is to be a full-service provider, bundling voice, data, and video over one wire and sending you one bill at the end of the month. It is not, however, a new vision.

The Long and Winding Road

The floodgates of telco entry into the video business really opened with passage of the Telecommunications Act of 1996. It gave the telephone industry not just formal legal approval to expand its business, but it was the final crescendo of what had been a building chorus of political philosophy that almost uniformly endorsed competition in the telecommunication sector over government control and separation of industries. The FCC, the White House, and both parties in Congress were, to a greater or lesser extent, embracing the ideology of the open marketplace and committing themselves to the notion that competition was better for the consumer than regulation.

It was not always so. The Justice Department, through its consent decree with AT&T, had effectively blocked the telephone company from entering the cable business and other information services in 1956. As the telephone industry, and especially AT&T, eyed cable TV in the 1960s, the fear then, as today, was that the telco would use the river of revenues from its protected monopoly telephone business to deliberately underprice new competitive ventures like the cable business with an eye toward driving out the competition. There was even concern that the telephone company would raise residential rates above normal levels in order to fund construction of competitive cable systems. This cross-subsidization would give the company an unfair advantage over almost everyone else by providing access to huge amounts of interest-free capital and giving it the ability to offer below-cost service, undercutting competitors' rates and driving them out of business. Cable companies were at an additional disadvantage because of their dependence on the telephone companies for pole space to string their wires. A telephone company attempting to offer competitive cable service could, by raising pole attachment fees or imposing burdensome technical requirements, force the local cable company off the poles, as the telephone industry in fact tried to do in the mid-1960s.[11] Those efforts, aimed at forcing local cable companies to lease telephone company facilities for the provision of TV service, are again what led the FCC in 1970 to tighten the restrictions on the Bell System and the independent phone companies.[12]

The FCC 1970 prohibitions on telco-delivered television were codified in the Cable Communications Policy Act of 1984. With some minor exceptions (e.g., rural services) the phone companies now were prevented both by Congress and the FCC from entering the video business. Finally, the provisions of the Modification of the Final Judgment (MFJ), which split up AT&T in 1982, additionally frustrated any RBOC efforts to enter cable service. But the winds of political change were blowing strong in the 1980s. The doctrine of deregulation, then un-regulation, that began under the Carter administration expanded during President Reagan's eight years in office.

In 1987 the Reagan Justice Department released a report on the status of the MFJ, recommending that the RBOCs be released from their restrictions. While lifting many of the constraints imposed on the companies, the court initially declined to allow them into the information services business and only did so following the directive of a higher court.[13] By 1991, therefore, the Baby Bell companies had cut one of the cords that bound them. (The MFJ was formally rescinded in April of 1996, quietly vanishing after more than ten years of momentous and controversial life.)

Meanwhile, the FCC began a series of proceedings designed to loosen their restraints on the RBOCs. In 1988, Alfred Sikes, then head of the National Telecommunications and Information Administration (NTIA), presented a report calling for the creation of what would become a Video Dial Tone service.[14] Under Video Dial

Tone (VDT), the telephone companies would be able to provide video services in their territories on a common carrier basis, that is they could be access providers but could not hold ownership interests in the content. When Sikes was named Chairman of the FCC in 1989, he took the idea with him. The Commission's declaration in 1988 that the cross-ownership ban should be lifted set the stage for the 1992 FCC decision to implement VDT and recommend to Congress that the 1984 Cable Act be amended to permit telephone companies even greater control over programming "subject to appropriate safeguards."[15]

The RBOCs did not wait around for Congressional action but won a series of court fights that struck down, on First Amendment grounds, the statutory ban on the provision of video service. Bell Atlantic's victory on this issue in 1993 was only the first in a series of judicial decisions that struck down the Cable Act prohibition for RBOCs nationally. And while the cable industry and others appealed those rulings, passage of the Telecommunications Act of 1996 made the issue moot by giving the telephone industry even wider latitude to diversify into new communications fields. The Act replaced VDT, under which the telephone companies were prevented from programming the local system themselves, with a concept called "Open Video Systems" or OVS.

Under OVS, telcos are permitted to offer their own programming, up to one-third of their channel capacity if demand exceeds supply. Moreover, operating under OVS rules, they are insulated from most of the state and local regulations that typically have attached to cable, including local franchising requirements and rate regulation. They do, at the same time, have to lease the remaining portion of their system to other programmers on a nondiscriminatory basis.

Although implementation of the OVS guidelines meant somewhat clearer sailing for the telephone industry as it moved into television, most of the Baby Bells had already stepped into those waters by the time the FCC formalized its rules. In fact, by 1998 some of the Bell companies had years of experimentation in home delivery of television. The following is an overview of the major efforts in telco TV.

US West

This Denver-based company provides local phone service to 25 million customers in fourteen states. When it purchased Hostetter's Continental Cable, it became the country's third largest cable television operator. The acquisition was not, however, the company's first foray into cable. US West owns a 20 percent stake in Great Britain's largest cable operator, Telewest Communications. Jointly owned with TCI, Inc. and SBC, Telewest provides a combined cable and telephone service to 4.1 million subscribers.[16] In 1993, US West also bought 25.5 percent of Time Warner, Inc.'s Time Warner Entertainment Co., the holding company for Time Warner's cable properties and film studio. It was noted during the acquisition of Continental that US West, through its additional affiliation with Time Warner, had access to more cable television homes in the United States than any other company.[17]

As early as 1992, US West announced its intention to rewire some of the major markets in its service area, including Denver, Minneapolis, Phoenix, Seattle, and Portland. US West began in Omaha with a hybrid analog-digital FTTC system featuring seventy-seven basic cable channels and digital video-on-demand services. It attracted 13,000 customers to its system, but found the digital traffic more complicated and demanding, as well as more expensive, than it had expected and by mid-1996 had postponed its plans for rolling out high-end systems beyond Omaha. The company's plans seemed to refocus on the development of traditional cable systems in the near term.

SBC/Pacific Telesis

Of the two partners in the SBC–PacTel combination, PacTel has been the more aggressive in moving into video services. It announced ambitious plans in late 1993 to rewire the entire state of California, but backed away from those plans and began looking at alternative delivery systems, including wireless cable (MMDS) and conventional cable franchises.

MMDS is one cost-effective way to get digitally compressed television into the home. Some RBOCs are looking at MMDS as an interim technology offering a number of benefits. Constructing wire-based systems or converting existing plant is expensive and time-consuming. It also may give the Baby Bells a chance to learn more about running multichannel television companies, a business in which they had very little expertise. Because of its limited interactivity, few saw it as the foundation for a fully integrated switched digital network, but as a shoe in the door of the cable customer's home, it is attractive in some situations. Part of the PacTel plan therefore was to enter the Southern California video market through the air. In 1995 it bought Cross Country Wireless for $175 million and was planning MMDS service to 4 million potential customers in Los Angeles and Orange counties in 1997.

While getting off to a quick start, SBC has been generally slower than some of the other RBOCs in venturing into broadband services. It was the first RBOC to purchase a cable company, buying two cable systems in the Washington, D.C. area from Hauser Communications, for $650 million, in 1993. (It sold the systems in 1997.) A subsequent effort to merge with Cox Cable, one of the country's leading MSOs, fell apart, however. By 1997, SBC had decided to reduce its activities in video, halting the PacTel cable operations in San Jose and San Diego, as well as its own SDV experiment in Richardson, Texas, and putting the Los Angeles MMDS initiative in doubt.

Bell Atlantic/Nynex.   In April of 1996, Bell Atlantic CEO Ray Smith and Nynex CEO Ivan Seidenberg announced the $21.4 billion merger of the two firms. It was the single biggest telecommunications merger in history. It joined two contiguous Baby Bells and created a telecom empire that stretched from Maine to Virginia, encompassing the entire northeastern seaboard and the huge metropolitan profit centers of Boston, New York, Philadelphia, Washington, D.C., Newark, and Richmond.

The new company had a stock market value close to $51 billion, 127,000 employees, and 36 million customers in twelve states.[18] Fundamental to the merger were the possibilities opened up by the large geographic spread of the new company and the long-distance market that it created. The Telecommunications Act of 1996, which made it possible for the Baby Bells to compete in long-distance, was credited as an important factor in the merger. Bell Atlantic now could be the local and long-distance carrier for all calls made within its region.

The attraction of the easy and lucrative long-distance market distracted the new company from its interests in video and may have slowed the pace of the telco's activities in the area. Video could wait while it established its local prominence in the long-distance market. But a flagging concern with video did not mean abandonment. Bell Atlantic maintained a healthy interest in telco television.

Of the two pre-merger companies, the original Bell Atlantic was the most active in television. Some observers marked the aborted merger of Bell Atlantic and TCI as the beginning of serious telco interest in cable. While the deal sank amongst the whitecaps of business and regulatory uncertainty, it nonetheless showed that the telcos were sailing. In fact, however, Bell Atlantic had been underway for some time. In 1992 the company joined with Sammons Cable to announce an experimental broadband full-service network in northern New Jersey to provide telephone and cable service to several towns in the area. Initially intended as a VDT network, Bell Atlantic subsequently dropped those plans and opened two new trials.

In the northern suburbs of Washington, D.C., it conducted a lengthy experiment with ADSL technological, supplying full Video On Demand to 1,000 customers. The VOD service, called "Stargazer," provided one of the first peeks at what a fully interactive pay-per-view system might look like. The Stargazer platform used high-capacity digital servers to store a library of more than 655 programs, including 200 films, 120 TV shows, and 120 children's programs. Prices for each program varied: A motion picture might cost $3 to $4, while a twenty-minute cartoon or a news feature clip from ABC's *Nightline* might run $1 or less. Some titles were sold for as little as 49 cents.[19]

A much more ambitious project in both technology and programming was conducted by Bell Atlantic in Dover Township, New Jersey. Bell Atlantic began commercial service over a 384-channel, digital FTTC system in early 1996, offering voice, data, and video. Originally devised as VDT system, Bell Atlantic already had contracted with a third-party programmer, FutureVision, to supply a 77-channel menu of cable and broadcast channels, but other programmers also rented space on the system. Bell Atlantic subsequently purchased FutureVision, taking full operational control and obtaining OVS status from the FCC.

For Bell Atlantic, however, Dover was just a start. Its next big step was the announced deployment of a full-service SDV system in its original home city of Philadelphia.[20] With Bell Atlantic's bold philosophy in video programming, the City of Brotherly Love was likely to become the first major metropolitan area in the country to measure the feasibility and potential of the new technology.

In the exploration of the possibilities of multichannel video, Nynex was as timid as Bell Atlantic was bold. While it does have extensive cable–telco holdings in the United Kingdom, its domestic wire-based television trials were restricted to relatively small-scale projects.

Bell Atlantic and Nynex also looked at MMDS delivery technologies, investing $100 million in CAI wireless in 1995 and announcing plans for digital wireless services in Boston and Hampton Roads, Virginia, beginning in 1997. Tests with the digital MMDS technology proved disappointing, however, as foliage from trees interferred with the digital signal. In late 1996 the telco suspended plans for the service.

Ameritech

About the only avenue Bell Atlantic did not pursue in its television activities was the outright creation of traditionally franchised, cable systems. This was the primary strategy of Ameritech, however, which eschewed the more expensive switched digital video approach. The Chicago-based company declared in 1993 that it would get into the switched broadband video business, but withdrew its Video Dial Tone applications in mid-1995, citing a cumbersome and time-consuming approval process. Instead, it sought and won local cable TV franchises throughout the Midwest, gaining permission to overbuild and compete with entrenched cable operators. Ameritech offered local municipalities a 5 percent franchise fee, a 750 MHz, HFC system featuring interactive banking and shopping services and a $1-per-year local government channel that could be used to generate revenue through advertising and infomercials.[21] It became the first Baby Bell to win its own local franchise in 1995 when it was granted the right to wire the Detroit suburb of Plymouth, Michigan. It went on from there to gain building rights in Ohio, Wisconsin, and Illinois.[22] While Ameritech continued to pursue cable TV franchises in the Midwest, its proposed acquisition by SBC put the future of its video activities in some doubt. SBC, as a corporate strategy, seemed to be moving away from the provision of video services, and it was unclear what impact, if any, this might have on Ameritech's cable operations.

BellSouth

BellSouth has, in some ways, maintained a lower profile in telco television than some of its RBOC brethren, but its has not been inactive. The company began experimenting with fiber and ISDN-based delivery systems in Florida as early as 1986. Like Ameritech, it has secured franchises for traditional cable systems in South Carolina, Alabama, and Florida. It has explored interactive HFC architectures for possible deployment in its top thirty Southern markets, and has been moving into MMDS systems and experimenting with LMDS.

GTE

With 18 million access lines in twenty-eight states, GTE was the largest non-Bell telecommunications company until 1998 when it announced plans to merge with Bell Atlantic. It began a highly publicized trial of interactive video services in Cerritos, California, in 1989, but the results proved disappointing, in part because of the undeveloped technology. The pre-digital test offered twenty on-demand movies but required employees at the GTE central office to scurry around and load video-tapes into twenty VCRs. GTE announced its intention to build OVS networks in sixty-six markets by 2005,[23] and was negotiating for cable overbuild franchises in Florida and California where it planned to build 750 MHz HFC systems.[24]

AT&T

With the deregulation of the industry, AT&T began moving enthusiastically into the local loop business, winning regulatory approval to offer local services and securing deals with competitive access providers that gave it a toehold in more than half the states for the joint provision of local and long-distance service. The largest of these deals was the acquisition of cable giant TCI. Whether AT&T planned to offer local video services, by itself or in concert with the local providers, was not immediately clear.[25] In early 1996 AT&T announced it was purchasing a 2.5 percent equity stake in DirecTV, with an option to buy 30 percent of the company. That move, coupled with the subsequent purchase of TCI, suggested the telephone company's intention to enter any video delivery business at least initially using existing platforms.

AT&T also divided itself into three separate companies to pursue more focused business interests. In the "tri-vestiture" AT&T spun off its computer interests, the manufacturing arm that had been Western Electric and its Bell Labs research component. The new AT&T would concentrate on telecommunications sectors, while the computer firm, recapturing its former NCR logo, tried to recover from disappointing results in that market. Through its newly spun-off and renamed equipment manufacturing company, Lucent Technologies, AT&T shareholders sought to become major turnkey equipment suppliers for the emerging full-service industry. The SBC trial in Richardson, Texas, was conducted on a high-end SDV system supplied by AT&T in conjunction with Broadband Technologies, Inc. The company also sold a full-service digital system to Walt Disney Co., which intended to make it part of its Disneyworld-like planned community, "Celebration, Florida," near the Orlando theme park.

Some observers felt the telephone companies, in their multibillion-dollar efforts to get into television, were driven in part by the popular frenzy of new technology and the glitter of Hollywood; utiltities such as telephone companies were seen on

Wall Street as steady but boring investments. Entry into television and data services was seen as a vehicle for moving the companies toward a more attractive, perhaps even exciting, position as growth stocks. Interest also was driven by the real possibility that the telephone industry could effectively compete in new markets in the next century with attractively priced, bundled information and communication services tailored to individual homes. Whatever the causes, the voice/data/video mantra was spreading from the RBOCs and long-distance companies down to the second tier telcos. Southern New England Telephone, for example, sought a cable television franchise for the entire state of Connecticut, and Carolina Telephone, in conjunction with Sprint, was building a VDT platform in Wake Forest, Georgia, challenging the existing Time Warner system.

The Utilities

Public utilities are interesting contenders in the contest for wireline television customers. The same deregulatory philosophy that affected telecommunications has also been opening the market for electric utilities. While still a minor player in the communications distribution game, the possibilities for the nation's power companies are beginning to expand, and they could become significant niche providers in the next century. In fact, if you live in Glasgow, Kentucky, or Lariat, Texas, you currently get your cable television, local telephone service, Internet access, and electric power all from the same company, the "power" company. Electric utilities were initially drawn to coaxial and fiber communication networks because they provided a means to monitor and control electrical usage and because utilities already had engineered a right-of-way conduit and wire path to all residences and businesses. Meter reading, connections and disconnections, immediate diagnoses of outages, load management, and even customer control of usage are all made possible by a telecommunications overlay using the company's existing network. Of course, these energy management functions take up only a fraction of the capacity of the broadband system. There's plenty of room left for MTV, CNN, fax, and voice traffic.

Only a handful of such operations currently exist. The Glasgow Electric Plant Board, noted above, began a pioneering effort in 1989. CSW Corp., a Texas utility, built a pilot system in Lariat in 1995 and was constructing a $300 million HFC system in Austin.[26] Deregulation, however, has touched the power industry in ways similar to the telecommunications field and utilities are looking at a variety of methods to leverage their existing and planned infrastructures into new business ventures.

Utility companies have little experience in telephone or video service, but are willing to contract out much of the expertise while providing the fiber backbone. Still, while the regulatory and technological changes of the last few years have made it easier for utilities to consider such systems, the likelihood of the industry becoming a major player in video and data services is uncertain.

BROADCASTING

Traditional Broadcasters

There are about 1,190 commercial broadcast television stations in the United States, 559 VHF stations (channels 2–13) and 635 UHF stations (channels 14–69). Most are owned by groups, although historically the number of stations any company can own, including the networks, has been limited by law. The Telecommunications Act of 1996 loosened these restrictions somewhat and an individual or group can now own any number of stations as long as their total audience reach does not exceed 35 percent of the national market.[27] The three major networks, ABC, NBC, and CBS, therefore, historically have controlled programming, but have been restricted in the number of stations they can actually own. In 1996, under the loosened regulations, CBS owned about seventeen television stations, ABC ten, and NBC six.[28] Most of the stations that run network programming are "affiliates" of the network, that is they have contractual arrangements for the carriage of the network schedules. Through the affiliates, the major networks reach nearly all the television homes in the United States. This extended reach allows them to sell advertising on a national scale and generate the millions of dollars necessary for the production and acquisition of high quality programming. Only a national network system (in both broadcast and cable television) makes possible the generation of revenue sufficient for the costly development of modern television programs.[29] Nonaffiliate stations, or "independents," typically subsist on a program diet of network reruns, old movies, talk shows, and game shows.

The FCC assigns station licenses across the country, in part, on the basis of market size. The larger the market, the more broadcast licenses have been allotted by the FCC, albeit with an eye toward reserving enough channels for smaller communities to support localism. The largest cities in the United State have ten or more stations, including all the major networks; smaller towns or cities may have only two or three stations, some only have one. Many towns in the United States have no assigned TV stations.

Cable has always had a competitive but symbiotic relationship with the broadcasting industry, because broadcasting represents not just a principle historic competitor to cable but also its chief source of programming. The long debate over "must carry" and "retransmission consent" regulations illustrates the roller-coaster relationship between the industries. Cable, initially, was dependent on the broadcast signal for its survival, but as cable penetration grew, broadcasters found they needed to be carried by the local system if they were going to be seen by a majority of their audience.

Some broadcasters began battling cable operators almost as soon as the first CATV antenna sprouted on the neighboring mountaintop. Broadcasters feared the competitive power of cable's multichannel technology, and with good cause. Cable television ultimately stole viewers and broke the national oligopoly of the three dominant television networks by fragmenting audiences. Cable's web of wires spread out through the towns and neighborhoods of the United States, and cable-only networks proliferated through the 1980s. As access to cable service increased, viewers voted with their remote controls; ratings and "share" increased for cable and decreased for the broadcast networks. (*Ratings* are the percentage of viewers watching out of the universe of people with TV sets; *share* is the percentage watching a particular program or network out of all those with their sets turned on at that time.) From 1979 through 1995, the combined prime time share for ABC, NBC, and CBS fell from above 90 percent to 53 percent.[30] The combined share of all basic cable, meanwhile rose, from less than 10 percent to more than 30 percent in all TV households and up to 42 percent in cable households. And these trends showed no signs of abatement.[31]

Cable and the New Broadcast Networks

Cable's basic programming services accounted for much of the viewer migration but not all of it. While cable was extending its reach, the networks also were challenged by the rise of independent television stations. In 1964 television set manufacturers were required to include UHF tuners in all sets so viewers would no longer have to buy separate devices. A change in FCC regulations made it easier to buy and sell stations and increased the number of stations a given company could own. Carriage by cable also made available UHF channel allotments more attractive and helped lead to an increase in the number of these stations around the country. While the new stations competed directly against existing network affiliates, they had an even greater impact by providing the base from which to build new networks. The first to do so was media mogul Rupert Murdoch, owner of News Corporation and 20th Century Fox movie studio. Murdoch began in the publishing business with a chain of Australian newspapers, expanding into British and U.S. publishing largely with sensationalist tabloids. In 1985 he entered the broadcasting business buying a group of U.S. television stations and half of the Fox studio (later acquiring the entire company), using them as the base to build his broadcast and cable programming networks. Murdoch relied heavily on independent television stations and exercised a keen marketing savvy that targeted younger audiences to create the "fourth" television network. Fox Broadcasting aired hit shows such as *Married with Children, The Simpsons,* and *Beverly Hills 90210.*

Cable's role in the development of the new network was twofold. First, carriage by cable of the local independent stations helped to give them greater visibility to the home viewer. Cable carriage, in many instances, improved the reception of the UHF signal, brought it into the homes of people who might not have been able to receive it over the air, and, most importantly, moved it off its "over-the-air" channel of, say, forty-eight, and brought it down on the subscriber's television dial to a channel below 13 and next to the network channels the viewer was used to watching. It helped establish a kind of home-viewing parity for the new independents. In addition, cable in some cases carried the new Fox network even when there was no local broadcast affiliate.[32] TCI struck a deal with Murdoch to carry the Fox network in markets that did not have an independent station to align with Fox.

Murdoch's success led to the launching of other broadcast networks. In 1993 both Warner Brothers and a partnership between Paramount and Chris Craft Broadcasting announced the start of broadcast networks. Warner Brothers began the WB network in 1994, and Paramount–Chris Craft started the UPN network in 1995, anchored by Paramount's hugely successful *Star Trek* franchise in its latest iteration, *Star Trek: Voyager*. While neither network generated large ratings, they did add to the general fragmentation of audiences and the continuing slide in the viewership of the previously dominant big three networks.

At the same time, it is important to note that although the ABC, NBC, and CBS networks are no longer the only players in the television universe, they are still the biggest. The combined prime time ratings of the top twenty basic cable networks in 1995 was only 22.4, less than half that of the combined ratings for the three broadcast networks.[33] The viewership of the USA network, consistently one of the most watched cable channels, is only about 2.3 ratings points, a fraction of that of any one of the broadcasters; only CNN, during the occurrence of important news events, generates ratings comparable to the broadcasters. Network broadcasting will likely remain a significant force in television, both as a delivery system and as a source for programming. In fact, much of the programming run on cable television remains old network material sold into syndication. Cable networks such as Nickelodeon, with its "Nick at Night" and "TV Land" schedules, has thrived almost exclusively on broadcast sitcoms from decades ago, featuring such pop cultural icons as *Bewitched* and *Mr. Ed*. ABC, CBS, and NBC will continue to be a dominant force in programming for many years because, more than anyone else, they require and generate an unending supply of original shows. "Nick at Night" can succeed on a steady diet of black-and-white reruns, NBC and CBS, obviously, cannot. The supply of original programming from the broadcast industry not only will continue, but will likely increase.

The New Broadcast Industry

The switch from analog to digital broadcasting will open up new program delivery possibilities for local and network broadcasters. As noted, while digital compression was once conceived of largely as a way to allow broadcasters to provide High Definition Television, the industry quickly realized that the same digital transmission techniques would allow them to broadcast several digitally compressed conventional television channels instead of one HDTV signal. It additionally offers the potential for providing nontraditional broadcast services such as paging and data delivery. Four or five channels of conventional television equate to equivalent multiples of advertising time and constitute a much more lucrative prospect than one channel of HDTV. Broadcasters began an intense and bruising political campaign in the early 1990s to allow them to use the new technology for delivery of multiple services. The FCC had set aside frequencies in the existing UHF band for the new digital broadcasting, but some in Congress felt broadcasters should be required to pay, up front, for the right to use that space. Many saw spectrum sales or auctions as one vehicle for helping balance the federal budget. The spectrum in question has been valued at anywhere between $12 billion and $70 billion and broadcasters were predictably chagrined at the prospect of having to pay for it. Broadcasters have not yet had to pay for their digital or analog frequencies, however. Stations throughout the nation's top 10 markets began digital broadcasting in 1998 using the UHF channels granted them by the FCC. At the same time, they will not have to relinquish their existing analog frequencies until 85 percent of the viewers in their market can receive digital signals. The FCC has authority to then auction off the returned analog channels.

Traditional broadcasters, therefore, are likely to become multichannel video and service providers using digital broadcast technologies within a few years. In some isolated cases this may make them more directly competitive with the local wire-based service. More likely, it will mean additional programming retransmitted by the local cable operator as the broadcaster places several channels, rather than just one, on the system.

In the long run it is unlikely that cable television will trigger the demise of broadcasting or the end of existing broadcast networks. Over-the-air television will continue to serve those who cannot, or choose not, to subscribe to cable TV or other paid, multichannel program services. Moreover, broadcasters will remain important content providers and, with additional channels made available to them, will increase their production of programming and their development of new telecommunications services. While maintaining their multichannel delivery systems they will likely concentrate their talents and energy in the development of programming, and so increasingly move to the software side of the business.

Wireless Cable

MMDS

The broadcasters' vision of being able to provide multiple channels of digital terrestrial broadcast programming is available in one sense today. MMDS (multichannel multipoint distribution service) has been around in some form for decades. The FCC initially envisioned a service providing spectrum access for specialized programming by school districts, religious organizations, and similar groups. For such organizations, the opportunity to transmit video programming proved attractive despite the cost of installing special antennas and converters at each receiving location. Because such organizations did not expect to transmit to the general public, the number of costly installations appeared manageable. Wireless cable when used in this way represented the FCC service category called Instructional Television Fixed Service (ITFS). Most ITFS licensees needed only one channel and typically did not operate continuously. The Commission subsequently recognized that it may have allocated too much spectrum for such a narrow application. ITFS licensees persuaded the FCC to allow sharing of their facilities and authorizations with commercial ventures as a way to secure needed funds. In time, commercial video services proliferated and their bandwidth requirements grew. The FCC accommodated such wireless cable service by allocating dedicated MMDS spectrum contiguous to the ITFS frequency band.

Initially, even MMDS lacked the kind of channel capacity sufficient to constitute the functional equivalent of cable television. Lacking compression technologies, MMDS primarily operated where cable television was unavailable, including urban areas where the politics of franchising and other factors delayed the construction of coaxial systems. The operator simply provided a handful of premium channels and was content to carve out a profitable and unobtrusive niche. Home Box Office, for example, used a single-channel MDS (multipoint distribution service) in the late 1970s and early 1980s to penetrate markets that were not yet wired for cable.

As an alternative to cable, MMDS has a number of advantages, chief among them being cost. Compared to cable, MMDS is very cheap, about $400 to $450 per subscriber, according to the industry. You do not have to build an expensive infrastructure nor maintain hundreds of miles of coax, fiber, amplifiers, and taps. The transmitter costs about a million dollars and the only other facilities expenses are subscriber dishes and converters. MMDS operators do not have to pay local franchise fees, nor are they subject to rate regulation. It is a very cost-effective business.

As long as MMDS was restricted to a few dozen channels, it never represented much of a competitive threat to cable, and was more typically used in large cities that had no cable service. As with other transport technologies, regulatory relief and digital technology are changing the picture, however. With digitally compressed signals, it is estimated that MMDS can deliver up to 250 channels. With its relative ease of installation, MMDS can quickly bring digital television and 200-plus channel service to market and at a relatively low operating cost. It is, in short, a way to get into the high-capacity transport business quickly and cheaply.

But MMDS also has its limits. Even with 250 channels, its capacity is dwarfed by the potential of a truly broadband wired network, which can provide, in its interactive form, a virtually unlimited number of program choices. In addition, MMDS is largely a one-way transmission path. Its interactivity is generally restricted to using conventional telephone lines as a return path. That is, a subscriber can select pay-movies and other services, but must place a telephone call to initiate the service. This is likely to prove awkward and overly burdensome to an audience raised on the instant gratification of the remote control and computer mouse. Importantly, MMDS is also prone to interference by physical objects, such as tall trees and buildings, which has limited its utility in some communities and is one of the reasons some proponents have backed away from it. In 1996 there were about 200 systems and one million MMDS subscribers in the country; revenues were about $272 million.[34]

The long-term potential for MMDS is unclear. Its most likely role is as an interim transport technology in locations where it is technically effective. It could be useful to cable companies as a way to extend their reach into more scarcely populated areas where sending a line is not cost effective. It may also be used by some telephone companies as a means of testing the multichannel video business. Some industry experts see a window of opportunity for MMDS to move in with digital services before wire-based systems can get up to full digital speed, but fade as wired systems mature.

LMDS and IVDS

The FCC also has allocated spectrum for a close cousin to MMDS, Local Multipoint Distribution Service (LMDS). This service operates in the 28 GHz band and will provide broadband video and wireless telephone services. Unlike MMDS, LMDS breaks its service area into small cells, each with a low-power transmitter covering a local area of two to six miles in radius. The shorter distance between sender and receiver means a smaller receiving dish than DBS or MMDS, from six to twelve inches across. Interactivity is possible using laptop-sized home transmitters to feed signals back to the system, and the cellular nature makes it possible to deliver different content in different cells, tailoring programming to the interests of a particular neighborhood. A digital LMDS system could provide several hundred channels of programming. In 1996, the FCC established a spectrum allocation plan that balanced the requirements of prospective LMDS and low Earth-orbiting satellite operators with existing satellite operators who use a portion of the band to transmit traffic and network control signals.

Interactive Video Distribution Systems (IVDS) present a yet to be proven narrowband (500 kHz) wireless option. With such limited spectrum, the services involve "bursty" digital data commands from subscriber terminals, rather than broadband downloading of content. Yet even a narrowband link into the home presents some promise for polling and interactive applications.

THE SATELLITE INDUSTRY

Industry Structure

Consumers using very large dishes have been watching satellite-delivered television for many years, and satellites will continue to be central to the distribution of national cable and broadcast programming. But only recently have higher powered satellite services made serious competitive inroads against cable television. Moreover, satellites have been expanding their base of consumer and business services, from international paging to position determination and navigation to interactive data. Satellites can distribute digital movies, but increasingly will supply your data and telephone needs as well. This section looks at the structure of the satellite industry, which is comprised of a number of specialized business segments, including satellite manufacturers, carriers, and program distributors.

Satellite Manufacturers

The domestic U.S. satellite manufacturing industry has consolidated into a tight oligopoly dominated by Hughes Space and Communications Company, with lesser market shares held by Lockheed Martin Astro Space and Space Systems/Loral. Heretofore, satellite manufacturing has involved an expensive, time-consuming development of a product line that is customized on a per-satellite basis to the particular requirements of an operator. Each satellite is one of a kind in the sense that satellite manufacturers do not establish and maintain an ongoing assembly line. The best a manufacturer can expect under current market conditions is the development of a uniform "bus" onto which different payload configurations attach.

Think of current satellite manufacturing as "designer" clothing: A relatively small number of any designer's creations reach the market. Satellite manufacturing began as a project-oriented, government-contracted project. Even now, the few satellites ordered in any year supports a "designer" satellite operation that can result in a two-year manufacturing timetable. The specificity of design and configuration means that the manufacturer cannot fully capture the kinds of economies of scale that might be available in cases where several different customers were ordering the same satellite model and technology could be standardized and applied across the manufacturing process.

Large constellations of satellites, such as low Earth-orbiting (LEO) satellites providing mobile services, present opportunities for the manufacture of "off-the-rack" or "ready-to-wear" satellites; a constellation of 66 Iridium and 228 Teledesic LEOs, for example, requires efficient, assembly line manufacturing of at least several satellites per month. Slashing production times makes the satellite construction business more like short-cycle automobile production, in which standard components can be installed on a number of modules that fit onto a single bus model.

Hughes Space and Communications Company.   Hughes Space and Communications (HSC) is a wholly owned subsidiary of General Motors and the principal owner of one of the two dominant DBS services, DirecTV. Since 1961, the company has manufactured over 150 spacecraft including more than 166 commercial communications satellites. HSC is engaged in the development and production of state-of-the-art space and communications systems for military, commercial, and scientific uses, including meteorological observations. The company designed and built the world's first geosynchronous communications satellite, Syncom, launched in 1963. It has manufactured more than 50 percent of the satellites now in commercial service worldwide.

Lockheed Martin Astro Space.   Lockheed Martin Astro Space has perennially run second in satellite sales to Hughes Space and Communications and has undertaken an aggressive campaign to bolster its manufacturing capability. The company has invested over $1 billion to close facilities in New Jersey and

Pennsylvania and to construct a state-of-the-art production facility in California. It also has announced plans to construct a $4 billion constellation of nine Ka-band communications satellites for service commencing in the year 2000.

Space Systems Loral. Space Systems Loral is a joint venture of Loral Space and Communications (itself the consolidated the satellite manufacturing capabilities of Ford Aerospace and Loral) and the European manufacturers Aerospatiale, Alcatel, Alenia, and Daimler–Benz Aerospace. The company has diversified into several different types of satellite product lines, including large general purpose satellites used by INTELSAT, and ones used for mobile telephony, DBS, air traffic control/weather observation and high-powered regional services, including video program delivery. The company also has agreed to provide a communications payload for a new line of Russian satellites.

In early 1996 Lockheed Martin Company and Loral Corporation announced a $10 billion strategic alliance. Primarily as a result of the slowdown in defense contracting in view of the Soviet Union's collapse, Lockheed Martin acquired Loral's defense electronics and systems integration businesses for approximately $9.1 billion. Additionally the companies will share in the ownership of a new venture, to be known as Loral Space and Communications Corp., that will own Space Systems/Loral and its telecommunication interests, including Globalstar.

Conversion from "Designer" to "Off-the-Rack" Manufacturing

The Global Information Infrastructure will stimulate a proliferation of services, frequencies, orbits, operators, and low Earth-orbiting satellite constellations containing dozens of space stations. The commercial communications satellite marketplace will continue to diversify in terms of products and markets. This industry no longer just supports the one-by-one manufacture of a few dozen satellites a year, with services provided by a few predominantly government-owned carriers participating in global or regional cooperatives. Instead, a variety of developing markets present the prospect for service diversity and perhaps even greater price competition. The option of procuring satellites, available in-orbit or for quick launch, has accelerated the development of a more diversified and maturing marketplace.

What an "off-the-rack" manufacturing process loses in terms of design flexibility, it gains in speedy deployment and economies of scale. Diverse markets and satellite roles require quicker turnaround in the manufacturing process, particularly when market opportunities occur within a "window" caused by short-term capacity shortages. Likewise, market opportunities will require different types of satellites, some containing less than the standard of twenty-four to thirty-six transponders, each with 36 MHz of bandwidth. "Lightsats" will operate in LEO satellite constellations by the dozens and as well can meet short-term capacity requirements while operating from geostationary orbital locations already occupied by a heavysat.

The Launch Industry

Very few companies launch satellites, primarily because of the substantial market entry costs and risk. The launch of a typical communications satellite into geostationary orbit costs $85 to $100 million. Until the decision to partially commercialize the industry, a few national governments or government-backed consortia monopolized the market. Even with a commitment by some nations to commercialize space, government enterprises still dominate. The pervasive and ongoing influence of government on this sector results because taxpayers have underwritten research and development of this essential component of modern intelligence-gathering. It persists now because incumbent operators like Araianespace and recent commercial market entrants in Russia and China are government-owned and governments in other nations worry that without quotas and price floors, government underwritten ventures will predatorially price launches and drive out private competitors.

Beginning in 1958 and running to the early 1980s, the United States government exclusively provided launch services for itself and for all civilian ventures. The decision to commercialize space resulted from an overall change in political philosophy as well as a pragmatic recognition that the government could not handle the entire demand for space shuttle and expendable launch vehicles. In quick order, the companies that had contracted with the U.S. Government became commercial operators.

The lead companies now involved in launching include Lockheed Martin and McDonnell Douglas (which merged with Boeing in late 1996). In the near future, launch operators will need to respond to diversifying satellite product lines. Most launches now insert one or two satellites into orbit. The LEO mobile satellite constellations will require launches of six or more space stations at a time, and the quick deployment of replacement lightsats.

Launch Insurance.   A satellite typically costs about $250 million to $275 million to construct and launch, and the technology of transporting several thousand pounds into a particular orbit 22,300 miles above earth has yet to become a routine endeavor. Launches also involve the ignition of highly combustible materials and the propulsion of large and heavy equipment that potentially could kill people and destroy property if a rocket were to go out of control. Because of the expense and risk in launching a satellite, most operators seek insurance rather than attempt to beat the odds. Launch insurance tracks historical launch failure rates and can vary from a low of about 7 to10 percent of total cost to a high of about 25 percent. Because so many factors can adversely affect a launch, the matter of an insurance payout can trigger disputes over who is liable when a launch fails. The launch provider may claim that the satellite manufacturer erred in the construction or installation of the satellite onboard the rocket. Likewise, the launch provider may blame a subcontractor, particularly one responsible for the construction of one of the several stages in a launch sequence that must ignite and successfully propel the satellite to a particular intermediate location en route to its final orbital slot.

Insurance typically pays for construction and launch of a replacement satellite but not lost revenues and profits. A satellite operator that has suffered a launch failure may have to scramble if it has not negotiated with the initial launch provider for an early replacement launch. Even if an operator has such a commitment, the launch operator may have to delay a relaunch until such time as it can determine what went wrong. Such delays have triggered litigation over expenses and lost profits.

Satellite Carriers

Satellite carriers managed the construction, launch, and operation of commercial satellites. They lease transponders for the life of the bird, as well as for shorter fixed terms and on an occassional use basis. The number of domestic U.S. satellite operators also has declined with mergers and acquisitions distilling the industry into three major operators: Hughes Communications, Inc. (HCI), GE Americom, and Loral Space and Communications Ltd.

HCI.   HCI, a subsidiary of General Motors, has the dominant market share with seventeen satellites owned, or individually managed on behalf of international customers. The company all but created the commercial satellite manufacturing business as prime contractor for the INTELSAT-1 (Early Bird) satellite. HCI operates ten satellites for domestic service and other subsidiaries of the company have a major market share in satellite manufacturing, and direct broadcast satellite service (DirecTV) in the United States with strategic joint ventures for DBS in other regions, including Latin America and Japan. In 1996 Hughes agreed to pay $3 billion to acquire PanAmSat Corp., the first private satellite operator to have operational facilities in each of the three major ocean regions.

GE Americom.   GE Americom now operates a business previously served by affiliates of RCA, Contel, GE, and American Satellite, Inc. The company has plans to diversify by increasing the number of communication satellites, acquiring 80 percent of a "little LEO" system, Starsys, that will provide data, position determination, and messaging services.

Loral Space and Communications.   In 1996 Loral Space and Communications acquired AT&T's Skynet system for $712.5 million. AT&T had operated four Telstar domestic satellites, primarily for video program distribution, but also for other business applications including teleconferencing and data transmission. Loral Space plans to invest an additional $700 million to expand Skynet with an eye toward more aggressively competing with Hughes.

Teleport Operators

Satellite users may own their own ground facilities for sending and receiving satellite transmissions. Teleports, however, provide this relay function for those who prefer to delegate it to a full-time professional organization, or whose service requirements do not justify the capital outlay in Earth stations and other facilities. Teleports provide more than simple uplinking and downlinking, they are more than just "antenna farms." The successful teleport operator provides a number of sophisticated multimedia services, including the processing of signals originating on terrestrial wireline networks to make them optimized for satellite transmission. This processing may involve digital compression, signal encryption, the addition of foreign language tracks, inserting advertisements, and coordinating with other satellite carriers abroad. Teleport customers include universities, programmers, radio and television stations, government agencies, and corporations.

Network Externalities in Satellite Telecommunications

Satellite-delivered telecommunications can enhance consumer welfare by generating higher value as a satellite serves increasing numbers of users and points of communication.[35] Satellites can provide such expanded access without increased costs and often without higher user rates.[36] Once a carrier incurs the substantial sunk cost to make its footprint available, the incremental cost for it to serve an additional point of communication and additional users via another Earth station approaches zero. An additional point of access requires users to install or interconnect with an Earth station, acquire domestic facilities to link their premises with the Earth station, and pay space segment charges.

The value of satellite service accruing to users therefore can increase as the satellite serves more Earth stations and more users, often without higher charges to reflect the increased utility.[37] The concept of direct network externalities reflects this enhanced value.[38] The benefit is considered an externality, because standard economic analysis and the pricing of service may not take into account this outcome. Indirect network externalities result when increasing coverage and market penetration result in more plentiful, lower costing complementary goods. For example, consensus on technical standards for Earth stations accessing INTELSAT and Inmarsat satellites can promote industry-wide equipment compatibility and help manufacturers achieve economies of scale by having to support fewer product lines with different technical standards.[39]

Hot Birds and Hot Slots

Massive startup costs and the large inventory of transponder capacity in new generations of satellites also create incentives for satellite operators to compete for the business of video program distributors. Video programming occupies a large portion of satellite capacity as compared to voice and data traffic. A satellite operator can achieve certain financial success by convincing video programmers that a particular satellite will become the preferred target for the Earth stations operated by cable and broadcast television operators. Because a single satellite Earth station typically can receive programming from only one satellite, broadcasters and cablecasters have a financial incentive to limit the number of satellite sources of video programs. The "Hot Bird" concept reflects the interest in pointing a single Earth station to one satellite for all video programming.

Satellites become Hot Birds when their operator has the good marketing fortune of attracting a key video programmer who can serve as an "anchor tenant." Once an operator attracts a key video programmer, whose content viewers expect to receive, other programmers follow suit. These follow-on programmers join the bandwagon with the expectation that once a broadcaster or cablecaster points an Earth station to a particular satellite to access the key anchor tenant, they will become more likely to contract to carry somewhat less desirable programs that happen to occupy transponders on the Hot Bird. In effect, providers of somewhat less desirable programming can ride the coattails of the most desirable program simply by occupying space on the "right" satellite. A programmer occupying transponders on a less desirable satellite may find cablecasters reluctant to install yet another Earth station simply to receive its programming.

Hot Birds help make certain satellite orbital slots the preferred location to which Earth stations point. A satellite operator who succeeds in loading a satellite with video programming also typically succeeds in making the orbital slot that the satellite occupies an essential point. Cablecasters lock in Earth stations to that orbital slot. Simple inertia and the cost of repositioning the Earth station would tend to keep them pointed to that particular orbital slot. But additionally the Hot Bird operator works to institutionalize that orbital slot as one of the key "Hot Slots" for access to cable television programming.

The Hot Slot concept has another characteristic in the DTH/DBS marketplace. DTH/DBS operators in Europe have launched more than one satellite into the same orbital slot to provide an even larger inventory of programs via a single Earth station. These operators deploy satellites that operate on adjacent frequencies. Rather than interfering with one another, the satellites operate much like a number of different television stations all serving the same locality but transmitting on different channels. The satellites collectively provide a larger bandwidth of frequencies with each satellite's operating frequencies segueing into the other to create a continuous range of transponders.

Digital Television Distribution

Satellites, which have distributed analog television signals to broadcasters and cablecasters for years, are now providing similar links for distribution of digital television signals. Many program providers, such as HBO and Showtime, send fully digitized signals to local and national home providers. DBS services and digital MMDS platforms maintain a digital signal to the subscriber; most cable systems translate the digital signal to conventional analog form before putting it on the system (conversion to full digital cable delivery will be a gradual process).

Some programmers choose to use a digital distribution service instead of digitizing the signal themselves. TCI has invested substantially in satellite distribution as part of the company's vision of a digital future. TCI's "Headend in the Sky" (HITS) service is part of its National Digital Television Center near Denver. Originally slated to begin operation with the delivery of digital set-top boxes in 1994, operations were delayed along with arrival of the decoders until late 1996. The HITS service uses digitization and compression technology to feed its own headends, and the headends of any other companies that wish to purchase the programming, with a plethora of cable networks and pay-per-view entertainment options. Programming services using this distribution option can feed HITS a digital signal or have HITS convert their analog feed.

Even DBS operators can play a role as distribution "middlemen." In addition to direct-to-home service, DBS services, along with such businesses as HITS, can deliver bundled digital feeds to local providers such as MMDS and satellite master antenna systems serving apartment houses (see more on SMATV systems below). Such a delivery scheme can save digital MMDS operators a substantial amount of money that would otherwise be necessary to encode the signals.

Direct-to-Home Satellite Television

Subscribers to DirecTV, PrimeStar, or one of the several other DBS/DTH services take part directly in satellite television. After failing in the early 1980s, DBS operators, providing service to dishes less than one meter in diameter, achieved a successful debut in 1995 with 1.4 million new subscribers. With a collective annual advertising budget of more than $400 million, DirecTV, United States Satellite Broadcasting, PrimeStar, and EchoStar succeeded in converting satellite-delivered television into a mass market and one of the success stories of the mid-1990s. By 1998, satellite television services had more than 6 million subscibers.

Previously, most satellite television reception occurred in rural locales unserved by cable television. The expense, complexity, and size of the television receive-only (TVRO) terminals operating at C-band meant that hobbyists with some technical know-how dominated the market. The medium-powered DTH and high-powered DBS satellites opened the market with smaller, cheaper dishes and cablelike packages of programming networks. The service particularly thrives where consumers have endured years of limited channel choices and where terrestrial options, like cable television, have been slow to materialize. DBS use of digital technology also meant crisper pictures on the home receiver and digital compression made it possible to increase the capacity of each transponder many times over, providing DBS distributors hundreds of available channels.

True DBS, as opposed to the use of satellites licensed to provide Fixed Satellite Service, operates in orbital slots optimized for full continental U.S. coverage, and separated from another DBS satellite by 9 degrees. The three primary DBS slots in the United States are at 101, 110, and 119 degrees West Longitude. The newly recognized value of these slots is evidenced by the fact that MCI bid $682.5 million dollars in an auction to obtain the 110 degrees West Longitude (W.L.) slot. The following looks at the current major DBS distributors.

DirecTV/USSB. Hughes Communications, Inc., operates DirecTV in a shared satellite access arrangement with United States Satellite Broadcasting, an affiliate of Hubbard Broadcasting. Hughes has two DBS satellites operating at 101 degrees W.L. The number of channels it can offer depends on FCC frequency assignments, not simply the number of transponders it has available from dedicated satellites. DirecTV has twenty-seven available frequencies at 101 W.L. and USSB has five. Both DirecTV and USSB provide service to compact, pizza-sized 18-inch Ku-band satellite terminals.

Hughes has invested about $1 billion in DirecTV. By 1998 it had 3.3 million subscribers and expected to reach a breakeven operational point with three million. As noted, AT&T also has an equity interest in the company. The service provides access to over 150 channels of programming, 60 channels of which are allocated to pay-per-view. Service packages are priced from $6 to $30 and offer most cable, movie, broadcast, and sports networks, with some programming, such as NFL football, available on an à la carte basis. USSB, with fewer channel offerings than DirecTV, has emphasized access to premium movie channels. It reported about 850,000 subscribers in early 1997.

PrimeStar/Tempo. PrimeStar Partners, a venture owned by several cable MSOs—including TCI, Time Warner, Continental, Comcast, Cox, Newhouse, and Viacom—operates medium (DTH) and high-powered (DBS) services. The company serves about 1.9 million subscribers and uses compression technology to provide more than 150 video and audio channels to satellite terminals with 13.5-inch (high-powered service) to 48-inch (medium-powered service) dishes.

Under the name Tempo, TCI also holds DBS licenses in the 110 and 119 degree W.L. slots and had sought to develop its own independent DBS service. In 1996, Tempo tried to acquire the Construction Permit of Advanced Communications, Corp., which had failed to meet due diligence deadlines for constructing, launching, and operating a DBS service. Rather than permit the transfer of the Permit, the FCC offered the license to the highest bidder, which turned out to be MCI. Tempo then executed a sale–lease back agreement with Telesat Canada, whereby Telesat would have acquired two Tempo satellites in exchange for the rights to use two Canadian DBS satellite orbital slots and the lease of twenty-seven of the available frequency channels. The FCC ultimately rejected the proposal, however, because it concluded that Canadian content restrictions denied effective competitive opportunities to U.S. programmers. TCI subsequently decided to launch a high-powered satellite into its 119 degree W.L. slot and provide high-powered service as an adjunct to Primestar.

Echostar.   Marketing itself as "The Dish Network," Echostar offers the standard menu of basic services and premium channels plus pay-per-view options, for an additional charge, on a 160-channel service. It began operations in the Spring of 1996 with a cut-rate package of cable channels designed to appeal to cost-conscious consumers. In 1998 it had about one million subscribers. The high-powered service has two satellites at 119 degrees W.L., each with sixteen transponders, although it has long-term licenses for only twenty-one of the thirty-two frequencies it currently uses. It also holds licenses for frequencies in the 61.5 degree W.L. and 175 degree W.L. slots. In addition to its consumer operation, EchoStar offers a twelve-channel business service used in corporate training.

Through the late 1990s, Rupert Murdoch, head of News Corp., attempted to enter the DBS business via several avenues, initially proposing a separate DBS service, ASkyB, along the same lines as his BSkyB British satellite television operation. This idea was replaced by a failed effort to merge with EchoStar. Subsequently, Murdoch bought into PrimeStar, trading an orbital slot and two satellites for an equity interest in the company.

Some DBS services have been developing plans to carry local broadcast signals in some markets. The proposal appeared to require government approval on copyright issues. If approved it would help neutralize the advantage held by MMDS and cable in the provision of local broadcast channels.

Shrinking Satellite Dishes

DBS is only one of a number of services that satellite distribution is making possible. As these services proliferate, businesses and households may have multiple Earth stations, or Earth stations configured for different uses, including video programming, real-time position determination and navigation, cellular radio-like telephone service, digital audio radio, Internet access, distance learning and teleconferencing, and data communications. DBS service received a boost from the FCC in 1996 when the Commission limited the ability of local authorities to restrict homeowners from setting up dishes on their property. Some cities have used zoning ordinances to control satellite dish proliferation. At the same time, the price and complexity of home reception equipment has had to drop to a level equivalent with other consumer electronic devices, before homeowners were willing to purchase them. They must be widely available and require little technical know-how to install and operate.

In fact, satellite Earth stations have shrunk in size and cost. Part of the reduction in size results from the migration upwards in power and frequency, from C-band to Ku-band and now onward to the Ka-band. As satellite power increases, dish size can decrease. Lower costs also have resulted from scale economies brought on by mass production. Thomson Consumer Electronics, using the RCA logo and the trade name Digital Satellite System (DSS), introduced a retail, ready-to-install DBS receiving package for less than $1,000 in 1995. With increased production and the onset of competition from Sony, Toshiba, Uniden, and Hughes Network Systems, the cost to the consumer dropped to below $200 in early 1997. PrimeStar provides customers with the option of not having to purchase the receiving equipment by paying a somewhat higher monthly subscription rate, although they do levy an installation fee of from $100 to $200, and as with the other DBS service, outlets for additional television sets in the home cost extra. Competition among the providers continues to drive down dish and installation prices, which are absorbed into the monthly service fees, and may soon be near zero.

TVRO and SMATV

While DBS is an industry in ascension, at least for the next few years, TVRO and analog SMATV are competitive providers in decline. TVRO is "television receive only," satellite receivers operating in the C-band. The large dishes, up to ten feet or more across, that dot the country's rural landscape are used to pick up the hundreds of channels directed at Earth by the various kinds of communications satellites. TVRO became popular in the late 1970s and early 1980s, initially with hobbyists who could peek at television signals not meant for home consumption, including network feeds to local stations, sports programs in the network distribution system, and even movies being fed nationally to local cable systems. The equipment was cumbersome and expensive. In addition to the dish, owners needed expensive electronic tuners and the more enthusiastic would purchase motorized mounts that allowed the dish to swivel and point to different satellites. As cable networks proliferated and equipment costs came down, TVRO became a common means of getting multichannel programming by people outside the reach of a city cable television system.[40]

In the mid- to late 1980s, the TVRO industry counted up to 3 million dish owners. Interest in the technology began to wane when the cable industry started scrambling and charging for its signals. Prior to about 1985, TVRO owners could get most of their programming unscrambled and for free, although many in the cable industry considered it signal theft. While initial industry efforts to scramble their signals were met as much with pirated decoder boxes and blackmarket descramblers as they were with stoic compliance, eventually most dish owners that continued the service paid monthly fees just like local cable subscribers, and subscriber counts increased. The rise of dedicated DBS further suppressed the interest in TVRO, however. For rural television consumers who simply wanted the convenience of cablelike service, the small dish and relatively low cost of DTH made more sense than the large TVRO dishes. At its height in 1985, there were about 4.5 million C-band subscribers, but that number had dropped to about 2.2 million by 1997. TVRO use is likely to continue, but recede to its roots as a pastime for hobbyists and serious television fans.

SMATV, or Satellite Master Antenna Television, is related to TVRO in that it is a satellite-based system. It can be conveniently described as a mini-cable system that serves an apartment building, "retirement village," condominium complex, or similar multidwelling structure or set of contiguous structures. The architecture is simple and cheap, consisting of little more than a TVRO dish to pick up the common cable channels and a set of wires to carry the signals through the complex. The roots of SMATV trace back to before the advent of community antenna television. Pre- and post-World War II apartment master antenna systems were functionally equivalent, although SMATV developed as a contemporary business in the early 1980s. SMATVs were a means to bring cable service to apartment houses before a full city-wide cable system was deployed. Even after cable was available, the SMATV service was often cheaper because of its lower operating costs.

Cable fought SMATV on legal and economic fronts, challenging the SMATV operators' right to operate without a franchise in the first instance and offering expanded services at attractive prices in the second. By 1990 there were only about 250,000 SMATV customers in the United States. Existing analog SMATV operations are attractive marketing targets for DBS and MMDS services. There are 6 million apartment units in the United States (in buildings with 200 or more units) and both satellite and MMDS providers seek to replace the analog C-band dishes with digital multichannel service, sharing revenue with the SMATV operator.

DANCING IN THE DARK

If Hostetter's elephants' waltz was a dance contest, the winner was far from certain, and in many ways the contestants are just stepping out onto the floor. There are a number of considerations in handicapping the dancers. Working for the cable industry and providing a hopeful note, perhaps, for Massillon Cable is the fact that following the 1996 Telecommunications Act, the attention of the RBOCs was drawn away from television and toward the much more lucrative long-distance market. Bell Atlantic, for example, can generate more than a billion dollars in annual revenue simply by picking off 10 percent of the long-distance traffic that originates in its region. RBOCs are much more readily equipped to enter this line of business both technologically and in terms of expertise. Because the equipment and experience already is in place, the long-distance market can be tapped more quickly and more cheaply than the broadband services. The Baby Bells, therefore, have turned their interest in television down to a slow simmer while bringing long-distance activities up to a rolling boil. The RBOCs could be expected to build high-end wired systems in some of the major markets over the next few years, but not venture far beyond them soon.

Meanwhile, cable and DBS services will continue expanding their digital capacity. By the estimate of one set-top chip manufacturer, there will be 20 million customers taking digital service by the end of 2000, about 20 percent of all television households (see Figure 8-2).

Despite the inroads of digital DTH, it could be well beyond 2000 before the 500-plus channel universe is a reality for most consumers. In the meantime, the public will, probably, as a result of intense advertising and marketing by all providers, begin thinking about which kind of company they will trust to deliver bundled services. Some in the cable industry once predicted that basic cable penetration would eventually reach 80 percent, citing studies that show 80 percent of today's high school students say they will sign up when they're adults. By the time they are adults, however, the other providers will be knocking on their door and, cable's public image is not strong. One recent survey showed that only 4 percent of those polled would trust their local cable operator with an integrated service of voice, data, and television; 21 percent said they would buy such a package from their local Bell operator, and 50 percent said they would trust the service to AT&T.[41] The group that conducted the study suggested that cable companies partner with firms that had better public relations records.

The price of service appears to make a difference, but even then the public currently privileges the telcos over cable. Another consumer poll reported that 36 percent of those asked would switch their telephone service from their current phone company to a cable provider if it saved them $2 a month. But 59 percent would drop their cable company and take television service from the phone company for the same $2 savings.

One result of this looming competition are forecasts that show the new distribution services pulling viewers away from cable television. Several independent predictions call for basic cable subscription to peak at around 64 million in 1999, under 70 percent penetration, even accounting for an expanded TV universe, and then be-

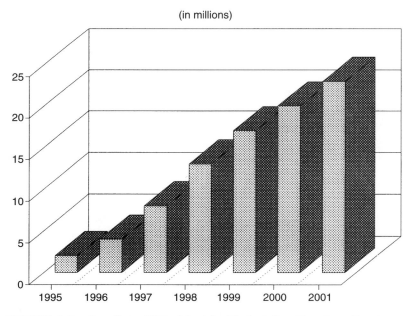

FIGURE 8-2   Predicted Worldwide Digital Set-Top Box Deployment

Source: "C-Cube Bites Back," *Cable World,* 8 April 1996, 22.

gin to fall, with viewers lured away principally by DBS and wireless cable. Industry analysts from Kagan Associates predict total basic cable viewership will then drop to 60.8 million by 2005 as viewers migrate to the program offerings of these digital broadcast services.[42]

The combined market for entertainment, data and Internet access, voice, and assorted other interactive services is expected to expand dramatically over the next few decades, but the pie will remain nonetheless finite, and one of the questions is how much erosion can cable or any of the alternatives stand. MMDS or telco wire-based providers do not have to siphon off all the cable subscribers in a given town, only enough to drive penetration levels below a certain margin. At some point, the dwindling subscriber base will be insufficient to maintain a cash flow that makes the business worthwhile. Important market questions include how much erosion can a given system take from the combined competition of DBS, wireless cable, and telco overbuilders and, additionally, how much revenue loss can be offset by income streams from new services such as cable telephone and Internet access.

While technology deployment, service, consumer loyalty, pricing, and cash flow will all figure in the resolution of the competition, the only thing sure about the outcome is that it will take at least several years to start to reveal itself. There are many questions yet to be resolved about the number and nature of competitive services the market can support. There are, however, some issues on which most observers and participants agree. Consumer choice in video services will expand with the deployment of digitally-compressed programming services, consolidation of companies providing multichannel television will continue, and those companies will press to develop bundled services of video, voice, and data to the home.

NOTES

[1]Kim Mitchell and Vince Vittore, "Hostetter: 'Companies of Size Will Survive,'" *Cable World,* 4 March 1996, 1.

[2]Rich Brown, "US West Buys Continental," *Broadcasting & Cable,* 4 March 1996, 12–13.

[3]Ben Bagdikian, *The Media Monopoly,* 4th ed. (Boston: Beacon Press, 1992).

[4]Brown, "US West," 13.

[5]As of November 1995, there were 11,586 systems; 973 of them independents and the rest held by 645 MSOs.

[6]Liberty is held as a separate tracking stock by TCI shareholders.

[7]Kim Mitchell, "Telco–Cable Crunch Time," *Cable World,* 19 February 1996, 56.

[8]Pablo Galarza, "Happy Independence Day," *Financial World,* 22 April 1996, 40.

[9]On satisfying a fourteen-point FCC checklist designed to ensure fair interconnection and competition.

[10]Service Areas: **SBC/PacTel:** California, Nevada, Texas, Oklahoma, Missouri, Alaska, Kansas; **Bell Atlantic/Nynex:** New York, New Hampshire, Rhode Island, Maine, Connecticut, Massachusetts, Vermont, Pennsylvania, Maryland, New Jersey, Virginia, West Virginia, Delaware; **Bell South:** Kentucky, North Carolina, South Carolina, Georgia, Mississippi, Alabama, Louisiana, Florida, Tennessee; **Ameritech:** Wisconsin, Michigan, Illinois, Indi-

ana, Ohio; **US West:** Montana, Washington, Oregon, Utah, Wyoming, North Dakota, South Dakota, Nebraska, Minnesota, Iowa, Colorado, Idaho, New Mexico, Arizona.

[11]See Thomas Hart, "The Evolution of Telco-Constructed Broadband Services for CATV Operators," *Catholic University Law Review,* 34: (1985): 697.

[12]Report & Order, 21 FCC 2nd 307.

[13]See *United States v. Western Electric Co.,* 767 F. Supp. 308 (D.D.C. 1991) and 900 F.2d 283 (D.C. Cir. 1990).

[14]Anita Wallgren, "Video Program Distribution and Cable Distribution: Current Policy Issues and Recommendations," National Telecommunications and Information Agency. U.S. Dept. of Commerce, June 1988.

[15]Second Report and Order, Recommendation to Congress and Second Further Notice of Proposed Rulemaking, 7 FCC Rcd, 5781, 5784 (1992).

[16]Landler, Mark, "Rivals Yawn at US West Cable Deal," *New York Times,* 29 January 1996, D-1.

[17]Landler, "Rivals Yawn."

[18]Mark Landler, "Nynex and Bell Atlantic Reach Accord on Merger," *New York Times,* 22 April 1996, 1.

[19]Richard Tedesco, "Bell Atlantic Blows Its VOD Horn," *Broadcasting & Cable,* 25 March 1996, 69.

[20]Glen Dickson, "Tele-TV Due for Digital MMDS in Fall," *Broadcasting & Cable,* 11 March 1996, 80.

[21]Carl Weinschenk, "Ameritech Scores a Telco First in Landing Cable Franchise," *Cable World,* 3 July 1995, 1.

[22]Ameritech ran into anticipated resistance from the local cable companies, especially Continental Cablevision, which held existing franchises in several of the towns, and had to back away from some areas because Continental owned exclusive local rights to Home Box Office and Cinemax through a system-wide, and legally controversial, arrangement with Time Warner.

[23]"GTE Expands Reach of Disney," *Telecommunication Reports,* 14 August 1995, 31.

[24]"GTE Close to Florida Cable Deals," *Broadcasting & Cable,* 6 May 1996, 9.

[25]Vince Cittore, "AT&T's Local Telephony Push," *Cable World,* 22 April 1996, 33.

[26]Jim McConville, "Utility Looks to Be Cable Player," *Broadcasting & Cable,* 15 April 1996, 70.

[27]Telecom Act. sect. 202.

[28]*Broadcasting & Cable Yearbook, 1996* (New Providence, NJ: R. R. Bowker, 1996).

[29]See, Bruce Owen and Steven Wildman, *Video Economics* (Cambridge: Harvard University Press, 1992).

[30]"The Drop Continues," *Broadcasting & Cable,* 25 March 1996, 10.

[31]National Cable Television Association, *Cable Television Developments,* Spring 1996, 5.

[32]Laurie Thomas and Barry Litman, "Fox Broadcasting Company, Why Now?" *Journal of Broadcasting & EM,* 35 (Spring 1991): 139–157.

[33]"USA Makes It Six in a Row," *Broadcasting & Cable,* 1 January 1996, 39.

[34]"The Handbook for the Competitive Market, Blue Book Vol. III," *Cablevision,* 1996, 4.

[35]For an introduction on satellite technology see: Andrew F. Inglis, *Satellite Technology: An Introduction* (Boston: Focal Press, 1991); Donald M. Jansky and Michel C. Jeruchim, *Communications Satellites in the Geostationary Orbit* (Norwood, MA: Artech House, 1987).

[36]See Michael L. Katz and Carl Shapiro, "Technology Adoption in the Presence of Network Externalities," *Journal of Political Economy* 94 (1986): 822; Michael L. Katz and Carl Shapiro, "Network Externalities, Competition, and Compatibility," *American Economics Review* 75 (1985): 424.

[37]INTELSAT typically does not engage in price discrimination on the basis of demand elasticity and user desire to lease capacity on a particular satellite. Private operators typically do. The "Hot Bird" concept reflects the added value and commensurately higher lease prices for satellites that become home to the most desirable video programs and networks. Because users have a financial incentive in limiting the number of Earth stations they need to install and maintain, they prefer to access only a few satellites for their complete inventory of video programming. Private satellite operators who have executed transponder leases with programmers having the most desirable video product find that other programmers, perhaps offering less attractive fare, want to lease capacity and possibly exploit the benefits of being more widely accessible.

[38]"There are many products for which the utility that a user derives from consumption of the good increases with the number of other agents consuming the good." Katz and Shapiro, "Network Externalities."

[39]See Carmen Matutes and Pierre Regibeau, "'Mix and Match': Product Compatibility without Network Externalities," *Rand Journal of Economics,* 19 (1988): 221.

[40]Homeowners in the cities who wanted the additional channels TVRO offered were sometimes frustrated by local codes and ordinances that prohibited the large and unsightly dishes in residential neighborhoods.

[41]Alan Breznick, "Time to Buddy Up?" *Cable World,* 29 April 1996, 8.

[42]Alan Breznick, "Some Sobering Predictions," *Cable World,* 15 April 1996, 4.

9

The Structure of the
New Media Industry

John V. Pavlik
Columbia University

> *If I were to give you an army of 10*
> *thousand people, could you build a pyramid?*
> *A computer gives the average person, a*
> *high school freshman, the power to do things*
> *in a week that all the mathematicians who*
> *ever lived until 30 years ago couldn't do.*
> *—ED ROBERTS[1]*

ON THE HOLODECK

Emerging technologies are rapidly transforming the media landscape. Advances in the Internet and the World Wide Web, wireless communications, and digital video technology are creating an entirely new communication environment in which the roles of media consumer and content creator often blur and interactivity becomes a reality. Multimedia technology, virtual reality, and flat-panel displays are redefining the media experience, transforming the narrative structure of media images, sound, and text into nonlinear, immersive, hypertext communication. Media consumers have unprecedented choice and control over the media experience, selecting not just what they watch, read, or hear, but when and where they do so. Nomadic computing is rapidly becoming more than a buzzword; it's becoming a twenty-first-century way of life. Journalists may find their methods of news gathering transformed by light-weight, wearable technologies (such as augmented reality, which adds layers of visual and other information onto "reality" as viewed through a head-mounted display) linked to massive databases through high-speed wireless technologies. Professor Steven Feiner at Columbia University has already developed a working prototype of an augmented reality system for use on the Columbia campus, where the wearer can walk through the campus and "see" architectural and other information superimposed on buildings such as the historic Low Library. Imagine reporting from the scene of a building explosion, surveying the wreckage with an augmented reality viewer, and quickly determining the inner structure of the building. The Center for New Media (CNM) at the Columbia University Graduate School of Journalism is developing a Mobile Journalist Workstation (MJW) that will incorporate Feiner's and other new media technologies into a single integrated system for advanced nomadic news reporting. This research is being conducted in collaboration with a number of programs at Columbia, including Engineering and Computer Science, in an attempt to blend the process of technology development and content creation in an interdisciplinary Engineering Research Center (ERC). Another important development is the miniaturization of mobile satellite phones, which just a decade ago were so cumbersome they required a sea-chest and a very strong back for portability. Introduced in 1996 is a notebook-sized Mini-M satellite phone from NEC Corporation that uses the Inmarsat satellite communications system to allow anyone anywhere in the world instaneous high-bandwidth, 25 Mbps capability for delivering fax, data, voice, and e-mail communications. The system fits in a standard briefcase, weighs a remarkable 2.6 kg (about five pounds) and runs on a built-in rechargeable lithium-ion battery pack, car battery, or AC power.[2]

The commercial media system itself is undergoing what Roger Fidler calls a "mediamorphosis," as well, moving away from passive, scattershot content delivery, toward highly targeted messaging, blending the best of both push and pull network technology. A double-edged sword, this new media engine may present both a marketer's paradise and a consumer's privacy nightmare.

Much media content in the years ahead will still consist of packaged products of news, information, entertainment, and advertising manufactured by highly centralized media organizations, but tomorrow's media will increasingly target in real-time the demands, tastes, and preferences of ever more specialized niche audiences spread over diverse geographic audiences. The new media system will not rigidly divide along the traditional lines of delivery such as print, broadcast, and cable, but will become true multimedia technologies, involving new forms of mediated communication, ultimately embracing the tactile technology of emerging virtual reality systems. Shared media experiences, although increasingly rare on a mass scale, will take on an entirely new meaning, one in which audiences anywhere around the globe will be enveloped in a total sensory media experience created at least in part by those audiences. Increasingly, each member of the new media audience will have direct access to this information superhighway through lightweight, portable, wireless multimedia devices, totally enveloping multisensory datasuits, or communal media technologies featuring multidimensional images and stereophonic sound not unlike the holodeck on the Starship Enterprise featured in *Star Trek: The Next Generation.*

Of course, not every media experience will be of this Buck Rogers type. Consumers will spend much of their media time reading newspapers printed on traditional newsprint. They will still read leatherbound and paperback books. They will still listen to the radio, watch TV, and get advertising circulars in the mail. And the Publisher's Clearing House will probably still proclaim half of America "Winners" in its multimillion dollar lottery. Moreover, legal and regulatory frameworks will continue to evolve mechanisms to monitor and control the new media system. With the policy-making process frequently lagging well beyond the more rapidly changing new media technology landscape, one can't help but recall a story told by Kenneth M. King, former president of EDUCOM. "A turtle was mugged by a gang of snails in Central Park. When making his report to the police, the turtle lamented: 'It all happened so fast.'"[3]

Freedom of expression issues will take on even greater significance in the new media environment. The Internet and other media technologies are empowering members of virtual communities around the globe. They are providing a new electronic age printing press that costs little to operate and reaches audiences of millions in almost instantaneous fashion. John Siegenthaler, a Pulitzer prize-winning newspaper editor and former chairman of The Freedom Forum First Amendment Center, says the information superhighway already is being dominated by eighteen-wheelers, including the baby Bells, cable TV companies, and other corporate players who are used to working in a regulated environment.[4] These companies are likely to compromise on First Amendment issues, he cautions. News organizations, journalism educators, and other guardians of the First Amendment will need to be vigilant in the new media environment if we, as a society, are to preserve free speech values. This is especially important, Siegenthaler adds, if it is true that a free press is one of the cornerstones of democracy.

The social and cultural consequences of these new media technologies are profound. They are creating unprecedented opportunities for political participation, through electronic town halls, direct access to political leaders and, potentially, online voting. At the same time, issues of equitable access and cost considerations are challenging the very political viability of creating a new information infrastructure. Umberto Eco, noted Italian author and inaugural visiting scholar at the Italian Academy for Advanced Studies in America at Columbia University, observes that we are likely moving into a society with three classes: those who don't have access to the Internet, those who have access but it is mainly passive (i.e., they just surf the 'Net) and those who know how to control it (what the Russians call the proletariat).[5] Social fragmentation is only one of the many potential negative consequences of the new technologies that are increasingly leading media consumers into online worlds and away from their geographically defined communities.

User Control and User Choice:
New and Improved Media

For the media consumer, perhaps the most important difference between old and new media is greater user choice and control. Unlike any time before, media audiences will have ever greater choice and control over media content and the media experience in general. Video-on-demand, including pay-per-view movies, news on demand, educational programming, and documentaries will all be available over the information superhighway. The shift in the media paradigm is from strict source or media control over content delivery to increasing user control. Emerging in the new media age is what can be described as nothing less than ubiquitous news and information. With the growth of Internet-based news and information products, ranging from broadcast-type services such as PointCast to on-demand news products on the World Wide Web, anyone with Internet access can obtain nonstop comprehensive news and information about anything from breaking news to news analysis. With a variety of wireless devices now available to link handheld PDAs to the Internet and the Web, such on-demand news is available anytime and anywhere around the globe.

Simultaneously, media audiences will enjoy increasing interactivity on the information highway. They will have opportunities to interact with media content, selecting different options, from preset video library menus to battling enemy starships in videogames. Audience members will also be able to participate in the process of content creation, sending messages, home video, or data files to anyone else on the system. Over time, the superhighway will offer increasing opportunities for moving beyond two-way communication and into an n-way media environment in which hundreds, thousands, even millions will participate in a rich communication smorgasbord. Virtual worlds will be created by media audiences around the world in which the dimensions of that world are limited only by the imaginations of those within it. The seeds of this n-way communication world can already be seen on the World Wide Web, increasingly graphical and three-dimensional multi-user domains (MUDs) and high-quality, low-cost videoconferences.

Does all this mean the end of the couch potato? Not at all. Not only will traditional passive media consumption continue, but it will thrive in an increasingly complex and stressful world demanding occasional if not frequent mindless escape. But the interactive, on-demand world of personalized communications will become a ready choice. Of course, too much interactivity could produce the era of the mashed potato.

Driving this user-controlled, interactive, multimedia world are the technological forces of digitization, compression, and the broadband packet-switched telecommunications network. Through advances in computer technology, we are rapidly moving toward a united state of media in which all communications, from voice to data to full-motion video, are available in digital form, computer-readable 1s and 0s. Compression technology has made it possible to compact that digital data, especially full-motion video, into smaller and smaller packets. The convergence of telecommunications and cable, along with the deployment of advanced optical fiber, has provided a high-capacity electronic superhighway to transmit and provide access to all that compressed digital data.

A final technological factor contributing to the transformation of the media landscape is wireless communications. As the forces of digitization and compression have inexorably advanced, research has helped create an increasingly broadband packet-switched network that is not dependent on wires. Instead, we are moving toward a telecommunications highway universally available over the high-frequency wavelengths of the radio spectrum. By connecting to satellite and wired networks, this wireless network will provide a complementary and perhaps competitive alternative multimedia information superhighway. Although engineers have not yet achieved the necessary compression algorithms to distribute full multimedia communications via the wireless spectrum in a wide-area network environment, they have done so in wireless local area networks. Moreover, they have developed increasingly efficient use and allocation of the wireless spectrum, including spread spectrum models that allow spectrum sharing for different applications and users. One interesting approach to high-speed communications in a wireless local area network is known as fiber-in-the-sky from CellularVision. It delivers up to 2Mb of bandwidth, making it possible to distribute broadcast-quality MPEG-2 digital video over a wireless local area network. When connected to a wired high-speed wide-area network, fiber-in-the-sky makes possible a phenomenon called *nomadic computing*. *Nomadic computing* means using a computer-based device, from a PDA to a laptop computer to access the information superhighway from any location, anywhere, anytime. Someday, we may see emerge global media nomads. We are already witnessing the application of nomadic computing and communications in state-of-the-art navigational systems for luxury automobiles. Cars such as the Acura, BMW, Cadillac, Lincoln, and Oldsmobile all offer increasingly sophisticated dashboard navigational systems that rely on global positioning satellites (GPS), which can pinpoint a vehicle's location within one hundred yards.[6] These systems offer a variety of services, including on-screen maps and voice-activated navigation, as well as roadside assistance. Handheld GPS devices are also now available, and are increasingly popular among hikers, sailors, and pilots. The GPS 4000 from Magellan, for instance, is smaller than a walkie-talkie and weighs about ten ounces.[7] The federal government has launched a $40 million program to challenge cities to build even more sophisticated nomadic navigational systems. The program is designed to foster "intelligent transportation systems" in New York, Phoenix, San Antonio, and Seattle, and will use Web sites, interactive television, and navigational devices in cars to facilitate commuting.[8] One of the critical issues to resolve involves building complete interoperable network environments that support easy access (via the main methods of connecting to the Internet, Point-to-Point Protocol, or PPP, which is more reliable—and has error corrrecting features—than the older Serial Line Internet Protocol, or SLIP), regardless of one's geographic location.[9]

PARALLEL OR DIVERGENT UNIVERSES?

What price will a digital universe exact? No one really knows. Projected costs to build the new communication infrastructure range from hundreds of billions to several trillion dollars, just for the United States. Cost estimates are also in the hundreds of billions to create new information infrastructures in Japan and many other countries. Those developing new media products and services say that the actual price the consumer will pay will be modest. If it isn't then none of the products will succeed. Telecommunications expert John Carey suggests that the estimates for the new information infrastructure may not really be as expensive as some in the industry claim. In the area of interactive television, "it turns out that much of the cost associated with building the new infrastructure, particularly for telephone companies, involves investments that the companies would make regardless of any interactive television services," Carey explains.

> In other words, the incremental costs of building a network for interactive television are a modest addition to normal replacement and upgrading costs for their networks. So, when a telephone company says that it will spend $17 billion to build a telecommunication superhighway for ITV and other advanced services, it usually means that they plan to spend $2 billion more than they would otherwise spend for normal replacement and upgrading of their network. Further, the plans typically allow them to scale back the additional costs if market demand for new services is lower than expected. For cable operators, incremental costs are greater. However, they too can scale back investment if demand is lower than expected. Further, the investment will yield other benefits such as lower operating and maintenance costs.[10]

But there are other costs, perhaps more significant than dollars. Among these are issues of access to the technology. Two principles that have guided public communication policy for most of the century are universal and equitable access. Unless these two principles apply equally well in the new media environment, the social costs will be high. Among the likely losers will be women, minority groups, inner-city and rural dwellers, children, the elderly, the homeless, and people with disabilities. Other social costs may include social fragmentation, digital isolation, and a falloff in political participation.

A related cost consideration involves the cost of building or rebuilding a public telecommunications system increasingly dominated by massive traffic on the Internet. The telecommunications network in the United States was built to support circuit-switched communications, primarily used for voice communications. "In spite of the great changes in technology, the basic concept of telephony has changed little over this century," observes Robert W. Lucky, Corporate Vice President of Applied Research at Bellcore, and the inventor of the "adaptive equalizer," a distortion-correction technology used in all high-speed data transmission today.[11]

Suddenly, a new paradigm has swept the world. Instead of two people speaking to each other in real time over a switched analog channel, asynchronous messaging and hyper-linked sharing of multimedia objects have become the objectives that must be supported by the future infrastructure.

This will not come without a substantial investment—by someone. In the past it would have been the phone company, once a heavily regulated monopoly. Today, it is unclear who will pay the cost. "There is tremendous investment in the present infrastructure, which is not cost-effective for these new objectives," Lucky cautions. "The question is: How do we get from here to there?"

The Consequences of Technology Convergence

One of the most basic trends in the new media environment is the convergence of multimedia and online, or networked, communications. As these systems converge, a truly unique and powerful new medium of public communication will emerge. Its commercial and cultural implications are as profound as they are remarkable. It is likely to transform virtually every social institution, from education to government, medicine to law, politics to religion, at home and abroad. This new medium will influence the process of human communication, the process by which social change occurs and the processes and mechanisms controlling both the United States and the world economy. The three most significant unanswered questions are:

- Will these changes be for the better or worse?
- What will be the cost and for whom?
- What will be the timetable for change?

Countervailing Forces

Countervailing technological forces may also be at work, however, in the new media universe. One of the almost sacred primordial forces driving technological change during the past quarter century has been the dramatically falling price of computing power. Recent evidence suggests this trend may soon be slowing down, if not drawing to a close completely. As computer chip manufacturers have created ever smaller chips capable of ever greater calculation, the price of computing has fallen remarkably. Manufacturers today, however, may be reaching the theoretical limit to computer chip miniaturization. "The problem is that life gets harder for chip makers as dimensions shrink below a micron in size," reports Gary Stix.[12] "At about 0.05 micron, the dimensions of the individual devices will be so small that quantum effects will disrupt their behavior. Then a new technology based on probabilistic laws will be needed." Producing reliable chips has also become increasingly complex and costly, as reflected in the initially flawed, super-fast Pentium chip. State-of-the-art chips now house some 16 million memory bits and require 200 processing steps. By 2001 reliable production techniques may require manufacturing devices as small as

15 to 50 nanometers, "less than the width of a coiled DNA molecule."[13] Moreover, as the cost of chip manufacturing has fallen, the cost of chip design and manufacturing technology has risen. Gordon Moore, the former chairman of Intel, the world's largest chip manufacturer, noted that his company's first chip manufacturing plant in the late 1960s cost $3 million.[14] "Today that is the cost of one piece of equipment in one of our plants," Moore observes. The next generation of chip manufacturing plants will exceed $1 billion in price, and by 2000 may cost ten times that. The effect on the semiconductor business is that returns on investment are threatened, and the drive to manufacture even smaller chips may stall.

If this trend toward chip miniaturization does draw to a close, projections for the future will change dramatically. It will not be safe to assume that super-powerful computing devices will become ubiquitous in the early twenty-first century. Information appliances will not become the consumer standard many hope for. The potential for video delivery and processing will fall dramatically, and the price will stabilize. Commercial investment in the new media, as a result, will slacken and economic growth will slow.

How likely is this dire scenario? Unless there is a breakthrough in chip design, it is fairly likely. Optical technology, however, though still in the laboratory research stages, is one of the most intriguing avenues for the future of computing. Optical, or photonic, computing, based not on the flow of electrons in a silicon-based computer chip, but on pulses of light in a new silicon environment, may unleash vast new opportunities to decrease the cost of computing power and dramatically increase computing power and speed—the theoretical limit is the speed of light, 186,000 miles per second. Moreover, if optical technology can be combined with some preliminary but theoretically sound research on organic neural networks, the next generation may reach new thresholds in computing power and intelligence. As an alternative to such designs, some companies are experimenting with three-dimensional microchips. Unlike traditional two-dimensional designs in which the chip is approximately 5 microns in height and the conducting wires and transistors lie across the insulating silicon base, Mitsubishi, IBM, Siemens, and Toshiba are developing chips 20 to 30 microns in height with wires, conductors, and transistors all layered atop an insulating base of silicon.[15] Such chips could eventually lead to the development of supercomputers the size of a sugar cube.

If computer speed, processing power, and memory do continue to increase, the possibilities are seemingly boundless. Some selected predictions for 2000 include:

- Personal "Crays" capable of emulating any desktop, from Macintosh to PC with the power of today's supercomputer in a portable handheld device, making nomadic computing and communications universal and ubiquitous
- Smart TVs that remember past viewing patterns and suggest new shows that match tastes and preferences
- Telephones that instantaneously translate callers speaking in any of a dozen or more languages

- Artificial intelligence applications so smart and humanlike that they can replace entire corporate departments such as accounting or finance[16]

Bandwidth Challenged

A related problem involves bandwidth limitations in today's telecommunications networks. Although compared to the networks of a decade ago the capacity of today's networks is considerable, few anticipated the exponential growth in bandwidth demand brought on by users of the Internet and World Wide Web in the 1990s. As networks clog and routers collapse, many see a potential hardening of the telecommunications arteries, despite the many millions of miles of high-bandwidth optical fiber now circling the globe. Notably, however, an international consortium of research groups at AT&T, Fujitsu, and Nippon Telegraph and Telephone (NTT) demonstrated a system in early 1996 that could increase bandwidth by as much as a thousandfold by 2000.[17] Transmitting one trillion bits of information in a single second over a single strand of optical fiber, the new technology was surpassed a few months later by a team at NEC Corporation, which transmitted two trillion bits in a second over a single strand of optical fiber.

DIGITAL PUBLISHING

The evolution of multimedia products in an online environment will push traditional and new media providers to explore new publishing frontiers. New media publishers will not only have opportunities to reach global audiences with multimedia products in real time, but will also be able to completely rethink their relationship with advertisers and audiences. Further, they will have the unique opportunity to completely rethink their internal processes of content creation. No longer will they be constrained by traditional modes of product development. Conversely, the world of digital publishing will present considerable uncertainty for companies already unsure of themselves and their business future. All bets are off in the business of new media. Competitors will arise from every corner of the market and the world. Even the audience will be inclined and able to get in on the action in a computer-driven media world. One of the great question marks is how "secure" will the online communications world become. Today, the forces of government and the private sector are battling over whether to permit government eavesdropping on online communications, or to create a strong encryption technology for networked communications. The outcome will substantially affect the growth of both commerce and communication on the Internet. Strong encryption will foster a robust communication and commercial environment, where information and transactions flow on a national and international scale unparalleled in history. Nano-transactional models where micro-payments for information and intellectual property as well as other digital objects, such as digital cash, will become commonplace.

If the government wins the encryption war, the growth of commerce and communication on the Internet will slow, and perhaps even grind to a halt. Today's electronic mail travels over the Internet much as a postcard travels through traditional postal services—anyone along the route can read its contents. Encryption such as PGP provides something akin to an electronic envelope, making it impossible for someone to see what's inside. Few consumers will be willing to send their credit card numbers around the globe knowing that it might be intercepted by anyone along the way. Conversely, should the government lose the struggle, various high-tech criminals will find the Internet a safe haven for their illicit communications and transactions. From drug dealers to tax evaders, a secure online environment means freedom from the watchful eye of law enforcement.

Without the wisdom of Solomon, the solution to this dilemma may never be found. One federal judge, however, has issued a landmark ruling against the federal government in an important encryption case. The U.S. State Department had ruled in 1993 that Daniel J. Bernstein, then a graduate student at the University of California at Berkeley and now a University of Illinois mathematician, "would have to register as an international weapons dealer if he wanted to publish an encryption program or discuss it at academic conferences that foreigners might attend," reports John Markoff.[18] Judge Marilyn Hall Patel of the U.S. District Court in San Francisco ruled in December 1996 that the State Department limits were an unconstitutional prior restraint on freedom of speech (prohibited in the classic *Near* v. *Minnesota* case ruled on by the U.S. Supreme Court). Although the encryption issue is far from settled, the early evidence is weighing in the favor of strong network encryption. Adding to this building momentum is the law of economics. Today, because the United States dominates the global information marketplace, there is great incentive for the federal government to provide mechanisms to support this continued economic advantage. Unless U.S. manufacturers and software developers are allowed to export their strong encryption technologies (many of the best encryption technologies, such as PGP, were developed by U.S. researchers), the marketplace will quickly become dominated by international players, where strong encryption is already available. It is likely the federal government in the United States will ultimately be swayed by the economic forces that mandate strong encryption if Internet commerce is ever to thrive and if U.S. companies are to compete effectively in the international market for encryption technology.

Digital Security

Security in cyberspace will become a dominant issue in the years ahead. Consumers and businesses will need to be vigilant in protecting their communications, electronic products, and commercial transactions in cyberspace. The cost of publishing online will rise as a result of security concerns and measures, at the same time increasing the cost of downloading electronic products and conducting electronic transactions and communications for the consumer. Similarly, the demand for electronic security will spawn new industries and trigger growth in existing companies involved in computer security. One possible new field will be insurance for electronic products, as a guard against electronic theft, vandalism, or destruction of electronic property.

Publishers or "Content Providers"?

One of the growing debates in the new media world involves what values dominate the content production process. Will content producers continue in the tradition of the great publishers of the newspaper or magazine publishing world, placing concerns about freedom of expression, privacy, and democratic processes high on the communication agenda? Will the values of the broadcast industry prevail? Where will concern about the public interest fit in this new scenario? Will everyone be reduced to the role of "content provider?" At a conference held in 1994 in Atlanta, heads of several hundred media publishing interests gathered to discuss the prospects for publishing on the information superhighway. When one participant encountered the president of the Chicago Bears, one of the two oldest National Football League franchises (the other being the Green Bay Packers), he asked him why he was attending the conference. His response was a simple, "Because we are a content provider."[19]

Verifying Information

Journalism also faces another imminent threat on the global information grid. On a digital information superhighway characterized by a laissez-faire marketplace in which information is openly exchanged and computer network security is difficult if not impossible to guarantee, how does a media organization—or any other organization—verify the accuracy of data? How does it protect its intellectual property? The world's largest news service recently ran headlong into this problem. On Monday, April 4, 1994, a remarkable news story appeared exclusively on the global Reuters news service. In the wake of the assassination of Colosio, the leading presidential candidate in Mexico's 1994 elections, the story alleged that President Salinas was about to rewrite the Mexican constitution to allow him to run for another term in office. The story, however, was false. Someone had cracked the Reuters network and placed the fictitious report on the news wire.

The "FBI" Solution: A Digital Fingerprint

One possible solution has been introduced by a British company offering an electronic signature ID. Nottingham-based MOR Ltd. has developed a digital technique it calls "FBI" that combines a header, electronic "fingerprints," and an alphanumeric ID sequence imprinted throughout an image or data file.[20] The digital ID is completely transparent and hidden from view and is nearly impermeable to tampering. When used, it would provide a nearly permanent encoding system that publishers and other new media content providers could use to verify the source of a message and to determine whether a video or audio segment was pirated from an original feed.

Digital watermarks are under development at a number of corporate and educational research institutions. One particularly interesting digital watermark is being developed by a research team at Columbia University led by Professor Shih-Fu Chang and involving the Center for New Media at the Graduate School of Journalism. Unlike other digital watermarks, the Columbia project involves a digital signature that not only protects copyright, but authenticates the source of an image or document, and, at the click of a mouse button, can identify the probability that a document has been tampered with and how. Such authentication is critically important in an era of digital image manipulation, eroding news credibility, and a public disillusioned and mistrustful of most institutions. The Columbia digital watermark survives network transmission, compression, and the most grueling of digital editing. Its ultimate test will likely be whether teenage computer hackers will be able to crack its digital shield.

The Confluence of Information and Entertainment

Despite the allure of digital technology, it is important not to get caught up in the hype surrounding the information superhighway and new media technologies. Media entrepreneurs have been drawn by the siren call of new technology in the past, only to lose millions of dollars on failed technology applications. Many are already urging caution in investing huge sums in as yet unrealized technologies. Mark Stahlman, president of New York-based New Media Associates, is one entrepreneur sounding the alarm. He recently wrote in *Wired* magazine:

> *All the headlines about the digital, interactive, 500-channel, multi-megamedia blow-your-socks-off future are pure hype. Yes, all the wild Wall Street, through-the-roof, Crazy Eddie, cornucopia, shout-it-out-loud promo jobs are pure greed. It's all a joke.*
>
> *It's now official. I'm announcing the beginning of convergence backlash. There will be no convergence. There will be no 500-channel future. There will be no US $3 trillion mother of all industries. There will be no virtual sex. There will be no infobahn. None of it—at least not the way you've been reading about it.*
>
> *Sure the technologies are real. Digital compression and digital phone lines are real. Those 100-MIPS micros are real. Multimedia and high-speed networks are real. In fact, the technology is so real that it's almost obvious. Unfortunately, the businesses to exploit these technologies are anything but obvious.[21]*

Tomorrow's News

Although newspaper readership has been declining steadily for nearly four decades, does this mean people are less interested in reading the news? Does the decreasing audience for network television news mean people want to watch less televised news? Research suggests the answer to both these questions is no. One recent study shows that three out of four adults in the United States are still "very interested" in getting the latest news about current events. There is also much anecdotal evidence to suggest that people still have an insatiable appetite for news. Today there are more newsletters (10,000 in print and even more in electronic form), magazines (10,000), ethnic newspapers (500), and other successful printed news products than ever before. Moreover, the national newspaper *USA Today,* the Cable News Network (CNN), C-SPAN, the ever vigilant eye on Congress and Washington, and CourtTV were all launched after 1980. Although few of these news and information products capture major audience shares, they have all carved out important niches.

If you are still not convinced, consider this scenario for one possible news product of the not-too-distant future. Imagine pulling out of your bookbag an eight-ounce electronic tablet about the size of a notepad. Unfolding the flexible tablet, you say, "Let's see this morning's newspaper." As the tablet's voice recognition software interprets your command and identifies your voice pattern, the screen is quickly transformed into a full-color electronic version of your local newspaper, if you still wish to call it a "newspaper." It's really a hybrid news product. The design still looks like a newspaper, with a front page, headlines, text, pictures, and graphics. But it's really much more. A touch with the attached light pen, and a news photo comes to life, with full-motion video and audio. Another touch brings up a detailed historical analysis of today's top news story. Reading a related editorial, you react strongly. Again using the light pen, you activate the tablet's microphone, which allows you to record a voice mail message to the editorial page editor, letting her know how you feel. PCS technology integrated into the tablet automatically sends your voice mail to the editor, who later hears your response, and sends you an equally strongly worded voice mail response. A classified ad catches your eye, and you use the light pen to extract more information about the product for sale. After seeing a three-dimensional picture of the product, you decide against making the purchase. As you look up, you see that you've reached the 116th stop on the number 1 line, and you put your tablet back in your bag and exit the subway, heading off to your graduate seminar in new media journalism at Columbia University in New York.

Network TV Online

The rise of electronic online information services does not signal the end of traditional print forms of communication, such as network television, newspapers, and magazines. "On-line services will coexist with print for the foreseeable future and maybe forever," says Stephen B. Shepard, editor in chief of *Business Week.*[22] Print is still highly portable and relatively inexpensive, and previous predictions of a paperless office have failed to materialize. In fact, the opposite has occurred. By the end of the 1980s, after a decade of computerization in the workplace, "we had four times the amount of paper being created in offices," says Rich Karlgaard, editor in chief of *Forbes ASAP,* a technology supplement to *Forbes* magazine.[23] Television is still well produced, widely available, generally entertaining and never suffers from delays due to limited bandwidth.

Despite that, traditional programmers such as the major television networks have experimented with the delivery of their broadcast programming via the Internet. ABC TV, for example, has used streaming video products such as VivoActive to promote their new fall programming, offering snippets of shows such as *Spin City* to worldwide audiences on demand. NBC has even launched a specialized service called NBC Desktop Video, which brings video-on-demand to the desktop for many executives in the financial world, who have particular interest in tuning in to press conferences of the federal reserve board, and so forth.

What these efforts reveal, however, is that video on the Internet is not television. Rather, video on the Internet is a new communication tool that will never replace traditional television programming. Network capacity and configuration will likely never support the on-demand delivery of broadcast-quality digital television. Rather, video on the Internet will evolve into a distinctive form of multimedia communication, on-demand, customizable and interactive, three qualities not possible in traditional television. These capabilities will lead the Internet, and its delivery of multimedia content, to mature in a fashion complementary to traditional multimedia forms of news and entertainment delivered in broadcast fashion via terrestrial, satellite, and cable transmission.

A BUSINESS MANAGER'S GUIDE
TO DIGITAL PUBLISHING

Although no one knows the exact parameters of the emerging new media environment, the basic topography of that world has begun to take shape.[24] New media products, regardless of their content, audience, or means of delivery, will be in digital form. Products will migrate rapidly toward the multimedia format, especially on the Internet and the World Wide Web. Content will evolve more slowly from extensions of the old media into more experimental and novel categories. Today's online services "are the Model Ts, the horseless carriages of the information future," says Bob Ingle, executive editor of the *San Jose Mercury News.*[25] The new media content patterns beginning to emerge include:

- Customizing and personalizing content
- Layering information to provide increased depth and detail to those with specialized interests
- Creating dynamic virtual worlds where users can enter immersive three-dimension environments, experience simulations, and discover unexpected or

serendipitous information, providing a new media version of one of the hall-marks of the traditional media—the "eureka" of a chance news encounter

Content providers will respond to the intellectual property challenges of the digital age in a number of ways, including branding, electronic signature identification (i.e., the digital watermark), and international partnerships. Audiences are likely to be defined not as much by geography or political boundary, but by lifestyle, psychographic, and generational factors. Perhaps more importantly, audience members will become important providers and shapers of content. Although most will remain in the passive, couch potato mode, many, especially in the younger audience segment, will enter into an interactive participatory mode, much as now prevails on the Internet. Content delivery will evolve increasingly toward a networked environment. Initially, many products will be on CD-ROM and other optical media, although magnetic formats will persist. Still, the efficiency of online delivery and the growing reach of online technologies, especially with the advent of wireless technologies, in concert with improved compression, encryption, and legal protections for intellectual property rights, will help online technologies prevail and become the dominant mode of delivery. Importantly, dominant multimedia production technologies now provide built-in, automatic translators for Web publishing. MacroMedia Director, the leading authoring environment for CD-ROM, introduced in late 1995 a product called Shockwave for creating similar multimedia content for the Web. Marimba has produced a new network product called Castanet that works in alliance with Macromedia Shockwave.[26] In beta testing until early 1997, Castanet is an Internet delivery system that incorporates both a client (Castanet Tuner) and a server (Castanet Transmitter). Together, these client and server software tools enable end-users to subscribe to Internet "application channels" built on the Castanet system. Rather than relying exclusively on an on-demand, pull network approach, Castanet delivers Web content to the local end-user (i.e., the channel resides locally on the client or subscriber computer), permitting the end-user to access the site without reloading the site each time. Updates are automatically downloaded and installed, but require minimal bandwidth because only that portion of the site that is new is refreshed. Sites currently using the Castanet technology include HotWired, CMP Media, Tribune Media, and Sportsline. Castanet and similar technologies offer a possible solution to the network congestion problem emerging with the 1990s growth of the Internet.

To sum up, publishers should consider the following ten new media guidelines:

- **Digital multimedia,** including a combination of full-motion video, audio, hypertext, and data, all fully manipulable on either optical or online format
- **Online versions** of media products do not seem to cannibalize print or broadcast versions. Experience, in fact, suggests that use of online products on the World Wide Web on the Internet generally enhances interest in traditional format products, especially when the online and traditional versions are not strict

duplicates of each other. Online offerings, however, are most effective when they offer original content, and not simply repurposed or repackaged content from other media

- **True interactivity,** featuring "upstream" capability
- **Flexible cost structure,** to allow consumers extensive choice in designing their own information system
- **Intellectual property rights protections and limitations,** to insure the integrity, credibility, and maximum lifespan of their content creations—many multimedia projects have already stalled over the complexities and cost of copyright considerations
- **Security,** including encryption, to protect communications in a public network environment
- **International partnerships,** which will enable domestic companies to effectively enter and succeed in foreign markets where local expertise is essential
- **Original, quality content,** without which consumers will have no significant reason to turn to new media offerings—this will cost more to produce, but ultimately will be worth the extra investment
- **Privacy protections** for not only the general public but for employees and individuals around the world
- **Freedom of expression protections,** without which the new media environment will be destined to whither and die

Although these general guidelines may suggest an optimistic view of the future, those entering the world of digital publishing would be wise to exercise caution. As of this writing few of the technologies examined in this book are settled. Most are in an active process of evolution. Technical standards vary not only from region to region, but from country to country, and show little chance of settling down anytime soon. Legal and regulatory structures are rapidly evolving and the competitive environment is in a great state of flux. Much of the audience has almost no idea what to make of the new technologies. Many audience members find them fascinating, but unsure whether they will be worth the cost or offer any real advantages over existing sources of media entertainment, news, and information. Content creators are also uncertain of how to proceed. So far, there are few truly original offerings in the new media environment. Most are simply adaptations and extensions of existing products and have about as much appeal as movie sequels, if that much. The new rules of content production are also up in the air. No one knows exactly what a multimedia "script" is worth, how long it will take to produce, and whether it will ultimately turn a profit. One thing is certain: Many entrepreneurs bold enough to leap into the new media world will lose much of their investment. Some will probably make a great deal of money. As one experienced corporate sponsor once said: Half of my advertising is extremely effective. I just don't know which half. It may be that half of the new media products put into the market will succeed; unfortunately, no one knows which half.

The Intrepid Entrepreneur

The intrepid new media entrepreneur will integrate a considerable amount of re-search into his or her marketing efforts. Using both formative (i.e., diagnostic) and summative (i.e., end results) evaluation will greatly increase the efficiency of any new media marketing efforts, and provide the competitive edge and adaptability needed to survive and even thrive in a highly volatile market.

A variety of media entrepreneurs have offered their prognosis for the future. Among the most visionary of the new media entrepreneurs is Reese Schonfeld, president and CEO of The National Food Network. Schonfeld, the cofounder of CNN, has been promoting the virtues of the information highway since the mid-1980s, long before most had even heard of the idea. Schonfeld admits he does not know what final shape the information superhighway will take, but he knows what it should be: It should be digital, packet-switched, and designed with an open architecture to allow everyone to produce content for it.[27]

In agreement is John Malone, president and CEO of TCI, and "the most power-ful man in television" adds premier media critic Ken Auletta.[28] "A full-access uni-versal network is really what we're talking about—broadband, fully interactive, bidirectional, and universally available," says Malone.[29] "I see it happening in the next three to five years."

James C. Kennedy, chairman and chief executive officer of Cox Enterprises of Atlanta, is convinced that newspapers have a place on the information superhigh-way, but to secure that place they will need to demonstrate creativity and commit-ment to change.[30] "If we don't have the courage and creativity to take these risks, we won't have to worry about the public trust we enjoy today," Kennedy told members of the Newspaper Association of America on June 27.

Amidst the swirling hype and hope of the digital revolution, Neal B. Freeman, a Peabody award-winning television producer and chairman of the Blackwell Corpo-ration, stands among those convinced of the promise of the information highway. "The digital era of communications is here, and its essence is this: Vastly more people will have vastly improved access to vastly more information."[31] Freeman's conclusion is based on an analysis of the political economy of the digital era, in which he believes we are at "one of those rare moments in techno-economic history when it becomes clear that some players will win big and many other players will win at least a little. The zero-sum, scarce-spectrum game is over, and real growth is at hand." What does he base his analysis on? Five factors:

- The increased power of special interests, with dozens of groups having formed, for example, their own networks, ranging from The Caribbean Satellite Net-work to The Crime Channel to The Gaming Network
- The retreat of telecommunications regulation, as the Clinton–Gore administra-tion continues the momentum built during the Reagan–Bush years marked by the 1984 Modified Consent Decree divesting the Baby Bells from behemoth

AT&T (note that in late 1996 NTT, the Japanese equivalent of AT&T announced its parallel division into three smaller parts)

- The loss of America's cultural hegemony, as the global information network slowly erodes U.S. dominance in the creation of popular culture
- The rise of the multinational corporation, making once exotic "supranationals" such as Rupert Murdoch the norm, as it is the exceptional company that does not systematically move its rising young executives around the global markets
- The emergence of the digital press, as online, multimedia newspapers and magazines take hold, redefining the concept of news and markets no longer limited by geographic or political boundaries

At the same time consumers will have access to an increasing flow of raw data feeds from electronic media of all types. The need for information filters will rise dramatically. Traditional news media organizations will have an opportunity to expand their interpretation function. Smart agents will rapidly move into our digital midst. One fascinating Israeli company has already introduced three classes of intelligent agents for the Internet. LiveAgent, SearchAgent, and LiveAgent Pro were released in 1997 by AgentSoft Ltd., each of which performs customizable, routine tasks on the World Wide Web. LiveAgent, for example, is a personal agent on the Web, observing one's browsing behavior (which sites one visits, what information one obtains or clicks on) and then replicates those behaviors, routinely returning updated information, and so on. The next generation of intelligent agents will fall into a new class called *adaptive agents*. Adaptive agents will not only observe one's online behavior, but extend it to new arenas. For example, an adaptive agent might watch as we browse three news sites, observing the categories of stories we are most interested in (e.g., information technology). The adaptive agent would then visit other similar sites (i.e., news sites we did not visit) and obtain additional information technology stories, even compiling a "natural language" (i.e., English) summary of the essential facts as well as the notable differences or contradictory facts reported at each site. A collaborative project involving the faculty from the Department of Computer Science and the Center for New Media at Columbia University is in fact already working on a test of such a "smart" application.

Careers in the New Media: The Educational Mandate

Anyone planning a career in new media should be prepared for change, adaptation, and convergence. Few new media technologies are settled into their final form. As the technology continues to evolve, content production processes will continue to change. Moreover, as the new media of the digital age grow in importance, individuals with a rich understanding of technology convergence will have an advantage. New media products will become increasingly multimedia in format, with text, data, audio, and motion video blending in a single communications environment. Students preparing for new media careers should take courses both in the liberal arts and in all aspects of human communication. Medium-specific courses or degrees will have decreasing value in the emerging new media environment. Instead, the next generation of students will need to combine basic skills in thinking and writing with new media coursework emphasizing all aspects of human communication, from interpersonal and group communication to mediated and networked communications.

The Business Forecast

*"You acted unwisely," I cried, "as you see
by the outcome." He calmly eyed me;
"When choosing the course of my action,"
said he, "I had not the outcome to guide me."*[32]

Against a backdrop of considerable optimism and enthusiasm for the coming new media age, there is still profound commercial and cultural risk in investing millions, even billions, of dollars in staking out territory on the new media business frontier. Although there is no way to completely remove the risk from entering the new media marketplace, there are ways to minimize that risk. One set of tools comes from the field of financial analysts, commercial high rollers accustomed to risk-taking. One of the premier financial analysts specializing in the media is J. Kendrick Noble, a veteran media analyst, who recently completed a senior fellowship at The Freedom Forum Media Studies Center. Noble's fellowship research included developing a methodology for conducting a business forecast for the media industry. Based on an examination of data for a variety of media and communication fields, including newspapers, magazines, cable TV, and telephony, for much of the twentieth century, Noble suggests that reliable forecasts for new media technologies are possible, at least under limited circumstances. Perhaps most importantly, the forecasts must be based on accurate historical time-series data. Moreover, any forecast should be extended for no more than one-third the time frame of the original data. That is, if historical data are available for thirty years, then any forecast or prediction should be limited to the next ten years. For example, if data are available for 1965–1995, then a reliable forecast can be made through 2005. Beyond that period, the forecast is subject to many unexpected factors and likely to vary widely from the observed or actual pattern. By inference, the time-series data available for World Wide Web commercial ventures is no more than about three years, making predictions beyond a year highly uncertain.

Noble further notes that mathematical curves known as "S" curves are among the most commonly used tools for such forecasting. Such so-called "growth curves" are based on mathematical models for describing growth rates among biological organisms, such as humans or microorganisms. Logistic (or Pearl) and Gompertz curves are among the most widely used growth curves, which Noble argues are effective for conducting new media forecasts.[33] Others have used such biological models in describing media growth patterns, as well, including studies of media specialization and niche publishing. In Noble's research, a logistic curve provided an accurate description of the household penetration of the telephone from 1877 to 1931, but as a result of the Great Depression, underestimated the ultimate penetration level of the telephone in the 1980s (i.e., the model predicted telephone penetration would top out at about 40 percent, when it actually reached close to 95 percent in the 1980s). Use of a Gompertz curve provided a somewhat less accurate description of the adoption level of the telephone during the first half of the twentieth century, but accurately forecast the penetration level of the 1980s. Assuming the Gompertz curve provides a more reliable long-term forecast for media household penetration, Noble's analysis suggests that cable TV will achieve in 2040 the same household penetration achieved by telephony in the 1980s (i.e., roughly 95 percent).

Given the utility of these financial forecasting methods, new media entrepreneurs should consider employing logistic and Gompertz curves to project the possible market for new media technologies. The results might help steer them away from huge financial blunders and into more productive, even if smaller-scale ventures. Still, a word of caution comes from an unlikely theological source. The Reverend Donald Shriver, former president of the Union Theological Seminar in New York, warns that a forecast for the future of the media, an institution central not only to the functioning of our economy but to our cultural and political process, may have greater value if it is contrasted against an alternative prediction, or based on clearly outlined conditions in an if/then fashion.[34] Typically, Noble observes, financial analysts must forecast a single projection, because it is what the clients demand. If their forecasts are right, they will succeed and make a lot of money. If they are wrong, they will need to find a new line of work. Intrepid new media investors should consider both the best and worst case forecasts before investing heavily in new media technologies.

A CONSUMER'S GUIDE
TO DIGITAL COMMUNICATION

As the world of digital communication continues to evolve, media consumers will need to develop a new form of electronic media literacy. Central to this literacy are understanding the dimensions, grammar, and commercial nature of multimedia and cyberspace communications. As these two forms of digital communications converge, or collide, in the emerging information superhighway the new literacy will also continue to evolve. The rules and guidelines offered here are merely a starting point, and will require continual updating as the technology and its uses evolve.

"Seeing is believing" is an adage many have subscribed to for centuries. But in today's digital media age it can no longer be relied on. Digital image processors have made synthetic video commonplace. As a result, new media consumers need to be both aware of the new rules of the game, as well as how new media content producers will respond. Outlined below are ten rules, or commandments, to guide consumers navigating the world of digital communications. The first three rules apply generally to digital media, and the rest apply to cyberspace and beyond.

Rule 1: Question everything that is seen, heard, read, or watched in the new media environment. Digital processors and those who own one make detecting synthetic content almost impossible, and there is no government agency like the Federal Drug Administration (FDA) charged with evaluating media content, partly as a result of the First Amendment, partly a result of the complexity and scope of the existing communication system, and largely because of technology itself.

Rule 2: Conclude that almost everything in the new media environment is created to make money for someone. The few media products that truly do not have a commercial basis are as rare as a VCR that never blinks 12:00.

Rule 3: Assume that every new technology is a potential threat to your privacy. Every interactive system from your cable TV to the telephone to the World Wide Web has the ability to record every interaction you engage it in. The question you must ask yourself is: Is the convenience it provides worth the loss of privacy? The questions to ask the service provider are: What information about me and my use of your service are you recording, how will you use it, and will you make the information available to anyone else, to whom, and for what price?

Exploring the Limits of Cyberspace: The Possible and the Impossible

Cyberspace is the domain of networked communications (most often the Internet) that today encircle the globe, and tomorrow may stretch well beyond planet Earth. Although its beginnings were meager and the applications generally limited to electronic mail and file transfers, today the boundaries of cyberspace are rapidly expanding. Electronic bombs are sometimes as frequent as electronic mail, commercial transactions are almost as common on some systems as document transfers, and electronic publishing is challenging commercial printing as the state of the art in reaching both niche and mass markets. Moreover, the frontier nature of cyberspace also abounds with villains, outlaws, and heroes. Together, these patterns lead to **Rule 4:** Assume there are no boundaries in cyberspace, other than your own or someone else's imagination.

The following rules are especially important for parents, but apply to anyone concerned about the digital world.

Rule 5: Apply all the rules of conventional media literacy to digital communications. In other words, be aware of what your children are tuned into, whether going online, exploring multimedia, or simply playing videogames. Guide them in their selections, but also let them explore and enjoy freedom in making their own decisions. Debrief them periodically on their new media encounters.

Rule 6: Expect the unexpected. Because the limits of cyberspace are unknown and expanding, there will always be surprises. This is much of what attracts young people to explore the online world, the Internet, and the World Wide Web. It is participatory, evolving, and allows connections to people all around the world.

There are many benefits possible, including cultural enrichment, education, and cognitive development. But there are also dangers, some of which are outlined below. As a corollary to this rule, consider what many have dubbed the Year 2000 Problem. Many software programs and computers run on an internal calendar based on a system of two digits (e.g., DD-MM-YY). As a result, many are concerned about what will happen to many of the world's computers and computer programs at the end of this century when the year becomes 00. Programs that use the year to make calculations (e.g., accounting) are especially susceptible to the problem. The Social Security Administration estimates that it will need to revise some 50 million lines of code to correct this problem in its own system.[35] Expect the unexpected in the year 2000!

Rule 7: Never assume that if your child is using their computer that they are necessarily engaged in something educational. Although it is tempting to think that using the computer is better than watching television, it's not necessarily the case. Pedophilia in the online world is not uncommon. Sexual content is among the most commonly transmitted digital material on the Internet. Children should always be monitored when using their computer, especially if their system has an online connection, including a modem and a phone line. It's wise to talk to your child after they use the computer to find out what they have been doing. Or, better yet, join them in their computer explorations and game playing. When buying computer games, always read reviews and make sure that the content is suitable for your child. Many games are fun, educational, and harmless. But many are equally filled with violence, sexual exploitation, and even racism. Many of both the best and worst games can be obtained through cyberspace. Monitor your child's computer use to make sure the material they may be downloading is appropriate for them and meets your standards. Also, make sure that your child is not obtaining pirated material, such as digital recordings of copyrighted music or video. This is not only potentially dangerous, but is illegal. If you do find pirated material, talk to your child about how they received it and delete the files. A variety of online resources are available to help parents screen out unwanted online content, including software filters such as SurfWatch, Cyber Patrol, and Net Nanny. Similarly, a variety of Web sites provide site reviews to give parents a sense of what sites are not only most suitable for children but will meet their children's needs and tastes. Cnet.com is one site that provides not only reviews of "the best of the Web," but also for CD-ROM offerings.

Corollaries to Rule 7:
- Beware of anyone bearing uninvited gifts, anything free, or anything that sounds too good to be true—because it probably is. The Internet is filled with hucksters, charlatans, con artists, and worse. The discussion below examines the dimensions of the lawless nature of the electronic frontier.
- Never give out your name, address, or phone number, and instruct your child to do likewise, and to never give out the name of their school.
- Don't respond to angry or obscene online messages; report them to the manager of the online service you or your child uses.
- Know the online service(s) your child uses, and see if blocking is available.

Rule 8: Encourage the spirit of the First Amendment in cyberspace. Freedom of expression is perhaps the strongest positive force to countervail against many of the potentially negative forces at work in cyberspace. By promoting more communication, not less, participants in the global online community will enjoy a more robust communication environment, one in which truth will likely prevail over falsehood. Such platitudes may seem naive in today's somewhat cynical age, but they reflect the importance of reaffirming the Constitutional guarantees on the electronic frontier.

Rule 9: Think twice before buying the first, or even second generation of any new media technology. Chances are great that the early generations may have bugs or technical problems. Subsequent versions are likely to be considerably less expensive and work better, often having more features and being less complicated. Also, new technologies will tend to evolve toward a more unified set of standards, allowing greater compatibility among software from different companies or suppliers. This is not a hard and fast rule, but it tends to be the case.

Rule 10: Experiment with and enjoy the technology. Test and explore the limits of cyberspace. If you have children, encourage them to do the same, and don't be afraid to *ask them* for help and advice. Chances are your children may know more about using many of the new media technologies than you do. Seeking their advice will not only be educational, but it will show them respect, help build their self-esteem, and encourage them to share future electronic discoveries with you. Research at the Pathways for Women in the Sciences program at Wellesley College suggests three ingredients are especially important in creating a user-friendly environment that will encourage girls to explore new media technology: hands-on experience, teamwork, and relevance.[36] Following these rules may not insure a safe, enjoyable, and learning new media environment, but they will increase the chances of electronic success.

Scenario for Tomorrow: Knowbots, Virtual Reality, and Cyberpunks

Because it is neither owned and controlled by anyone, nor regulated by government (the CDA not withstanding), the Internet has served as a hotbed for unrestrained communication and an information free-for-all. Although philosopher John Locke may have been pleased to see his notion of a marketplace of ideas come to digital fruition, he may have been equally concerned about some of the emerging patterns of abuse.

Anarchy and Lawlessness on the Electronic Frontier

Technology reporter Peter H. Lewis writes that "Turks and Armenians have brought their decades-old hatred to the digital stage, accusing one another of using electronic mail forgeries and software that seeks and destroys an enemy's messages to the broader community."[37] Elsewhere on the "net," computer programmers are preparing "electronic mail bombs" to damage other users' computers, pedophiles are going online to recruit young boys for sex, pornographic images are transmitted in large volume. Many long-time users are worried that the free and open atmosphere that has existed on the Internet and fostered an intellectual climate rich in diversity will be replaced by one chilled by obscenity and pandering to the lowest common denominator, where prejudice and promiscuity become the norm.

Strategies to protect the Internet community have been few, and some have given up hope. "Certainly there will never be any consensus to establish a regulatory body for Usenet (largest news group on the Internet)," writes Mr. Botz in an e-mail.[38] "And no, the existing defenses are clearly not adequate. So what will happen? The Net as we know it will die."

Others see a technological solution. "What people will probably do is invent 'site kill files,'" writes David Hayes, a Usenet participant who works at the National Aeronautics and Space Administration's Jet Propulsion Laboratory in Pasadena, CA.[39] "Site Kill Files" allow a user to block selected computer messages or specific parts of the network. At the same time, site kill files could be used to censor politically unpopular views, not just obscene messages or unsolicited advertisements.

Virtual Reality

Jaron Lanier, the creator of the first virtual reality device, says that passive entertainment will always have a place in the media world, but he believes there is also a much more engaging place for virtual reality. Virtual reality is in use in a variety of applications, including industry, design, education, medicine, art, and entertainment. In Germany, virtual reality technology is helping in the redesign of the city of Berlin, with VR technology controlling construction robots. In Japan, department store shoppers use VR applications to design their own kitchen, try it out, and have it delivered. In the United States, Medical Media Systems of New Hampshire is using virtual reality to enhance surgical tools. The company's VR technologies integrate magnetic resonance imaging (MRI) with live sensory data to give a surgeon a three-dimensional view of the body. Conjuring up images of the science fiction film classic *Fantastic Voyage,* starring Raquel Welch, surgeons also use an instrument called endoscopic surgery, in which a tiny optical fiber is inserted into the body to control microinstruments. By remotely controlling this device, the surgeon virtually experiences the interior of the body. "It is like a zone for a fighter pilot," says Lanier.[40]

Although the passive couch potato may not quickly become a thing of the past, historians of the next millennium may someday need to write a virtual media history. Shaping that future is research scientist Brenda Laurel, whose work at Interval Research, a new Palo Alto, California, think tank, is creating virtual reality products generally not held in high regard in the commercial sector because they do not involve killing.[41] Laurel's virtual reality creations include a "virtual environment for two" at the Banff Center for the Arts in Canada, which lets visitors don computerized helmets and hand sensors to take a simulated trek to a mountain cave and step into the bodies of a snake, fish, spider, or crow.

Sonification

As we move into an era dominated by information, we are threatened by an increasingly complex and bewildering array of data. T. S. Eliot once asked, "Where is the wisdom lost in knowledge? Where is the knowledge lost in information?" Anthony Smith today asks, "Where is the information lost in data?" "Sonification" may provide at least a partial answer. "Sonification" refers to the notion of making scientific data audible. Introduced into the technical literature in 1952, the notion has surfaced from time to time since then. Recently, a sonification research program emerged at the National Center for Supercomputing Applications (NCSA) at the University of Illinois. "If you work in the field of computer music, representing data with sound is a pretty obvious idea," says Illinois composer Robin Bargar.[42] The group at NCSA has developed sonification software that uses an IBM-compatible PC and a MIDI synthesizer to turn just about any data into sound. Gregory Kramer, a musician similarly intrigued by the notion of sonification, has developed a system in which sound represents several variables at once. Clarity, the company he founded in Garrison, New York, is designing a sonification system for operating rooms, which will broadcast the patient's vital signs, including blood pressure and oxygen levels. The trick to sonification systems is developing a trained ear for sound, but it's a problem that training can overcome. Says Kramer, "You know when your car is running well just by listening to it. A certain noise, like a rattle, might also tell you what's wrong. Sounds in a well-designed sonification system could be interpreted in much the same way.[43] In the next decade, specialized applications of sonification technology might allow physicians to analyze complex patient data simply by listening to their audio representation. Perhaps sports fans one day may digest complex sports statistics simply by listening to an audio representation of the data on their personal digital appliance.

Artificial Life

Notions of artificial life, or living beings created by human hands, have dwelled in man and woman's imagination for more than a century. Victorian novelist Mary Shelley envisioned an artificial lifeform in her classic novel of Gothic horror, *Frankenstein*. More recently, Hungarian mathematician John Von Neuman described the automaton, a robotic machine capable of self-replication and other lifelike qualities. Logician Alan Turing outlined the foundation for machine-based life in his creation called the Turing Machine.

As a scientific discipline, the field of artificial life is in its infancy, however, with the first formal conference held in 1987.[44] Nevertheless, a number of computer scientists have conducted pioneering research to create computer-based life forms, artificial life, or a-life, which exhibit many of the qualities commonly associated with "real" life. These qualities include the ability to see, to eat, to reproduce and engage in sexual activity, to make decisions, to adapt to a changing environment, to demonstrate processes of natural selection. Since these artificial beings are capable of dying, then conversely they are also capable of living. Tomorrow's media world may be populated more heavily by electronic a-life forms than by their human counterparts. Many of these a-life forms will be acting as personal assistants, or knowbots, seeking the information their human masters desire, making or breaking appointments, or even conducting transactions at the bank or the supermarket, based on rules that we have established for them. At the same time, many of these electronic creatures may be less socially acceptable. One of the most notorious forms of artificial life is the computer virus. Although invented as an academic exercise, the computer virus has evolved to become a powerfully destructive force. Beyond the computer virus, future forms of a-life may exceed even a science fiction writer's most devilish imagination.

Most Wanted in Cyberspace

When Willie Sutton once was asked why he robbed banks, he replied, because that's where the money is. If cyberspace's most wanted cyberpunk were asked why he turned computer hacker, would he respond in like fashion, because that's where the information is? We may soon find out. Computer wizard Kevin Mitnick became the FBI's most wanted computer hacker for allegedly stealing software and data from more than a half dozen cellular telephone manufacturers.[45] After being hunted for violation of a Federal probation requirement that he not enter computers illegally, Mitnick was apprehended when the San Diego SuperComputer Center's Tsutomu Shimomura, a well-known security expert, helped federal authorities track him down. Mitnick had hacked into the home computer of Shimomura, raising his ire. Shimomura then turned his own computer security talents to tracking Mitnick and eventually led authorities on an electronic manhunt to Mitnick's Raleigh, North Carolina apartment. Shimomura has since signed substantial (reported to be for more than $1 million) book, film, and CD-ROM contracts to tell the story of how he helped catch Mitnick.

Reflecting on the strange case, *New York Times* technology reporter John Markoff reports that as a teenager, Mitnick used a computer and modem to:

- Secretly read electronic mail of computer security officials at MCI Communications
- Access telephone company central offices in Manhattan and the phone switching centers in California, allowing him to listen in on phone calls and engage in high-tech hijinks like reprogramming home phones so that callers would hear a recording asking for a deposit of 25 cents

- Break into a North American Air Defense Command computer, foreshadowing the 1983 movie *War Games*

Some see Mitnick as a cyberspace hero, and a victim of the Internet-mania of the mid-1990s. Chris Gulker reports at the Random Access web site, "Is Kevin Mitnick a dangerous criminal apprehended by an ingenious high-tech detective? Or a sad, if annoying, loner who was set up by shrewd manipulators cashing in on Internet hype?"[46]

THE GLOBAL INFORMATION INFRASTRUCTURE: GORE

One of the emerging benefits of the new information age is the development of a global information infrastructure (GII). The GII refers to the emerging network of advanced telecommunications, computing, and information technologies around the world, particularly the Internet. Although the GII will not reach all communities, countries, and computers simultaneously and in equal fashion, it will—in fact, it already does—reach many millions of people around the world. The GII will make it possible for people in even remote regions to stay in constant electronic touch. It will enable low-cost, high-speed commercial transactions from any location in the world, as long as they are connected to the GII. It will provide electronic access to diverse resources located throughout the world.

Important questions about the GII include:

- Who will have access?
- What will be the cost of access and use?
- Who will pay for the construction of the GII?
- How will the GII be controlled or regulated?
- What guarantees for freedom of expression will exist in the GII?
- How will regional differences in GII policy be managed in an international arena?

A Global Virtual Digital Library

From a cultural perspective, one of the most important opportunities the GII affords is the creation of a global virtual digital library. Such a library is already developing, as electronic resources such as those at the OCLC, the U.S. Library of Congress, and at countless libraries and public institutions connect to the global computer network known as the Internet. This library is virtual in the sense that its collection, as it were, is housed in no single physical location. Rather, it exists in digital format in many decentralized locations, in computers in libraries, schools, offices, and elsewhere. Each digital location acts as a communication portal, or file server, providing electronic access, browsing, or downloading of material to any location in the world connected to the GII. Important questions about this global virtual digital library are many, and parallel those outlined above regarding the GII.

A New Athenian Age of Democracy

Perhaps even more important than the development of virtual libraries are the implications of digital communications for the political system. For more than a century, political pundits have pondered the role of electronic media in the democratic process.[47] Today, Vice President Gore proclaims that networked communications may signal the beginning of a new Athenian Age of Democracy. Lawrence Grossman, former president of NBC News and PBS, echoes this view in his book *The Electronic Republic,* suggesting that new media technologies are rapidly transforming the democratic system from one of representation to direct democracy. Armed with their computers, modems, and WebTVs, citizens increasingly have direct access to the political process. Not only can they communicate directly with political candidates and elected officials, but they can vote on referenda and other legislative issues. Such a political transformation may be both a good and a dangerous thing. Although direct-access technology may enhance political participation, it may also lead to political decisions based on little more than the emotions aroused by dramatic television images.[48] More alarmingly, the selective development and diffusion of new technologies, the lack of access to the poor, and the difficulty in using many new technologies may also lead to political tyranny of the majority, with minority voices being lost in a digital cacophony.

Electronic Town Meetings

For more than two centuries, town meetings have been a vital part of democracy in America, making the electoral process a participatory rather than a spectator sport. French philosopher Alexis de Tocqueville observed how town meetings gave Americans a hands-on education in democracy. Brandeis University Professor Jeffrey Abramson notes that the town meeting was originally designed to meet three purposes:

- To educate citizens about common concerns
- To empower citizens to self-government
- To engage citizens in an open and universally accessible process[49]

Of course, since their inception, town meetings have failed to meet these goals fully, sometimes restricting participation based on race, gender, church membership, and property. Still, the town meeting has been pursued as a democratic ideal. In its most recent incarnation, it emerged during the 1992 and 1996 presidential campaigns in a new, technologically driven form called the *electronic town hall.* Texas Businessman Ross Perot trumpeted the electronic town hall as the platform for a new era of democracy. Others hailed the electronic town hall as a twenty-first-century technique to reintroduce face-to-face communication in a media society. But electronic town meetings are not necessarily a panacea. Not everyone may have access to the technology needed to participate fully. There is a tendency for "push button" democracy to take hold, where, rather than meet and discuss, participants may do little more than push a button on a telephone handset or a remote control to indicate approval or disagreement.

Abramson argues that three conditions are necessary for effective deliberation at a town meeting:

- Citizens should be able to explore political messages of substance at length and in depth, without limiting exchanges to ever-shrinking soundbites
- Citizens must be able to reflect on those messages, and not respond instantaneously
- Citizens should be able to interact and exchange views and ideas, to test each other's reactions, and weigh their opinions against those of others

Although face-to-face meetings can clearly satisfy these conditions, how well electronic town halls fare is a matter of how they are designed and executed.[50] Technology may make it possible to bring together many participants at remote and scattered locations, but it can also encourage instantaneous response and a lack of substantial communication.

Abramson outlines six critical issues in designing electronic town meetings to satisfy the above criteria for effective political deliberation.

- **Venue.** New media technologies enable us to hold electronic town meetings on a national, regional, or local level. The choice of venue depends on both the issue or political campaign, as well as citizen access to the relevant technology.
- **Issue.** Every electronic town meeting should be devoted to a single, clearly stated issue, such as national health care or the federal deficit.
- **Agenda-setting/Editorial Control.** Setting the issues for the town meeting is a complex matter and research by Abramson suggests two models. The primary model is for the organization hosting the meeting, such as a news organization, to choose the issues and plan the event, including selecting moderators, experts, and so forth. Alternatively, it is sometimes effective for a nonprofit group to set the agenda.
- **Audience/Participants.** Rarely will a town meeting, electronic or face-to-face, satisfy the demands of scientific sampling and representativeness of the broader population. Instead, audience members are typically self-selected, and represent only politically active groups. Thus, Abramson recommends building an audience in two stages. First, there will naturally be the primary, self-selected audience, often limited to those who can come to a TV studio. Second, a

broader audience should be invited to participate through the use of interactive technology such as the telephone, through 800 or 900 numbers or through online communications such as an Internet forum.

- **Choice of Interactive Technology.** Interactive technology provides three main options for providing audience involvement and participation. First and most basic is touch-tone telephone dialing, particularly 800 and 900 networks provided by carriers such as AT&T and MCI. These networks can process more than 10,000 calls in 90 seconds. For national town meetings, it is essential to provide sufficient 800 network capacity. The CBS *America Online* special during the 1992 campaign frustrated many callers by providing too little capacity—only 314,786 calls got through out of some 24.6 million attempts.

  Second are two-way cable systems, which were inaugurated in the Warner Amex Qube experiment in the 1970s in Columbus, Ohio, and are today increasingly common. Interactive systems in San Antonio, Texas, Minneapolis, Minnesota, Portland, Oregon, Upper Manhattan, New York, Reading, Pennsylvania, Orlando, Florida, and Fairfax, Virginia all allow the viewer to send messages upstream using a remote control as well as receive TV programming. Lack of access to nonsubscribers is a limitation of this approach.

  Finally, online services provide a third technological option for electronic town meetings. Online computer forums are in fact already common on the Internet and on commercial services. They allow in-depth discussion of issues, as well as direct communication and exchange of ideas. Moreover, through the Internet it is possible to provide a forum for holding for the first time an electronic town meeting in an international global venue. As we move toward McLuhan's global village, this may become an increasingly important issue. Moreover, online forums are inexpensive, since telecommunication charges are only local. The biggest drawback to online network approaches is the limited availability of computers and online services among the general citizenry. Even in an information society such as the United States, only some 36 percent of U.S. households have a computer and even fewer have a network connection. This situation, however, may rapidly change with the proliferation of powerful, inexpensive videogame players and the convergence of telecommunications, cable, and computers, as well as the increased availability of Internet access through schools, libraries, and other public spaces. Other emerging technologies such as DBS and PCS may also provide a technological infrastructure for electronic town meetings by the end of the decade. Importantly, pioneering online voter information services were implemented via the Internet during the 1994 elections in California, including the Voter Online Information and Communications Exchange (VOICE) sponsored by two major national organizations, the League of Women Voters and Project Smart Vote.[51] The 1996 campaign saw even greater online forums on the World Wide Web, with an increasingly diverse cross-section of the voting public accessing voter information at both official campaign sites as well as from reliable online news sources.

- **Voting from Home or Other Audience Locations.** This is in many ways the natural conclusion of the electronic town hall. One of the most significant problems in electronic voting, however, is the ability of individuals to vote multiple times. Similarly, it is important to provide multiple individuals at *a single location* the ability to cast their votes. A potential solution to these problems is to provide a personal identification number (PIN) to each participant to electronically monitor voting, assuring that each town hall participant could vote only once, and that each person at a location could cast a vote. Moreover, this approach would lay the foundation for full voting activity electronically, assuring that each ballot cast was entered by a registered voter. The security of each PIN would become imperative in such a system. Advanced systems could use optical scanners to verify voter identification through fingerprints or retinal scans, although at present the cost of the necessary technology would be prohibitive. One of the important limitations of voting at electronic town meetings is generalizability beyond the meetings' participants. Participation in town hall meetings, whether traditional or electronic, is not representative of the population at large, and any results from a vote can not be fairly generalized to the broader population.

THE NEXT GENERATION:
CHILDREN AND TECHNOLOGY

Understanding the uses and consequences of new media technology ultimately hinges on understanding the next generation. Today's children and youth are the heaviest users of new media technology. They enjoy the highest comfort level with the technology. For them, many seemingly foreign and obtuse technologies are second nature and completely transparent. They often have an intuitive grasp of new media technologies. Whether programming a common house device like a VCR or accessing the Internet, many youth travel in and out of the cyberworld as easily as most adults get in and out of a car. Even toddlers two to three years old can learn to use a mouse and control a computer. One interesting Web site designed just for kids, Internet-For-Kids, offers children of all ages a variety of customized educational and entertaining interactive tools and applications.[52] Under the leadership of company founder and president, Victoria Williams, the site is a road sign to the future.

To many older adults, the idea of talking to your computer, much less a banking machine, may seem like fanciful science fiction if not downright dangerous. But to the next generation, calling in to an automated banking machine and simply telling the computerized system what transactions you wish may be as simple as using an ATM is to most Americans today. One major bank in New York is already conducting a test with voice-response tele-banking. You dial in and simply say "representative" for the operator, or any of a number of other terms to select those banking options. The system works simply, easily, and reliably. What's around the corner is anybody's guess. But one thing is certain: The next generation will glide as easily through this high-tech world as today's average household gourmet operates a microwave oven. The next generation's new media habits will also continue the transformation of new media technology. Their behavioral preferences and patterns and content choices will influence the design, look, and feel of tomorrow's media. The nature of interactivity will reflect the next generations' lifestyle and attitudes.

Jaron Lanier, the recognized "father" of virtual reality offers this view of the importance of the next generation:

> *The digital superhighway is much more than a highway system. It's actually the construction of an entirely new virtual continent in which the highway runs. In the future, we will live part of our lives in cyberspace, in the world of virtual reality. We could bequeath few gifts to future generations more important than getting this right. It's critically important to balance public and private interests, much as it's very important to do so in land use, where even private land owners have certain obligations to the public.*[53]

No one can predict with any certainty the future of the media world. Many elements will be new and unexpected, while perhaps most will continue to reflect the best and worst of today's media system. Commercial interests will no doubt continue to dominate, but there will be room for not-for-profit cultural forces. As we already see in the Internet, the role of an electronic public space will be profound. The future of the media world may not be ours entirely to shape, but it is ours to discover. Lord Tennyson once offered these encouraging words:

> *Come, my friends, 'Tis not too*
> *late to seek a newer world.*
> —*LORD ALFRED TENNYSON*[54]

NOTES

[1] Levy, Steven, "We Have Seen the Content, and It Is Us." *The Media Studies Journal,* Winter, 1994.

[2] NEC Ad number 162, *Scientific American,* January 1997: 21.

[3] Kenneth M. King, "Computers, Man and Society Seminar Remarks," Columbia University, December 18, 1996.

[4] Siegenthaler, John, Leadership Institute, The Freedom Forum Media Studies Center, June 23, 1994.

[5] Eco, Umberto, "From Internet to Gutenberg," speech, Italian Academy for Advanced Studies in America at Columbia University, November 12, 1996.

[6] Krebs, Michelle, "Cars That Tell You Where to Go," *New York Times,* December 15, 1996.

[7] Bodo, Pete, "How to Find Yourself, or Not Get Lost," *New York Times,* December 15, 1996.

[8] Levere, Jane, "Travel Systems Use Technology to Ease the Commute," *New York Times,* December 23, 1996.

[9]Leonard Kleinrock, "Nomadic Computing," Presentation at The Heritage of Marconi's Invention and the Future of Telecommunication, Columbia University, December 9, 1996.

[10]Carey, John, "Media Research and the Information Highway: Setting a Research Agenda," February 14, 1994, Speech, The Freedom Forum Media Studies Center.

[11]Robert Lucky, "Reinventing Telephony as Internet Comes of Age," Presentation at The Heritage of Marconi's Invention and the Future of Telecommunication, Columbia University, December 9, 1996.

[12]Stix, Gary, "The Wall: Chip Makers' Quest for Small May Be Hitting It," *Scientific American,* July 1994, p. 96, 98.

[13]Ibid., 96.

[14]Ibid.

[15]Markoff, John, "Chip-Making Towers of Power," *New York Times,* Nov. 8, 1994: C1.

[16]*Business Week* special report "Some Gigachip Milestones to Look for," July 4, 1994: 88.

[17]Gibbs, W. Wayt, "Bandwidth, Unlimited," *Scientific American,* January 1997: 41.

[18]John Markoff, "Judge Rules Against Curbs on Export of Encryption Software," *New York Times,* December 19, 1996.

[19]Dennis, Everette E., Technology Studies Seminar, The Freedom Forum Media Studies Center, April 6, 1994.

[20]Fitzgerald, Mark, "Invisible Digital Copyright ID," *Editor & Publisher,* June 25, 1994.

[21]Stahlman, Mark, "Backlash: The Infobahn Is a Big, Fat Joke," *Wired,* March 1994: 73.

[22]Rifkin, Glenn, "Seeing Print's Future in a Digital Universe," *New York Times,* May 9, 1994: D8.

[23]Ibid.

[24]Ibid.

[25]Moeller, op. cit., 1994: 25.

[26]www.marimba.com

[27]Schonfeld, Reese, Speech, IRTS seminar Feb. 11, 1994.

[28]Auletta, op. cit., 1994: 52.

[29]Tynan, Daniel, "PC Meets TV." *PC World,* February 1994: 139.

[30]Thalhimer, op. cit., July 6, 1994.

[31]Freeman, Neal B., "Populism + Telecommunications = Global Democracy," *National Review,* November 15, 1993: 50.

[32]Bierce, Ambrose, *The Collected Works of Ambrose Bierce.* New York: The Neale Publishing Co., 1909.

[33]Martino, Joseph P. (1993), *Technological Forecasting for Decision-Making,* 3rd ed. New York: McGraw-Hill. Noble, Jr., J. Kendrick, "U.S. Daily Newspapers: Past, Present and Prospects, 1958–2008," research report, presented at Fellows Seminar, May 26, 1994.

[34]Shriver, Rev. Donald, Speaker, Fellows Seminar, The Freedom Forum Media Studies Center, May 26, 1994.

[35]www.sandybay.com/pc-web/Year_2000_Problem.htm

[36]Hafner, Katie, "Getting Girls On-Line," *Working Woman,* April 1994: 61.

[37]Lewis, Peter H., "Sneering at a Virtual Lynch Mob," *New York Times,* May 11, 1994: D7.

[38]Ibid.

[39]Ibid.

[40]Lanier, ibid.

[41]Hermelin, Francine, "Feminizing Virtual Reality," *Working Woman,* April 1994: 54.

[42]Nadis, Steve, "Artificial Intelligence: The Sound of Data: Data May Fill Your Ears Rather Than Your Eyes," *Omni,* January 1994: 26.

[43]Ibid.

[44]Levy, Steven, *Artificial Life: The Quest for a New Creation.* London: Penguin Books, 1993.

[45]Markoff, John, "Cyberspace's Most Wanted: Hacker Eludes F.B.I. Pursuit," *New York Times,* July 4, 1994.

[46]www.gulker.com/ra/hack/

[47]Carey, James (1989), op. cit.

[48]Schudson, Michael (1992), "The Limits of Teledemocracy," *The American Prospect,* 11 (3): 41–45.

[49]Abramson, Jeffrey B., and Charles M. Firestone, *Electronic Town Meetings: Democratic Design for Electronic Town Meetings,* The Aspen Institute, 1992.

[50]Arterton, F. Christopher (1987), *Teledemocracy.* Beverly Hills, CA: Sage. Becker, Theodore (1993). "Teledemocracy: Gathering Momentum in State and Local Governance," *Spectrum: The Journal of State Government,* 66 (2): 14–19.

[51]Lewis, Peter H., "Electronic Tie for Citizens and Seekers of Office," *New York Times,* Nov. 6, 1994: 15.

[52]www.internet-for-kids.com

[53]Tynan, op. cit., 1994: 139.

[54]Tennyson, Alfred, *Ulysses.* London: Moxon, 1869.

10

The Structure of the Internet Industry

Jeffrey H. Brody
California State University, Fullerton

Ours is a brand-new world of all-at-onceness.
Time, in a sense, has ceased and space
has vanished. Like primitives, we now live
in a global world of our own making, a
simultaneous happening. The global village is
not created by the motor car or even the airplane.
It is created by the instant electronic information
movement. The global village is at once as wide
as the planet and as small as the little town. . . .
MARSHALL McLUHAN, McLUHAN ON
McLUHANISM, *1966.*

The Internet is at the center of the integration of
a new media ecology. . . . The economic struggle
among firms attempting to control and dominate
this complex is the outer and visible edge
of deeper transformations in the structure of
nations and other forms of social organizations.
JAMES CAREY, THE INTERNET AND THE END OF THE
NATIONAL COMMUNICATION SYSTEM: UNCERTAIN
PREDICTIONS OF AN UNCERTAIN FUTURE, *1998.*

Howard Stern loves to boast that he is the "King of All Media." The brash, outspoken Stern hosts a nationally syndicated radio show and cable television program. He has written a best-selling book, starred in a feature film, and appears in a weekly entertainment show on the CBS television network. Stern may have a point about dominating media. But when it comes to discussing the power and potential of media, especially comparing old media to new media, the Internet reigns supreme. Where else can one view text, photographs, animation, and video, listen to music and radio, watch television and motion pictures, make telephone calls, participate in audio conferences, talk by e-mail, and navigate within a three-dimensional world. All of this can be accomplished by jumping from one hypertext link to another as bits of information are transferred from one part of the world to the other. In just a few clicks of a mouse, one can visit the website of a bank in Africa, a newspaper in Asia, a scientific outpost in Antarctica, a bed-and-breakfast in Australia, a museum in Europe, a music store in North America, and a university in South America.

The integrative powers of the Internet overwhelm all other forms of media and, as Carey argues, it is a new media ecology that's best described by the metaphor of McLuhan's global village. More than 100 million people around the world were connected to the Internet by the end of 1997.[1] In *Being Digital,* Nicholas Negroponte, director of MIT's Media Lab, says that Internet use is growing at the rate of 10 percent per month, a rate that, if possible, would put the total number of Internet users at greater than the world's population by the year 2003. The professor estimates that 1 billion people will use the Internet by the year 2,000. The demographics of the Internet, according to Negroponte, will mirror "the demographics of the world," and create, along the lines of Carey and McLuhan, " a totally new global social fabric."[2]

Surveys of Internet use confirm these predictions. A 1998 report by the Worldwatch Institute disclosed that web use is growing geometrically in Latin America and Asia, and that 4 million people are expected to be online in China by the millennium. The World Wide Web is on its way to becoming a worldwide phenomenon. Forecasts show that the United States share of Internet use will drop from 56 percent in 1997 to 40 percent by the year 2002, as less technologically advanced countries connect to the net.

At the same time, children between the ages of 2 and 22 are being labeled the "Net Generation," much like baby boomers were called the "television generation." These young people are using the net in school the same way the baby boomers used encyclopedias, and are relying on e-mail to communicate with each other the same way baby boomers relied on the telephone.[3] A Gallup survey in March, 1998, found that the major difference between baby boomers and the young generation in Internet use is that baby boomers restrict themselves to gathering news and information, whereas young people rely on the Internet for all types of communication and social interaction. Furthermore, universities have initiated net-based courses and are beginning to require that students purchase laptop computers with Internet access for their classwork. These net skills will provide the foundation, and the intellectual capital, for the next generation to tap into business and explore new possibilities for the growth and expansion of the Internet.[4]

With all the technological wonder and prophesy, it's important to remember that the Internet is a relatively new industry and phenomenon. The first successful test to link computers at different locations took place in 1969 when the pioneers of the Internet, the U.S. government's Advanced Research Project Agency, set up a network among host computers at Stanford University, UCLA, University of California, Santa Barbara, and the University of Utah. That experiment led to the birth of the Internet, which was primarily used for e-mail and the exchange of information among university researchers and students. The Internet came of age as a communications medium with the creation of the World Wide Web—the Internet's graphical interface—by British engineer Tim Berners-Lee in 1991, and the invention of the first graphical browser in 1993 by Marc Andreesen and his team at the University of Illinois. Two decades of networking computers laid the foundation for the future of communications, but the groundwork that sparked the communications revolution, the World Wide Web, is actually less than a decade old.

The transmission of information in this century has evolved from analog telephone calls over copper wire that carry less than one page of information per minute to optical fiber as thin as a human hair that can transmit the equivalent of more than 90,000 volumes of an encyclopedia in a single second over a high-speed network.[5] The shift from analog to digital technology, from the telephone to the Internet, has occurred so quickly that one MIT researcher predicts that "the Internet will carry more communications traffic than conventional telephone voice circuits by the end of 1998."[6] With the introduction of smart phones that process e-mail and display web pages, the telephone has joined the personal computer and the television set as an Internet connection. Personnel at companies across the country communicate with e-mail and receive company correspondence through net-based technology. Commenting on a study that showed homes connected to the net watch 15 percent less television, an NBC executive said that the networks have to prepare for the convergence of television and the Internet.[7]

There has been a convergence, and consensus in thinking about the potential of the Internet, among intellectuals, venture capitalists, and business executives. Without a doubt, communications theorists, computer specialists, media moguls, telecommunications leaders, and Wall Street investors have found common ground in the belief that the Internet is evolving into the premier medium of the twenty-first century. Because of its ability to convey both sequential and nonsequential writing, e-mail, audio and visual images, animation, three-dimensional virtual reality, audioconferencing, and multimedia presentations, the Internet has become the embodiment of the much talked about information superhighway. As personal computers become as ubiquitous in the home as they are in the workplace, the prominence of networked computers becomes paramount to capital, communications, and commerce.

The Internet, to echo Malcolm Forbes, has become a capitalist tool. In its brief history, the thrust of growth generated by the Internet has shifted from academicians and technophiles to hard-core businesses and venture capital, especially after the National Science Foundation, which monitored the Internet, lifted restrictions against commercial use of the net in 1991. A little more than 50 percent of the total venture capital invested in the United States goes to information technology.[8] Small wonder that Bill Gates, touted as the richest entrepreneur in the world, shifted the thrust of his Microsoft empire to the network paradigm and is battling the government of the United States over an Internet anti-trust issue. Two Stanford University graduate students, David Filo and Jerry Yang, became multimillionaires by creating Yahoo, a directory of "cool sites" on the web, and turning it into an Internet portal that boasts 6.35 million weekly viewers.[9] America Online, which purchased Netscape and has partnered with Sun Microsystems, repositioned itself from a proprietary network to become the nation's number one Internet service provider. Even online sex sites generate almost $1 billion in revenue per year.[10] David Abrahamson in *The Visible Hand: Money, Markets, and Media Evolution* envisions an Internet that will be privatized, market-driven, supported by advertising, and concentrated in the hands of fewer and larger companies.[11] That appears to be the direction that the Internet is headed. Revenue generated from the Internet will mushroom from $14 billion in 1996 to about $327 billion by the year 2,002, according to Forrester Research Inc. A 1998 report by the U.S. Department of Commerce states that investment trends show that $327 billion figure is on the mark, and three companies alone—Cisco, Dell, and General Electric—each did $3 billion in Internet commerce in 1997 and each expect to conduct more than $17 billion in Internet commerce within three to five years.[12]

As *Business Week* notes in its 1998 annual report on information technology:

> *Without a doubt, the Internet is ushering in an era of sweeping change that will leave no business or industry untouched. In just three years, the Net has gone from a playground for nerds into a vast communications and trading center where some 90 million people swap information or do deals around the world. Imagine it took radio more than 30 years to reach 60 million people, and television 15 years. Never has a technology caught fire so fast.[13]*

Business Week's analysis is underscored in the lament of a Netizen who decries in an alternative publication that business has conquered the Internet: "And the veteran denizens of the Internet—dismissed variously as geeks, losers, elitists . . . — are witnessing with trepidation the upheaval of their online world. No one knows quite what the Internet will look like once the dust settles, but one thing is clear: the free market has indisputably arrived."[14]

In almost every part of the industrialized world, trade shows and conferences have been organized on almost a monthly basis to promote Internet commerce. More than 1 million e-commerce transactions—the direct buying and selling of merchandise across the Internet—occur each day.[15] That humanity has exploited communications technology for commerce, probably more so than for high culture, dates to 3100 BC, in ancient Mesopotamia, where the oldest surviving evidence of a writing system, pictorial symbols on clay tablets, lists commodities and business transactions.[16]

Today, Internet stocks have spurred a frenzy of speculation that some money managers compare to the 1849 goldrush. In the summer of 1998, America Online, Yahoo, Amazon.com, Excite, and Lycos reached a combined market value of $45 billion, compared to Chrysler's $38 billion. This has generated concern because some Internet companies, such as online newspaper publications, have yet to make money and their price/earning ratios remain negative. The stock price of Amazon.com, for example, soared from $12 to more than $100 per share in one year (July, 1997–July, 1998), even though the company doesn't plan on making a profit until after the year 2000.[17] Amazon.com shareholders learned a lesson in speculation when its stock price dropped more than 25 percent in two days during the market correction of September, 1998. About two-thirds of the 50 companies listed in the Internet Stock Index, a key indicator of Internet business activity, are losing money or barely breaking even.[18]

Is hype a part of hypertext? Is there a need for caution in speculating about a new digital future? Are critics correct in asserting that "the only thing we know for certain about the future and impact of the Internet is that we know nothing"?[19] This is what must be kept in mind as one examines the nature and scope of an industry that is transforming the world so quickly that much of the information gathered about it can be speculative and out-of-date by the time it's published.

HYPE IN HYPERSPACE

While the Internet is without question in ascendancy and commerce has become the generating force behind the Internet's spectacular growth, researchers must maintain some skepticism about the prophecies that seem to abound on the net and in the media about the Internet industry. The Internet after all is in its infancy as an industry and as a communications medium. The experiences of two of the Internet's most well-known and respected pioneers, Harold Rheingold and Louis Rossetto, serve to illustrate the pitfalls of banking on the Internet as an info-highway to sure success. Both authorities on cyberculture, Rheingold and Rossetto overextended themselves and failed in Internet ventures.

A consultant to the U.S. Congress Office of Technology and Assessment and author of *The Virtual Community* and *Virtual Reality,* Rheingold founded "Electric Minds" in 1996 with $1 million start-up capital to serve as a virtual community on the web. Rheingold envisioned a site on the net where anyone and everyone could meet and chat. While the idea of creating a virtual community in cyberspace may have appeared fine on paper, Rheingold failed to get enough subscribers or advertisers to pay for "Electric Minds," which fell apart within a year, despite critical praise of the site's content. Rheingold wasn't the first and won't be the last web entrepreneur to learn that the quality of a site is no guarantee of success.

The energetic and electrifying Rossetto founded *Wired Magazine,* which became an acclaimed commercial success. Known for its distinctive graphics, *Wired* has been praised as one of the magazine industry's most avant-garde high-tech publications. Rossetto's vision of moving from old media (print) to new media (the net) failed to find financial backers. Wall Street turned a deaf ear to Rossetto when it came to supporting his electronic ventures on the World Wide Web to the tune of $400 million. Rossetto was unable to garner support for an initial public offering of his Wired Ventures, Inc. He lost control of the celebrated and distinctive *Wired Magazine* at the end of 1997 after selling it to Advanced Publications in order to obtain capital to keep the online operations afloat. Following that debacle Rossetto remarked: "It turns out euphoria is not a business strategy."[20]

Yet, those who are quick to criticize the net need to beware. Clifford Stoll in *Silicon Snake Oil,* a 1995 net-bashing book, warned that most businesses would go broke on Internet ventures—but then admitted if his bicycle ever broke down, he'd like to buy a car online without haggling. Not only is that now possible, Stoll can buy online airline tickets, hot sauce, and a copy of his own outdated book.[21]

Because of the dynamism of the industry, and the ability of people to log onto the Internet from millions of computers around the world, analysts have experienced difficulty gathering accurate and timely data. The decentralized nature of the net makes it nearly impossible to categorize its content and to analyze with certainty what exactly is on the net at any given moment in time. With more than 320 million web pages, researchers have been stymied in their efforts to index the web—even with the use of sophisticated search engines. And the problem is expected to grow worse as the number of web pages expand by 1,000 percent in the next few years.[22] The web has become so unwieldy that even the best search engines fail to index a majority of the web pages on a given subject, and even when they come close the results are often overwhelming because a typical search can come up with several thousand hits. Content on the Internet encompasses the content of other media, including online newspapers, television news reports, and magazines. Tracking the amount of e-mail messages sent over the net would be a daunting, if impossible, task.

A report by Nielsen Internet Demographics, whose parent company has extensive experience measuring audience share and viewership in the television industry, concludes that the Internet poses challenges for researchers and is a very difficult medium to measure. As mentioned, the U.S. Commerce Department and Forrester Research Inc. projected net commerce to reach $327 billion by 2002. In April, 1998, ActivMedia Inc. predicted net commerce to generate more than $1.2 trillion in revenue by 2002. Founded in 1994, ActivMedia claims to be the oldest market research firm on the web and has conducted five annual surveys of net commerce. That ActivMedia can boast to be the oldest market research firm shows how new market research on the web is.[23] The best conclusion that one can reach is that net marketing is in its infancy.

It is much easier to gather data and information about the established communications industries—magazines, newspapers, television, radio—than the Internet. Take subscribers or users, for example. In 1996, six studies in the United States and two worldwide by respected research organizations failed to agree on the number of people using the Internet and disagreed in one case by more than 600 percent.[24] Contrast this with the newspaper industry, which has long relied on the independent Audit Bureau of Circulation to come up with accurate figures on the number of subscribers for each daily newspaper in the United States.

In fairness to Internet researchers, the Audit Bureau of Circulation monitors a mature industry that literally has grown up with the country. The bureau keeps tabs on some 1,600 daily newspapers with an estimated total circulation of a little less than 60 million. Compare that with the challenge of auditing more than 11,000 Internet service providers in the United States, including the largest, America Online, which claims membership of 12 million. Furthermore, the number of daily newspapers has declined over the past three decades in the United States, while the Internet is growing and has been changed overnight by innovators coming up with new software, products, and ideas. Just keeping track of Internet start-up companies is daunting. The number of Internet-related exhibitors at Comdex, the world's largest computer-technology trade show, nearly doubled from 290 in 1995 to 550 in 1996 and continues to mushroom each year. Mecklermedia, publishers of *Internet World,* sponsors conferences in major cities across the globe that feature dozens of industry-leader speakers and hundreds of exhibitors. In 1998, Mecklermedia sponsored conferences in 23 countries, including Argentina, India, Sweden, and the United Arab Emirates. The beauty of Internet commerce is that it can take place 24 hours per day, simultaneously in every time zone across the globe. In all of history, no merchant or corporation has ever been able to do that. The global nature of the Internet will allow someone to read an online magazine or purchase products from any place in the world.

ADVANTAGE OF INTERNET COMMERCE

Robert Hertzberg, editor of *Internet World,* posed a question to readers at the beginning of 1998.[25] He asked if the good old days of Internet time—short product cycles and rapid-fire acquisitions—were dead. In Hertzberg's analysis, the big boys, the Fortune 1000 companies, misunderstood the tremendous commercial potential of the Internet from about 1993 to the middle of 1995. That strategic misunderstanding enabled start-up companies to flourish and develop products and services at lightning speed. Hence, the designation, Internet time. By 1998, according to Hertzberg, the industrial giants had awakened from their sleep and stepped into the Internet marketplace. It will only be a matter of time before every Fortune 1000 company has a functioning website that gives that company a business address and commercial presence on the Internet. University graduates with skills in designing and maintaining websites have found themselves inundated with job offers. Hertzberg asks if there is room for small companies and start-ups to overcome the capital advantage of the large corporations. It remains to be seen whether start-up companies will remain competitive once the giants in the industry move in. The question is whether Amazon.com, which touts itself as the world's largest bookstore, will be able to compete when the major book publishers and retailers develop online sites themselves. Time will tell. But the advantages of Internet commerce remain a certainty for small businesses as well as multinationals.

First of all, Internet commerce eliminates traditional time/space restrictions on business. An Internet user can access sites wherever and whenever he wants, from at home, in the office, or even a coffee shop down the block. Airports, convention centers, and hotels are increasingly providing for high-speed online connections, so users can obtain e-mail and surf the net. Website and e-mail addresses are becoming commonplace on business cards, stationery, and advertising. The monthly cost of maintaining a website is cheaper than renting physical space for a store, and the ability to look up information, purchase goods, and complete transactions without going through a middleman saves time and money for both the buyer and the seller.

In 1996, Southwest Airlines found it could save a windfall by allowing passengers to purchase tickets on its website—that started a ripple in the airline industry that has spread like a wave to other airlines and created Internet travel services that allow customers to bid on tickets and purchase discount tickets for select routes posted on the Internet.[26] The Internet poses a threat to the travel-agent industry and others like it that process requests from customers who, if the technology were available, would be willing to look up the information themselves. Just ask the owner of a bed-and-breakfast in Alaska who routinely books requests over the Internet from vacationers in the lower 48 states. For the price of a local phone call (the Internet connection), one can communicate with regions of the world once limited to airmail or expensive long-distance telephone calls. It is certainly conceivable that sending information over the Internet could put a crimp in the overnight mail delivery business. Forecasters already predict that rental video stores will be antiquated when band-width technology enables inexpensive and quick transmission of motion pictures over the Internet.

Daniel Minoli and Emma Minoli in their *Web Commerce Technology Handbook* point out the benefits of electronic commerce, including reduced costs to buyers, reduced costs to suppliers, reduced time to complete business transactions, reduced inventories and increased market analysis, increased access to a client base, improved product analysis, and increased information access.[27] What this means is that consumers, wholesalers, and retailers can use the Internet to reduce costs. At the same time, sellers can take advantage of Internet technology to improve service and products. They can also gather marketing data electronically, reducing reliance on focus groups, survey research, and questionnaires. A major debate over privacy on the net is taking place because companies that maintain websites can collect and store personal information about web users. Companies have taken advantage of Internet technology to sell data about web users and to track the surfing behavior of web users for advertising purposes, so advertisers can launch direct marketing campaigns over the net to individual users.

The Dell Computer Corporation serves as a case study of the net's commercial potential. According to the Commerce report: "Dell saw the advantages of the Internet and began exploiting them before others in its industry. In July 1996, Dell's customers could configure and order a computer directly from Dell's website. In six months' time, Dell was selling $1 million worth of computers via the Internet each day. It's volume doubled a few months later. Dell reports having sold $6 million per day several times during the 1997 holiday selling season."[28] Selling directly on the Internet eliminates the cost of maintaining a store—cyberspace, in effect, replaces physical space. And the consumer gets the convenience of being able to make a purchase without leaving home or being hassled by sales personnel.

In addition, the Dell website answers more than 120,000 technical support queries per week via e-mail, and about 20,000 customers use the website each week to check the status of their orders, reducing labor costs and time spent on the phone. Other companies have found similar success. Federal Express saves $10 million per year by allowing customers to track packages. Cisco systems started allowing customers to purchase its routers, switchers, and other networking devices on the Internet in 1996, and in 10 months generated more than $1 billion in sales.[29] The Internet has enabled Dell and Cisco to increase both business and customer satisfaction. Information technology companies are in the forefront of Internet commerce, mainly because their customer base is technologically oriented. As more people become connected to and familiar with the Internet, business in other sectors of the economy will expand.

TYPES OF COMMERCE

Four types of commercial activity take place on the Internet. The first is related to the development of the Internet itself—the building of the Internet backbone and the related computer, software, and information technology that enables people to use the Internet. The other three are related to commerce—direct business-to-business transactions on the net, the sale of commercial products, and the electronic delivery of goods and services.

Analysts have claimed that the information technology has fueled U.S. economic development and that the Internet industry will provide the backbone for U.S. economic expansion in the twenty-first century. The Internet infrastructure includes the necessary hardware, services, and software needed to wire the world. A popular television commercial depicts children in a remote village of Africa communicating over the net with children from the United States. Doug Fine, a writer and film director who has reported for the *Washington Post,* discovered just how true this is when he visited Toksook Bay, a Yup'ik Eskimo village in Western Alaska. The isolated village, 400 miles from Russia, did not have telephones until 1980. But thanks to wireless technology, villagers now produce their own web pages and "chat" with the rest of the world over the Internet at much less cost than the phone system. Fine remarked that the largely subsistence village has leapfrogged over the "Telephone Age" to the "Digital Age" with cutting edge, wireless technology.[30] The market is global, and the race is on to connect the world. As the Commerce Department report noted: "To meet this increased demand, consumer electronics companies, media giants, phone companies, computer companies, software firms, satellite builders, cell phone businesses, Internet service providers, television cable companies, and, in a few cases, electric utilities, are aggressively investing to build out the Internet."[31] Companies are competing to sell the hardware (computers, televisions, telephones), the transmission media (cable, wire, switches, routers, antennas, and satellites), and the remote access devices (modems, cable modems, and wireless modems) that are needed to hook up to the Internet. Consumers today have the option of connecting to the Internet by computers, television, telephone, and even portable digital assistants that send and receive e-mail and faxes.

The two most important factors that affect consumer use are price and bandwidth (the speed of the connection). As the price of Internet technology decreases, more consumers are expected to connect to the net. The lower the price, the greater the demand. Bandwidth governs the speed at which information can be downloaded and transmitted and makes the difference between whether the Internet works like a speed boat or a tug. Measured in bits per second, bandwidth determines the rate at which data moves on the network. Manufacturers have rushed to increase bandwidth and provide high-speed residential Internet access, knowing that consumers don't want to wait 15 minutes to download a file. Fierce competition has arisen within the telecommunications industry to provide high-speed Internet connections through fiber optics, cable modems, and wireless and satellite systems. One reason communications giant AT&T purchased the cable television company, Tele-Communications Inc., in the summer of 1998 was to capitalize on the cable firm's high-speed Internet link, @Home. The merger signals the marriage of television with the net. The race is on between telephone-wire systems and television-broadcast systems (cable, wireless, satellite) for domination of the net. And victory may go to the swiftest. Work is underway to build a new superfast network, called Internet 2, that will transmit the contents of the 30-volume *Encyclopedia Britannica* in one second compared to the 27 hours it would take to transmit those volumes using a conventional 28.8-kilobit modem.[32]

Thousands of companies, known as Internet Service Providers (ISPs), have sprung up to connect consumers to the net. These ISPs are companies that own or rent bandwidth on the Internet backbone and then provide a platform for users to access the Internet. The company that dominates this market is America Online with 12 million subscribers, nearly four times as much as its nearest rival. However, most

ISPs are local providers that service a small geographical area and gain access from larger regional or national providers.[33] It appears that many ISPs will fade in the next decade. Stiff competition has brought down the price of connecting to the net. ISP's can no longer charge high fees for service by the hour; most offer unlimited service for a set monthly price. Some of the smaller companies have survived by stressing reliability—America Online and other big ISPs have experienced problems handling prime-time demand for their services. Others have established niche operations—stressing software, for example, that excludes pornographic sites, a marketing measure that appeals to concerned parents. Earthlink Network Inc., a California firm that grew from 30,000 subscribers in 1995 to more than 450,000 in 1998, offers customers the option of designing a personal web room that allows them to get e-mail, chat online, and display a 300-photo scrapbook.

America Online has joined Yahoo and other search engine companies in establishing itself as an Internet portal. These service companies are competing for the strategic position of being a home page, the first page a user sees when logging on. Internet portals provide e-mail, search engines, and other consumer services designed to attract users and, of course, advertisers, to their sites. In a world with literally hundreds of millions of web pages, the advantage of being the home page cannot be understated. To create a portal that encompasses a user's communications and research needs and can be tailored to an individual's wants is the challenge. Home-page exposure is equivalent to a prime-time slot on television, the front page of a newspaper, the cover of a magazine, or a billboard over Times Square.

That is why the battle between Microsoft and Netscape over the market for Internet browsers is so significant. The browser, which is the software that connects users to the net, has been designed to show up on computers as a default home page. Both Microsoft and Netscape have tailored their browsers to include features that one would find on an Internet portal; hence, eliminating the need for users to change their home page. This is more than a matter of convenience. It is a strategy for boosting revenue from advertisers—hundreds of millions of dollars are at stake.

The U.S. Justice Department has accused Microsoft of cutting off Netscape by incorporating its Internet software as part of its Windows operating system. Since Windows runs about 90 percent of the world's personal computers, and Microsoft's Internet Explorer is part of Windows, there is no incentive for consumers to buy another browser. The government wants Microsoft to drop its Internet software from Windows or allow competing systems to be part of the Windows operating system. "This is a step backwards for America, for consumers and for the personal-computer industry that is leading our nation's economy into the 21st Century," Microsoft Chairman Bill Gates said after the suit was filed in May 1998. But Attorney General Janet Reno said Microsoft had "restricted the choices available for consumers in America and around the world." In 1996, Netscape controlled more than 90 percent of the browser market. At the time the Justice Department suit was filed, its share of the market had dropped more than a third, to less than 60 percent.[34] While it is not the purpose of this chapter to debate the merits of the suit, which may not be settled for years, it is clear that Gates wants to capitalize on the Internet and Internet technology. The software pioneer made his fortune by developing and marketing the premier operating system for the world's personal computers. But in the mid-1990's, Microsoft realized it was losing position in the third wave of the computer revolution—the move from mainframe computers to personal computers to networked computers that talk with each other. Mosaic, the first web browser, was introduced in 1993, and a year later, in April 1994, Netscape Communications was founded as Mosaic Communications. Six months later, Gates wrote a memo called "Sea Change" that turned his company around. In August 1995, Microsoft shipped Windows 95, which included the Internet Explorer browser. Gates' strategy was to incorporate the price of the browser within Windows, effectively offering it for free.[35] In doing so, the Justice Department accused Microsoft of putting a choke hold on the browser market, effectively strangling competition on the net. It remains to be seen whether Microsoft will be able to dominate the Internet the same way the company dominates computer operating systems and software.

COMMERCE BETWEEN BUSINESSES

Commerce between businesses is one of the strongholds of the Internet. Net technology enables businesses to communicate with each other, eliminating steps that used to take up time in direct person-to-person contact, telephone calls, memorandums, and faxes. Posting a call for bids at a company's website expands the pool of potential contractors beyond the purchasing agent's Rolodex. It also expands the base of potential clients beyond the geographic territory of the firm's sales force. The net has helped companies consolidate purchasing, streamline their bidding procedures, and expand business opportunities. Forrester Research reports that almost half of all durable goods manufacturers will conduct business-to-business commerce over the Internet by 2001, and that wholesalers of office supplies, electronic goods, and scientific equipment will garner a projected $89 billion worth of business by 2001. General Electric, for example, bought $1 billion worth of supplies over the Internet in 1997, and saved 20 percent on material costs because the company expanded its pool of suppliers by using the net. And Boeing has booked $100 million in orders by setting up a website that handles airlines' spare-parts requests.[36] Just as the net has challenged the domination of the proprietary networks providing information and entertainment for consumers, such as AOL, Compuserve, Prodigy, and Genie, the net is expected to cut into Electronic Data Interchange, a proprietary network that manufacturers use to conduct business-to-business commerce.

The experience of Dell and Cisco Systems has been replicated by smaller regional companies. SED International, a computer parts firm, has been called the quietest billion-dollar company in the Atlanta region. The company boosted its business by establishing an online sales operation. "We have found that sales online are more profitable than sales the traditional way through salesmen," SED International vice president Jim Andracchi told the *New York Times.* "What we found was that there is a breed of buyers for whom the price is not so important as other factors— getting the right-size order quickly, on a certain date. For those people, the salesman relationship is not needed, and it helps for them to be able to place orders 24 hours a day not just when a salesperson is handy."[37]

The public sector also has benefited. The 1998 *Business Week* "Info Tech Annual Report" touts the example of Chris Barnes, Los Angeles County's head of procurement. By consolidating purchases through an Internet-based system, the county expects to close its antiquated central warehouse and save $38 million over the next five years. The net enables county employees to save prices by comparison shopping and staying on top of inventory.[38] Instead of stockpiling inventory, the net allows merchants and businesses to streamline their warehouse operations. Eliminating inventory that ties up capital is one of the major advantages of net-based commerce.

The net has changed the way businesses search for personnel and has helped individuals find jobs in their neighborhood and around the world. Human resource departments have used the Internet to expand their search for job candidates by posting positions on the web. Help-wanted advertising has found a new home on the web. A number of entrepreneurs have established job banks. America's Job Bank (www.ajb.dni.us) lists some 700,000 jobs, and Yahoo offers about 200,000 free classified ads (www.classifieds.yahoo.com). Web-based classifieds may challenge newspapers, headhunters, and other traditional ways of finding work.

COMMERCIAL SALES OF GOODS AND SERVICES

Most Americans remember former Surgeon General C. Everett Koop as a folksy, white-haired avuncular figure. If the good doctor's latest venture takes off, he will make a name for himself in cyberspace. In July 1998, Koop launched a website, Dr. Koop's Community, that "lets consumers refill prescriptions online and pick them up at a local Rite Aid pharmacy." Koop has found a home on the web that allows him to offer views about health and earn money, too.[39]

Online commerce is swiftly evolving. In its early days consumers used the web to find computer parts, books, and travel-related services. Today, the web has become a global shopping mall, offering a cornucopia of goods and services for every consumer need, even groceries. Harried Christmas shoppers can avoid holiday traffic and packed shopping malls by ordering fruitcakes (www.sosupreme.com), ornaments (www.ornaments.com), wreaths (www.mwv.org/mckinnon), and live trees from Vermont (www.apbt.com/dayspring/treepage.htm) on the web. For general gifts, they can visit the Internet mall (www.internetmall.com), the virtual emporium (www.virtualemporium.com), and the netmarket (www.netmarket.com). They can place a bid for goods at an online auction or retrieve discount coupons (www.coolsavings.com) for greater savings.[40] These are some of the ways the

Internet is revolutionizing retail. In July 1998, *Time Magazine* featured a cover story entitled, "Kiss Your Mall Goodbye—Online shopping is faster, cheaper and better." By the year 2000, online consumer sales will reach $20 billion, an increase of 233 percent over 1998's projected totals, according to the Gartner Group. While *Time* relies on the Gartner Group's projections, the Commerce Department cites the more conservative Forrester Research and Robertson Stephens, which each predict about $7.35 billion in retail sales by the year 2000.[41] No matter which prediction approximates the truth, the net offers consumers a new way to shop without ever leaving their homes.

NetSmart, a New York-based market research firm, conducted a survey of 520 Internet users in 1996 and found that 54 percent had bought merchandise online and that 18 percent said the web is the first place they go to shop.[42] The average online shopper is a 33-year-old single person, college-educated with a median household income of $59,000, according to Jupiter Communications.[43] Andersen Consulting predicts that online shopping for groceries and household goods will soar as some 20 million U.S. households, some 15 percent of all U.S. households, shop online, generating some $85 billion in the purchases of goods and services by the year 2007.[44]

The sales-generating potential of the web has troubled traditional sales and service industries, including automobiles, travel, insurance, and financial services. These businesses are worried that online shopping in many cases eliminates the need to go to a store or to seek advice from sales representatives. Small wonder that according to a recent survey almost half of all auto dealers see the Internet as a threat. J. D. Powers & Associates underscored their concern by predicting that more than one-fifth of all new car and truck buyers will use the Internet by 2000. Online services allow car buyers to place a bid on a vehicle without haggling or high-pressure tactics from sales personnel. Online trading of stocks and mutual funds, bolstered by the amount of financial information available on the Internet, threatens to take commissions away from traditional brokerage houses. Push technology allows investors to monitor the market like a stockbroker and receive continuous quotes at their office terminals. Insurance executives, according to the Commerce Department study, "believe that within five years, their customers will prefer to purchase and receive auto and term life policies online to purchasing from an agent." Banks are following suit with websites that provide a full array of financial services.[45] "Any industry where dissemination of information was the 'value added' is likely to be shaken up by the Internet," Jill Frankel, an International Data Corps analyst, told *Computer World*. "It's really empowered consumers. The Internet has become the middleman."[46]

The web provides the chance for small companies to go national or even global and compete with large manufacturing firms. Raymond Cohen, CEO of Cardiac Science Inc. of Irvine, California, told the *Los Angeles Times* that a website helped boost his company's international sales of defibrillators and heart monitors to 85 percent of its total business.[47] The online site for 1-800-Flowers contributed 10 percent of the company's $300 million in revenues in 1997. About 15–20 percent of the online business comes from Americans working overseas who send flowers to their friends and family in the United States.[48] One need not forget an anniversary or a birthday with the net. Many retail operations serving specialty items, such as hot sauce or even wine, have boosted national sales by creating a niche for themselves on the web. Carl Levinson calls himself a cyber-merchant. Operating out of a $600 per month Indianapolis warehouse, he sells Italian silk ties and oxford cloth shirts through his Ties@Cost and Shirts@Cost websites.[49] Land's End, the Gap, and other clothing outfitters have established sites on the web for consumers to make purchases and special orders. So have toy makers. Toys 'R' Us is online and Mattel Inc. maintains a Barbie website at www.barbie.com.

The biggest downside to net commerce is the perception among some potential customers that confidential information is not secure on the net. The fear that hackers can invade one's privacy by stealing credit card information conveyed over the net has inhibited consumers. Yet, net advocates are quick to point out that consumers have no problem giving out credit card information over the phone or to gas station and restaurant employees. A 1998 Harris poll found that most people who have made purchases online believe their credit card information could be used by others to make improper purchases. There is a fear that hackers or unscrupulous employees can gain access to private information, despite encryption technology designed to protect data transmitted over the Internet. For commerce to flourish, security must be guaranteed. Businesses must also take precautions to protect personal information conveyed over the net. Surveys have shown that consumers are concerned that personal data could be sold to marketers for the purpose of conducting personalized, direct mail-style advertising campaigns over the web.

CASE STUDY: ONLINE NEWSPAPERS

The newspaper industry, which is used to double-digit profits, has experienced anxiety about the net. On the one hand, publishers envision saving delivery and production costs by going online. On the other hand, publishers fear the loss of advertising revenue and the reluctance of consumers to subscribe to online newspapers. Nevertheless, the public's taste for online news is increasing as more Americans turn to the Internet during times of crisis and breaking news stories. A Pew Research Center survey estimates that some 36 million Americans went online for news in 1998 compared with 11 million in 1996.[50] The convenience of reading the news at a workstation terminal cannot be understated. The question of whether advertisers and consumers wish to pay for the service remains to be answered. Media executives, who remember the collapse of Knight-Ridder's electronic teletext service, Viewtron, which cost $50 million and attracted only 50,000 subscribers, remain worried about the profitability of online newspapers. Failure to find a common formula for delivering online news was reflected in the demise of the New Century Network, a partnership of nine leading newspaper companies that was formed in 1995 to bring newspapers into the Internet age. The network, composed of companies that own 196 daily newspapers, collapsed in 1998 after the companies decided to go their own way in establishing online operations.[51]

The number of online newspapers in the United States, however, continues to grow as publishers hedge their bets by establishing a web presence, even if the site loses money. Publishers say they are forced to go online, to defend their position as the content providers for news and classified advertising. Newspapers fear the presence of electronic media on the web (MSNBC, CNN) and worry about losing their lock on classified advertising to online automobile and real estate sites. More than 2,066 newspapers published online editions in 1997, compared to 745 in 1996 and 496 in 1995.[52] Nearly all of the online sites suffer from a lack of advertising and only a handful of online editions charge subscriber fees. About 120 newspapers have closed their sites because they couldn't attract enough advertising.[53] Furthermore, there appears to be a limit to the amount of advertising viewers will tolerate at a website. It is unlikely viewers will adjust to a formula that displays full screens of advertising between web pages or tolerate a web page jammed with banner ads. To make money, newspaper executives have engaged in novel strategies that go beyond the mainstays of generating advertising revenue and charging for circulation. The Times Mirror corporation purchased Auction Universe, a virtual auction house, and has located an auction site at the online edition of the *Hartford Courant,* one of the newspapers the chain owns. The *Courant* site encourages readers to purchase goods by electronic auction. The *Gainesville Sun,* a newspaper owned by the New York Times Corporation, has launched a sports boutique, touting the University of Florida's Gator football team, at its website.[54] Newspapers have even merged advertising and editorial, establishing links between bookstores and featured book reviews at their online sites. This type of practice could be extended to the travel section or the home section where a story about Hawaii would have links to Hawaiian hotel sites or a story about roofing would have links to roofers' sites. Some journalists have questioned the propriety of this practice, but newspaper executives maintain that editorial integrity is not affected and the practice is the same as placing a bookstore advertisement in the book review section.

Besides selling products, newspapers have established themselves as Internet service providers and online archives that allow people to purchase stories and research information. By becoming ISPs, newspapers hope to fortify their presence on the net as a home page with links to revenue-generating commercial sites. Establishing archival sites on the web allows newspapers to recycle and package stories, extending their shelf life beyond one edition. Newspapers can offer readers entertainment guides, restaurant guides, travel guides, demographic information, and stories related to topics of direct interest.

ADVERTISING ISSUES

The newspaper industry shares a common problem with the owners of other commercial websites—how to attract advertising. In 1997, the total advertising dollars spent on the Internet reflected less than 1 percent of the total spent on advertising for all media.[55] Newspapers, magazines, radio, and television all depend upon advertising revenue. The older, established media have proven themselves in their ability to attract an audience that advertisers can measure for results. On the web, newspapers have sold display advertising, classified advertising, and sponsorships of their websites as strategies to generate revenue. Advertisers enjoy sponsorship because it establishes a presence, literally planting their corporate flag, at another company's website. There is skepticism, though, about the efficacy of placing a web banner ad. So much so that advertisers have demanded they only pay for ads when visitors click on their sites. This "pay per clickthrough model" would be the equivalent of an advertiser placing a print ad in a newspaper and only paying for it if a reader visited his store. Some advertisers want to go further and establish a "pay per transaction" model in which a purchase must be made at the site. The Internet today is a buyer's market with sellers forced to accept rates and conditions that would be unacceptable in an old media market. One of the biggest problems is attracting national advertisers to the net.

Advertising executives believe the Internet has a long way to go before it can legitimately compete for dollars spent on broadcast and print. Seven executives interviewed by *Internet World* magazine echoed time-honored skepticism about unreliable website ratings, inadequate demographic data about website visitors, and the overall effectiveness of advertising on the web. Advertisers believe the numbers generated are soft and that software designed to track web use comes up short in providing hard data about the number of people who view advertisements. "Advertisers want companies to measure reach and frequency of each visit, demographics, and want the site to be audited and have consistent reporting and cross-site comparisons," said Tim Stehle, director of online marketing analysis for the Knight Ridder New Media Center.[56] Despite these reservations, online advertising is expected to grow. Portal sites are particularly attractive because of their high usage and visibility. Other sites can follow the example of magazines and niche marketing. Newspapers want to maintain their share of the classified market and can offer discounts for placing an online advertisement along with a print ad.

GOVERNMENT AND COMMERCE

The policies of federal and state governments, as well as governments around the world, have direct impact on commerce and the Internet. In coming years, governments will have to tackle major legal issues involving copyright, gambling, taxation, libel, censorship, privacy, obscenity, free speech, trademarks, encryption, fraud, and domain names. Treaties will have to be established to regulate commerce in cyberspace and determine rules governing a medium that is truly worldwide. The net was conceived in the spirit of anarchy—a system with no central controls. As it grows and matures, laws and regulations will be made to clarify and protect the rights of individuals, businesses, and nation-states. Just in the area of taxation alone, the nation's governors have complained about losing sales tax revenues because of net commerce. They have grumbled about taxing sales on the net, although the federal government placed a three-year moratorium on net taxes and fees in June 1998. While the United States has a moratorium on taxes, there is no predicting what other countries will do. Conflicts among nations are bound to arise over what constitutes free speech, the regulation of gambling and sex sites, and policies regarding libel and slander. Rules governing commerce and trade among nations need to be worked out for cyberspace.

CONCLUSION

Every new medium has a moment when it comes into its own. For television news, the continuous coverage of the Kennedy assassination marked its ascendancy. For CNN, the cable news network, its on-the-spot, real-time coverage of the Gulf War proved it could play in the same league as the national networks. The Internet's baptism of fire was the September 11, 1998, release of Kenneth Starr's 425-page report on President Clinton's alleged misconduct in office. The net performed admirably (the backbone held up to record traffic) and proved its importance to public affairs. Congress, in choosing to release the entire report on the Internet, allowed the public to obtain an unmediated evaluation of Clinton's sexual affair with Monica Lewinsky. Estimates are that more than 20 million people may have looked at the report on the Internet—CNN claimed a record 34.26 million page views on the day the report was released.[57] The display of the report on government and news media websites showed the versatility of the Internet as a vehicle for mass communication.

In using the Internet, Congress allowed the world to read a report that would have typically been disseminated to a few hundred people on its initial release date. Because of the time and effort to photocopy a 425-page report, very few people outside of the news media would have been given a copy. Congress showed the world the power of the Internet. The age of information technology has truly arrived. Business leaders, educators, legislators, and futurists have recognized the power and commercial potential of the Internet. The foundation has been laid for a new social order. Fueled by commerce, the Internet will transform the world, ushering in the global village of the millennium.

NOTES

[1]NUA Internet Surveys, http://www.nua.ie/surveys.

[2]Nicholas Negroponte, *Being Digital* (New York, Vintage Books, 1995): 6, 158, 159.

[3]"Internet Economy Index," *The Industry Standard,* 13 July 1998: 47; "Techwatch," *Time Magazine,* 25 May 1998: 32.

[4]Don Tapscott, *Growing Up Digital: The Rise of the Net Generation* (McGraw-Hill, New York, 1998): 61.

[5]"The Emerging Digital Economy," U.S. Department of Commerce, Washington, D.C., 1998: 4.

[6]Adam Clayton Powell III, "Internet Rapidly Overtaking Telephone Traffic," *Freedom Forum Online,* www.freedomforum.org/technology/1998/3/11traffic.asp.

[7]"Wired Homes Watch 15 Percent Less Television," Mike Snider, *USA Today,* August 13, 1998: A1.

[8]"The Emerging Digital Economy," Appendix 2, U.S. Department of Commerce, Washington, D.C., 1998: A2-5.

[9]Saul Hansell, "There Is a Why? In Yahoo," *The Orange County Register,* February 15, 1998: B1

[10]Frank Rose, "Sex Sells," *Wired Magazine,* December, 1997: 221

[11]David Abrahamson, "The Visible Hand: Money, Markets, and Media Evolution," *Journalism Quarterly,* Spring, 1998: 14.

[12]"The Emerging Digital Economy," U.S. Department of Commerce, Washington, D.C., 1998: 21

[13]"Infotech Annual Report," *Business Week,* June 22, 1998.

[14]Wyn Hilty, "How the Web Was Lost," *OC Weekly,* Sept. 20–26, 1996: 10.

[15]David Noack, "E-Commerce and Online News," *Mediainfo.com,* Nov., 1997: 18.

[16]Mitchell Stephens, *A History of News,* (Fort Worth, TX: Harcourt Brace, 1997): 45.

[17]David Rynecki, "Frenzy over Net Stocks Sparks Fear," *USA Today,* July 7, 1998: A1; "Amazon.com Is Risky Play, But What of Plane Builder?" *Los Angeles Times,* July 14, 1998: D7.

[18]"Internet Shares' Mixed Results Show There's Caution on the Cutting Edge," *The Orange County Register,* September 2, 1998: B2.

[19]James W. Carey, "The Internet and the End of the National Communication System: Uncertain Predictions of an Uncertain Future," *Journalism Quarterly,* Spring, 1998: 28.

[20]Kirk Andersen, "The Digital Bubble," *The New Yorker,* January 19, 1998: 30.

[21]Clifford Stoll, *Silicon Snake Oil* (New York, Anchor Books, 1995): 106.

[22]"Finding Web Pages Keeps Getting Harder," www.internetnews.com/bus-news/1998/04/0301-usa-find.html.

[23]"Report: E-Commerce Revenues to Top $1.2 Trillion by 2002," *Electronic Commerce News,* www.internet.com.

[24]Andrew W. Kantor and Michael Neubarth, "How Big," *Internet World,* December 1996: 48.

[25]Robert Hertzberg, "The End of an Era?" *Internet Week,* January 19, 1998 www.internet.com.

[26]"The Emerging Digital Economy," Appendix 4: 26

[27]Daniel Minoli and Emma Minoli, *Web Commerce Technology Handbook* (New York, McGraw-Hill, 1998).

[28]"The Emerging Digital Economy," Appendix 3: 14–16.

[29]"The Emerging Digital Economy," Appendix 3: 12.

[30]Doug Fine, "Eskimos Warm to the Digital Age," *The Washington Post,* August 9, 1998: C1.

[31]"The Emerging Digital Economy," Chapter Two: 8.

[32]"500 Million Industry Grant Announced for Super-Fast Internet 2 Service," http:www. freedomforum.org/technology/1998/4/14internet2.asp.

[33]Leon Salvgail, Steven K. Besler and Sacha Mallais, *Internet Server Connectivity* (Indianapolis, New Riders Publishing, 1996): 21.

[34]"U.S. States Sue over Windows," *The Orange County Register,* May 19, 1998: A1.

[35]Kathy Rebello, "Inside Microsoft," *Business Week,* July 15, 1996: 56.

[36]"Infotech Annual Report," *Business Week,* June 22, 1998: 128.

[37]Ernest Holsendolph, "The Art of the Internet Deal: Business-to-Business," *The New York Times,* March 30, 1998: B1.

[38]"Infotech Annual Report": 134.

[39]Laura Rich, "Former Microsoft Exec to Launch Drugstore.com," *The Industry Standard,* July 27, 1998: 19.

[40]Greg Hardesty, "Ho-Ho-Ho.com," *The Orange County Register:* B1.

[41]Michael Krantz, "Click Till You Drop," *Time Magazine,* July 20, 1998: 36. "The Emerging Digital Economy," Endnotes, Appendix 5: 18.

[42]"Bits & Bytes," *Business Week,* January 20, 1997.

[43]Krantz: 38.

[44]"Bits & Bytes," *Business Week,* February 23, 1998.

[45]"The Emerging Digital Economy": 33

[46]Sharon Machlis, "Channel Conflicts Stall Web Sales," *Computer World,* February 16, 1998: 2.

[47]Marla Dickerson, "Going Global by Going Online," *Los Angeles Times,* February 11, 1998: D1.

[48]"The Emerging Digital Economy," Appendix 5: 17.

[49]Marla Dickerson, "Yes, We're Online," *Los Angeles Times,* October 21, 1996: D1.

[50]"Americans Reading News on the Internet Have Tripled in 2 Years," *Los Angles Times,* June 9, 1998: D3.

[51]"Newspapers' Internet Partnership Ceases," *Orange County Register,* March 11, 1998: B2.

[52]Erik Meyer, "An Unexpectedly Wider Web for the World's Newspapers," *American Journalism Review,* www.newslink.org/emcol/10.html.

[53]Scott Kirsner, "Profits in Site?" *American Journalism Review,* December, 1997.

[54]David Noack, "E-Commerce and Online News," *Mediainfo.com,* November, 1997: 19.

[55]"Total Ad Dollars Spent on the Net," *Business Week,* October 6, 1997.

[56]Jodi B. Cohen, "Measuring the Web Audience," *Editor & Publisher,* June 29, 1996: 37.

[57]Maria Seminerio, "Starr Report Could Be Most-Read Web Item Ever," www.zdnet.com/zdnn/stories/zdnn, Sept. 14, 1998.

Index